THE WORLD ENCYCLOPEDIA OF
CRUISERS

THE WORLD ENCYCLOPEDIA OF
CRUISERS

- An illustrated history of the cruisers of the world, from the American Civil War
to modern-day missile cruisers, spanning a period of almost 150 years

- Features a directory of over 250 warships with 650 identification photographs

BERNARD IRELAND

LORENZ BOOKS

This edition is published by Lorenz Books, an imprint of
Anness Publishing Ltd, Hermes House, 88–89 Blackfriars Road,
London SE1 8HA; tel. 020 7401 2077; fax 020 7633 9499;
www.lorenzbooks.com; www.annesspublishing.com

Anness Publishing has a new picture agency outlet for images for
publishing, promotions or advertising. Please visit our website
www.practicalpictures.com for more information.

UK agent: The Manning Partnership Ltd; tel. 01225 478444;
fax 01225 478440; sales@manning-partnership.co.uk
UK distributor: Grantham Book Services Ltd; tel. 01476 541080;
fax 01476 541061; orders@gbs.tbs-ltd.co.uk
North American agent/distributor: National Book Network;
tel. 301 459 3366; fax 301 429 5746; www.nbnbooks.com
Australian agent/distributor: Pan Macmillan Australia; tel. 1300 135 113;
fax 1300 135 103; customer.service@macmillan.com.au
New Zealand agent/distributor: David Bateman Ltd;
tel. (09) 415 7664; fax (09) 415 8892

Publisher: Joanna Lorenz; Senior Managing Editor: Conor Kilgallon;
Senior Editor: Felicity Forster; Copy Editor and Indexer: Tim Ellerby;
Cover Design: Nigel Partridge; Designer: Design Principals;
Editorial Reader: Jay Thundercliffe; Production Controller: Claire Rae

ETHICAL TRADING POLICY
At Anness Publishing we believe that business should be conducted
in an ethical and ecologically sustainable way, with respect for the
environment and a proper regard to the replacement of the natural
resources we employ. As a publisher, we use a lot of wood pulp to
make high-quality paper for printing, and that wood commonly comes
from spruce trees. We are therefore currently growing more than
500,000 trees in two Scottish forest plantations near Aberdeen –
Berrymoss (130 hectares/320 acres) and West Touxhill (125 hectares/
305 acres). The forests we manage contain twice the number of trees
employed each year in paper-making for our books. Because of this
ongoing ecological investment programme, you, as our customer, can
have the pleasure and reassurance of knowing that a tree is being
cultivated on your behalf to naturally replace the materials used to make
the book you are holding. Our forestry programme is run in accordance
with the UK Woodland Assurance Scheme (UKWAS) and will be
certified by the internationally recognized Forest Stewardship Council
(FSC). The FSC is a non-government organization dedicated to
promoting responsible management of the world's forests. Certification
ensures forests are managed in an environmentally sustainable and
socially responsible basis. For further information about this scheme,
go to www.annesspublishing.com/trees.

NOTE: The nationality of each cruiser is identified in the
specification box by the national flag that was in use at
the time of the vessel's commissioning and service.

PAGE 1: *Diadem*. PAGE 2: *Prinz Eugen*. PAGE 3: *California, Virginia*
and *South Carolina*, supported by *Leahy/Belknaps*.

Contents

Introduction

Of the main categories of warship, the cruiser has enjoyed by far the least attention from historians and researchers. The reason is probably one of definition. Battleships and aircraft carriers, destroyers and submarines all have clearly defined identities and duties; the dates of their introduction and/or demise being likewise apparent. In contrast, the cruiser was a category that emerged, rather than being conceived for some specific purpose.

Until the mid-19th century, the term "cruiser" was applied to a "cruising ship", one that was not tied to the battle line. "Seventy-fours" and smaller, down to frigates, might be given independent commissions, joining corvettes, sloops, cutters and lesser craft in the general discomfiture of the enemy and his trade. The freedom of such commands yielded experience (and prize money) that founded many an illustrious naval dynasty.

During the long period that followed the fall of Napoleon, the duties of the cruiser were again best defined by its label in that they revolved around maintaining the peace and "showing the flag" throughout the far reaches of an often restive empire. Categorized as "colonial sloops" or "corvettes", these small ships, their machinery still very much auxiliary to sail, were the "cruising ships" of the time.

By virtue of sheer weight, the introduction of the ironclad resulted in the demise of the multiple gundecks of the all-wooden era. The armoured single-decker (strictly speaking, a frigate) became the new line-of-battle ship. Continuous and rapid improvement in artillery, in protection and in machinery

TOP: **Typical of the screw corvettes that policed the world's empires, the German *Augusta* dries sails at anchor. As her gundeck is not covered, the gunports are clearly visible.** ABOVE: **All ocean raiders face the common problem of eventually requiring skilled dockyard assistance. The Confederate cruiser *Alabama* was thus apprehended outside Cherbourg in June 1864.**

began to give designers broader options in specification but due to weight, forced compromises on them. There began a clear divergence between vessels bearing heavy armament and protection, and others that favoured speed, with their gun battery and armour reduced accordingly. Here lay the origins of the Victorian battleship and the great armoured cruisers which could eclipse them in both cost and size.

Cost, in this protracted period of peace, became an ever more dominant factor. Smaller cruisers were required, a process facilitated by two further innovations: the essentially Italian concept of the protective deck and the availability of heat-treated, "cemented" steel armour with greatly improved resistance to penetration. For the same degree of protection, armour plate could now be thinner and lighter.

A choice of cruiser types was now possible: First Class armoured ships to act as a fast wing of the fleet and to undertake opposed reconnaissance; Second Class, usually

protected, types for general fleet duties and trade protection; small Third Class vessels, lightly protected, for colonial policing, and a new category of Scout Cruiser, from which emerged the Destroyer Leader.

The hard experience of World War I swept aside most of these categories. Successive inter-war treaties resulted in the new classifications of "heavy" and "light" cruisers. The former type was used by the Japanese with particular imagination and effectiveness, almost as latter-day Second Class battleships.

To their still-relevant roles of reconnaissance, tracking and reporting, cruisers found further roles during World War II. Widespread amphibious operations saw them indispensable in fire support. Convoys to Malta and North Russia, and American fleet activities in the Pacific, were conducted in the teeth of enemy air superiority, resulting in the continuing development of the new-style anti-aircraft cruiser.

Kamikazes and German stand-off, guided bombs brought about the requirement for guided anti-aircraft missiles. American construction programmes had produced scores of identical gun-armed cruisers but, although for the most part little used, it proved uneconomical to convert them to guided-missile ships. Block-obsolescent, their disposal was slowed only by the continuing threats of the Cold War. Their going effectively marked the passing of the conventional cruiser.

From a multiplicity of guided-missile systems emerged the essentially anti-aircraft "destroyer" and anti-submarine "frigate". Combine their systems and function, adding an anti-surface ship-guided weapon for good measure, and one arrives at the current definition of the cruiser, highly expensive, highly complex and multi-purpose.

ABOVE LEFT: **One of the nine Eclipse-class protected cruisers, HMS _Minerva_ dated from 1895. Note the auxiliary spotting top to assist the ship in her defence of the Suez Canal.** TOP: _Scharnhorst_ **coaling at Valparaiso shortly after von Spee's victory at Coronel in 1914. Note the mix of 21cm/8.3in and 15cm/5.9in guns.** ABOVE: **The beauty of a cruiser at speed is caught well in this image of the Italian heavy cruiser _Fiume_ of 1930. One of four Zara-class ships, she exceeded 35 knots on trials. Together with two sisters, she was sunk at Matapan in 1941.**

ABOVE: **As can be appreciated from this 1960s photograph of the USS _Chicago_, hopes that early missile systems could be fitted easily into war-built cruiser hulls were misplaced.**

The History of Cruisers

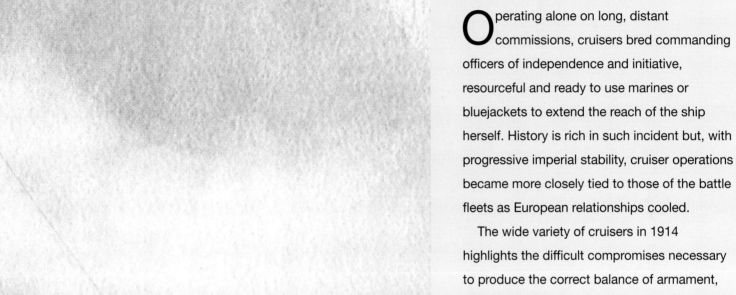

Operating alone on long, distant commissions, cruisers bred commanding officers of independence and initiative, resourceful and ready to use marines or bluejackets to extend the reach of the ship herself. History is rich in such incident but, with progressive imperial stability, cruiser operations became more closely tied to those of the battle fleets as European relationships cooled.

The wide variety of cruisers in 1914 highlights the difficult compromises necessary to produce the correct balance of armament, protection and propulsive power. With considerable success, they assumed the roles of sailing frigates in patrolling, reconnaissance, tracking and reporting. During World War II, their long range and independence exploited good intelligence to hunt down the enemy's auxiliary raiders and the supply ships upon which they depended.

In wartime, the major threat to cruisers turned out to be not other cruisers but aircraft and submarines. The answer to the former was the guided missile, and it was the rapid development and proliferation of these that signalled the demise of the conventional cruiser. Today's ideals are technological excellence and lean crews.

LEFT: **The turn of the 20th century marked the peak of British maritime supremacy. Here, the crew of a three-master, snubbing at her anchor, cheer the passage of an armoured cruiser, a product of the Naval Defence Act, in full Victorian livery.**

Early cruisers

The origins of the term "cruiser" lay more in a ship's function than in its type. In general, it was applied to ships too small to lay in a line of battle and which were engaged on independent duties. A cruiser might, thus, be a frigate scouting or reconnoitering on behalf of a battle fleet, a corvette engaged in the policing of distant stations, a sloop safeguarding commerce from the depredations of privateers or even a cutter patrolling to counter a lucrative smuggling trade. These and similar duties greatly occupied the Royal Navy of the early 19th century and it is not surprising, therefore, that the service was responsible for many of the developments that eventually refined the cruiser into specific types.

By the middle of the 19th century, in the absence of major wars, the most important duty of cruisers was the policing of colonial territorial waters, generally "showing the flag" and deterring local belligerents with aspirations to disrupt any part of a worldwide British trade network from acting.

Where improvements in iron construction and in propulsion machinery were being applied to the battle fleet on a continuous basis, change came slowly to the colonial cruisers for very practical reasons. One was that early examples of this new machinery was inefficient, burning large quantities of coal, of which the ships could stow little and at a time when the full network of imperial coaling stations had yet to be established. Ships might spend many years on a single station, being serviced in the region and rotating crews at specified intervals. Such vessels needed a high degree of reliability and long

TOP: **The combined mass of all-metal hulls, machinery and bunkers, and heavier guns, enforced the end of the multi-decked warship. HMS *Warrior* and *Black Prince*, designed to lay in a line-of-battle, were, nonetheless, single-deckers and therefore technically large frigates.** ABOVE: **Despite the technical advances of ships such as the above, guns were still mounted on the broadside. The 254mm/10in gun shown fired explosive shells, but was still mounted on a wooden carriage with old-style breechings to contain its recoil.**

endurance, so their machinery was regarded as auxiliary to sail, under which they spent the greater part of their time. Often referred to as "captains under God", their commanding officers in these days of slow communications were of necessity accustomed to making decisions without reference to higher authority, and were accustomed to independent action.

This apparent reluctance to change also resulted from the fact that colonial cruisers frequently worked in extreme climates, usually tropical but occasionally in high latitudes.

A wooden vessel was infinitely more comfortable for her crew than an early "iron pot" which, poorly insulated, sweated unhealthily. Even when iron construction became more general, it remained common for colonial cruisers to be of so-called "composite construction", i.e. wood planked on an iron frame. A further incentive was that a copper-sheathed wooden hull fouled less quickly in tropical waters than an iron one, a consideration of some significance with respect to both speed and to the remote possibilities of regular dry-docking on distant stations. Finally, the woodworking trades still comprised a high proportion of a dockyard's manpower, and the scarcer metal workers were more efficiently employed on major warships.

In 1860 there were 34 screw frigates and corvettes, 76 screw sloops and 24 "gun-vessels" in the Royal Navy's establishment. Many were unprotected, others described as "ironclad" by virtue of the addition of a waterline belt, typically of 114mm/4.5in of wrought iron backed by 660mm/26in of teak. This was rarely tested in action.

Guns were fewer but had increased in size considerably. Typically, there were eight 100pdr muzzle-loading smooth bores, disposed four to each broadside. They were concentrated amidships in what was termed a "central battery", protected by sides and transverse bulkheads, again of 114mm/4.5in iron backed by teak.

Fully rigged and typically of 3,251 tonnes/3,200 tons displacement, a screw corvette would have steam reciprocating machinery developing some 1,305kW/1,750ihp. With a clean hull this might be good for nearly 12 knots. Her complement of up to 270 would include a marine detachment and/or a company of bluejackets well-trained in military skills to be used for intervention ashore as required.

In Pacific territories, an administrator might have responsibility for scores of widely scattered islands, and the station cruiser afforded him not only transport but underpinned his authority. Many a British vice-consul, overtaken by a local insurrection, has owed his life to the timely arrival of the Navy.

TOP: **Iron screw corvettes were diminutives of the frigates usually lacking a deck over the broadside battery. Here, the *Active* of 1869 leaves Portsmouth under sail, passing the famous *Victory*, all-wood, obsolete and representative of the "Old Navy".** ABOVE: **The *Swiftsure* of 1870 carried ten 229mm/9in, muzzle-loading, rifled shell guns. In order to protect these with the thickest feasible armour, they were concentrated into an amidships, two-deck redoubt, this type of vessel becoming known as a "central battery" ship.** BELOW: **Also carrying her heaviest weapons amidships, the French *Victorieuse* shows differences from her British equivalents. Note the use of sponsons to gain a measure of axial fire, the short forecastle, and the vestigial navigating bridge forward of the funnel.**

The influence of the American Civil War

During their long years of war against Great Britain, the French employed large numbers of privateers which, given legitimacy by Letter of Marque, preyed to great effect on British commercial shipping. From 1861, with the onset of civil war, American Union ships quickly blockaded the ports of the Confederate South, which resulted in the latter responding by the licensing of approximately 80 privateers. Although these succeeded in taking many Union prizes it proved impossible to realize their value by condemnation before a prize court. The South's own ports were blockaded and those of all major maritime powers were unavailable because, by the 1856 Declaration of Paris, privateering had been declared illegal in International Law. As the only available option was now to sink any capture, the profit motive disappeared and with it the majority of would-be privateers. These now turned instead to the risky but highly lucrative trade of blockade-running.

Driven more by altruism than by the prospect of personal gain, however, some Confederate skippers continued to cause considerable disruption to Union shipping. Notable among these was Captain Raphael Semmes, who commanded the *Alabama,* one of a pair of fast screw sloops built to disguised account by the British firm of Laird. In a wide-ranging two-year cruise Semmes took 69 prizes but finally, in June 1864, was obliged to call at the French port of Cherbourg for essential machinery repairs. Upon leaving port, the *Alabama* was met by the protected Union ship *Kearsarge* and destroyed in a protracted gunnery duel.

Between them, the *Alabama* and other notable raiders, such as the Laird-built *Florida* and the *Shenandoah*, accounted for about five per cent of Northern shipping. Although it made

no difference to the eventual outcome of the war, it caused the Union to lay down several fast cruising vessels capable of hunting down the fastest raider. Built of wood, with some iron reinforcement, these differed from ship to ship but collectively, were known by the name of the lead ship, *Wampanoag*. For the sake of endurance they were fully rigged but their *raison d'être* was speed, and nearly one half of their lean hulls was devoted to machinery. The *Wampanoag* herself could sustain a then world record speed of 16.7 knots. Her four outsized funnels and three masts made for a very impressive appearance and, to the particular interest of Britain and France, both of whom had profited considerably from the war, it was let known that the function of the ships was, primarily, to apprehend Confederate raiders but, in the case of foreign intervention, to raid enemy commerce.

Completed after the cessation of hostilities, the Wampanoags proved to have weak hulls, and their machinery unreliable and expensive to operate (not least because of the

ABOVE: **Under the command of Captain Raphael Semmes, the *Alabama* became the most successful Confederate raider. All such cruisers must, however, return to port at some stage for essential repairs and maintenance. As with many raiders yet to come, this would prove to be her undoing.**
LEFT: **At the time of the Civil War, America still depended upon Europe, both as a source of specialist heavy engineering and as an important market for its goods. Merchantmen carrying the latter, vital to finance the war, were vulnerable to commerce raiders such as the Confederate *Alabama*.**

LEFT: Concerned by the success of commerce raiders during the American Civil War, the British Admiralty began to replace its many wooden frigates with large iron frigates with considerable speed for the day. Typified by the *Inconstant* of 1868, they proved to be too expensive.

ABOVE RIGHT: Last of the Confederate raiders, the *Shenandoah* wreaked havoc on the Union-based whaling industry in the Northern Pacific. Difficulties in apprehending her led directly to the United States acquiring naval basing rights in the Samoan Islands. LEFT: Although nowhere near as spacious as this impression suggests, the *Merrimack*'s slope-sided topside construction is evident. Two of her eight 229mm/9in Dahlgren rifled breech-loaders are shown. Despite her superior firepower, her celebrated duel with the turret-equipped *Monitor* proved inconclusive. BELOW: Best known of the big Union wood-built cruisers was the *Wampanoag*, typifying the type that the *Inconstant* (above) was designed to counter. Although setting an early world speed record of nearly 18 knots, she was so expensive to operate that she worked almost exclusively under sail.

necessary number of stokers). Congress, which saw little justification for a fleet at all, saw even less for these ships but, nonetheless, the fact that they could out-run anything that they could not out-fight caused considerable concern in British and French naval circles, who both built in direct response.

Recognizing that the long wooden hulls of the Americans lacked longitudinal stiffness, both countries countered with large iron frigates. Launched in 1868, the British lead ship was the *Inconstant*, whose 5,873 tonnes/5,780 tons considerably exceeded the *Wampanoag*'s 4,283 tonnes/4,215 tons. Despite that, she was unprotected and, as contemporary iron plate had a bad reputation for shattering when struck by heavy shot, she was sheathed externally in timber. About a knot slower than the American, the *Inconstant* was, nevertheless, by far the better ship. Two variants, the larger *Shah* and smaller *Raleigh*, were also built but all proved expensive to run in peacetime.

Much delayed by the 1870–71 war with Prussia, the French produced the *Duquesne* and *Tourville*. Where the British ships

mounted their ten heavy guns broadside in central batteries, the French located some weapons in sponsons to give a measure of end-on fire.

In order to afford some protection, these large iron frigates were designed with coal bunkers flanking their machinery spaces.

The origins of the protected cruiser

Completed in 1875, the British unprotected frigate *Shah* was deployed as flagship of Commander-in-Chief, Pacific, Rear Admiral Algernon de Horsey. Accompanied by the unarmoured wooden screw corvette *Amethyst*, she arrived in Callao, Peru, in May 1877 to find that, following a mutiny aboard, the Peruvian turret-ship (or monitor) *Huascar* was taking armed action against foreign interests. Intent on her capture, de Horsey came up with her off Ilo on May 29.

The *Huascar* had been built by Laird 12 years previously and, in contrast with the British ships' mainly broadside armament, mounted two 254mm/10in weapons, firing 136.3kg/300lb projectiles, in a revolving turret. Her armoured belt varied between 114mm/4.5in and 64mm/2.5in in thickness, while the turret armour was 140mm/5.5in thick. Her stem was also reinforced for ramming.

Far larger, the *Shah* mounted two 229mm/9in, sixteen 178mm/7in and eight 64-pounder guns, the *Amethyst* adding fourteen more 64-pounders.

Refusing a summons to surrender, the *Huascar* sought shallow water, obliging her deeper-draught adversaries to fire, for the most part, at long range. During a three-hour action the *Huascar* tried once, unsuccessfully, to ram the *Shah*, while her inexperienced gunners failed to score a single hit.

For their part, the British ships made 70–80 hits from between 1,372m/1,500yds and 2,286m/2,500yds. Of all these, only one pierced the *Huascar*'s armour. During the action the *Shah* launched a Whitehead torpedo, the first such instance, but missed, due to its inaccuracy and low speed.

TOP: **Like the Confederate *Alabama*, the Peruvian turret ship *Huascar* was British-built. Taken over by renegade elements, she was intercepted in a policing action by the British iron frigate *Shah*. In the only big-ship action fought by the Victorian Navy, the *Shah* failed to sink the pirate.** ABOVE: **Benedetto Brin, the great Italian constructor, pioneered the vaulted protective deck, crowned by a cellular layer, as a lighter and more effective alternative to vertical side armour. Laid down in 1877–78, his battleships *Lepanto* (seen here) and *Italia* dispensed completely with belt armour.**

De Horsey thus failed to apprehend the renegade, while his actions caused misgivings at home for, had the *Huascar* been competently handled, she would have given the British the choice of retreating or being sunk. Clearly, cruising ships required protection but, due to their weight, vertical side belts were out of the question. However, the great Italian constructor, Benedetto Brin, was designing battleships with a new, and lighter, means of protection, already partially adopted by the British Admiralty in the turret battleship *Inflexible*, completed in 1881 and a command of the redoubtable John Fisher.

LEFT: **The French protected cruiser** *Tage* **here demonstrates a "harbour furl" (or "harbour stow") whereby her square canvas is gathered to the centre of the yard, a method which allows the sails to dry. Her three funnels are indicative of the number of boilers necessary even for auxiliary machinery.** ABOVE: **The British** *Inflexible* **of 1876 swiftly adopted Brin's ideas. She was not, of course, a cruiser but note here the low freeboard hull with unarmoured ends, and the powerfully armoured citadel with the two twin 406mm/16in muzzle-loader turrets placed** *en echlon.*

Brin reasoned that no side armour could withstand hits from the huge 432mm/17in guns that he was specifying. He therefore abandoned it entirely in favour of thinner horizontal protection, made lighter through using not-too-reliable steel plate. The "horizontal" protective deck was actually vaulted, its 76mm/3in plate abutting a ship's sides some 1.83m/6ft below the designed waterline. Above it, a flat unarmoured deck was located some 1.52m/5ft above the waterline. The space between these decks was subdivided into small compartments, or cells, some coal-filled, some void.

At ranges then considered practicable, projectiles followed fairly flat trajectories. Any penetrating the side, or shell, plating about or below the waterline would contact the convex curvature of the protective deck at a very shallow angle and be deflected upward, to expend their energy within the cellular layer. Despite some resultant flooding, it was unlikely that this would be sufficient to submerge the upper level of the cellular structure. Compartments above and below the cellular level would not, therefore, be flooded, the ship retaining adequate buoyancy and stability.

For cruising ships, the Admiralty began by partially adopting the idea, initially in the first-of-class *Comus* of 1878. Being far smaller than the *Inflexible*, her protective system was also on a smaller scale. The protective deck, flat rather than curved, was 38mm/1.5in in thickness, and located only 0.91m/3ft below the waterline, extending over only the central machinery spaces and magazines. The cellular structure was only a half-deck in depth but screened down either side by coal-filled bunker spaces. The *Comus* had a steel frame clad with iron plate, the latter being wood-sheathed and coppered as was customary for colonial cruisers.

ABOVE: **Last of the sailing corvettes built for the Royal Navy, the C-types (***Cordelia*** here) were also the first with all-metal hulls. Steel-framed, iron-clad, and wood-sheathed, they had a 38mm/1.5in steel protective deck over their machinery.**
BELOW: **First French cruiser to be built with a protective deck, the** *Sfax* **of 1884 slightly pre-dated the** *Tage* **(top left) and her sister** *Cécille.* **She was capable of a then-respectable 17 knots and with the** *Tages* **comprised the commerce-raiding squadron. Note how the heavy rig is no longer used for sailing.**

With this class of 11 ships, a new breech-loading 152mm/6in gun made its appearance. The final pair, *Calliope* and *Calypso*, mounted four of them in sponsons, French-style, to improve axial fire.

Early belted and armoured cruisers

There is rarely a definitive solution to the problems posed by warship design and, despite Benedetto Brin's concept of horizontal protection attracting one school of design, another still preferred and justified vertical protection. This, in what were still considered "line-of-battle ships", was necessarily massive. Faster than such vessels, a "cruiser" would logically decline action and her protection could be on a lighter scale. The question was one of how best to apply it. A given weight of armour could be spread fairly thinly over full length vertical belts, more thickly over shorter belts that protected only vital areas, or distributed in a compromise of vertical belting and protective deck. As a result two types developed; the "belted" and the "armoured" cruiser, although the latter term was often used to describe either type.

The Russians are credited with building the first belted cruisers with the launch of the General Admiral in 1873 and the Minin in 1878. Their full-length belts were, respectively, 152mm/6in and 178mm/7in thick, leaving the gun batteries, one level above, unprotected. The General Admiral's six 203mm/8in main battery weapons were breech-loading rifles (BLRs) and were concentrated in an amidships box with high bulwarks. The four corner guns could be traversed to fire either ahead or on the beam. In contrast, the Minin adopted French ideas with pronounced tumblehome and her four 203mm/8in BLRs located in four quarter sponsons, the weapons being capable of limited traverse to enable them to fire ahead or to work on the beam or axially for the purpose of chase fire.

TOP: **Russia's** *General Admiral* **had a shallow armoured belt protecting the waterline over its entire length. Just discernible is the open-topped box redoubt amidships, the ship's six 9.1-tonne/9-ton guns firing over a low armoured bulkhead only 0.76m/30in in height.** ABOVE: **The** *Shannon* **(if this is indeed her, for she was completed with a vertical stem) was the Royal Navy's first armoured cruiser. Her waterline belt stopped 18.3m/60ft from the stem, terminating in a 229mm/9in bulkhead. An armoured deck continued forward. Except for forward fire, the battery was unprotected.**

The launch of the General Admiral resulted in the laying-down of the Shannon, Britain's first armoured cruiser although, as this term was not yet generally accepted, she was classed as a "broadside armour-belted cruising ship with the status of a Second Class battleship", terminology, which reflected the still uncertain purpose of such vessels.

In both armament and armour, the Shannon was interesting. Of her seven 229mm/9in muzzle-loading rifles (MLRs), six were in the open and fired broadside, while the seventh, beneath the poop deck, could traverse sufficiently to fire through embrasures on either quarter. For the purposes of pursuit, two 254mm/10in MLRs fired forward through a transverse iron bulkhead. Up to 229mm/9in thick, this also served to protect the gundeck from raking fire from ahead (betraying tactical thinking from the still-recent sailing ship era).

The ship's belt armour, of similar thickness, extended from right aft to the transverse bulkhead, which continued down two levels to close it off. The belts were roofed by a 38mm/1.5in thick protective deck, one level beneath the gundeck. Forward of the lower edge of the bulkhead a 76mm/3in protective deck sloped downward, terminating in reinforcement for the ram. For further protection, this deck was overlaid by deep (if inaccessible) coal bunkers.

Over-ambitious and overweight, the *Shannon* was judged to be too weak to serve in a battle line yet too slow to be an effective cruising ship. This appears to have been anticipated prior to her launch as her two follow-ons, *Nelson* and *Northampton*, were laid down at 40 per cent larger by displacement. Their belts extended over only the centre section of the hull but were closed off by armoured bulkheads at either end. The extra power required twin shafts, each fitted with two propellers, which imposed considerable drag when the ships were under sail.

Powerful rivalry still existed between the British and French navies and, despite the reservations of the former toward the large armoured cruisers, the French followed suit in 1882 with the launch of the *Vauban* and *Duguesclin*. These displaced about 5,995 tonnes/5,900 tons compared with *Northampton*'s 7,722 tonnes/7,600 tons, and differed in having their armour disposed in a similar way to that of their recently completed battleship *Amiral Duperré*. Their belts were full length but shallow, leaving a margin to provide protection for four barbette-mounted 240mm/9.5in breech-loading rifles (BLRs). Barbette mountings left the guns exposed but, lacking heavy overhead shielding, permitted the weapons to be mounted higher above the waterline.

ABOVE: **Together with her near-sister *Vettor Pisani*, the Italian Navy's *Carlo Alberto* was not completed until 1898. Her side belt was of 152mm/6in plate amidships, tapering to 114mm/4.5in at the extremities. The main protective deck was 152mm/6in thick, with a 51mm/2in secondary deck above.**

BELOW: ***Nelson* and *Northampton* (shown) were larger derivatives of the *Shannon*. The deep embrasure was for one of the four symmetrically disposed 18.3-tonne/18-ton guns which fired axially through armoured bulkheads. Eight 12.2-tonne/12-ton guns fired on the beam through the unarmoured side above the belt. Compare the rigging with that of the *Alberto* (above).**

ABOVE: **A further solution to deploying four heavy guns was afforded by the French *Amiral Duperré*. Two single 343mm/13.5in, 48.8-tonne/48-ton guns were barbette-mounted on sponsons forward of the funnels, with two more on the centreline further aft and covered by a light spar deck.**

LEFT: **The Nelsons had "soft", or unarmoured, ends in order to concentrate protection amidships. Loss of buoyancy in the ends, if holed in action, was minimized by utilizing them for water-excluding spaces along the waterline, such as coal bunkers and water tanks.**

The Naval Defence Act of 1889

The Royal Navy of the 1870s and 1880s was a service in transition. Its well-organized, well-proven fleet of wooden, broadside-armed sailing ships had been assailed by technological development. How best to absorb and combine developments such as iron or steel, horizontal or vertical steam engines, paddles or screws, barbettes or turrets, muzzle or breech loaders? Each development attracted enthusiasts and in one form or another, these technologies found their way into new vessels, even if only for evaluation. The net result was an eclectic range of oddities and one-offs that lacked any sort of coherence and which were a logistical nightmare.

Technological development was not, of course, limited to Great Britain and growth in foreign fleets, particularly those of France and Russia, was a matter of some concern. To maintain battle fleets at home and in the Mediterranean, and to cover its worldwide imperial commitments, the Navy required adequate numbers of effective fighting ships; these it now obviously lacked.

The full extent of the Navy's weaknesses was first highlighted during 1884 in a series of articles in the influential Pall Mall Gazette, and the resulting public interest was skilfully exploited by interested parties. One such person was the junior Sea Lord, the then Captain Lord Charles Beresford, who prepared a detailed memorandum for the Board of Admiralty

> "Most of what you see is mere ullage." Admiral Hewitt describing the
> Royal Navy's ships at the 1887 Golden Jubilee Review

TOP: **Between 1899 and 1902 the new protected cruiser HMS *Crescent* acted as flagship on the Royal Navy's then North America and West Indies Station. Wearing a courtesy ensign, admiral's flag and jack, she is seen leading a squadron at an American review at Bar Harbor, Maine.** ABOVE: **Although rather similar in appearance to the Crescents, *Blake* and *Blenheim* (seen here) were rather larger, mounting a second 234mm/9.2in gun in lieu of a couple of broadside 152mm/6in guns. She is pictured in the uniform grey livery adopted from 1902, and disarmed, is serving as a depot ship, probably during World War I.**

demonstrating the complacency engendered by long years of freedom from major maritime war. For example, since the abolition of the old Navy Board there was no organization to oversee the conduct of war. Neither was there any intelligence-gathering service, nor a plan for the direction of merchant shipping in war, or for the transport and strategic stockpiling of essentials such as coal and ammunition.

To the Admiralty's embarrassment, this highly confidential assessment found its way into the columns of the same Pall Mall Gazette, raising public interest still further. Ever the opportunist, Beresford resigned his position on the Board early in 1888 to use his parallel occupation as Member of Parliament

ABOVE: **HMS *Blanche* was one of the four Barracouta-class Third Class cruisers which spent much of their lives in the Channel and Atlantic fleets, sometimes leading a division, or half flotilla, of torpedo boats. Note the navigating bridge, located aft, and what appears to be auxiliary canvas, bent on the after side of the masts.** RIGHT: **Destroyed by an internal explosion while visiting the Cuban capital, Havana, the USS *Maine* became the catalyst for the war against Spain. An armoured cruiser, she mounted two twin 254mm/10in turrets, the forward offset to starboard, as seen here, the after to port.**

> "There is no doubt that, had we gone to war with France in those days, we might well have been swept off the face of the globe... The Naval Defence Act saved the country."
> **Admiral Bacon in *A Naval Scrap Book***

to lobby the Navy's case for coherent, planned expansion. From so controversial a figure, who attracted both detractors and supporters in equal measure, the Service might have appreciated less support, but he was certainly effective.

Less obvious, but equally influential, was an 1887 report by the Assistant Controller, William White (later Sir William, Director of Naval Construction), anticipating the need to replace 72 warships during the ensuing four years. Where it was customary for the Chancellor of the Exchequer to inform the First Lord of what he could expect by way of annual vote, it was apparent that what was now required was a fully funded, multi-year construction plan. Needless to say, the Treasury baulked.

Then, early in 1889, a committee of three adjudicating flag officers reported unfavourably on the conduct of recent naval manoeuvres. It highlighted the poor performance of various types of ship and went on to exceed its brief in a reasoned redefinition of the purpose and scope of British sea power. The Royal Navy, it stated, was "altogether inadequate to take the offensive in a war with only one Great Power". The fleet, in fact, needed the strength to take on a combination of the next two largest fleets, the so-called Two Power Standard.

Between them, Beresford, White and the adjudicators could take credit for the Government appreciating the gravity of the situation and funding what was passed as the Naval Defence Act of 1889.

ABOVE: **Wearing the jack of the Kaiserliche Marine, the *Victoria Louise* was classed as a heavy cruiser. Note the stepped arrangement of the secondary 15cm/5.9in weapons, maintained right through to the final Scharnhorsts.** LEFT: **The Victorian Royal Navy was noted for "spit and polish" in preference to target practice, evidenced by this view of the after 234mm/9.2in gun aboard the *Edgar*. A reliable weapon, weighing about 23.4 tonnes/23 tons, the 9.2 fired a 172kg/380lb projectile. With only two guns per ship, a slow rate of fire, and no fire control, the weapon was not very effective.**

Among 70 new warships to be spread between the 1889–94 Programmes were no less than 42 cruisers. Of what were already being termed the First, Second the Third Classes they brought much-needed standardization, creating a force against which foreign fleets had to measure themselves. The bulk were constructed in White's reorganized and newly efficient royal dockyards.

The formal adoption of the Two Power Standard gave the Royal Navy an exact size but, with developments abroad, it would prove to be too expensive a goal to maintain.

First, Second and Third Class protected cruisers

All of the Defence Act cruisers, irrespective of class, would be "protected", as opposed to "armoured" or "belted". This was the result of an assessment of the preceding armoured cruisers, whose protection had generally followed that of contemporary battleships, and which had not been considered successful. Leading the way with these were the *Imperieuse* and *Warspite*, a pair which, completed in 1886 and 1888 respectively, were greatly influenced by the new French Marceau-class battleships, many of whose features they copied on a smaller scale. Difficult to classify, they were known officially as "armour-plated steel barbette ships" but, in adopting a partial 254mm/10in belt and 38–76mm/1.5–3in protective deck, they came out near 1,016 tonnes/1,000 tons overweight. This was serious for, of the 2.4m/8ft depth of the belt, 1m/3.25ft should have given above-water protection. As it was, the upper edge of the belt was near the waterline, so that the ships depended mainly on their coal bunkers and protective deck for protection.

While the *Imperieuse* and *Warspite* were building, the seven-ship Orlando class was laid down. These were designed at 5,690 tonnes/5,600 tons compared with *Imperieuse*'s 8,636 tonnes/8,500 tons yet they still carried a pair of guns of the same 234mm/9.2in calibre. This class, too, was belted and, as the general rule of thumb for vertical armour was to make it of

ABOVE: **Lead ship of a class of seven, *Orlando* was a "belted" cruiser which, for her length, carried a heavy armament. Her forward 234mm/9.2in and five starboard 152mm/6in guns, all in open shields, are clearly visible. Note how the forward and after 152mm/6in weapons are sponsoned to supplement axial, or "chase" fire.**

similar thickness to the primary gun calibre, they carried the same 254mm/10in belt over two-thirds their length. This was closed by 305mm/12in transverse bulkheads, roofed by 50mm/2in plate and continued to either end in the form of a 76mm/3in protective deck. It is small wonder that, with a full load of fuel aboard, their belt was totally submerged.

None of the Orlandos was ever tested in action, so their limitations remained unexposed. In service they were judged to be a success, being fitted with innovative horizontal triple-expansion machinery delivering a speed of 18 knots. It was apparent, however, that too much was being attempted on too limited a displacement. Nonetheless, by accepting a displacement of approximately 6,706 tonnes/6,600 tons and a slight reduction in speed, the Americans followed suit with the *Maine*, launched in 1888. Mounting four 254mm/10in guns in two echeloned twin turrets, she looked the part, being often referred to as a "Second Class battleship". The French, however, had reservations, and were preparing a revised design which would point armoured cruiser development in a new direction.

LEFT: **In the mid-1880s the torpedo was still something of a novelty weapon. With six fixed above-water tubes, firing on the beam, forward, amidships and aft, the seven Archers were classed as "torpedo cruisers". High bulwarks and many boats obviously made loading these fragile weapons a tricky process.**
ABOVE: **The eight Astraeas (*Hermione* seen here) were enlarged and improved Apollos. Despite her imposing appearance she mounts only a single 152mm/6in gun forward and aft, and eight 119mm/4.7in guns firing on the beam. Both classes were worn out and obsolete by 1914.**

ABOVE: **Nearly 50 Third Class cruisers were built in the 20 years after 1885 for the purposes of commerce protection. The *Pallas* (shown here) of 1890 led a nine-ship class of which five were transferred to the Royal Australian Navy. The final 11 (Pelorus class) had a reduced armament.** BELOW RIGHT: **French influence was evident in the *Warspite*, which carried the new 234mm/9.2in at either end and on the beam, necessitating pronounced tumblehome.**
BELOW: **Of the 21 Apollos built in 1890–91, only eight survived to serve during World War I, seven of them converted to minelayers. The *Retribution*, shown here, was scrapped in 1911. Several of the class were expended as blockships, notably at Zeebrugge and Ostend.**

Even before the completion of the Orlandos, expert opinion in Britain had swung in favour of the protected cruiser in offering a more balanced design. All cruisers resulting from the 1889 Act were thus of the protected type, resulting in a hiatus in armoured cruiser production. For extended range, British cruisers required large coal bunkers, while increased magazine space was needed because guns of 152mm/6in calibre and below now fired fixed ammunition as "quick-firers". Cruisers had, in any case, no business fighting armoured ships, so weight earlier devoted to belts was better allocated to coal and ammunition. This premise was satisfactorily proven in the building of the 9,297-tonne/9,150-ton *Blake* and *Blenheim*, launched in 1889 and 1890 respectively.

The largest cruisers ordered as a result of the 1889 Act were the nine Edgar-class vessels which, at 7,468 tonnes/7,350 tons, were slightly scaled-down Blakes. Rated First Class, they were intended for duties attached to the battle fleet. Two groups of Second Class cruisers were also built, comprising eight Hermiones of 4,430 tonnes/4,360 tons and no less than 21 Apollos of 3,455 tonnes/3,400 tons. Ships of either class could make about 20 knots and the function of both was primarily trade protection. Finally, there were four 2,621-tonne/2,580-ton Pallas-class cruisers, tacked on to a further five built to serve the Australian states. Rated Third Class, the British units were intended for colonial duties.

All the new ships adhered to a basic cruiser layout established with the Orlandos, with a large gun forward and aft complemented by six, eight or ten smaller weapons firing from protected broadside casemates.

Cruisers and naval brigades

A major duty for a Victorian colonial cruiser was to be able to put ashore fully trained and equipped "bluejacket" contingents suitable to meet any reasonable degree of unrest. All ranks were given regular military-style training – small arms drill twice weekly and, once per week, drill with cutlass, field guns and landing parties.

Irrespective of the size of a ship's contingent, it was termed a "naval brigade". With a crew even larger than that of a contemporary battleship, a large armoured cruiser would be expected to be able to field a fully self-supporting force of 400 men. Of these, 200 seamen and 80 marines would be organized in four or five companies of riflemen. Eighty seamen and marine artillerymen would be responsible for two 76mm/3in 12-pounders and one machine gun, all on wheeled mountings. In addition there were pioneers and ammunition carriers, medical staff and stretcher bearers, armourers, signallers and buglers. What amounted to about half the ship's complement was commanded by up to 20 officers. In the absence of such a force, their ship would need to be withdrawn temporarily from frontline duties. A Third Class cruiser would muster an equally self-contained force of about half the above size. Ships were sometimes immobilized in order to provide more men.

> "By ten o'clock the 100 bullocks and 60 horses were spanned-in to the guns and wagons. Commander Limpus reported that he was ready. I sounded the advance from the Town Hall, the band played 'A Life on the Ocean Wave', and the little army started." Captain Percy Scott's own account of the Navy's departure from Durban

For those deployed at the "sharp end", the long era of *Pax Britannica* could be anything but peaceful. Naval interventions were numerous and quite often on a considerable scale, as was the case when a massive Afrikaner incursion into Natal precipitated the Second Boer War in October 1899. The British had anticipated this event, so that the Royal Navy's South Africa squadron was reinforced by the timely arrival of the two large "white elephants" *Powerful* and *Terrible*. The former, her crew looking forward to home leave following a three-year China Fleet commission, had instead been diverted to Mauritius to collect a half-battalion of British troops for passage to Durban. Interestingly, these ships were credited with 22 knots, but this nine-day run, averaging 595km/370 miles per day, or about 13.4 knots, was considered a good sustained performance.

ABOVE: **The appropriately named armoured cruiser *Good Hope* laying in Table Bay during the South African War. In July 1907 the vessel became the flagship of the gunnery enthusiast Admiral Sir Percy Scott. Her secondary 152mm/6in shooting was then "without parallel in the British Fleet". Seven years later she was destroyed by gunfire at Coronel.**

Commanding the *Terrible*, which arrived at Cape Town on October 14, was Captain Percy Scott, a passionate gunnery specialist. On his own initiative he put ashore several of the ship's long-barrelled 76mm/3in 12-pounders and oversaw the dockyard's mounting them on improvised carriages for transport up-country.

A considerable British military force quickly found itself invested in the town of Ladysmith. Its field artillery was outranged by that of the Boers and the Navy was requested to provide the means of redressing the balance.

Within 24 hours, Scott had landed two 119mm/4.7in guns and had them fitted to carriages. These, together with their 20.4kg/45lb ammunition, sailed immediately for Durban in the *Powerful*. From there, a 284-strong brigade from the cruiser travelled with the guns directly to the Ladysmith area in two special trains, the final stretch under enemy fire. The two 119mm/4.7in guns, accompanied by four 12-pounders and four Maxims, found themselves immediately in action at Lombard's Kop. The enemy repulsed, the guns were then relocated in the town's defences, the 12-pounders in a battery, the 119mm/4.7in guns individually. All were capable of being moved at short notice.

Ammunition was short, and the sailors often found themselves serving as infantry, but the Navy's excellent

ABOVE LEFT: **All "bluejackets" of Victoria's navy were trained in military arts and usually relished the prospect of a "run ashore" to offset the routine of life afloat. It can only be noted, however, that, to marksmen as skilled as the Boers, the white uniforms made their practice considerably easier.** ABOVE: **The US Navy, too, was ready and able to land armed contingents to maintain or restore law and order, as evidenced by this party from the cruiser *Philadelphia* in Samoa. The United States sought basing rights in the island, but their interests clashed with the more colonial objectives of Great Britain and Germany.**

gun-laying endlessly disrupted the Boers' own batteries and troop concentrations. This contributed greatly to the effort of keeping the town in British hands until finally relieved in February 1900.

Scott, meanwhile, had satisfied Army requests for a 152mm/6in gun on a field mounting, together with several 119mm/4.7in guns on flat railway wagons. There was also an improvised armoured train, complete with searchlight.

By September 1900, when hostilities ended, the *Terrible* had already replaced the *Powerful* on the China station – just in time to become deeply involved in the Boxer Rebellion. Having exchanged their khaki battle dress for the more familiar blue, the contingents from the two cruisers were replaced by those from others, notably the *Forte, Philomel* and *Tartar*.

LEFT: **As far back as 1882 the Royal Navy had improvised an armoured train in the course of the Egyptian campaign. Less than 20 years later similar trains were used in South Africa. This short-barrelled 406.4kg/8cwt, 76mm/3in 12-pounder is well protected but apparently rather limited in traverse.**
ABOVE: **Percy Scott, then commanding the *Terrible* at the Cape, records that "we had on board long-range 12-pounder guns, specially supplied for use against torpedo boats". Mounted on "a pair of Cape wagon wheels and an axle tree" they looked "rather amateurish" but outranged anything available to either side.**

Later armoured cruisers

British reservations on belted and armoured cruisers were not shared by the French. Trials using new medium-calibre, quick-firing (QF) guns had impressed them with the damage that could be inflicted upon unprotected topsides. Such punishment would effectively disable a protected cruiser engaged on commerce raiding, a strategy important to the French. They established that a fairly modest thickness of armour would defeat or greatly reduce the effect of QF weapons and so, in 1890, launched the 6,604-tonne/6,500-ton *Dupuy de Lôme*, whose hull was totally clad in 100mm/3.9in armour from 1m/3ft 3in below the designed waterline right up to main deck level. To emphasize her role, the French reversed usual practice by locating a heavy 194mm/7.64in gun on either side in the waist and three smaller 164.7mm/6.48in firing axially at either end. Satisfactory arcs of fire were obtained by the use of exaggerated tumblehome, which also saved some topside weight but reduced the ship's stability range.

The *Dupuy de Lôme*'s immediate successors, the four 4,775-tonne/4,700-ton *Admiral Charners* of 1892–94 and the slightly larger *Pothuau* of 1895, reverted to a more orthodox armament layout.

The Russian cruiser *Rurik* was launched in 1892, but completed at a leisurely rate. At approximately 11,122 tonnes/10,923 tons she was nearly twice the size of the *Dupuy de Lôme*. Probably well-placed rumour credited her with an impressive range of 30,577km/19,000 miles, a threat against

ABOVE: **Of the ten-strong Monmouth class of armoured cruiser only the nameship became a war casualty. The *Kent* (shown here) is passing the Downs as a sailing merchantman engages a tow for the London Docks. She gained fame at the Falklands in 1914 by overhauling and sinking the German cruiser *Nürnberg*.**

commerce that the British could not ignore. In response, they launched in 1895 the then-enormous 14,427-tonne/14,200-ton *Powerful* and *Terrible*. Although classed as protected cruisers they were considerably larger than contemporary battleships, with the forecastle deck extending right aft. The resulting high freeboard made them good seaboats while giving sufficient depth to mount an impressive sixteen 152mm/6in secondary weapons in double-decked casemates. They were inordinately expensive to operate and their 4-knot advantage over the *Rurik* and her two follow-on vessels was bought at the expense of protection.

In total contrast to the *Dupuy de Lôme* the Americans launched the one-off *New York* in 1891 to a sound, unfussy design that put a twin 203mm/8in turret forward and aft, and a single 203mm/8in on either side of the waist. She was followed by the slightly larger *Brooklyn* of 1895, which continued the "lozenge" layout but mounted four twin turrets.

With the Powerfuls, however, the British had started a trend that led directly to the apotheosis of the armoured cruiser. Their 48 boilers demanded four funnels, whose impressive silhouette prompted a French series that began with the six-funnelled

Jeanne d'Arc of 11,329 tonnes/11,150 tons, launched in 1899, and finished, 18 ships later, with the two Waldeck-Rousseaus of 14,072 tonnes/13,850 tons in 1907–08. All had boiler spaces and, therefore, funnels, split into two distinctive groups. Early units continued the practice of mounting a heavy gun at either end, with an essentially broadside-mounted secondary battery. Later vessels moved to single-calibre armament, mostly turret-mounted.

By using more effective and thinner nickel and chrome-based cemented armour, the British returned to the armoured cruiser with the six Cressys of 1899–1901. Between then and 1906 they built 35 ships in steadily escalating size, culminating with the 14,834-tonne/14,600-ton Minotaurs, which carried four 234mm/9.2in guns in two twin centreline turrets, and ten 191mm/7.5in guns in single turrets sided in the waist.

With the six Californias of 1904 the Americans produced powerful equivalents. Although these were followed by the slightly smaller trio of Charlestons, size then increased again to the four impressive 14,733-tonne/14,500-ton Tennessees, with four 254mm/10in guns and sixteen 152mm/6in guns.

Although the "naval race" with Germany was, by 1906, having a great effect on British capital ship policy, this was not true with respect to armoured cruisers. Of these, the Germans had but half a dozen reckonable units. The two pairs of Prinz Adalberts (1901–02) and Roons (1903–04) had four 21cm/8.2in and ten 15cm/5.9in guns apiece, but their two 11,786-tonne/11,600-ton derivatives, the Scharnhorsts, mounted a formidable eight 21cm/8.2in and six 15cm/5.9in guns.

Development came to an abrupt halt in March 1908 with the completion of the *Invincible*, the first battlecruiser. Larger, faster, more heavily armed, she made the armoured cruiser obsolete overnight.

ABOVE: **Showing her ram forefoot as she pitches in a swell, the Cressy-class *Euryalus* looks all of her 12,193 tonnes/12,000 tons. Detail on the starboard side of her hull is clearly visible, including the two-level casemates of the secondary 152mm/6in guns. Note the row of ventilators paralleling the funnels and the docking bridge aft.** BELOW: **Battlecruisers, such as the prototype *Invincible*, were not really cruisers but fast, virtually unprotected battleships for use in opposed reconnaissance. Against armoured cruisers they were deadly, but they were themselves vulnerable to heavy-calibre gunfire.**

LEFT: ***Scharnhorst*, and her sister *Gneisenau*, represented the latest and best of German armoured cruiser design in 1914. That they were overwhelmed by the 305mm/12in gunfire of battlecruisers appeared to vindicate Fisher's dictum that speed and firepower were sufficient protection in themselves.** BELOW: **The six American Pennsylvanias of 1903–04 carried four 203mm/8in and fourteen 152mm/6in guns on a 14,072-tonne/13,850-ton displacement. For a further 711 tonnes/700 tons, the four following Tennessees carried four 254mm/10in and sixteen 152mm/6in weapons. All, including the Pennsylvania-class *California*, were renamed after cities, this ship becoming *San Diego*.**

Scouts and the origins of the light cruiser

The British Admiralty's practical experience with steam turbines began with the destroyer *Viper* in 1899. Following successful service in several significant merchant vessels, it was then decided to install this type of machinery in a cruiser. Existing Third Class protected cruisers were limited by their triple expansion reciprocating engines so that minor increases in speed were only possible by designing longer and finer hulls. One of the final groups of such ships, the Topaze class, was selected to evaluate steam turbine propulsion, the *Amethyst* being thus completed in 1904. Although an inefficient direct-drive, un-geared installation, it still developed some 22 per cent more power, delivering an extra 1.5 knots.

At about the same time, a case was made for a new type of small cruiser, a Scout, capable of assisting in a traditional close blockade by assuming the sailing frigate's role of watching the enemy's harbours. Destroyers were also developing rapidly and it was envisaged that flotillas of 24 such craft would make mass torpedo attacks on an enemy battle line. To control such a pack a senior officer would need to be embarked on a larger craft, capable of keeping pace while carrying heavier quick-firing (QF) guns to deter any counter-attack by enemy destroyers. It was mainly with this role in mind that the Admiralty had four pairs of scouts built, to a similar specification but individual design of the manufacturing yards. The preferred result was the Armstrong-built *Amethyst* design, completed in 1905. This displaced 2,713 tonnes/2,670 tons and could make 25.5 knots with reciprocating machinery. For service requirements, the Admiralty had this basic design stretched to 3,353–3,505 tonnes/3,300–3,450 tons, the

TOP: **Both British and German fleets produced series of effective "fleet" cruisers named after their respective towns. Earlier British classes, such as the Bristols (*Gloucester* seen here) had a protective deck. With the generally short range encounters that developed, the later classes were fitted with belts.** ABOVE: **The eight Arethusas (*Aurora* seen here) were smaller than the fleet cruisers, and intended to work with the then-usual large destroyer flotillas. Particularly associated with the Harwich Force, they led to the numerous "C" class of light cruiser. Note the sturdy tripod mast.**

resulting Boadicea and Active classes making 26 knots with turbines, and carrying up to ten 102mm/4in guns.

Although fewer, the German Third Class protected cruisers were similar to their British counterparts, and formed the basis of their first group of "Towns" in 1904–05. Then, at a rate of two or three hulls per year, they evolved rapidly, with steam turbines being generally adopted in 1909. Their 10cm/3.9in guns were greatly superior to the 102mm/4in of the British ships and they also had a 50mm/2in protective deck, which the contemporary Boadiceas lacked.

In 1910–11, therefore, the British completed the five Bristols, some 15.2m/50ft longer than a Boadicea and with

displacement increased from 3,455 tonnes/3,400 tons to 4,877 tonnes/4,800 tons. This allowed the ten 102mm/4in guns to be complemented by a pair of single 152mm/6in weapons that were better able to stop a destroyer. In addition, they had a partial 50mm/2in protective deck and, with 25 per cent more power and partial oil firing, a maximum speed of 26 knots.

The British "Towns", like their German equivalent, comprised a series of continuously evolving groups. They totalled 18 ships, of which the final trio, the Birminghams of 1915–16, displaced 5,527 tonnes/5,440 tons and mounted nine 152mm/6in guns. Interestingly, they exchanged a protective deck for a 76mm/3in side belt, capable of stopping a 10cm/3.9in projectile and indicative of the expectation of close-range action.

The Birminghams could make 25.5 knots but, for their successors, the Staff Requirement was 30 knots. The resulting Arethusas were smaller and finer-lined; although nominally 27-knot ships, they were good for 29 knots if forced. Already termed "light cruisers", they had a 25mm/1in protective deck worked in, similar to the latest German practice. This, in addition to an armoured belt, technically made them small armoured cruisers.

From the Arethusas evolved the first group of the extensive C-class which, in a series of related sub-classes, comprised 30 ships, themselves slowing evolutionary improvements.

Of the original pure "scout cruiser", little more was seen. Exceptions were the trio of American Chesters of 1907 and the later, and much enlarged, Omahas. During World War II, the Italians introduced their handsome *Capitani Romani*, described officially as *esploratori oceanici*, while the Germans commenced work on their the uncompleted *spähkreuzer* (reconnaissance cruisers).

ABOVE: **Designed more specifically to operate individually as scouts, the USS *Chester* (shown here) and her two sisters were given unusually high freeboard to assist in maintaining speed in a seaway. Not intended for serious fighting, their armament and protection was very light.** BELOW: **Completed in 1918, the Kölns represented the ultimate stage of development of the German "Towns". They had both belt and protective deck, 15cm/5.9in guns in place of 10.5cm/4.1in and geared steam turbines. Confusingly, later ships repeated names of those sunk earlier, the previous *Köln* being lost at Heligoland Bight.** BOTTOM: **The only successors to the US Navy's Chester-class scouts were the ten Omahas of 1920–24. Twice as large and 10 knots faster, they had a powerful chase armament of six forward-firing 152mm/6in guns. These were disposed in a twin gunhouse and four single casemates.**

The pursuit of the *Goeben*

As Europe stumbled toward war in 1914 the British Mediterranean Fleet, commanded by Admiral Sir Berkeley Milne, comprised one squadron each of battlecruisers, armoured cruisers and light cruisers together with 16 destroyers. Allied with the French these would have to meet the combined strength of the Austro-Hungarian and Italian navies together with a German contingent bound by the planned Triple Alliance. Germany's contribution was just two ships but, of these, the battlecruiser *Goeben* had firepower and speed that outclassed any British or French ship in the Mediterranean.

The First Lord of the Admiralty, Winston Churchill, was well aware of this point and, on July 30, six days before war erupted, gave Milne broad instructions which stated, specifically: "Do not at this stage be brought to action against superior forces, except in combination with the French ..."

On August 1, the *Goeben* and the light cruiser *Breslau* were at Brindisi. To shadow them, Milne despatched two battlecruisers, while Rear Admiral Ernest Troubridge was sent with his four armoured cruisers to patrol the Otranto Strait at the entrance to the Adriatic.

> "Being only able to meet *Goeben* outside the range of our guns and inside his, I have abandoned the chase with my squadron..."
> Troubridge to Milne, timed 04:49 hours, August 7, 1914

TOP: **HMS *Chatham* was one of only four light cruisers available to Admiral Sir A. Berkeley Milne's Mediterranean Fleet in August 1914. The picture shows how her fine lines demand a multitude of timber shores to stabilize her when stemmed in dry dock, here only partly emptied.** ABOVE: **Consort to the *Goeben* was the light cruiser *Breslau*, also completed in 1912. The escape of the pair to Constantinople, and their continued existence, ostensibly under the Turkish flag, was a source of continuing concern during the Anglo-French Dardanelles campaign, as a foray was constantly threatened.**

Arriving at Messina on August 2, the German Rear Admiral Wilhelm Souchon received the disappointing news that Italy, after all, intended to remain neutral. Without waiting to complete with coal, he departed with some urgency. His absence was quickly noted and reported to Milne by the light cruiser *Chatham*. Troubridge was promptly ordered westward, leaving only the *Gloucester* and destroyers to watch Otranto. Indecisive, Milne then ordered Troubridge to return, and the *Chatham* to join the battlecruisers in their search.

ABOVE: **The island harbour of Mudros was the major base for British and French forces during the operations around the Dardanelles. The Cressy-class armoured cruiser is either *Bacchante* or *Euryalus*. Used for reconnaissance and spotting, the airship is a non-rigid Sea Scout "blimp" of the RNAS.** RIGHT: **The dogged but, ultimately, unsuccessful Allied campaign on the Gallipoli peninsula resulted in a continuous stream of troop convoys to and from the theatre. Having evaded German cruisers, such as the *Emden*, in the Indian Ocean, these Anzac troops now had to be protected from the *Goeben*.**

Souchon, meanwhile, anticipating a declaration of war with France, headed for North Africa in order to disrupt the recall of French military forces. News of war with both France and Russia came on August 3, and, early next morning, the *Goeben* bombarded the embarkation port of Philippeville, while the *Breslau* attacked Bona. The operation was brief and limited but inflicted psychological damage.

Souchon was now informed of a new German alliance with Turkey and ordered to Istanbul (then Constantinople). Needing coal, he made for Messina but, at 10:30 hours on August 4, encountered the British battlecruisers. Not yet at war, the British made to shadow the Germans but unable to match their speed, were quickly shaken off. At midnight, a British ultimatum to Germany expired and the two nations were at war.

Early on August 5, Souchon arrived again at Messina but, as a belligerent, was allowed only an insufficient 24 hours to coal his ship. He duly sailed on August 6, passed the *Gloucester,* watching the southern end of the strait, and headed eastward. As Austria-Hungary had not yet declared war, his situation was precarious. Occasionally harried by the *Breslau*, the *Gloucester* successfully trailed the fugitives as far as Cape Matapan before being ordered back due to lack of coal.

Although much slower, Troubridge's armoured cruisers had been well placed to make an interception. Uncertain, however, of exactly what constituted a "superior force", he desisted. In doing so he almost certainly avoided a Coronel-style defeat, but his action resulted in Court Martial proceedings.

Milne was now thoroughly confused by conflicting Admiralty telegrams regarding Austria-Hungary's participation. For 24 hours the hunt for Souchon lost momentum, allowing the Germans to take aboard emergency coal at an Aegean rendezvous. Unaware of Souchon's true destination, Milne disposed his forces to safeguard the Greek coast, enabling the enemy to safely enter the Dardanelles on the evening of August 9, to the consternation of the Admiralty.

ABOVE: **Much in her original condition, the *Goeben* is seen here under Turkish colours as the *Yavuz*. She served until the 1960s and, as the sole surviving example of a major World War I combatant, should have survived as a museum ship. Despite widespread protest, however, she was scrapped.** BELOW: **Another of Milne's light cruisers, the *Gloucester* under the command of Captain Howard Kelly, performed a classic cruiser role in shadowing and reporting the progress of the Germans. Alone, and occasionally exchanging fire with the *Breslau*, she desisted only when bunkers became low.**

There followed the charade of the two German ships taking Turkish names and colours, and their crews donning Turkish uniform. They proved to be a considerable nuisance to Russian interests in the Black Sea, but although a continuous threat to Anglo-French operations in the eastern Mediterranean, they mounted only one damaging raid. This, in turn, proved disastrous for them, the ex-*Breslau* being sunk by mines and the *Goeben* fortunate to regain sanctuary following heavy mine damage.

Coronel and the Falklands

Most significant of the detached German naval forces in August 1914 was the East Asiatic Squadron, based at the Chinese enclave of Tsingtao. Commanded by the very able Vice Admiral Graf von Spee, it comprised the latest armoured cruisers *Scharnhorst* and *Gneisenau*, and the light cruisers *Emden, Leipzig* and *Nürnberg.*

Once Japan entered the war supporting Britain in accordance with its treaty obligations, von Spee knew that Tsingtao would be indefensible so, already on a Pacific cruise, his squadron never returned. Detaching the *Emden* to conduct war against commerce in the Indian Ocean he, and the remainder of squadron, headed eastward toward South America, his progress marked by sudden raids on islands in quest of coal and provisions. Eluding the British, Commonwealth and Japanese warships that were seeking him, von Spee linked up with a further cruiser, *Dresden*, at Easter Island on October 12.

The only British force in South American waters was a scratch group commanded by Rear Admiral Christopher Cradock. Its two armoured cruisers, *Good Hope* and *Monmouth*, unlike the German ships, had only recently been mobilized. Their crews consisted largely of reserves and new recruits. Cradock also had the pre-Dreadnought *Canopus* but, believing her too slow to fight an action, neglected to concentrate on her. Aware of von Spee's progress, he sent ahead his only modern cruiser, the *Glasgow*, to seek intelligence upon which he could base his next move.

On October 31, the German admiral learned that *Glasgow* was at the small Chilean port of Coronel and, believing her

TOP: **Flagship of Read Admiral Christopher Cradock's South American Squadron, the armoured cruiser *Good Hope* had been recently commissioned with a large proportion of reservists. Not efficiently "worked-up", she was totally outclassed by von Spee's seasoned cruisers.** ABOVE: **Von Spee's nemesis at the Falklands, the battlecruiser *Inflexible* leads the armoured cruiser *Minotaur* and two others. The two battles proved little more than the old dictum that "a good big 'un will always beat a good little 'un".**

unsupported, moved to intercept. When, late the following day, he made contact, he found her in company with the *Good Hope*, *Monmouth* and the armed liner *Otranto*. Although the *Canopus* was 300 miles distant, Cradock immediately detached the *Otranto* and sought action.

His situation was hopeless from the outset. His big ships had had little gunnery practice and in heavy seas they were unable to work the guns in their lower casemates. They were further disadvantaged by being sharply etched against the afterglow of the sun sinking behind them, while their opponents were near-invisible against the darkening eastern horizon.

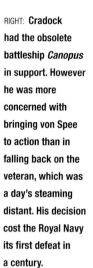

RIGHT: **Cradock had the obsolete battleship *Canopus* in support. However he was more concerned with bringing von Spee to action than in falling back on the veteran, which was a day's steaming distant. His decision cost the Royal Navy its first defeat in a century.**

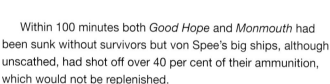

Within 100 minutes both *Good Hope* and *Monmouth* had been sunk without survivors but von Spee's big ships, although unscathed, had shot off over 40 per cent of their ammunition, which would not be replenished.

Although courageous, Cradock had, in the circumstances, acted foolishly. Sixteen hundred had perished in what had been the Royal Navy's first defeat in over a century. At the Admiralty the new First Sea Lord, Fisher, acted decisively with his political superior, Churchill, and in great secrecy detached three battlecruisers from Jellicoe's Grand Fleet. Von Spee was obviously headed homeward and to guard against the possibility that he would use the newly opened Panama Canal, the *Princess Royal* was sent to North American waters. It was thought more likely however that he would double the Horn and be tempted by the large coal stocks maintained on the Falkland Islands. Vice Admiral Sir Doveton Sturdee was therefore despatched with the *Invincible* and the *Inflexible*, collecting en route the cruisers *Bristol*, *Carnarvon*, *Cornwall*, *Kent* and the Coronel survivor, *Glasgow*.

Sturdee arrived at Port Stanley on December 7, and was still engaged in coaling when, less than 24 hours later, von Spee approached. Berthed in the harbour was the *Canopus*, and a speculative 305mm/12in salvo from her deterred the enemy, who made off into open ocean.

The British were quickly in pursuit and, in unusually clear conditions, steadily overhauled the fugitives. *Inflexible* opened fire at 12:50 and, half an hour later, von Spee ordered his light cruisers to scatter *sauve qui peut*. Each, however, attracted its own pursuer and, long out of dock, were caught and destroyed, only the *Dresden* escaping.

In destroying the *Scharnhorst* and *Gneisenau*, Fisher's revolutionary battlecruiser concept was totally vindicated, their superior speed and firepower overwhelming von Spee's gallant defence and by extension signalling the obsolescence of the armoured cruiser.

TOP: **The captain of the *Gneisenau* was reportedly at odds with von Spee over the latter's decision to attack the Falklands. As it was, the German cruisers, long out of dock, were neither able to out-run nor out-gun Sturdee's battlecruisers.** ABOVE: **HMS *Bristol*, with an engine opened for repair, nearly missed the Falklands action. She was eventually despatched together with an auxiliary to round up von Spee's accompanying colliers who it was feared conveyed a landing force to occupy the islands.**

ABOVE: **Sole German survivor of the Falklands action, the *Dresden* went to ground in the maze of waterways around the Magellan Strait. When eventually run to earth in Chilean territorial waters, British cruisers ignored neutrality laws to effect her destruction.** BELOW: **Sisters of the ill-starred *Monmouth*, *Cornwall* (seen here) and *Kent* both participated at the Falklands. In company with the *Glasgow*, survivor of Coronel, the *Cornwall* sank the *Leipzig*, while *Kent* overhauled and disposed of the *Nürnberg*.**

Blockade and the Tenth Cruiser Squadron

At 03:00 hours on August 2, 1914, Rear Admiral Dudley de Chair broke his flag aboard the cruiser *Crescent* at Portsmouth. One hour later an Admiralty telegram ordered him to take his Tenth Cruiser Squadron (10th CS) to Scapa Flow "with all despatch". Its task on declaration of hostilities would be to initiate a sea blockade of Germany. Maintaining a permanent patrol line from the Orkneys to the Norwegian coast, it would first snare any returning German-flag shipping and then, as this inevitably diminished, intercept neutrals attempting to break the blockade with the intention of confiscating contraband cargo.

"Contraband" is not an exact term but here is understood to mean any goods that would directly benefit the enemy military or Germany's capacity to wage war. Cargoes destined for the civil population were exempt although successive British Orders-in-Council considerably extended the list of what constituted contraband.

The Admiralty's objective was to make all neutral shipping proceed via the restricted Dover Strait where it could be efficiently regulated. The official view was that any proceeding via the northern route had some reason for evasion. The British assumption of a right to stop and search caused widespread resentment among neutrals, particularly the United States. In deference to the latter, the content of forthcoming Orders-in-Council were first discussed with them.

De Chair's ships, Crescent- and Edgar-class cruisers dating from 1893–94, were among the navy's oldest. "Short-legged", mechanically unreliable, crowded, wet and uncomfortable, they proved totally unable to cope with the first northern autumnal gales. Badly damaged, some barely surviving, they were exchanged in November 1914 for the first of what would be a total of about two dozen ex-passenger liners. Armed with old 152mm/6in guns, these were far better able to cope with the

"If anything more strikingly demonstrating the value of sea power can be given [than the work of the 10th CS], I do not know of it." Speech by Sir Eric Geddes, First Lord of the Admiralty, on opening the post-war Sea Power exhibition

ABOVE: **Neutrals could be encountered anywhere in British waters, and here a destroyer is preparing to send away her seaboat to examine a Nederland Line passenger vessel.**

endless storms of these northern latitudes. They had capacious bunker capacity and comfortable accommodation, not only for their own crews but also for the many extra hands required to form "prize crews" for the purpose of taking neutrals into the examination anchorages at Kirkwall or Lerwick. A ship might have a dozen or more armed parties away at any time and not expect to recover them for weeks on end. Their transfer by open boat could be hazardous, so the ships, known officially as Armed Merchant Cruisers (AMCs), carried Newfoundlanders, who were second-to-none in the art of small boat handling.

LEFT: **Like the *Alsatian*, flagship of the Tenth Cruiser Squadron, the 10,754grt *Virginian* belonged to the Allan Line, later subsumed into Canadian Pacific. She and the *Victorian* were the first steam-turbine passenger liners on the North Atlantic service.** BELOW: **Two P&O liners served in the blockade service, the 9,500-tonne/9,350-ton *Moldavia*, dating from 1903, and the 10,885grt *Mantua* of 1909. The *Moldavia* is seen embarking peacetime passengers by tender.**

ABOVE: **Admiral de Chair's flagship, _Crescent_, and the supporting Edgar-class cruisers were among the oldest in the navy, and manifestly unsuited to protracted patrols in Northern waters. Breakdowns, structural damage and casualties persuaded the Admiralty to retire the ships in favour of armed liners.**

That the blockade was hurting the enemy was evident in his continual complaints regarding its legality, and his trying to justify the employment of still-illegal unrestricted U-boat warfare as a consequence.

The AMCs were not escorted, and it was a constant mystery why the Germans never specifically targeted them. Several, however, were lost to torpedo, others through stress of the unremittingly foul northern weather.

From March 1916 the 10th CS was under the command of Rear Admiral Reginald Tupper. His workload began to be eased at about this time through the introduction of the so-called Navicert, a certificate issued by naval authority to a ship and cargo at its port of origin, identifying the eventual end-user and obviating the requirement for further search.

Further relief came in April 1917. American ships and cargoes, particularly cotton, had been something of a delicate issue, now solved by that nation becoming a combatant. Neutral shipping was in business to make a profit and, for the

ABOVE: **Admiral de Chair's flagship, _Crescent_, and the supporting Edgar-class cruisers were among the oldest in the navy, and manifestly unsuited to protracted patrols in Northern waters. Breakdowns, structural damage and casualties persuaded the Admiralty to retire the ships in favour of armed liners.**

most part, would trade with either camp. The endless British problem, therefore, was how to stifle the flow to the enemy without causing diplomatic opprobrium, while at the same time realizing that "playing safe" reduced the value of the blockade.

In round figures, nearly 13,000 interceptions were made. Some 2,000 of these proceeded voluntarily for examination and a further 1,800 went under armed guard. It was believed that about 650 ships evaded the patrols, but this represented just 5 per cent of movements.

The loss of materials to Germany was debilitating, civilian morale suffering further from the feeling of encirclement. Indeed, as the government tended to blame the blockade in order to disguise its own failings, this impression was exacerbated.

ABOVE: **_St. George_ was the odd one out, being the only Edgar not involved with 10th CS, having been converted to a destroyer depot ship pre-war. By coincidence, she had been an earlier appointment of de Chair, when he was a commander and she was flagship C-in-C, South Atlantic.**
RIGHT: **Designed for the long-haul Australasian service, Orient liners were comfortable and of great endurance. Four, including the _Orvieto_, seen here, served with the Tenth Cruiser Squadron, the _Otway_ being lost by torpedo.**

German experience in World War I

In August 1914, there existed enormous potential for German cruisers to damage Allied commercial shipping. The British Admiralty believed that the time-honoured defensive measure of convoy had been made redundant by the advent of steam propulsion. Traffic thus followed well-defined routes, which created focal points of high shipping density. Despite advice for caution, commercial considerations encouraged masters to deviate little from normal peacetime routine.

To support cruiser warfare, however, Germany lacked the British advantage of worldwide bases and coaling stations. Extended operations would depend upon how reliably cruisers could obtain coal and provisions and, if required, ammunition and repair facilities. As a result, well before the war probable theatres were identified and a representative – vice consul, commercial attaché or equivalent – appointed to organize

ABOVE: **Detached from von Spee's squadron at the outbreak of war the *Emden*, under her resourceful commanding officer, von Müller, pursued a brief but successful raiding career in the Indian Ocean. Her boldness was typified by a surprise bombardment of oil storage tanks at Madras (now Chennai) on September 22, 1914.** BELOW LEFT: **Von Müller's decision to destroy the cable station on Cocos Island sealed the *Emden*'s fate. A radioed alarm brought the Australian cruiser *Sydney* (shown here) quickly to the scene. A Chatham-class cruiser, her eight 152mm/6in guns totally outclassed the German's ten 10.5cm/4.1in weapons.**

requirements. Despite international law regarding supply to combatants by neutrals, high profit would always justify high risk for some operators.

Reflecting their lack of experience in maritime warfare, the Germans in fact had only modest plans in place, initially involving only three regular cruisers and a handful of auxiliaries. In the Indian Ocean, the light cruiser *Emden* had been detached from the German East Asiatic Squadron to conduct a campaign against commercial shipping. For three months her commanding officer, Karl von Müller, skilfully evaded hunting forces by constantly changing his location. The *Emden* took 23 prizes, totalling over 100,000 gross registered tons (grt) with all captured personnel being scrupulously well-treated before being transferred to neutral ships. Inevitably von Müller was apprehended, his nemesis on November 9 being the Australian cruiser *Sydney*.

ABOVE: **Pictured at Dar-es-Salaam, where she was German East Africa station ship, the *Königsberg* complicated matters in the Indian Ocean by embarking on a commerce-raiding cruise while the *Emden* was still at large. Fortunately, she went to ground in the Rufiji delta, where the Royal Navy blockaded and destroyed her.** RIGHT: **As a variation on commerce raiding, the Germans used commercial ships as minelayers from the outset. The very first shots of the naval war were fired on August 5, 1914, when the cruiser *Amphion* and two destroyers of the Harwich Force intercepted and sank the *Königin Luise* (shown in the foreground).**

The light cruiser *Karlsruhe* was in the Caribbean. Being a new ship, fresh out of dock, she outpaced intercepting British cruisers on two occasions. Like the *Emden*, she supplemented her supplies from prizes which she used to extend her line of search. Her commander, Köhler, operated primarily in the teeming focal point off north-eastern Brazil, accounting for 16 ships of some 73,000grt before the *Karlsruhe* was destroyed by an internal explosion on November 4, 1914.

The third German light cruiser at large was the *Königsberg*, based in East Africa. She had taken but one prize when, reputedly short of coal, she holed-up in the fetid, shallow delta of the Rufiji River to await supplies. Searching British cruisers intercepted her collier, learned of her location and blockaded her until she could be destroyed by indirect bombardment.

Included in this first wave of raiders were several auxiliary cruisers mostly passenger liners armed by appointment in August 1914. In total they accounted for a further 100,000grt of Allied shipping but led a limited, fugitive existence. Within months, those not intercepted and sunk were compelled by mechanical problems to seek sanctuary and internment in neutral ports, where they remained for the duration.

An unquantifiable bonus for the Germans was the very considerable disruption caused to trade through a raider being at large and the number of regular warships removed from other duties for the purpose of hunting her down.

Although the U-boat soon became the principal means by which the Germans conducted their campaign against commerce, auxiliary cruisers continued to be used to considerable effect. Regular warships had proved to be over-ambitious in the role, as ordinary merchantmen with concealed armament aroused little suspicion and were inexpensive to

BELOW: **Converted from a merchantmen, the successful German raider *Möwe* laid mines off Cape Wrath in January 1916. These claimed the pre-Dreadnought *King Edward VII*, seen here. That sovereign had stipulated that she should always be a flagship; this had been her first voyage as a "private" ship.**

convert and to operate. Most successful was the *Möwe* whose mines, laid early in 1916, accounted for several ships including the pre-Dreadnought battleship *King Edward VII*. During a later foray she accounted for a record 25 ships of some 123,000grt. Another auxiliary *Wolf,* actually cruised for a single period of 15 months without being apprehended. Making considerable use of a small embarked floatplane, she sank about 114,000grt.

Experience gained during 1914–18 enabled the Germans to prepare an even more formidable campaign during World War II, conducted almost exclusively by auxiliary cruisers supported by a well-organized force of supply ships.

LEFT: **The Battle of Jutland in 1916 destroyed the reputation of both battle and armoured cruisers, the Royal Navy losing three of each. Caught on the engaged flank of the British battle line, the *Defence* came under a hail of German 28cm/11in and 15cm/5.9in fire, causing her to blow up with the loss of all 903 crew.**

Goodenough at Jutland

On May 31, 1916, as Jellicoe's Grand Fleet and Scheer's High Seas Fleet headed for the clash that would be Jutland, each was preceded, at a distance of 48–63km/ 30–40 miles, by its respective battlecruiser force. Their task was armed reconnaissance and they, in turn, had light cruiser screens pushed out ahead and around.

Admiral Beatty's "eyes" were the 13 ships of the First, Second and Third Light Cruiser Squadron (LCS) which were disposed on a line of bearing as the whole formation headed SSE. At 14:20 hours, the easternmost cruiser, *Galatea*, sighted what proved to be Admiral Hipper's advance force. Against standing instructions, all nine of the First and Third LCS peeled off to investigate. This left just Commodore William ("Barge") Goodenough's Second LCS in company. Wearing his broad pendant in the *Southampton*, he led *Birmingham*, *Nottingham* and *Dublin*.

Correctly suspecting the presence of a larger enemy force, Beatty pressed on to the south. Goodenough was positioned on his starboard bow while the remainder, on rejoining, fell in on the port quarter. At 15:40 Hipper's battlecruisers were sighted and the light cruisers kept to Beatty's disengaged side as a vicious and prolonged gun duel developed. In the course of this, as Hipper sought to entice Beatty's squadron on to Scheer's greater force, two British battlecruisers, *Indefatigable* and *Queen Mary*, blew up catastrophically.

This exchange was still in progress when, at 16:30, the *Southampton*, some three miles ahead, sighted and reported "sixteen battleships with destroyers disposed around them". This was Jellicoe's first warning of Scheer's approach. Beatty immediately reversed course to lure the German forces in turn on to the Grand Fleet. Goodenough, however, held on toward Scheer in order to confirm his earlier observation. As the Second LCS closed the enemy battle fleet at a combined speed of about 45 knots, not a shot was fired for, end-on, the enemy was uncertain of his identity. With the range at just 10,973m/12,000yds, Goodenough's commander said "If you're going to make that signal, sir, you'd better make it now. You may never make another…"

That done, at 16:48, the Second LCS turned away. In doing so it presented its distinctive profiles, attracting a storm of fire. There began an hour and more of misery as the older battleships at the German rear, their 28cm/11in guns unable to range the British capital ships, used the trailing Goodenough for practice. Deluged with water and shell fragments, the cruisers survived by "chasing the salvoes", or weaving to confuse the enemy gun-layers. These manoeuvres also caused Goodenough's navigating officer's dead reckoning to be increasingly in error, influencing the Commodore's reports.

LEFT: **Having received over 20 heavy calibre shell hits and at least one torpedo, the German battlecruiser *Seydlitz* arrived back at Wilhelmshaven with an estimated 5,385 tonnes/5,300 tons of water aboard and her two after turrets burned out. Note how the roof and guns of the forward turret have also been removed.** BELOW LEFT: **German heavy calibre guns fired a total of 3,597 recorded rounds at Jutland, of which 122 scored direct hits. British figures were 4,480 and 123 respectively. Commodore Goodenough's *Southampton* took 21 hits, one 28cm/11in, two 15cm/5.9in and the remainder 10cm/3.9in.** BELOW: **On a day notable for poor signalling and reporting, comprehension and initiative, "Barge" Goodenough and the Second Light Cruiser Squadron were an exception, doing all that could reasonably have been expected of them.**

ABOVE: **The presence of considerable numbers of obsolescent fighting units suggests that Admiral Scheer really did not expect to fight a major battle. Having already extinguished a potentially serious fire caused by two 152mm/6in hits, the *Frauenlob* capsized following a torpedo hit from *Southampton*.** BELOW: **At Jutland, the *Canterbury* (shown) and *Chester* were attached to *Hood*'s devastated Third Battle Cruiser Squadron. The *Chester* would be heavily damaged but *Canterbury* attached herself to the Third Light Cruiser Squadron. Despite a busy day, she escaped with just one hit.**

At 18:15 hours the great battle line of the Grand Fleet came into sight across the northern horizon and it soon became Scheer's turn for discomfort. As the battle became general Goodenough tucked his squadron in at the rear of the British line, firing on the enemy's light units as opportunities were presented.

Scheer's priority was now to extricate himself and, in conditions of fitful visibility, he succeeded admirably. As darkness fell, the British, still in battle formation, were effectively between the Germans and their base, however during the night Scheer's forces moved through the tail of Jellicoe's line resulting in violent clashes.

Stationed to the west of the Grand Fleet battleships, Goodenough suddenly encountered the enemy's Fourth Scouting Group, whose half-dozen light cruisers were under 805m/880yds distant. Both sides opened with searchlights and rapid salvoes. The *Southampton* sank the *Frauenlob* with a torpedo but, brightly illuminated, was in turn swept by fire. To an earlier hit by a spent 28cm/11in shell was now added two by 15cm/5.9in shells and about 18 by 10cm/3.9in shells. The ship's 76mm/3in belt resisted the smaller projectiles but fragments scythed the upper-deck and exposed gun crews. Her communication aerials destroyed, she signalled *Nottingham* by lamp: "My wireless is shot away. Answer calls for me and report the action."

The demise of the armoured cruiser

As related earlier in this book, armoured cruisers had by the 1880s developed into a type of Second Class battleship, the true capital ship having the maximum practicable armament and protection, being complemented by large cruisers with medium-calibre weapons, lighter protection and higher speed.

Not convinced of the benefits of the latter expensive ships, the British Admiralty concentrated in the Naval Defence Act classes on protected cruisers of more modest size.

The French, however, persisted in building large and fast cruisers aimed primarily at war on commerce. Newly developed Krupp cemented steel armour with its improved stopping power permitted much thinner and lighter protection and so the Admiralty reverted to vertical belt armour in addition to protective decks. As a result, the British armoured cruiser was reborn.

Necessary speed translated into many boilers, many boilers into length. Extra length permitted extra displacement and the adoption of the 234mm/9.2in gun forward and aft. These, with

ABOVE: **Some of the last pre-Dreadnought battleships, the King Edward VII class of 1903–05 (shown here) were about 138.4m/454ft in length. Contemporary Devonshire-class armoured cruisers were nearly 6.1m/20ft longer. The latter were 4 knots faster but mounted only 191mm/7.5in rather than 305mm/12in main-calibre guns. Their vertical protection was proof against only cruiser gunfire.**

casemated, 152mm/6in guns along either beam, followed the armament layout of contemporary capital ships. It was then but a short step to the proposal of using armoured cruisers as a fast wing of the battle fleet, tasked with conducting reconnaissance in force, finishing off damaged enemy ships and even engaging smaller enemy capital ships.

Once accepted as an element of the battle fleet as opposed to commerce protection, the armoured cruiser rapidly increased in size and cost. Compare, for instance, the armoured cruiser *Black Prince* and the battleship *King Edward VII*, launched 1903/04:

> "She tore past us with a roar, rather like a motor roaring up hill on low gear, and the very crackling and heat of the flames could be heard and felt. She was a mass of fire from foremast to mainmast, on deck and between decks. Flames were issuing out of her from every corner..."
> Eyewitness account from destroyer *Spitfire* of *Black Prince*'s final moments, Jutland night action

	King Edward VII	*Black Prince*
Displacement	15,881 tonnes/15,630 tons	13,717 tonnes/13,500 tons
Length overall	138.2m/453ft 9in	154m/505ft 6in
Armament	4x305mm/12in	6x234mm/9.2in
	4x234mm/9.2in	10x152mm/6in
	10x152mm/6in	
Complement	777	789
Cost (£)	1.38 million	1.20 million

In terms of cost and manning, the two types were almost equal and, at a time when naval strength was commonly measured by the yardstick of capital ship numbers, more armoured cruisers simply meant fewer battleships.

Controversy was resolved with the launch in 1907 of the first of Fisher's revolutionary battlecruisers (initially termed "large armoured cruisers"). With eight 305mm/12in guns and a 3-knot speed advantage these were the natural predators of armoured cruisers, which were effectively made obsolete. However, as only four of the new "Town"-class light cruisers were in service in 1914, existing ships still had their part to play.

Action soon found them wanting. In heavy seas at the battle of Coronel, the *Good Hope* was unable to use her lower casemated 152mm/6in guns to defend herself. (Four years later, the 13,920-tonne/13,700-ton American *San Diego* flooded and foundered when her lower casemates were submerged by a list of only 9.5 degrees.) Under ideal conditions, the 234mm/9.2in gun was a reliable and accurate weapon, but in action, just two barrels and no fire control greatly degraded this potential.

At the Falklands, Fisher's battlecruiser concept was triumphantly vindicated when Sturdee's two battlecruisers used their speed and gun range to destroy von Spee's two crack armoured cruisers almost at leisure.

Jutland marked the end of the armoured cruiser as an integrated battle fleet unit. In accordance with Grand Fleet Battle Orders to "push on and gain touch with the enemy's battle fleet", Arbuthnot's First Cruiser Squadron succeeded only too well. At just 7,315m/8,000yds in indifferent visibility it was swept by fire from Scheer's mainforce, the *Defence* blowing up and the *Warrior* foundering later. This vulnerability to heavy-calibre gunfire was underlined when a third, *Black Prince*, blew up from a pre-Dreadnought's gunfire in a nocturnal clash.

In contrast, the new light cruisers proved remarkably resistant. None was sunk at Jutland although several were hard hit (e.g. *Southampton* by one 28cm/11in, two 15cm/5.9in and eighteen 10cm/3.9in shells; *Chester* by seventeen 15cm/5.9in shells; *Castor* by about ten 15cm/5.9in and 10cm/3.9in shells, etc). By the end of the war British armoured cruisers were mostly relegated to trade protection and service on distant stations. Ironically their nemesis, the battlecruiser, had likewise been discredited in the supreme test of major action.

ABOVE: **The one-off *Blücher* was built by the Germans on the basis of faulty intelligence regarding the capability of the then-secret British battlecruisers. Really an armoured cruiser, she was nonetheless attached to Hipper's battlecruiser squadron and paid the price at Dogger Bank.**

TOP: **Dating from 1901–03, Cressy-class armoured cruisers (*Euryalus* seen here) were no longer fit for front-line duty during World War I. The class was somewhat unfairly damned when three, not comprehending the new rules of submarine warfare, were destroyed together by one boat.** ABOVE: **The final class of armoured cruiser built for the Royal Navy were the three Minotaurs of 1908 (*Shannon* seen here). Into their slender 158.2m/519ft hulls were packed two twin 234mm/9.2in turrets and 10 single 191mm/7.5in turrets, the latter sided in the waist. Capable of only 23 knots, they were rendered obsolete by the battlecruiser.** ABOVE LEFT: **With the six Pennsylvanias of 1903–04 and the four Tennessees of 1904–06, the US Navy's armoured cruisers were every bit the equal of their British counterparts. With the decision to reserve "State" names for battleships, all were "demoted", the *California* (CA.6) becoming the *San Diego*, seen here.**

Inter-war treaties and their effect on cruiser development

Following World War I the victorious nations lapsed into an insupportable capital ship "naval race". The reasons for this were various, but included American suspicions of Japanese intentions in the western Pacific, the determination by the American "big fleet" lobby to bring about a US fleet "second to none" (which upset the British, still committed to a Two Power Standard in fleet strength) and the perennial rivalry between France and Italy in the Mediterranean.

To halt the enormously expensive capital ship construction programmes that resulted, representatives of the five nations met in Washington in 1921–22. Although the resulting treaty, binding until 1936, was aimed primarily at capital ships, it was also the first of several to fundamentally affect the cruiser category, in terms of numbers, size and armament.

With the peace, the Royal Navy had scrapped all pre-war cruisers but, although this left about 50, most were of the small "fleet" type, in which endurance had been subordinated to speed and firepower. For peacetime operation the service needed rather larger ships, for trade protection, whose characteristics were diametrically opposite. At Washington, therefore, Britain refused to accept limitations on the number of cruisers "not connected with or required for fleet action".

The treaty limited individual cruiser size to 10,160 tonnes/ 10,000 tons displacement, carrying guns of no greater than 203mm/8in calibre. Both parameters were in excess of anything yet constructed (excepting the discredited and discontinued armoured cruiser) and had the unintended effect that each signatory began to build up to them. With

no global tonnage limit agreed, a new "treaty cruiser" race developed. These ships, too, were extremely expensive. The Royal Navy had to build them to avoid being out-classed but they soaked up scarce funding while being unnecessarily large for required purposes.

Great Britain lobbied hard to limit the 203mm/8in treaty cruiser but attempts at compromise failed at Geneva in 1927. In 1930, therefore, the London Naval Conference tried again, this time successfully. Its subsequent treaty defined a cruiser as a surface ship of war, other than a capital ship or aircraft carrier, exceeding 1,880 tonnes/1,850 tons and carrying guns exceeding 130mm/5.1in calibre. In deference to British requirements for small "fleet" cruisers and larger "trade" cruisers, the treaty sub-categorized them into ships carrying guns of greater or less than 155mm/6.1in calibre.

Global limitations were placed on overall cruiser tonnage and also on each of the two sub-categories, popularly termed "heavy" and "light" cruisers. Agreed ceilings were as follows:

	Heavy cruisers tonnes/tons	Light cruisers tonnes/tons	Total tonnes/tons
British Commonwealth	149,156/146,800	195,284/192,200	344,440/339,000
United States	182,888/180,000	145,803/143,500	328,691/323,500
Japan	110,140/108,400	102,062/100,450	212,201/208,850

As can be seen, the larger proportion of the British allocation was for light cruisers, any number of which could be built within the total agreed tonnage. In heavy cruisers, the

LEFT: **Having been allied to Great Britain and the United States during World War I, Japan felt slighted by what she felt was a meagre tonnage allowance permitted under the Washington Treaty. *Chokai* was one of 16 powerful cruisers constructed as a substitute for capital ships.**

ABOVE: **Naval occasion – the complement of HMAS** *Australia* **formally drawn up during a royal review at Spithead. The spacious proportions of the County-class cruisers are evident. Comfortable ships, they were ideal for independent cruiser operations.**
BELOW: **Late treaty restrictions on light cruisers reduced the number allowed to the Royal Navy. Numbers were maximized by reducing individual displacements to a minimum. The four Arethusas were really Improved Leanders less one twin turret, and represented the minimum effective size. The nameship is shown here.**

ABOVE: **Eleven Counties were built for the Royal Navy, with a further pair,** *Australia* **and** *Canberra* **for the expanding Royal Australian Navy.** *Australia*, **here seen as a flagship, had a busy time during World War II, her three funnels apparently making an irresistible target for Japanese kamikazes.**
INSET LEFT: **The Vickers-pattern 152mm/6in gun, used in British light cruisers, was a relatively simple but reliable weapon, firing a 45.4kg/100lb projectile. In full flash gear and gas mask, a loading number is seen ramming home the separate charge.** BELOW: **The American Brooklyn-class light cruisers with 15 guns were built in direct response to Japanese developments. After 1945 they were the only American light cruisers to be transferred to foreign flags, Argentina, Brazil and Chile each receiving a pair. This is the Brazilian** *Tamandaré*, **ex-USS** *St. Louis* **(CL.49).**

actual number of hulls was stipulated, consensus following tough bargaining. By the end of 1936, it was agreed, the United States could build 18, the British Commonwealth 15 and Japan 12.

The London Treaty was, in its entirety, to remain in force for no longer than the end of 1936, when the remaining clauses of the Washington Treaty also lapsed. With the mid-1930s seeing an accelerating pace of rearmament, a Second London Naval Conference was convened in good time with the hope of maintaining some control over construction. In the subsequent treaty, signed in March 1936, there were several articles of critical importance relating to cruiser design. Individual displacements were now to be limited to only 8,128 tonnes/8,000 tons. Until January 1, 1943, guns of greater than 155mm/6.1in calibre were forbidden. One can see in these parameters, for instance, the origins of the British "Crown Colony" class and its derivatives which, on that displacement, mounted an ambitious twelve 152mm/6in guns in four triple turrets, later reduced to three.

The treaty also divided light cruisers into two sub-categories, i.e. greater or less than 3,048 tonnes/3,000 tons displacement, with either carrying guns of up to 155mm/6.1in calibre. This covered new classes of "super-destroyer", favoured particularly by the French.

The River Plate action

Dubbed "Pocket Battleships" by the popular press, Germany's Deutschland-class armoured ships were built for commerce raiding. Cruising at 13 knots, their range was greater than 30,578km/19,000 miles. Well-protected, mounting six 28cm/11in and eight 15cm/5.9in guns, they were destined to out-fight anything that they could not out run.

Supported by a dedicated supply ship, the *Admiral Graf Spee* sailed for the South Atlantic before hostilities commenced and, by December 7, 1939, she had destroyed nine merchantmen. Then, having evaded a total of eight hunting groups, she made for the shipping focal point off the estuary of the river Plate, which separates Argentina from Uruguay. Here, early on the December 13, she encountered Commodore Henry Harwood's South American Division. Wearing his broad pennant in the light cruiser *Ajax*, he had in company her sister, *Achilles* (largely New Zealand-manned) and the small 203mm/8in cruiser *Exeter*. It was unfortunate that his largest unit, the 203mm/8in *Cumberland*, had been detached to the Falklands.

On a clear summer morning the three British cruisers immediately adopted Harwood's stated plan of splitting the enemy's fire by operating in two divisions. When first sighted, the German was to the north-west of the British and headed toward them on an approximately south-easterly course. As the range was about 17,374m/19,000yds, both sides opened fire immediately. *Exeter* turned on to a westerly heading to get

ABOVE: **This impression of the River Plate action implies a close-range encounter. Harwood, however, with ships of** superior speed, selected ranges to divide the enemy's fire and to keep at a distance where smaller calibre guns would still be effective against armour. Not an easy compromise. ABOVE RIGHT: A boat crew from the *Graf Spee* assists the ship in coming to a buoy in this pre-war shot. Note the "Wappen", or arms, of the original Vice Admiral Maximilian Reichsgraf von Spee, who died with the *Scharnhorst* at the Falklands in December 1914.

on to the *Graf Spee*'s starboard flank, while the two light cruisers worked up to full speed to work around to the north of the enemy to engage him from the opposite side. As they worked across the *Graf Spee*'s bows, they successfully headed her off, her course being quickly changed to east and then under smoke to the north-west.

The German commanding officer, Captain Langsdorff, initially divided his fire as Harwood intended, but soon realized that the *Exeter* constituted the major threat. Concentrating on her with his 28cm/11in main battery, he quickly hit her three times, putting "B" turret out of action and causing the ship to be conned from the emergency after steering position. To ease the pressure, *Exeter* fired torpedoes but was hit three times more. After some 35 minutes she had one turret left operable and, with an increasing list from flooding, was barely able to stay in the action.

By now, *Ajax* and *Achilles*, the former with her aircraft spotting, had closed the enemy, only lightly opposed by the *Graf Spee*'s secondary armament. They were hitting freely although their 152mm/6in projectiles bounced "like turnips" from the German's armour. In contrast, the *Exeter*'s three hits on the *Graf Spee* had penetrated deeply.

> "As things turned out, I am delighted that you did not have the *Cumberland* with you – even if you had sunk the *Graf Spee*, it would not have been so glorious an affair."
> Personal letter to Harwood from the First Sea Lord, Sir Dudley Pound, January 11, 1940

ABOVE: *Cumberland* (see here) and *Exeter* had both spent time at Port Stanley in the Falklands for essential maintenance. *Cumberland* was still there when Harwood's ships sighted the enemy but sailed immediately. She arrived off the River Plate as reinforcement, having steamed at full power for 36 hours.

LEFT: In one of the best-remembered images of World War II, the gutted wreck of *Graf Spee* burns out in shallow water off Montevideo. Two secondary 15cm/5.9in guns are visible by the wrecked funnel and, far right, the barbette of the after triple 28cm/11in turret has been displaced by a magazine explosion.

BELOW: HMS *Achilles* was one of only two cruisers fully manned by New Zealanders. Endorsed by Commodore Harwood, their Commanding Officer's report read that "New Zealand had every reason to be proud of her seamen during their baptism of fire." Four died and three were injured.

Langsdorff made extensive use of smoke and course changes to upset the light cruisers' gun-laying and, having effectively put the *Exeter* out of action, began to concentrate fire on the lighter ships. These undoubtedly saved the *Exeter* from destruction, although the *Ajax* was caught by a 28cm/11in shell which immobilized two turrets, half her main armament.

Better to observe the scattered action, Captain Langsdorff had forsaken his armoured control position for the exposed fore top, where he was lightly wounded by splinters and probably concussed by blast. To the puzzlement of the British, he maintained a wavering westerly heady directly for neutral South American waters. His ship had suffered three 203mm/8in and eighteen 152mm/6in hits but with the exception of a large hole right forward, she was not significantly damaged. His 35 dead and 60 wounded weighed heavily on the German commander, however, who made for Montevideo in Uruguay, trailed at a respectful distance by Harwood's two light cruisers.

As a belligerent, Langsdorff was allowed 24 hours in a neutral port but, to effect repairs and seek medical assistance, a further 72 hours were granted. The British Admiralty, meanwhile, was despatching every possible warship to the area. Langsdorff knew that he had no chance of fighting his way back to Germany. Politically, internment was not an option so, having gained Berlin's sanction, he sailed into the Plate on the December 17 and destroyed his ship by exploding the magazines.

ABOVE: Both *Ajax* (here) and *Achilles* came close to torpedoing the *Graf Spee* as her attention was distracted by *Exeter*. A single 28cm/11in hit put both *Ajax*'s after turrets out of action but her fire, although rapid, was of an accuracy affected by sudden, necessary and radical changes of course.

Armed merchant cruisers in World War II

Inter-war treaty limitations and political parsimony combined to guarantee that the Royal Navy entered the new war with too few cruisers. On the pre-war assumption that the United Kingdom would experience no shortfall in mercantile tonnage, the Admiralty therefore planned to plug the gap with 50 Armed Merchant Cruisers, or AMCs. These were requisitioned by October 1939, their cargo capacity immediately being lost to the nation.

In time of war, passenger liners are valuable particularly as troop carriers and, too complex to be built at such a time, needed to be husbanded carefully. Six, however, had already been lost by the time of the fall of France in June 1940. The 41 of the type taken by the Admiralty were required for long-range patrolling and to give convoys a measure of defence against attack by surface raiders. For armament, they were given aged 152mm/6in and 119mm/4.7in guns retained from discarded cruisers of World War I.

> "An immense expense and also a care and anxiety." First Lord of the Admiralty (Winston Churchill) to First Sea Lord (Admiral of the Fleet Sir Dudley Pound) on the subject of AMCs, January 1940

ABOVE: **Pre-war, the *Worcestershire* was one of the stately Bibby Line four-masters providing a liner service to India and Burma. In her wartime guise of Armed Merchant Cruiser (AMC) she has landed two masts and had her funnel shortened. She has both air and surface search radar and six antique 152mm/6in guns.**

Under some pressure, the Admiralty released nine but allocated no less than 25 to a Northern Patrol. As in the previous war, it was aimed at contraband control, and the interception of returning enemy merchantmen and outgoing raiders. It was successful in both. During the first four months of hostilities over 300 neutrals were sent in for examination but when, in November 1939, the AMC *Rawalpindi* sighted the fast German battleships *Scharnhorst* and *Gneisenau*, she could do little more than raise the alarm and demonstrate how to die bravely. Her warning caused the enemy to abandon his planned foray but patrolling AMCs then proved vulnerable to U-boat attack, losing six more of their number during 1940.

To reduce this rate of attrition, AMCs were based on Halifax, Nova Scotia, from the end of the year. From here they escorted eastbound convoys as far as meridian 25 degrees West before refuelling in Iceland and patrolling the Denmark Strait in the course of their return.

LEFT: **A unit of the patrol line in the Faeroes-Iceland gap, the ex-P&O liner *Rawalpindi* encountered the German battleships *Scharnhorst* and *Gneisenau* in November 1939. Although the AMC was quickly destroyed, her report of the enemy's position caused him to abandon his planned Atlantic foray.**
ABOVE: **The German auxiliary cruiser *Thor*, which sailed in June 1940, encountered the AMCs *Alcantara* in July and *Carnarvon Castle* (seen here) in the December. Both British ships suffered considerable damage but were not able to inflict sufficient to cause the enemy to abandon his cruise.**
LEFT: **Sole escort to a 37-ship Atlantic convoy when it was attacked by the "pocket battleship" *Admiral Scheer*, the *Jervis Bay* sold her life dearly, buying sufficient time to allow her charges to scatter. As a result, losses were limited to just five merchantmen.**
BELOW: **Protracted cruises by German auxiliary raiders depended greatly upon meeting regularly with supply ships and tankers. One of these, *Weser*, was destroyed by the Canadian AMC *Prince Robert* (seen here) off Mexico in September 1940.**

By February 1940 the Admiralty had 46 AMCs, mostly ex-passenger liners, in commission and spread between Halifax, Freetown (West Africa), the Mediterranean, and the Indian and Pacific Oceans.

Armed with obsolete weapons removed from long-scrapped warships, and with only the most rudimentary fire control, it was obvious that what the Naval Staff termed "indispensable auxiliaries" were unable to engage even the weakest of enemy raiders on anything approaching equal terms. Yet, deployed to intercept just this category of opponent, the ex-Royal Mail liner *Alcantara* encountered the German *Thor* off the Brazilian coast in July 1940. Badly damaging the British ship, the *Thor* escaped to continue her cruise. Still in the South Atlantic in the December, she met up with the AMC *Carnarvon Castle*, with a similar result. Both AMCs had been totally outranged, but little could be done to improve matters, better equipment being unavailable.

AMCs also continued to escort convoys. Sole escort for 37 merchantmen, the *Jervis Bay* found herself fighting off the *Admiral Scheer* in November 1940. Selling her life dearly, she bought sufficient time for her charges to scatter with the loss of only five. Her commanding officer was awarded the Victoria Cross.

Unstinting valour could not disguise the vulnerability of the AMC, underlined when the *Thor*, on her second cruise, easily destroyed the *Voltaire*.

Increasing numbers of escorts permitted a July 1941 reorganization of the North Atlantic. Here, and soon afterwards on the West African station, AMCs were withdrawn for other duties, more suited to their purpose.

With the build-up of American and Canadian troops in the United Kingdom, and the resumption of the Allied offensive, troopship capacity became inadequate and so, during 1942, a further dozen AMCs reverted to this role. Of the remaining 23, all returned to troopship duties during 1943–44 save those retained for specialist service, such as heavy repair and depot ships, or Landing Ships, Infantry (LSIs).

Having exchanged their bright peacetime liveries for grey Admiralty "crabfat", the liners fought their war courageously and at considerable cost but were never considered the equals of a regular warship and proved ultimately to be more valuable in the role for which they had been originally designed – people carrying. Most survived to give long post-war service.

The German raiders

Experience during World War I, particularly with the *Wolf* and *Möwe*, proved to the German Navy that innocently disguised, armed merchantmen made more effective commerce raiders than warships. The latter were more expensive, ever in short supply, demanded large crews and needed frequent dockyard attention. On the other hand, a merchantman's designed cargo capacity could accommodate fuel and stores for considerable endurance, while through paint and canvas, she could quickly assume a false identity before shifting location.

During World War II, despite the service being under strength, surface warships still conducted a number of raiding cruises, leading directly to the loss of the *Graf Spee* and the *Bismarck*. Plans existed, however, for the conversion of 26 auxiliary raiders. In the event, only half of these were actually taken in hand, of which nine made cruises.

The intention was for them to operate in more remote theatres, such as the South Atlantic and Indian Oceans, where Allied shipping, particularly British, was plentiful but where regular German surface combatants could not safely venture. Both Japan and Soviet Russia (until June 1941) rendered considerable assistance. Further support was given by a network of German supply ships stationed at remote oceanic locations. The major function of these was the replenishment of long-range U-boats to extend their patrols still further but they could also offer limited mechanical assistance.

Merchantmen selected for conversion comprised good-quality tonnage from the major companies, notably Hamburg-Amerika, Norddeutscher Lloyd and Hansa lines. Typically of 7,000–8,000grt, although some were considerably smaller, they

TOP: **Typifying the innocent appearance of German auxiliary cruisers, the** *Orion* **appears to be any nondescript, disruptively painted merchantman. Formerly the** *Kurmark* **of Hamburg-Amerika she mounted six 15cm/5.9in guns and, in total, was credited with sinking 61,342grt of Allied shipping.**
ABOVE: **The usual quarry for an auxiliary raider was the independently routed merchantman, normally encountered in remote areas of ocean not covered by the regular convoy network. Any attempt by a victim to transit an "RRR" raider warning would result in heavy fire and casualties.**

varied greatly in appearance, some being steam propelled, others motorships. Their ingeniously concealed armament usually included six 15cm/5.9in guns and two to six torpedo tubes. Most carried two floatplanes to extend their search horizon, and several hundred mines, which were planted in small clutches at focal points, positions calculated to cause maximum loss and disruption.

Badly delayed by the unusually severe winter of 1939–40, the first raiders, *Atlantis* and *Orion*, sailed in March and April 1940. During May and June the *Widder*, *Pinguin* and *Thor* also broke out successfully. Last of the "first wave", the *Komet*, which had been fitted out at Murmansk, was escorted by Soviet icebreakers to gain the Pacific by the northern route.

The raiders' commanding officers were selected from older regular personnel, usually with considerable experience of the merchant service. Their normal mode of operation was to close with a selected victim, disclose their identity and demand complete compliance, particularly that no radio be used. Any defiance was met by 15cm/5.9in gunfire into the bridge structure. British Admiralty instructions, however, were that a ship was to transmit a raider warning before submitting, an

LEFT: **The AMC *Carnarvon Castle*'s attempt to apprehend the German raider *Thor* resulted in her receiving heavy damage. Guns issued to AMCs were, as seen here, aged weapons removed from long-scrapped warships of an earlier war. Fire control was also rudimentary.** ABOVE: **Following resupply from the auxiliary raider *Kormoran*, a U-boat (*U-124*) strikes down a torpedo. *Kormoran* was disguised as the Japanese freighter *Sakito Maru*, with the Rising Sun flag displayed on each side of the hull and authentic Japanese markings which they had taken with them from Germany.**

ABOVE LEFT: **The final encounter between the *Kormoran* and the Australian cruiser *Sydney* took place about 241.4km/150 miles south-west of Carnarvon, Western Australia. On abandoning ship, one of the *Kormoran*'s boats capsized but the remainder safely made the Australian coast, where the survivors were made prisoner.** ABOVE: **Cadet O'Hara on the SS *Stephen Hopkins*, a US Liberty ship engaging the German auxiliary cruisers *Stier* with *Tannenfels* on fire on September 27, 1942.** BELOW: **Suspicious of the *Kormoran*, which was disguised, the fully alert *Sydney* unwisely took position on her beam and at less than a mile's range. She was suddenly swept by gunfire and torpedoes. Answering in kind, she inflicted mortal damage on the raider but headed away, never to be seen again.**

order that resulted in the death of many courageous radio officers, who transmitted despite warnings.

The "second wave" comprised the raiders *Stier*, *Kormoran* and *Michel* together with the *Thor*, making a further cruise. They were the last as, by 1943, the interlocking Allied patrol and escort system made such operations increasingly difficult, not least for the targeted supply network.

The majority of raiders were destroyed, but their experience was varied. Three (*Komet*, *Atlantis* and *Pinguin*) were intercepted and sunk by British warships. Another, *Kormoran*, engaged in a duel with the Australian cruiser *Sydney*, an exchange that resulted in the destruction of both. The *Stier* was likewise sunk in a mutually destructive duel, this time with the American merchantman *Stephen Hopkins*, which defended herself valiantly with a single 127mm/5in gun. The *Thor* proved to be something of a scourge for the weakly armed British Armed Merchant Cruisers (AMCs), fighting off and badly damaging first the *Alcantara*, then the *Carnarvon Castle*, before finally sinking a third, the *Voltaire*. She was, herself, destroyed by explosion while refitting in Yokohama.

Despite the huge disruption caused by German merchant raiders (Italian and Japanese hardly figured), they accounted for only 133 ships of about 830,000grt, about 3.8 per cent of total war losses. Most successful was the *Atlantis* with 22 ships of about 146,000grt.

LEFT: **HMS *Exeter*'s Walrus amphibian secured and ready for hoisting aboard. Visible are the two starboard-side 102mm/4in guns on high-angle mountings and capable of long-range barrage fire against aircraft. By World War II aircraft were already too fast to be accurately tracked by such weapons.** ABOVE: **Virtually useless against attacking aircraft, the quadruple 12.7mm/0.5in machine gun was still being widely specified for newbuildings into World War II. Together with the 2-pounder "pompom" cannon and high-angle 76mm/3in 12-pounders they comprised a range of standard weapons that fell far short of satisfactory.**

The introduction and development of the anti-aircraft cruiser

Although by the end of World War I 76mm/3in guns on high-angle (HA) mounts had made a general appearance to provide an anti-aircraft capability, they lacked any sort of fire control and were virtually useless. To combat a high-flying bomber the problem was complex. Firstly, a gun with the necessary elevation and a high sustained rate of fire was required. This then needed to be linked to a control system capable of measuring an aircraft's present and predicted position. Manual estimation quickly proved to be too slow.

The 1930s saw the introduction of small multiple automatic weapons (for example the British 12.7mm/0.5in machine-gun and 2-pounder pompom, and the American 28mm/1.1in gun) for close-range defence but, for longer ranges, medium-calibre guns were required. Here, the British preference was for the

102mm/4in, whose 13.6–15.9kg/30–35lb fixed ammunition could be rapidly handled by hand. The Americans retained their trusted 127mm/5in gun, whose 24.9kg/55lb projectile tested the ability of strong men on a continuous basis.

New British light cruisers (i.e. 152mm/6in) of the 1930s were so strapped by treaty-imposed tonnage restrictions that only four 102mm/4in guns could be accommodated. The adoption of the very successful twin mounting reduced the space required for these but doubled the weight per gun. In those pre-radar days, the American 127mm/5in 38-calibre could range to the useful limits of visibility while still having a capacity against surface or shore targets.

As the 1930s progressed, the British Admiralty became concerned that neither convoys nor battle groups had sufficient anti-aircraft (AA) escorts. For the former, programmes of sloops and escort destroyers were put in hand, both classes armed with the ubiquitous twin 102mm/4in Mark XIX mounting. However, only the most recent of fleet destroyers had guns of high elevation, and with the desire for a steadier platform it was decided to convert the better of the elderly C-class cruisers for

LEFT: **In a post-war exercise HMS *Cleopatra*, a surviving Dido-class AA cruiser, puts up an impressive barrage against an attacking aircraft. Air-to-surface guided weapons were already in the inventory, however, against which even fast and accurate gunnery was largely ineffective.**

ABOVE: **A well-proven standard weapon, the American 127mm/5in 38 had a higher rate of fire than the British 133mm/5.25in, making their Atlanta-class cruisers (*Oakland* shown here) more effective against air attack than the Royal Navy's Didos. With gunhouses located on three levels, both types had high profiles.**

ABOVE RIGHT: **Twenty years old, the Royal Navy's C-class cruisers found a new and effective role converted into the first dedicated AA cruisers. Units such as *Curlew*, seen here, were given four twin 102mm/4in high-angle mountings with full director control. Ironically, the ship was destroyed by aircraft attack in 1940.**

an AA role. Their 152mm/6in and torpedo armament were landed in favour of 102mm/4in HA guns with full director control. They were effective but only six were converted before they were superseded by better, purpose-built ships.

During 1935 it had been decided that a new 133mm/5.25in projectile would be the best compromise between rapid HA fire and ship-stopping capability. Guns of this calibre mounted in twin turrets and capable of an 80-degree elevation were installed in the specialized Dido-class cruisers that followed. Considered a true dual-purpose weapon, the 133mm/5.25in gun comprised the entire designed medium-calibre armament for the ship which, uniquely, was designed with three forward mountings.

The commissioning of the Didos conveniently coincided with the introduction of radar. Although still primitive, its improved approximation of heights and ranges allowed the ships to use their armament effectively to the limit of its range. In practice, however, the 36.3kg/80lb fixed ammunition proved to be too heavy for rapid handling.

As the 133mm/5.25in gun was considered to be a light weapon, the Didos, themselves small, were given five twin mountings for maximum barrage fire. The weight of the three

forward turrets severely taxed the ships' generally light construction, so that most landed their "C" guns in favour of automatic weapons.

Much the same design philosophy governed the American Atlanta class. These were originally configured around no less than sixteen 127mm/5in 38-calibre guns, disposed in six centreline and two wing mountings. Together with radar gun direction, the proximity fuse provided the greatest improvement in the ability to cause damage of AA fire, as the projectile no longer had to actually hit a target to destroy it. Despite this huge advantage, the hitting power of the kamikaze saw the *Atlantis*'s wing turrets and torpedo tubes landed in favour of more 40mm/1.57in guns.

The aerial threat during World War II progressed from high level and dive bombing to radio-controlled glider bombs and suicide kamikazes. These last two threats needed to be completely disintegrated and not just disabled in order to stop the attack. The main post-war innovation was to temporarily exchange small-calibre automatic weapons for 76mm/3in, radar-laid guns as an interim measure while the first surface-to-air missile (SAM) systems were being developed.

LEFT: **The 40mm/1.57in Bofors and the 20mm/0.79in Oerlikon designs were the most effective AA weapons of World War II, and were produced under licence in huge numbers in the United States. A weakness of the quadruple 40mm/1.57in, as is here apparent, was the requirement for so many to feed it ammunition.**
ABOVE: **Experience in the Pacific was that low-level torpedo aircraft would synchronize their attack with dive bombers, splitting the available defensive fire. As seen here, a single aircraft would draw huge volumes of barrage fire. Proximity fusing was possible only in 76mm/3in projectiles and larger.**

The *Bismarck* pursuit

Although broad, the Denmark Strait between Iceland and Greenland is constricted by a permanent but variable icefield. It is in this area that the relatively warm Gulf Stream forms fogs and mirages on encountering the ice chill, which results in treacherously shifting visibility.

On May 23, 1941, the British heavy cruisers *Suffolk* and *Norfolk* were patrolling these difficult waters. Their purpose was to detect any attempt by the new German battleship *Bismarck*, accompanied by the heavy cruiser *Prinz Eugen*, to break through into the open Atlantic. Having sailed from Norway two days earlier, they were expected at any time.

From the rugged north-western extremity of Iceland a defensive minefield narrowed the strait further but the cruisers kept near the ice edge, where conditions were at their most variable and radar most useful. As no air patrols could be flown, the British were keeping an extra sharp watch to avoid being surprised.

At 19:22, in a clear patch, *Suffolk* suddenly made visual contact with the enemy at about 10,973m/12,000yds. *Norfolk* then emerged from a fogbank even more closely, to be greeted by a couple of warning salvoes. Using their extra speed and the patchy visibility to advantage, the two gained position on the quarters of the enemy. Following at high speed, they transmitted regular positional reports to Admiral Tovey who was endeavouring to intercept with the Home Fleet.

Well ahead of Tovey was Vice Admiral Holland in the battlecruiser *Hood*, accompanied by the new battleship

TOP: ***Suffolk**'s great asset was her effective new radar. In the capricious fog of the Denmark Strait, this allowed her and the Norfolk to trail the enemy from a safer distance. The appearance of the Counties was not improved by the unsightly hangar and the weight-saving measure of cutting down the quarterdeck.*
ABOVE: **Having given her pursuers the slip, the *Bismarck*'s fate was decided through a sighting by a Coastal Command Catalina. Known to its American builders as a PBY, its design dated back to 1933 but, proving enormously versatile, it flew throughout World War II. More than 3,300 were built.**

Prince of Wales. Vectored in by the cruiser's reports, these made contact at about 05:50 on May 24. Rear Admiral Wake-Walker, with the cruisers, anticipated his task complete and, from 24km/15 miles, watched the heavy ships engage. When, at about 06:00, the *Hood* blew up and the *Prince of Wales* was obliged to retire, his responsibilities became even greater as Tovey was still 482km/300 miles distant.

ABOVE: In perhaps the finest action picture ever of a battleship, the *Bismarck*'s own gunfire puts her in sharp relief. Her after turrets are trained on their extreme forward bearing as she engages the British ships, then on her port bow. Most of the action was fought on this bearing as *Hood* tried to close the range.

LEFT: The Abyssinian Crisis and Spanish Civil War saw the *Hood* retained in the Mediterranean as flagship, her planned modernization never being undertaken. By far the largest and most imposing vessel in the Royal Navy at that time, her loss was keenly felt. ABOVE: A Southampton-class cruiser such as the *Sheffield* is seen here in typical Atlantic conditions. Water could be driven through the smallest of apertures, creating electrical faults or flooding, and it was common practice to train the forward turrets abaft the beam in such conditions. BELOW: Against a dour Arctic sky, a silhouetted *Prinz Eugen* is seen loosing a salvo as heavy-calibre British shells fall to the right. The very similar profiles of *Prinz Eugen* and *Bismarck* led to some confusion with the British gunlayers, leading to doubt as to which ship was actually being engaged.

Unknown to Wake-Walker, the *Bismarck* had sustained damage sufficient to persuade her flag officer, Vice Admiral Lütjens, to abandon his foray and to make for a port in occupied western France.

During the night of May 24/25 the carrier *Victorious* mounted an unsuccessful air strike and Lütjens made several aggressive feints in an endeavour to shake off his trackers. These, of necessity, maintained a respectful distance and changes of course were frequent. At about 03:00 on May 25, Lütjens finally broke contact with his pursuers by making a radical change of heading, quickly detached the *Prinz Eugen* and made for Brest.

At this point Tovey was some 161km/100 miles adrift, but other British units were closing in. Urgent searches were mounted to re-establish contact, but it was not until 10:30 on May 26 that a PBY (Catalina) sighted the *Bismarck*, now just 1,127km/700 miles short of the sanctuary of Brest.

Interception was now only possibly by Vice Admiral Somerville's Force H, battling northward from Gibraltar in a rising gale. Somerville sent the cruiser *Sheffield* ahead to establish visual contact, but she was still 32km/20 miles short when the *Ark Royal*'s first air strike arrived. In appalling weather conditions, they attacked the *Sheffield* in error. By dint of furious manoeuvre the cruiser survived unscathed and, maintaining station, acted as a waypoint for the second strike. This put two torpedoes into the fugitive at about 21:00 on May 26, slowing her sufficiently to enable Tovey to engage at first

ABOVE: A pre-war impression of *Norfolk*, painted for Far Eastern service. In days before air-conditioning, the great hulls of the Counties, with well-ventilated mess decks, high deckheads and wood-sheathed weather decks, made them very suitable and popular ships for tropical use.

light with the battleships *King George V* and *Rodney*. Their heavy gunfire reduced the *Bismarck*'s topsides to a flaming shambles but, at the close ranges being employed, her hull was immune to fatal damage. Tovey's ships now very low on fuel pulled away, leaving the helpless hulk to be despatched by torpedo. This duty fell to a further cruiser, the *Dorsetshire*, which completed the task clinically with two torpedoes on one side and one on the other. Just 16km/10 miles distant was the *Norfolk*, which had seen the task through from the outset.

LEFT: **The amphibious landing on Guadalcanal, August 7, 1942, was the first of any size in the Pacific. Very much a shoestring operation, it was initially virtually unopposed. Within 48 hours, the USS *Chicago*, seen here covering the landing, would be fighting for her life.**
BELOW: **A Japanese impression of the Battle of Savo Island with, probably, the *Quincy* (left) and *Astoria* hopelessly ablaze. The ferocity and skill of the Imperial Japanese Navy in night-fighting came as an unpleasant surprise to the Allies, who had to embark on a steep learning curve.**

Savo Island

Commanded by Rear Admiral Richmond K. Turner, American amphibious forces hit Guadalcanal and neighbouring Tulagi in the Solomons on August 7, 1942. Japanese response was immediate; Vice Admiral Mikawa Gunichi sailing from Rabaul with five heavy and two light cruisers. His objective was to destroy the landing by attacking the vulnerable amphibious warfare ships laying off-shore. The operation proper had been covered by a three-carrier force under Vice Admiral Frank Jack Fletcher who controversially withdrew on the following day. This left Turner protected by a force of six heavy and two light cruisers and 13 destroyers. Two heavy and one light cruiser were Australian and the force's senior officer was Rear Admiral V.A.C. Crutchley VC of the Royal Navy.

Mikawa had to travel 966km/600 miles and, in the course of August 8, he was sighted at least twice. The reports, however, took 11 hours to reach Turner while the assessment of the enemy force was such that it was thought to only be capable of a daylight attack, which was anticipated for August 9.

Turner and Crutchley had little reason for alarm and made precautionary night dispositions, the 15 transports being herded into a guarded anchorage off Tulagi. The direction of Mikawa's advance was from the north-west down the 29km/18-mile-wide channel between Guadalcanal and Florida Island. This approach was divided by the round, 5km/3 mile-diameter island of Savo, a brooding volcanic cone towering to nearly 500m/547yds.

Crutchley, with Turner's agreement, divided his heavy cruisers to patrol north and south of Savo, placing the light cruisers further back to cover the approach to Tulagi. Beyond Savo, two radar-equipped picket destroyers patrolled across the strait.

> "It is difficult for me to understand how events could have occurred as they did, but it seems best to face facts." Turner to Crutchley in a preliminary assessment of the battle, August 12, 1942

Mikawa's plan was simple, to sweep in to the south of Savo, overwhelm the covering force with torpedo salvoes and gunfire, destroy the amphibious fleet and to "hightail it" out to the north of Savo to be well beyond Fletcher's carrier aircraft range before daylight.

Feeling secure against night attack, Crutchley and his flagship, the *Australia*, were absent with Turner when, at about 01:00 on August 9, the Japanese in line ahead swept past the picket destroyers without being noticed. If this was not serious enough, Mikawa's cruiser-launched floatplanes had been over-flying the amphibious force area for about 90 minutes without causing undue suspicion.

These suddenly dropped flares, throwing the cruisers *Canberra* and *Chicago* of the southern force into sharp relief. Still unsuspected, the leading Japanese ships snapped on searchlights, their instantaneous 203mm/8in salvoes following torpedoes already in the water. Blasted by two dozen hits and two torpedoes, the Australian was never in the fight. Her colleague, *Chicago*, took one hit each from shell and torpedo but, totally bewildered by what was happening, failed to warn the northern force of three cruisers.

As Mikawa swept around Savo his line lost cohesion in the darkness and confusion. Now effectively in two groups, it hit the northern force from two sides simultaneously. Smothered at close range by an enemy that they barely saw, the *Astoria*, *Quincy* and *Vincennes* were fatally damaged within minutes.

The *Chokai*, Mikawa's flagship, had suffered a single hit but this, to the charthouse, appeared to affect the Admiral's judgement. With his primary objective, the amphibious fleet, now virtually undefended, he now feared dawn retribution from Fletcher's carriers (in fact now almost beyond strike range). Throwing his chance of achieving annihilation to the wind, Mikawa led his squadron away, unmolested, into the velvety blackness of the tropic night.

Behind, he left four Allied cruisers sunk or sinking and over 1,000 Allied seamen dead. The action lasted barely an hour. Only the *Chicago* survived.

A subsequent enquiry absolved the Allied commanders of negligence but noted that their forces had not yet acquired that level of aggression and war-awareness that divided defeat from victory. That could, and would, be achieved only by constant action against a still underestimated, but able and resourceful, enemy who excelled at night-fighting.

TOP: **Seen here probably on builder's trials in the Clyde in 1927, the Australian cruiser *Canberra* was lost at Savo Island, literally without firing a shot. Even as she responded to the sudden appearance of Mikawa's force she was swamped by gunfire, taking "at least 24 shells" as the Japanese swept past.**
ABOVE: **As built, the Japanese *Kako* mounted her 20cm/7.87in guns in single**

turrets, as seen here. They were later twinned. As Mikawa's triumphant force withdrew, it passed the veteran American submarine S-44 which, from 640m/700yds, sank the *Kako* with four torpedoes.
LEFT: **Within the complex organization of the Imperial Japanese Navy, Vice Admiral Mikawa Gunichi was senior officer of the Outer South Seas Force of the Eighth Fleet. At Savo Island his judgement was faulty in that although he defeated the Allied cruiser force, he failed to destroy the transports, his primary objective.**

ABOVE: *Kinugasa* **(seen here) and *Aoba* were improved versions of the *Kako* and *Furutaka*, the four usually operating as a division. The *Kinugasa* was the tail-ender of the Chokai group, as the *Furutaka* became separated in the confusion. She suffered only four killed and one wounded.**
LEFT: **Just two months before she was lost at Savo Island, the cruiser *Astoria* was one of those acting as escort to the carrier *Yorktown* at Midway. With that carrier disabled, and later sunk, Admiral Fletcher transferred his flag temporarily to the *Astoria*.**

LEFT: **After World War II the US Navy disposed of its surviving pre-war tonnage. Of the nine Brooklyn-class light cruisers of 1936–38, only one had become a war casualty. Two more were scrapped and two each were transferred to Argentina, Brazil and Chile.** ABOVE: **Under the Argentinian flag, the *Boise* (CL.47) became the *9 de Julio* and the *Phoenix* (CL.46) the *17 de Octubre*. Following political upheavals she was renamed *General Belgrano* in 1956 (seen here) after Don Manuel Belgrano, hero of national independence and designer of the national flag.**

Phoenix/Belgrano – the life and death of a Pearl Harbor veteran

Four of the large new Brooklyn-class light cruisers were present in Pearl Harbor when the Japanese struck on December 7, 1941. Three were in the crowded Navy Yard but the fourth, *Phoenix* (CL.46), was anchored in the East Loch. Fortunate in not being made a torpedo target she made to get under way along with other ships. A signal from the flagship initially prohibited movement but, once this was countermanded, the *Phoenix* was able to slip down past Ford Island and the gutted wreckage of "Battleship Row" to gain the relative safety of the open sea.

Despite going on to serve at all the main southern amphibious landings, including Hollandia, Leyte, Lingayen and Mindoro, *Phoenix* survived the war. Prematurely aged by hard service, she, together with her sister *Boise*, was transferred in 1951 to Argentina. She assumed the name 17 *de Octubre* but, five years later with the collapse of the Peron regime, she was renamed for General Belgrano, hero of national independence.

Her life proceeded uneventfully until, in April 1982, Argentina invaded the long-claimed British Falkland Islands. Making clear her intention of recovering the territory, Britain quickly despatched a naval task force and declared a 644km/400-mile diameter Maritime Exclusion Zone (MEZ) about the islands. Ahead of the task force, unseen and unadvertised, sped three nuclear attack submarines (SSNs). These, *Spartan*, *Splendid* and *Conqueror*, arrived between April 12 and April 19.

The considerable Argentine military presence on the islands was largely dependent upon supply by sea. A plethora of

LEFT: **Survivor's view of the *Belgrano* foundering following two torpedo hits from the nuclear submarine HMS *Conqueror*. The sinking caused a political storm but, militarily, was absolutely correct in the establishment of moral superiority. The Argentine surface fleet gave no further trouble.**

LEFT: **The second Argentine cruiser, *9 de Julio*, (seen here), was deleted in 1979 and probably used as a source of spares to keep the 40-year-old *Belgrano* functioning. Although conventionally armed, the *Belgrano* had overwhelming firepower in comparison with that of the British warships.**

targets was thus available to the SSNs but the Royal Navy was bound by the principle of "minimum force" and, for the moment, rules of engagement permitted no attack. Nonetheless, although the British government insisted on terming the dispute a "conflict" rather than a "war", it was traditional naval strategy to hit first and to hit hard in order to establish a moral ascendancy over an adversary (compare with Heligoland Bight 1914 and Calabria 1940).

On May 1 the situation changed when intercepted signal traffic indicated that the Argentinian Navy was contemplating a major attack on the British task force. The latter, operating to the north-east of the islands, beyond the reach of enemy mainland-based air, found itself between two hostile task groups. To its north-west was one based on a carrier deploying A-4 Skyhawks. To its south-west, and skirting the MEZ, was a second, comprising the *Belgrano* and Exocet-armed escorts. The cruiser, although now elderly, shipped fifteen 152mm/6in guns which comfortably out-ranged the 114mm/4.5in armament of the British.

The Argentinians hoped that carrier-based air strikes with A-4s (superior in performance to the British Harriers) would cause damage and disorder from which the *Belgrano* group could take advantage.

Early on May 2 the two S-boats had located the carrier's escorts but not the carrier, their prime target. Meanwhile to the south of the islands the *Belgrano* group was being tracked by the *Conqueror*. London assessed the cruiser to be a direct threat and, despite her not having entered the MEZ and having turned on to a westerly course, ordered her sinking. The *Belgrano* had turned away on learning that due to lack of wind, the carrier air strike could not be mounted.

Unrushed, the *Conqueror* closed to within a 1.6km/1 mile before putting two torpedoes into the Argentinian which, poorly

TOP RIGHT: **HMS *Conqueror* was the first nuclear hunter-killer ever to sink a ship in anger. She used the elderly Mk8 torpedoes on the grounds of a close attack (under one mile) and for the odd reason that they would have "a better chance of penetrating the cruiser's armour and anti-torpedo bulges."** ABOVE: ***Phoenix* attempts to escape, passing Pearl Harbor's blazing oil tanks. In company with the *Detroit*, she was first ordered back to her berth before finally getting out to sea. She fired over 80 rounds of 127mm/5in against attacking Japanese aircraft and managed to escape damage.**

prepared, had no hope of survival. The British submarine easily evaded the depth charges expended by hopeful escorts but, despite her also not interrupting their subsequent life-saving efforts, a total of 321 were lost in the sinking.

The anti-war lobby in Britain subsequently made a maximum of political capital for the sinking yet, militarily, it was correct in signalling unequivocally to the Argentinians the consequences of any attempt at direct naval intervention. For the remainder of the short war, the Royal Navy was untroubled by the Argentinian surface fleet, which tended to remain in waters judged too shallow for the operation of SSNs.

The cruiser after 1945

Unable to win a war at sea fought by conventional means, Germany and Japan turned to the unconventional. As early as 1943 the Luftwaffe was deploying guided bombs against shipping while, during the following year, the less technologically advanced Japanese dispensed with the requirement for sophisticated guidance systems by employing suicide pilots. Either method was potentially lethal and highly accurate. Rapid-fire, radar-laid proximity-fused weaponry was the first response but the long-term solution lay in the surface-to-air missile (SAM), capable of eliminating such a threat at a safe distance.

First-generation SAM-systems were very demanding of space, with bulky missiles and handling arrangements and the need to direct each missile from launch to contact. Cruiser-sized hulls were required and although many nearly new war-built hulls were available, they did not lend themselves to easy conversion.

By the early 1950s, two viable American SAMs had emerged in the long-ranged Talos and medium-range Terrier. Accommodating the former required deep hull penetration and was expensive. Terrier, more compact, could be housed in a superstructure, although even this was bulky.

Reflecting the still-necessary flexibility of a cruiser, these early conversions were "single-ended", retaining their original forward gun armament. Their considerable extra "kudos" as

TOP: *California* (CGN.36) leads *Virginia* (CGN.38) with, possibly, *South Carolina* (CGN.37) to her starboard, and supported by *Leahy/Belknaps*. An all-nuclear navy appeared a possibility during the 1970s but, despite being able to steam indefinitely, nuclear warships still require regular topping-up with stores, ammunition and victuals. ABOVE: Following experience of air attack in World War II, and with the additional threat of Soviet Cold War developments of maritime bombers equipped with stand-off, air-to-surface missiles, Western fleets concentrated first on producing effective surface-to-air missiles, such as the 16.1km/10-mile ranged American Tartar. BELOW LEFT: Designed initially without guns, the *Long Beach* (CGN.9) later had a pair of single 127mm/5in 38 guns added, visible in the waist. The early Talos and Terrier missile systems were replaced by Standard, and Harpoon was added. Early plans to carry Polaris were not pursued.

missile carriers quickly made them popular as flagships, exacerbating the problem of inadequate accommodation space. With aircraft carriers needing to maximize volume devoted to aircraft, it was expected that area missile defence would be furnished by an escorting cruiser, although the latter was still expected to be flexible enough to operate independently in more traditional roles.

Despite the difficulties, the Americans produced the three Albany-class double-enders, incorporating both Talos and Terrier, and with a gun armament confined to just two 127mm/5in 38s. The two systems were also sold abroad but the resulting foreign conversions were few.

ABOVE: **When the Royal Navy's long-anticipated new attack carrier was cancelled in the early 1970s, a class of dedicated escorts was cancelled with her. HMS *Bristol*, the Type 82 prototype, alone survived. She had combined steam and gas-turbine propulsion and was designed around the Sea Dart SAM system.**

ABOVE: **"If a ship *looks* right, she usually *is* right." So runs the old tag and, unfortunately, the elaborate American missile cruiser conversions never "*looked right*". The 1960s rebuilds, such as the *Albany* double-ender, proved that purpose-designed vessels were ultimately better value for money.**
RIGHT: **Theoretically capable of 20 rounds per minute per barrel, the 152mm/6in guns of the British Tiger class were, mechanically, highly complex. Obsolete as all-gun cruisers, the ships were converted to carry ASW helicopters.**

Major World War II operations had highlighted the requirement for headquarters or task command ships. The considerable equipment and staff associated with their extensive command and control functions were located in mercantile hulls during the war but, for the peace, demanded the new concept of the "command cruiser", for which only purpose-design could really be satisfactory.

The cash-strapped British government was slow to introduce these new types of ship. An ambitious design for an 18,289-tonne/18,000-ton single-ender came to nought. Conventionally armed, unconverted cruisers found their way remorselessly to the scrapyards, while the three new Tigers, although completed with sophisticated, fully automatic 152mm/6in and 76mm/3in weapons, were obsolete before they were commissioned.

In place of the Sea Slug-armed 18,289-tonne/18,000-ton vessel and the large Type 82 escort for the projected new carrier, the Royal Navy received the County-class cruiser-sized destroyers. The Type 82s were terminated at one ship while the promised "command cruiser", following much inter-service and political wrangling, found final form in the *Invincible*, an ASW helicopter carrier in all but name.

Just a few good examples of the conventional cruiser were built post-war, notably pairs by France, the Netherlands and Sweden. Its last group, however, had to be the planned 24-strong Sverdlovs of the Soviet Russian fleet. At about 15,749 tonnes/15,500 tons and gun-armed they were fine ships and, although anachronistic, caused NATO planners problems in the area of trade protection.

For the US Navy, the extension of nuclear propulsion to surface ships removed the cruiser even further from its traditional concepts. The monstrous, all-missile *Long Beach* proved to be an evolutionary dead-end while her nuclear-powered escorts, although termed "frigates", were the size of earlier cruisers. Although they were eventually rerated "cruisers", their extra expense proved unjustifiable.

ABOVE: **France's last remaining conventional cruiser, *Colbert*, had been converted to a command ship by the early 1980s, serving as flagship for the Toulon-based Mediterranean Fleet. In this role she carried no gun larger than a 100mm/3.9in.** BELOW: **Missile systems are very demanding of space, and cruisers need to be designed around them. The Russian *Slava* of 1982 can accommodate 16 large SSM launchers forward, with eight vertical-launch silos for SAMs in the gap abaft the funnel.**

New technologies and mission changes have, for the moment, seen the end of the traditional cruiser, replaced by large, multi-function fleet escorts equipped with three-dimensional radar and a variety of missiles. This has been made possible by electronic micro-miniaturization, which has greatly increased potential without the parallel explosion in ship size.

Directory of Cruisers

Pre-World War I

In the period up to 1914 the cruiser emerged as a warship category in its own right. Its development was inevitably greatly influenced by the enormous technical advances of the era. From the cumbersome and heavy cylindrical boiler developed the water-tube types, lighter and more efficient. Compound armour advanced to proprietary "cemented" steels, giving greater protection for less weight. Horizontal and vertical steam reciprocating engines gave way to the smooth-running, compact steam turbine.

Our early examples are still sailing warships with auxiliary power, armed, mainly on the broadside, with muzzle- and breech-loading, smooth-bore and rifled shell guns. By 1914 we see 27-knot cruisers armed with quick-firing weapons, designed either to operate with the fleet or against commerce. During this period, armoured cruisers, as large and as costly as contemporary battleships, are still seen by some as a viable alternative. Cheaper and faster, protected cruisers emerged as the best "general purpose" type, equivalent to the old 74-gun Third Rate.

LEFT: **Small masted cruisers, such as the *Condor* of 1898, were the backbone of the Royal Navy's Pacific cruising fleet. Of several closely related classes, they were usually of composite construction, with iron or steel framing, clad in wood. The lower hull was sheathed in copper.**

Royal Oak, Hector and *Zealous*

A French order for four, steam-driven ironclads, placed in 1858, triggered immediate British reaction. Iron protection, however, was first added only to gundecks and machinery. Only with the *Royal Oak*, completed in 1863, was armour extended to a belt, above and below the waterline. Converted from a 91-gun two-decked Second Rate while under construction, she emerged as a "wooden-hulled iron frigate" as, eventually, did her six sisters.

Conversion involved lengthening by 6.4m/21ft and the plate, full-length over gundeck and waterline, was 64–114mm/ 2.5–4.5in in thickness. She was completed with eleven 178mm/7in, breech-loading rifled guns (BLRs) and twenty-four 30.8kg/68lb cannon. The great combined weight of plate and artillery, spread over the entire length,

imposed great hogging stresses on a timber-framed hull. She was, therefore, rearmed in 1867, with four 203mm/8in and twenty 178mm/7in guns (all of them muzzle-loaders). All except four of the latter calibre were concentrated around the centre of the ship.

Although technically a frigate, she was still considered to be "of the line", but her machinery was of low power, and she still relied mainly upon her full sailing rig. Effectively, she was a second-rate liner, with further third-rates (slower and weaker) ranked below her.

The *Zealous*, another converted two-deck 91-gunner, typified these latter ships. Experience had shown the problems attendant upon lengthening, so she retained her original dimensions. To save weight at the extremities, she had a full-length armoured belt, but sixteen

ABOVE LEFT: The *Royal Oak* as rearmed. Sheathed with 50–114mm/2.5–4.5in armour plate on her wooden frame, she and her near sisters were able to accommodate only one tier of heavy guns, technically making them frigates. The *Royal Oak* was faster under sail than under power. Note the canvas windsail ventilators. ABOVE: Unlike the *Royal Oak*, the *Zealous* was not lengthened on being converted from a two-decker. Her wooden frame was less strained by the concentration of sixteen of her twenty 178mm/7in MLRs in a central citadel. Note her funnel is lowered like that of the *Royal Oak*.

of her twenty 178mm/7in MLRs were concentrated amidships. Side armour on the gundeck was limited to this area, closed off at either end with a 76mm/3in transverse bulkhead.

Iron-on-wood was never satisfactory and the Admiralty was, at this time, hesitantly moving to iron-on-iron framing (the big Warriors were, as yet, incomplete). *Hector* and *Valiant*, completed in 1864 and 1868, heralded the new style.

ABOVE: Still new, the *Hector* in 1864 with funnel raised. Like the *Royal Oak* (above), she is barque-rigged, but with double topsails. She was the first Royal Navy ship to be built and engined by the same firm (Napier).

Royal Oak (as rearmed)

Built: Chatham Dockyard
Commissioned: May 28, 1863
Displacement: 6,451 tonnes/6,350 tons (designed); 7,112 tonnes/7,000 tons (full load)
Length: 83.2m/273ft (bp)
Beam: 17.4m/57ft
Draught: 7.4m/24ft 3in (normal)
Armament: 4 x 203mm/8in MLR and 20 x 178mm/7in MLR guns
Machinery: 2-cylinder, horizontal, single-expansion engine, 6 box boilers, 1 shaft
Power: 2,760kW/3,700ihp for 12.5 knots
Endurance: 559 tonnes/550 tons (coal) for 4,075km/2,200nm at 5 knots
Protection: 76–102mm/3–4in (belt), 76–114mm/ 3–4.5in (gundeck)
Complement: 585

LEFT: Naval occasion: the *Inconstant* with masts manned and dressed overall. Her ungainly lines are improved by the fine Victorian livery. Retired to serve as a static training ship in 1898, her iron hull was not scrapped until 1956. ABOVE: A good view of the *Shah* under both sail and steam. The ship gained fame in 1877 when, with the corvette *Amethyst*, she engaged the Laird-built pirate ironclad *Huascar* off Ilo, Peru. In the course of the action, *Shah* launched the first Whitehead torpedo in anger. It missed.

Inconstant, Shah and *Raleigh*

Civil War experience led the Americans to build the fast cruiser/commerce destroyers of the Wampanoag type. As is not uncommon, their actual performance was somewhat exaggerated but, although this was suspected by the British Admiralty, the ships posed sufficient threat to warrant a suitable response.

Thus, the *Inconstant*, was laid down in 1866 as the first of a new type of large "iron screw frigate". Speed, seaworthiness and endurance demanded a considerable length of hull and, in contrast to the longitudinally weak, wooden structure of the Wampanoags, the new ship was of all-iron construction. To reduce fouling (and, thus, to maintain speed and to increase time between dockings), the hull was sheathed in a double layer of oak, coppered from boot-topping downward. Design margins were very tight, so that the sheathing and deep, flanking coal bunkers constituted the ship's sole protective system. This method of protection was undoubtedly influenced by the British Admiralty's deep misgivings about the shattering effect of shot on iron plate.

Because of these doubts, the *Inconstant* was given an unusually large number of heavy-calibre weapons, to enable her to conduct a gunnery duel at ranges where she would incur little damage. Her mainly broadside armament was located on two levels, and she was given full ship-rig. Bunkers were sufficient for 43 days' steaming at 5 knots but only 54 hours at full speed.

Inconstant's great cost (for the day) was exacerbated by the new techniques involved in her construction. The second-of-class, *Shah*, was beamier and steadier, with greater bunker capacity and with a lighter armament. She proved to be 16 per cent cheaper but, despite this, the third and last of the type, *Raleigh*, was shorter, slower, yet more lightly armed and, generally, less capable for her designated role.

Inconstant, Shah and *Raleigh*

	Built	Commissioned
Inconstant	Pembroke Dockyard	August 1869
Raleigh	Chatham Dockyard	June 1874
Shah	Portsmouth Dockyard	December 1875

Inconstant (as built)

Displacement: 5,873 tonnes/5,780 tons
Length: 102.8m/337ft 4in (bp)
Beam: 15.3m/50ft 4in
Draught: 7.5m/24ft 7in (maximum)
Armament: 10 x 229mm/9in MLR and
6 x 178mm/7in MLR guns
Machinery: 2-cylinder, horizontal, single-expansion, trunk engine, 11 boilers, 1 shaft
Power: 5,490kW/7,360ihp for 16.2 knots
Endurance: 764 tonnes/750 tons (coal) for
5,149km/2,780nm at 10 knots
Protection: Nominal
Complement: 600

ABOVE: Smallest of the large iron frigates, *Raleigh* was more economical to man, consequently spending much of her life as a station flagship. She was reputedly the last Royal Navy ship to round the Horn under canvas and was scrapped in 1905.

Volage and Bacchante classes

Admiralty policy regarding the large, iron screw frigates was never made particularly clear. Assuming, however, that they were intended both to accompany high-value convoys and to patrol distant trade routes, it made sense to complement them with a smaller class of vessel, capable of undertaking similar tasks more cheaply in nearer waters. As more accurate detail of the American building programme emerged, it became apparent that their vaunted "commerce destroyers" were, in practice, not quite the threat that they had appeared. The Admiralty thus reduced its own programme, but did not stint on the quality of the remaining ships.

The *Volage* and *Active* were laid down in 1867, the year after the *Inconstant*, and described as "iron screw corvettes". This description was accurate inasmuch as the ships, besides being significantly smaller, carried their mainly broadside

armament on an open upper deck, protected only by high bulwarks. Both had iron hulls, sheathed in a single layer of oak, but attracted considerable criticism in being slower than the big frigates and, therefore, less effective in their cruising role.

It will be noted that, in line with British practice of the time, all were equipped with muzzle-loading rifles (MLRs). Early unfortunate experience with breech-loading (BL) guns had brought about a reversion to MLRs, but the obvious and increasing advantages of BL guns saw them generally reintroduced in the late 1870s. The two Volage-class corvettes were thus, as part of a general fleet programme, later rearmed.

The *Volage* design was improved for the following three Bacchantes. Although only 3.1m/10ft longer, these carried a far heavier armament, the gundeck being covered to protect gun crews from falling

ABOVE LEFT: **This photograph gives a clear view of the *Euryalus* in Mediterranean livery tended by the customary flotilla of Maltese dghaisamen. Both she and the *Bacchante* were straight-bowed.**
ABOVE: ***Boadicea* at Calcutta with awnings rigged. Her knee bow differentiates her from her two sisters. Although her class carried their armament on a covered gun deck, they were classed as corvettes, rather than frigates, owing to their limited complement and, thus, flexibility.**

debris. They varied considerably in detail and, despite having the more advanced compound engine, they were slower again than the Volage pair.

Volage and Bacchante classes

	Built	Commisssioned
Active	Thames Iron Shipbuilding Co, Blackwall	March 1871
Volage	Thames Iron Shipbuilding Co, Blackwall	March 1870
Bacchante	Portsmouth Dockyard	July 1879
Boadicea	Portsmouth Dockyard	May 1877
Euryalus	Chatham Dockyard	June 1878
Highflyer	Portsmouth Dockyard	Cancelled

LEFT: **Pictures of Victorian cruisers, such as the *Volage* seen here, are not so common. Full plain sail is supplemented by studding sails on the weather side. Smaller than the Bacchantes, both the *Active* and *Volage* had knee bows.**

Volage (as built)

Displacement: 3,129 tonnes/3,080 tons
Length: 82.3m/270ft (bp)
Beam: 12.8m/42ft 1in
Draught: 6.6m/21ft 6in (maximum)
Armament: 6 x 178mm/7in MLR and 4 x 160mm/6.3in MLR guns
Machinery: 2-cylinder, horizontal, single-expansion trunk engine, 5 box boilers, 1 shaft
Power: 3,379kW/4,530ihp for 15.3 knots
Endurance: 427 tonnes/420 tons (coal) for 3,426km/1,850nm at 10 knots
Protection: Nominal
Complement: 340

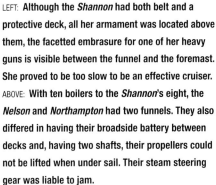

LEFT: **Although the *Shannon* had both belt and a protective deck, all her armament was located above them, the facetted embrasure for one of her heavy guns is visible between the funnel and the foremast. She proved to be too slow to be an effective cruiser.**

ABOVE: **With ten boilers to the *Shannon*'s eight, the *Nelson* and *Northampton* had two funnels. They also differed in having their broadside battery between decks and, having two shafts, their propellers could not be lifted when under sail. Their steam steering gear was liable to jam.**

Shannon and Nelson class

As the *Inconstant* was to the US Navy, so was the *Shannon* to the Russian, each the response to a perceived threat. Innovative designers, the Russians in 1873 launched the *General Admiral,* a new-style "belted cruiser" mounting six heavy guns in a central battery. Her design eschewed the usual protective deck in favour of a 152mm/6in armoured belt. British response was immediate, the *Shannon* being laid down even as the Russian was being launched.

In being equipped with both belt armour and protective deck, the *Shannon* may be assumed to be the first British armoured cruiser. Although extending fully aft, the belt terminated well short of the bows, being closed-off by a transverse bulkhead. Both upper and lower edges of the belts linked to protective decks, together creating an armoured box.

The *Shannon*'s battery was above the armour, devoid of cover other than that provided by reinforced bulwarks. Her two 254mm/10in MLRs fired forward along the facets, while three 229mm/9in MLRs fired on each broadside. A seventh 229mm/9in gun was located beneath the poop, firing astern.

Originally classed as a Second Class battleship, but capable of little over 12 knots, she was generally considered to be neither cruiser nor capital ship.

In recognition of the *Shannon*'s anticipated shortcomings, the two larger Nelsons were commenced just one year later. They adopted twin boilers (evidenced externally by two funnels), which enabled the steering gear to be located below the armoured deck.

A short belt left both bow and stern "soft", while creating a central armoured box, above which was a covered box battery. From its four corners, 254mm/10in guns could train either axially or abeam, while four 229mm/9in weapons fired on each broadside.

Like the *Shannon*, the Nelsons were considered over-expensive for their purpose, and could not be afforded in useful numbers.

Shannon and Nelson class

	Built	Commissioned
Shannon	Pembroke Dockyard	July 19, 1877
Nelson	Elder, Glasgow	July 26, 1881
Northampton	Napier, Glasgow	July 26, 1881

Shannon (as built)

Displacement: 5,542 tonnes/5,455 tons
Length: 79.2m/260ft (bp)
Beam: 16.5m/54ft
Draught: 6.8m/22ft 3in (mean)
Armament: 2 x 254mm/10in MLR, 7 x 229mm/9in MLR and 6 x 20lb BL guns
Machinery: 4-cylinder, horizontal compound engine, 8 boilers, 1 shaft
Power: 2,513kW/3,369ihp for 12.3 knots
Endurance: 589 tonnes/580 tons (coal) for 4,186km/2,260nm at 10 knots
Protection: 152–229mm/6–9in iron, backed by 254–330mm/10–13in teak (belt); 38–76mm/1.5–3in (decks)
Complement: 450

LEFT: **Later in her existence, the *Nelson* is seen with reduced, "military" rig and with large fighting tops added to fore- and mizzen-masts, supporting quick-firing guns. By the time of this photograph (the 1890s), she was reduced to trooping and training duties.**

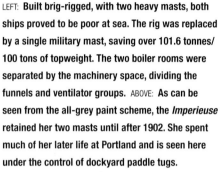

LEFT: **Built brig-rigged, with two heavy masts, both ships proved to be poor at sea. The rig was replaced by a single military mast, saving over 101.6 tonnes/ 100 tons of topweight. The two boiler rooms were separated by the machinery space, dividing the funnels and ventilator groups.** ABOVE: **As can be seen from the all-grey paint scheme, the *Imperieuse* retained her two masts until after 1902. She spent much of her later life at Portland and is seen here under the control of dockyard paddle tugs.**

Imperieuse class

Further building of large armoured cruisers by the Russians, and a deterioration of Anglo-Russian relations, resulted in the British Admiralty producing the two Imperieuse-class "steel barbette ships". They were intended to work on distant stations where they were more likely to be involved in a ship-on-ship gunnery duel than in a line action.

Recent French practice had been to arrange four heavy guns lozenge-style, i.e. one forward, one aft and one on either beam. The beam-mounted guns were located on shallow barbettes, sponsoned out over sides fashioned with pronounced tumblehome. This enabled (in theory at least) three of the four guns to bear forward, aft, or on either beam. Lighter than turrets, barbettes permitted higher freeboard. These two cruisers

became the only British warships to adopt these features.

Four of the new 234mm/9.2in BL guns (which would prove to be very reliable weapons) were mounted in open shields on the revolving armoured turntables of the barbettes. A full-length, but non-continuous, protective deck was stepped up by one level over the extent of the shallow amidships belt, roofing in above the machinery and boiler spaces.

Faulty design calculations saw the ships badly overweight. They were, however, the last armoured ships designed with square rig. In this case, the two-masted brig rig proved so inefficient that it was removed. Further weight was saved by the suppression of four of the intended ten 152mm/6in guns of the broadside secondary battery. Through being constructed of steel, the

ships' structure was already somewhat lighter than it would have been had it been made of iron. The protective deck was raised one level in way of machinery.

Relieved of two heavy masts and a bowsprit, the appearance of the pair was radically changed, with a single mast stepped amidships, between the funnels. Although castigated failures, both enjoyed long careers.

Imperieuse class

	Built	Commissioned
Imperieuse	Portsmouth Dockyard	September 1886
Warspite	Chatham Dockyard	June 1888

Imperieuse class

Displacement: 8,655 tonnes/8,500 tons (full load)
Length: 96m/315ft (bp)
Beam: 18.9m/62ft
Draught: 8.3m/27ft 3in (maximum)
Armament: 4 x 234mm/9.2in BL and
10 x 152mm/6in BL guns; 6 x 457mm/18in
torpedo tubes (6x1)
Machinery: 2 x 3-cylinder inverted compound engines
Power: 7,460kW/10,000ihp for 16.75knots,
12 boilers, 2 shafts
Endurance: 1,148 tonnes/1,130 tons (coal) for
12,965km/7,000nm at 10 knots
Protection: 254mm/10in with 254mm/10in teak
backing (belt); 51–203mm/2–8in (protective
deck); 203mm/8in (barbettes)
Complement: 555

LEFT: **In this view of the *Warspite*, the French-style tumblehome of the sides is visible. This enabled the amidships sponson-mounted 234mm/9.2in guns to theoretical fire along the ship's axis. In practice, the effects of gun blast greatly reduced the useful arcs of the weapons.**

ABOVE LEFT: **Painted for tropical duty, the *Calliope* lays to a buoy in Portsmouth harbour. Not apparent is the unusual combination of materials used in her construction – steel framed and iron plated, sheathed in wood and with underwater sections coppered.** ABOVE: **Ceremony played a great part in the life of the average colonial cruiser, as here with the *Comus*, seen in Canadian waters. The *Comus* was the only one of her class to have a uniform 152mm/6in breech-loading battery.** LEFT: **Seen undergoing repairs to her propeller shaft, the *Conquest* shows her underwater detail to advantage. Note the heavy wooden rudder and the parallel-sided aperture for the lifting screw.**

Comus and Calypso classes

During the 1870s, the French were still perceived to be Britain's most likely naval adversary. The Royal Navy was responsible for safeguarding Britain's teeming merchant shipping but, generally discounting convoy as being irrelevant to steam-powered ships, it was difficult to plan to counter a determined *guerre de course* (war against commerce), where raiders might be fast armed merchantmen. Even if not commandeered for fleet work, the handful of large "armoured cruisers" available could offer little effective cover on distant trade routes.

The answer was sought in larger numbers of small cruisers, individually smaller and more affordable than the *Volage* type, and of considerable endurance. Thus were conceived the Comus-class corvettes, later regraded "Third Class cruisers".

Designed to operate alone, they were expected to be able to fight and to withstand damage. On their limited displacement, belt protection could not be considered, so the Comus class became the first extended series of protected cruiser, with a light protective

deck 0.91m/3ft below the designed waterline, overlaid with a 1.22m/4ft deep subdivided (or "cellular") layer. Machinery spaces were flanked by coal bunkers, while the hull was given a double layer of teak sheathing, the bottom sections coppered.

For endurance, all were given a three-masted ship or barque rig, and were among the last Royal Navy ships to use sail on a regular basis.

As early 152mm/6in BL guns proved unsatisfactory, most of the class spent

the greater part of their careers armed with MLRs. Recognizing the trials of long, tropical commissions, the Admiralty did much to improve habitability, particularly with efficient ventilation and adequate sanitary facilities.

The enlarged pair of Calypsos, displacing 2,814 tonnes/2,770 tons, were built in parallel and were armed from the outset with 152mm/6in and 127mm/5in BL guns. They were the last type of fully rigged corvette to be built for the Royal Navy, signalling the demise of sail.

Comus and Calypso classes

	Built	Commissioned
Canada	Portsmouth Dockyard	May 1, 1883
Carysfort	Elder, Glasgow	September 15, 1880
Champion	Elder, Glasgow	December 7, 1880
Cleopatra	Elder, Glasgow	August 24, 1880
Comus	Elder, Glasgow	October 23, 1879
Conquest	Elder, Glasgow	April 18, 1885
Constance	Chatham Dockyard	October 3, 1882
Cordelia	Portsmouth Dockyard	January 25, 1887
Curaçoa	Elder, Glasgow	February 24, 1880
Calliope	Portsmouth Dockyard	January 25, 1887
Calypso	Chatham Dockyard	October 19, 1885

Comus class (with revised armament)

Displacement: 2,418 tonnes/2,380 tons
Length: 68.5m/224ft 8in (bp)
Beam: 13.6m/44ft 6in
Draught: 5.9m/19ft 3in (normal)
Armament: 2 x 178mm/7in MLR and 12 x 64pdr MLR
Machinery: 3 x 4-cylinder horizontal compound engine, 6 boilers, 1 shaft
Power: 1,865kW/2,500ihp for 13 knots
Endurance: 478 tonnes/470 tons (coal) for 6,075km/3,280nm at 10 knots
Protection: 127mm/5in (protective deck)
Complement: 265

LEFT: **A graceful knee bow differentiates the *Iris* from her sister. In this picture she still has her foremast crossed in her original barquentine rig. Her proportions were particularly pleasing, her underwater form being an early example of refinement through tank-testing.** ABOVE: ***Iris* with her later, light rig. Their fine form meant that they could not carry any great press of sail, but with over half their length devoted to boilers and machinery they achieved a very high speed for their day.**

Iris class

Although not incorporating the innovative protective deck system of the *Comus* that followed them, the *Iris* and her sister were significant in cruiser evolution. Not yet defined as a category, cruisers tended still to be in concept either reduced battleships or colonial police craft. Particularly with the latter, hulls were necessarily optimized more for their qualities under sail than for speed. To counter any determined French war against commerce, the Admiralty now required moderately armed, but fast, cruisers. Thus, the Iris design, dating from 1875, was that of a "fast corvette" but was referred to officially as a "despatch vessel", a misleading label almost certainly designed to disguise its true function.

Lightness of construction, a fine form, and plenty of power characterized the design. Lightness was bought by constructing each vessel completely out of still-expensive steel, which exhibited equal strength with iron for about 15 per cent less material. Carefully tank-tested (a further recent innovation), the hull had a slim length/breadth (L/B) ratio of 6.52 (cf. *Comus*'s L/B = 5.06). Propulsion was by twin screws, the engines being horizontal compound units, low enough to be accommodated below the waterline. Their only real protection was afforded by the deep flanking coal bunkers.

Although initially fitted with a light barquentine rig, they soon had this removed. The fineness of the hull precluded the two engines being installed conventionally, side-by-side. They therefore occupied adjacent spaces, separated by a watertight bulkhead and driving shafts of unequal length. As the boiler spaces were also subdivided, the whole contributed greatly to the ships' potential survivability.

Propeller design was still in its infancy and it was only after several changes that the pair realized their true capability, comfortably exceeding 18.5 knots, the fastest of their time.

Iris had a clipper bow, the *Mercury* a straight stem. Both were later termed Second Class Cruisers.

Iris class

	Built	Commissioned
Iris	Pembroke Dockyard	April 1879
Mercury	Pembroke Dockyard	September 1879

Iris (as built)

Displacement: 3,342 tonnes/3,290 tons (normal); 3,790 tonnes/3,730 tons (full load)
Length: 91.4m/300ft (bp); 101m/331ft 6in (oa)
Beam: 14m/46ft
Draught: 6.2m/20ft 6in (maximum)
Armament: 10 x 64pdr MLR (later, 13 x 127mm/5in BL)
Machinery: 2 x 4-cylinder, horizontal, direct-acting compound engines, 12 boilers, 2 shafts
Power: 4,476kW/6,000ihp for 17.5 knots
Endurance: 793 tonnes/780 tons coal for 8,150km/4,400nm at 10 knots
Protection: Nominal
Complement: 275

LEFT: **Seen in tropical livery, the *Mercury* still has her original heavy sailing rig and is pierced for her original, old-style armament of ten 64pdr muzzle-loaders. She was rearmed twice more before finishing her career as a depot ship. She was not scrapped until 1919.**

LEFT: *Leander* finished her career with a 16-year spell as a depot ship. The distinctive three pairs of cowl ventilators remain but, of her original rig, only the mainmast here survives, complete with W/T extension. The new stump foremast is set vertically and she has gained two light derrick posts aft. ABOVE: Seen in the early years of the 20th century, the *Amphion* is in her final (schooner) rig. The most forward and after guns on each broadside were located in sponsons giving them a measure of axial fire.

Leander class

Also initially rated "despatch vessel", but reclassed as Second Class cruisers while under construction, the four Leanders took the *Comus*'s protected cruiser concept a stage further. The latter had a thin, flat deck, located below the (normal) waterline, surmounted by a cellular layer extending above the waterline. The Leanders had a much thicker deck which extended only over the machinery spaces. There was no cellular layer but the protective deck, flat for over half its width, sloped at about 25 degrees along either side. The flat was just above the waterline and the slopes terminated some 0.91m/3ft below it. The idea was that close-range, flat-trajectory shot, hitting about the waterline, would be deflected upward. Of the two

schemes, that of the *Comus* probably offered better survivability, but was more space-consuming. As they were never equally tested in action, no meaningful comparison may be drawn.

Interestingly, the Admiralty Board was itself divided, with the chosen Leander design being an improved Iris. Installed power and speed were less, but considerably greater bunker space more than doubled its endurance, an important factor in commerce protection. Twin screws also gave redundancy in the event of damage.

Like the *Iris*, the Leanders were fitted initially with a light barquentine rig, removed at the first major refit, probably because of their reputation for tenderness when not under a press of sail.

Being built later than the *Iris,* the Leanders benefited by being armed from the outset with 152mm/6in BL guns. Ten were carried, five along either side of the upper deck. This was itself transitional in that the centre three fired on the broadside, with only the end weapons able to train anything like axially. In addition, the ships were credited with carrying up to 16 smaller weapons, a mix of Nordenfelts, Gardners and Gatlings.

Leander class

	Built	Commissioned
Amphion	Pembroke Dockyard	August 10, 1886
Arethusa	Napier, Glasgow	September 29, 1887
Leander	Napier, Glasgow	May 29, 1885
Phaeton	Napier, Glasgow	April 20, 1886

Leander (as built)

Displacement: 3,789 tonnes/3,730 tons (normal); 4,369 tonnes/4,300 tons (full load)
Length: 91.4m/300ft (bp); 96m/315ft (oa)
Beam: 14m/46ft
Draught: 6.2m/20ft 6in (mean)
Armament: 10 x 152mm/6in BL guns
Machinery: 2 x 2-cylinder, horizontal, direct-acting compound engines, 12 boilers, 2 shafts
Power: 4,103kW/5,500ihp for 16.5 knots
Endurance: 1,032 tonnes/1,016 tons (coal) for 20,372km/11,000nm at 10 knots
Protection: 38mm/1.5in (partial-protective deck)
Complement: 280

ABOVE: **Although of the same design as the *Amphion* (above) the *Arethusa* appears longer and lower by virtue of her earlier Victorian livery. She still has her canvas bent on. The light bowsprit is probably an aid to handling the old-fashioned stocked anchor.**

Torpedo cruisers

The French Navy's "Jeune École" movement, exploring the possibilities of torpedoes in conjunction with small warships, influenced the Royal Navy in directions other than in simply developing antidotes. One result was the so-called "torpedo cruiser", a small Third Class cruiser designed to work with the battle fleet, covering it against enemy torpedo boats while, itself, having the means to inflict injury if the opportunity arose. The application required an agile vessel armed with torpedoes and with numerous quick-firing (QF) guns capable of stopping a torpedo boat.

A first attempt produced the two 1,605-tonne/1,580-ton Scouts of 1886–87 with a single 356mm/14in torpedo tube forward and further "launching apparatus" in the waist. Only later fitted with 119mm/4.7in QF guns, they were not successful in that they were poor sea-keepers and, at 16.5 knots, too slow.

Built in parallel were the eight larger Archer-class ships. Unlike the Scouts, which were fitted only with a pair of military masts, the Archers reverted to a three-masted, fore-and-aft auxiliary sailing rig. Also too slow, and reputed to be sluggish seaboats, over-armed with six 152mm/6in BL guns, they found a useful role in colonial duties.

In 1888, as the last Archers were being completed, the keels were laid of the four Barracoutas. They were more closely related to the Scouts but, although similarly classed as Third Class protected cruisers, changed the former's horizontal reciprocating machinery for more efficient, but higher profile, vertical, triple-expansion engines. Their protective deck was heavier and, for small ships, innovative in running full length.

As cruisers, the concept proved to be a design dead-end, primarily because the power-to-weight ratio of reciprocating machinery was not in favour of small, fast hulls. Evolution continued, nonetheless, through the development of smaller "torpedo gunboats" of the Gossamer, Alarm and Dryad classes, totalling 30 units.

ABOVE: **Third Class protected cruisers, the Barracoutas incorporated the novelty of two 356mm/14in torpedo tubes, both above-water. Their main armament remained their six 119mm/4.7in guns. Note that the navigating bridge was abaft the mainmast, and that the hull had both raised forecastle and poop.**

Torpedo cruisers

	Built	Commissioned
Fearless	Barrow Iron Shipbuilding	July 1887
Scout	Thomson, Clydebank	October 1886
Archer	Thomson, Clydebank	December 1888
Brisk	Thomson, Clydebank	March 20, 1888
Cossack	Thomson, Clydebank	January 1, 1889
Mohawk	Thomson, Clydebank	December 16, 1890
Porpoise	Thomson, Clydebank	February 12, 1888
Racoon	Devonport Dockyard	July 1888
Serpent	Devonport Dockyard	March 1888
Tartar	Thomson, Clydebank	June 30, 1891
Barrosa	Portsmouth Dockyard	June 1890
Barracouta	Sheerness Dockyard	March 1891
Blanche	Pembroke Dockyard	February 1891
Blonde	Pembroke Dockyard	July 1891

Barracouta (as built)

Displacement: 1,609 tonnes/1,580 tons (normal)
Length: 67m/220ft (bp); 71m/233ft (oa)
Beam: 10.7m/35ft
Draught: 4.6m/15ft (mean)
Armament: 6 x 119mm/4.7in guns;
  2 x 356mm/14in torpedo tubes
Machinery: 3-cylinder, triple-expansion engines,
  4 boilers, 2 shafts
Power: 2,238kW/3,000ihp for 16.5 knots
Endurance: 163 tonnes/160 tons (coal) for
  6,297km/3,400nm at 10 knots
Protection: 25–51mm/1–2in (protective deck)
Complement: 160

LEFT: *Barrosa* **alongside. The aperture for the starboard, hull-mounted torpedo tube is forward of the brow ("gangway"). Note the 119mm/4.7in gun, trained to starboard, and the shuttered embrasure for a 3pdr. Note also the twinned, "torpedo-boat" type funnels, the large catting davit for the anchor, and the bow ornament.**

Vulcan

In 1883 the French Admiral Théophile Aube "father" of the Jeune École made, on the strength of one experience, the ambitious statement that his tiny 46-ton torpedo boats were capable of operating "self-sufficiently" and of navigating the Mediterranean or Atlantic alone. This arrant nonsense led to his navy specifying escorting gunboats and larger "defensive" torpedo craft to protect capital ships at sea.

Less than impressed by French claims, the British Admiralty was already evaluating larger, rival designs stemming from yards such as Yarrow, Thornycroft and White. Production also began on "Second Class torpedo boats", small craft designed to be carried aboard parent ships in place of earlier spar torpedo-armed picket boats. Lacking endurance and seaworthiness, these would be put afloat in the vicinity of the enemy.

This concept was first essayed in the *Hecla*, purchased on the stocks as a mercantile hull in 1878 and already converted to a naval auxiliary. Commanded 1881–84 by the redoubtable Captain (later Admiral of the Fleet) A.K.

Wilson, the "unhandy" *Hecla* was described by him as being a combination of armed transport and "torpedo store ship", carrying also mines, cables and six Second Class torpedo boats with facilities for their support.

With Wilson as its champion, the idea was deemed successful enough for Portsmouth Dockyard to lay down the purpose-designed *Vulcan* in 1888. The ship was an orthodox protected cruiser except for her light, and primarily defensive, armament of 119mm/4.7in QF guns and the extensive stowage aft for six Second Class torpedo boats. These were located on trolleys, which were rail-transferred to within the operating radius of either of two 20.3-tonne/20-ton Elswick-supplied hydraulic gooseneck cranes.

Rapid development in torpedo craft saw the *Vulcan* quickly made obsolete. Reduced to a depot-ship, then training-ship status, her long-lived hull existed until 1955.

ABOVE: **Despite her fine lines, the *Vulcan* was rarely able to make 20 knots. This picture clearly shows the complication of the anti-torpedo net protection. The cap in the stem covers two of the ship's six torpedo tubes.** LEFT: **A torpedo boat typical of the type designed to be carried by major warships, to be set afloat in close proximity to an enemy line. The torpedo launching gear is visible amidships. Note the protected cupola for the helmsman and the turtle-decked forward end.**

Hecla and Vulcan

	Built	Commissioned
Hecla	Harland & Wolff, Belfast	October 1878
Vulcan	Portsmouth Dockyard	July 1891

Vulcan (as built)

Displacement: 6,726 tonnes/6,620 tons (normal)
Length: 106.6m/350ft (bp); 113.6m/373ft (oa)
Beam: 17.7m/58ft
Draught: 6.9m/22ft 6in (maximum)
Armament: 8 x 119mm/4.7in QF guns; 6 x 356mm/14in torpedo tubes; 6 x Second Class torpedo boats each carrying 2 x 356mm/14in torpedoes
Machinery: Vertical, triple-expansion engines, 4 boilers, 2 shafts
Power: 8,975kW/12,032ihp for 16.5 knots
Endurance: 1,016 tonnes/1,000 tons (coal) for 22,224km/12,000nm at 10 knots
Protection: 51–127mm/2–5in (protective deck)
Complement: 430

ABOVE: **Dominated by her two enormous, 20.3-tonne/20-ton gooseneck cranes, the *Vulcan* is seen in all-grey Edwardian livery. She still retains her Bullivant nets but has lost her original ornate bow ornament. Most of her career was spent as depot ship or torpedo school vessel.**

Bramble, Condor and Cadmus classes

All "cruisers", in the then-prevailing sense of the word, were a late-Victorian collection of ship types described variously as corvettes, sloops and gun vessels or gunboats. Differences between these categories were far from clear cut and, until they were all eventually regraded Third Class cruisers, the primary significance of a category lay in its determination of the rank of commanding-officer and, hence, a ship's establishment. All were built for, or found their vocation in, colonial service.

Of those considered here, the smallest were the four Brambles which, at only 721 tonnes/710 tons displacement, were categorized First Class gunboats. They carried just two 102mm/4in and four 12pdr QF guns and were commanded by a Lieutenant. Following over 60 built of wood or of composite (wood planking on iron-framed) construction, these were the first boats of all-steel build. For smaller hulls, steel offered lighter construction, although this was offset by the sheathing

and coppering specified to retard fouling while on tropical service.

The Brambles were not equipped with sailing rig, so their bunker capacity limited their endurance, although machinery was also becoming more efficient and reliable. Sail training in the Royal Navy was also being scaled-down, so crews with these skills were becoming more difficult to assemble.

Where the Brambles had no true protection, the larger Condor and Cadmus classes had sufficient displacement to work in a protective deck over the extent of the boiler and machinery spaces. Longer than the Brambles by 7.3m/24ft and 9.1m/30ft respectively, they were still about the same length shorter than the earlier Comus- and Calypso-class steel corvettes and were, therefore, classed as "sheathed steel sloops". As such, they rated a Commander in command, in contrast to a corvette's Captain.

Designed for long commissions on distant stations, the steel sloops were fitted initially with sailing rig but, during their long careers, all had it removed.

LEFT: The *Condor* dries sails in the warmth of a Mediterranean port. A later commission saw her based on the Canadian Pacific coast. In December 1901 she left Esquimalt for Honolulu only to be immediately overwhelmed by a severe storm. Wreckage was found, but no survivors. Her heavy rig may well have contributed to her loss.

LEFT: **Colonial sloops retained their sailing rig for a considerable period. Here, the *Fantome* is rigged as a barquentine, canvas bent-on. Note the navigating bridge is located aft, also the conspicuous cowl ventilators, essential for the cooling of machinery spaces in the tropics. The spacious stern accommodation harks back to earlier days.** ABOVE: **Unlike the *Fantome*, the Condor-class *Mutine* is rigged as a barque. Despite their considerable draught, sloops of these classes were valuable during World War I in the Mesopotamia campaign, before being superseded by shallow-draught river gunboats. *Mutine* survived until 1932 as an RNVR drill-ship, being superseded by purpose-built shallow-draught river gunboats.**

Bramble, Condor and Cadmus classes

	Built	Commissioned
Bramble	Potter, Liverpool	June 1900
Britomart	Potter, Liverpool	June 1900
Dwarf	London & Glasgow	August 1899
Thistle	London & Glasgow	April 1901
Condor	Sheerness Dockyard	November 1, 1900
Mutine	Laird, Birkenhead	1900
Rinaldo	Laird, Birkenhead	1900
Rosario	Sheerness Dockyard	May 1899
Shearwater	Sheerness Dockyard	1900
Vestal	Sheerness Dockyard	1900
Cadmus	Sheerness Dockyard	1904
Clio	Sheerness Dockyard	1904
Espiegle	Sheerness Dockyard	1901
Fantome	Sheerness Dockyard	1902
Merlin	Sheerness Dockyard	1902
Odin	Sheerness Dockyard	1902

Cadmus (as built)

Displacement: 1,087 tonnes/1,070 tons (normal)
Length: 56.4m/185ft (bp); 64m/210ft (oa)
Beam: 10.1m/33ft
Draught: 3.4m/11ft 3in (normal)
Armament: 6 x 203mm/4in QF guns
Machinery: 3-cylinder, vertical, triple-expansion engines, 4 boilers, 2 shafts
Power: 1,044kW/1,400ihp for 13.3 knots
Endurance: 7,408km/4,000nm at 10 knots
Protection: 25–38mm/1–1.5in (partial protective deck)
Complement: 130

LEFT: **Although built with forced draught for their boilers, the Merseys still needed to have their funnels increased in height, as seen here on the *Severn*. This did not assist their reputation as heavy rollers, leading to their original sailing rig being removed.**

Mersey class

If it is accepted that the *Iris* and *Mercury* were the ancestors of modern cruiser design, then the four Leanders, laid down about five years later, were their first derivatives. With the same major hull dimensions as the straight-stemmed *Mercury*, they floated more deeply due to the addition of a partial protected deck. Constructed of 38mm/1.5in plate, this extended over only the boiler and machinery spaces, but the resulting extra displacement cost about 1 knot in maximum speed. To protect the machinery and to keep the weight of the deck at an acceptable height, horizontal, double-acting compound (i.e. double-expansion) engines were again specified.

Although the Leanders mounted ten 152mm/6in guns in the same arrangement as those aboard an Iris, they were all far more effective breech-loaders (BLs). The class was originally fitted with a barquentine rig (i.e square-rigged on foremast, fore-and-aft on main and mizzen) but, as it contributed to heavy rolling, it was later removed.

Rated Second Class protected cruisers, the Leanders were followed immediately by the four, further-improved Merseys. Good, evolutionary design saw these have a lower displacement on the same major dimensions despite having a full-length protective deck. They were also faster on much the same power.

The Merseys were the first cruisers built without a sailing rig, their consequent lack of bowsprit enabling a curved, ram bow to be adopted. Unusually the designers managed to exhaust their 12 boilers through a single funnel.

At about this time, the Admiralty's talented constructor William White, who had been associated with all these projects, left government employment to join Armstrong's at Elswick. He favoured small cruisers that sacrificed a measure of protection for improved speed and firepower. His legacy was to give the Merseys a single, over-large 203mm/8in BL gun on both forecastle and poop.

Mersey class

	Built	Commissioned
Forth	Pembroke Dockyard	July 1889
Mersey	Chatham Dockyard	June 1887
Severn	Chatham Dockyard	February 1888
Thames	Pembroke Dockyard	July 1888

Mersey class (as designed)

Displacement: 4,114 tonnes/4,050 tons (full load)
Length: 91.4m/300ft (bp); 96m/315ft (oa)
Beam: 14m/46ft
Draught: 5.9m/19ft 6in (full load)
Armament: 2 x 203mm/8in BL and 10 x 152mm/6in BL guns; 2 x 356mm/14in torpedo tubes
Machinery: 2-cylinder, horizontal, direct-acting, compound engines, 12 boilers, 2 shafts
Power: 4,476kW/6,000ihp for 18 knots
Endurance: 914 tonnes/900 tons (coal) for 16,205km/8,750nm at 10 knots
Protection: 51–76mm/2–3in (protective deck)
Complement: 325

LEFT: **From 1903 until 1920 the *Thames* served as a depot ship for submarines, as seen here. She was then sent to Simonstown as a training ship, finally being scuttled offshore after a career of over 60 years. Note the semaphore arms at the mainmast head.**

Orlando class

Having been created, the modern cruiser was now the subject of some indecision. The introduction of quick-firing armaments had suggested the likely riddling of a ship's hull and topsides. Assuming that resultant flooding was well-controlled, it appeared likely that these relatively small-calibre projectiles might lack a lethal punch, hence the *Mersey*'s carrying of a pair of 203mm/8in weapons, capable of piercing the belt of any cruiser antagonist.

As, however, these larger weapons were yet by no means universal, it could still be argued that the provision of a vertical belt, which would keep enemy projectiles out altogether, was preferable to a protective deck system, which would merely contain damage inflicted. The argument for the latter arrangement lay in its lightness.

Therefore, when the successor to the *Mersey* was being considered, sketch designs were prepared with alternatives of belt or protective deck. Somewhat surprisingly, the former was selected, probably influenced by current French and Russian designs of armoured cruiser, their most likely perceived opponents.

The new class, the seven Orlandos, were actually "armoured cruisers" in that their shallow, part-length belt was itself overlaid with a full-length protective deck. Probably with an eye to the available number of dry docks worldwide, the same hull length was again adopted, although beam was increased by a generous 3m/10ft. Despite this, the extra weight of protection, together with a heavy and over-ambitious 234mm/9.2in gun at either end, brought each to at least 406

tonnes/400 tons overweight, submerging the belt and totally negating its benefit.

Built with short funnels, which were soon lengthened, the Orlandos set the style for British cruisers over many subsequent classes. Their secondary 152mm/6in guns, later converted to QF, were carried at an effective height, sponsored for chase-fire. Although their masts were crossed by heavy yards, they were not designed for sailing.

Orlando class

	Built	Commissioned
Aurora	Pembroke Dockyard	July 1889
Australia	Napier, Glasgow	December 11, 1888
Galatea	Napier, Glasgow	March 1889
Immortalité	Chatham Dockyard	July 1889
Narcissus	Earle, Hull	July 1889
Orlando	Palmer, Jarrow	June 1888
Undaunted	Palmer, Jarrow	July 1889

Displacement: 5,690 tonnes/5,600 tons (designed); 6,110 tonnes/6,000 tons (full load)
Length: 91.4m/300ft (bp)
Beam: 17.1m/56ft
Draught: 6.9m/22ft 6in (full load)
Armament: 2 x 234mm/9.2in and 10 x 152mm/6in BL guns; 6 x 457mm/18in torpedo tubes (6x1)
Machinery: 3-cylinder, triple-expansion engines, 4 boilers, 2 shafts
Power: 6,338kW/8,500ihp for 18 knots
Endurance: 914 tonnes/900 tons (coal) for 14,816km/8,000nm at 10 knots
Protection: 254mm/10in (partial belt); 51–76mm/2–3in (protective deck)
Complement: 490

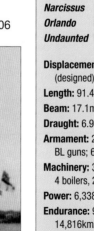

ABOVE: **Greatly improved in appearance and in boiler efficiency by longer funnels, the Orlandos established the general form of many subsequent British cruisers. *Aurora* is seen at the 1897 Diamond Jubilee Fleet Review.**

LEFT: **Completed with a rudimentary sailing rig, the Medeas had it removed later in their careers.** *Medea*, **seen here, retained her old, fidded topmasts, contrasting with the plain poles acquired by** *Melpomene* **(above). In action, the ship would be conned from the armoured position beneath the rather flimsy navigating bridge.** ABOVE: **The Medeas proved somewhat limited for independent operation and the** *Melpomene*, **seen here, went for scrap as early as 1905. She appears to be approaching an anchorage, with chart table set up on the starboard bridge wing and a leadsman on either side.**

Medea and Barham classes

For a short spell in 1883–85, William White broke his Admiralty career to work for Armstrong's at Elswick. At a time when cruiser design was in an important formative phase, therefore, there existed a strong cross-influence between "pusser" designs and those of what would become a long line of influential "Elswick cruisers".

Laid down in 1887, the five-strong Medea class were a cross between scaled-down Merseys and the Elswick-designed Italian cruiser *Dogali*. Originally classified as Second Class cruisers, they were regraded Third Class while under construction. Intended to be a small and inexpensive type to be built in numbers for trade protection, they proved to be too limited, despite carrying six 152mm/6in BL (later QF) guns.

Of the five, *Medea* and *Medusa* were equipped with vertical compound engines, the remainder with horizontal-

acting machinery. The latter trio were also wood-sheathed and coppered, making them slightly slower.

The Medeas, in turn, provided the basis for the Admiralty-designed Katoombas trio, commenced by Elswick in 1888 to Australian account.

White also produced a stretched version of his *Barracouta* design, intended to realize 19.5 knots on double the installed power. This could only be achieved under forced draught conditions where, even with fast and expert stoking, boilers and machinery were subjected to great stress, accidents and failures being common.

The two resulting cruisers, *Barham* and *Bellona*, were completed in 1889–90, but already looked dated with their two widely spaced funnels alternating with the three masts of a now-anachronistic sailing rig. When achieved, their designed speed was assisted by their

slim form, their 85.3m/280ft by 10.7m/35ft hulls giving a length/breadth (L/B) ratio of about 8.0, compared with the *Medea*'s 6.36. Their main armament was restricted to a manageable six 119mm/4.7in QF weapons.

Medea and Barham classes

	Built	Commissioned
Magicienne	Elder, Glasgow	February 11, 1880
Marathon	Elder, Glasgow	July 1889
Medea	Chatham Dockyard	May 1889
Medusa	Chatham Dockyard	June 1889
Melpomene	Portsmouth Dockyard	July 1889
Barham	Portsmouth Dockyard	July 1891
Bellona	Hawthorn Leslie, Hebburn	July 1891

Medea (as built)

Displacement: 2,844 tonnes/2,800 tons (full load)
Length: 80.7m/265ft (bp)
Beam: 12.8m/42ft
Draught: 5m/16ft 6in (normal)
Armament: 6 x 152mm/6in BL guns;
  2 x 356mm/14in torpedo tubes
Machinery: 2-cylinder, vertical compound engines,
  6 boilers, 2 shafts
Power: 6,711kW/9,000ihp for 18.8 knots
Endurance: 406 tonnes/400 tons (coal) for
  14,816km/8,000nm at 10 knots
Protection: 25–51mm/1–2in (protective deck)
Complement: 220

LEFT: **The two Barhams were an unsuccessful attempt to develop a small protected cruiser capable of 20 knots. The great proportion of length that was devoted to boilers and machinery is apparent here. As completed, the pair had a third mast amidships. Both had short careers.**

Pearl, Apollo and Astraea classes

The three Katoomba-type cruisers built at Elswick for Australian service were to form the first three of a new Pearl class of Third Class protected cruisers, essentially improved Medeas with an all-QF armament of eight 119mm/4.7in guns. Two more were constructed on Clydebank to complete the five-strong Australian squadron.

Following national agitation regarding the effective strength of the Royal Navy, Parliament passed the Naval Defence Act in 1889, providing for 70 new warships. At the same time, the so-called Two Power Standard was adopted, setting the Royal Navy's strength at equal to at least a combination of the next two most powerful fleets.

A first result was that four more Pearls were built for the Royal Navy. These were followed by 11 slightly enlarged and faster Pelorus class, spread over three programmes of the later 1890s.

No less than 29 Second Class protected cruisers were to be ordered, of which 21 were Apollos and the remainder of the larger Astraea class. The construction of so many Apollos represented huge confidence in a design which, at 3,455 tonnes/3,400 tons, was little more than an enlarged Medea. The layout remained the same, with a raised forecastle and poop, upon each of which was mounted a single, centreline,

152mm/6in gun. In the waist, behind high bulwarks at upper deck level, were located 119mm/4.7in QF guns, all essentially broadside weapons.

In their day, the Apollos were considered successful, if lightly armed. The eight follow-on Astraeas displaced a further 975 tonnes/960 tons and had a thicker protective deck. They were also flush-decked, allowing them to better maintain speed in adverse conditions and also to carry their eight 119mm/4.7in QF guns at a greater height.

Obsolete by World War I, these classes nonetheless played useful, if expendable, roles. Four were used as blockships at Ostend and Zeebrugge.

Apollo class

Displacement: 3,455 tonnes/3,400 tons (normal)
Length: 91.4m/300ft (bp), 95.8m/314ft 6in (oa)
Beam: 13.3m/43ft 8in
Draught: 5.5m/18ft; (maximum)
Armament: 2 x 152mm/6in QF and
6 x 119mm/4.7in QF guns; 4 x 356mm/14in torpedo tubes
Machinery: 3-cylinder, vertical, triple-expansion engines, 4 boilers, 2 shafts
Power: 6,898kW/9,250ihp for 20 knots
Endurance: 544 tonnes/535 tons coal for 16,668km 9,000nm at 10 knots
Protection: 25–51mm/1–2in (protective deck)
Complement: 270

Pearl, Apollo and Astraea classes

	Built	Commissioned
Katoomba (ex-*Pandora*)	Armstrong, Elswick	March 24, 1891
Mildura (ex-*Pelorus*)	Armstrong, Elswick	March 18, 1891
Ringarooma (ex-*Psyche*)	Thomson, Clydebank	February 3, 1891
Tauranga (ex-*Phoenix*)	Thomson, Clydebank	June 4, 1891
Wallaroo (ex-*Persian*)	Armstrong, Elswick	March 31, 1891
Pallas	Portsmouth Dockyard	July 1891
Pearl	Pembroke Dockyard	October 1892
Philomel	Devonport Dockyard	November 10, 1891
Pheobe	Devonport Dockyard	March 1892
Aeolus	Devonport Dockyard	January 6, 1894
Andromache	Chatham Dockyard	December 1891
Apollo	Chatham Dockyard	April 1892
Brilliant	Sheerness Dockyard	April 1893
Indefatigable	London & Glasgow	April 1892
Intrepid	London & Glasgow	November 1892
Iphigenia	London & Glasgow	May 1893
Latona	Vickers, Barrow	April 1891
Melampus	Vickers, Barrow	December 1891
Naiad	Vickers, Barrow	January 1893
Pique	Palmer, Jarrow	March 1893
Rainbow	Palmer, Jarrow	January 1893
Retribution	Palmer, Jarrow	May 1893
Sappho	Samuda, Poplar	February 1893
Scylla	Samuda, Poplar	April 1893
Sirius	Armstrong, Elswick	April 1892
Spartan	Armstrong, Elswick	July 1892
Sybille	Stephenson, Hebburn	May 1894
Terpsichore	Thomson, Clydebank	April 1892
Thetis	Thomson, Clydebank	April 1892
Tribune	Thomson, Clydebank	May 1892
Astraea	Devonport Dockyard	November 5, 1890
Bonaventure	Devonport Dockyard	July 5, 1894
Cambrian	Pembroke Dockyard	September 1894
Charybdis	Sheerness Dockyard	January 14, 1896
Flora	Pembroke Dockyard	March 1895
Forte	Chatham Dockyard	January 1895
Fox	Portsmouth Dockyard	April 14, 1896
Hermione	Devonport Dockyard	January 14, 1896

LEFT: **This image of *Dido* gives an idea of the complexity of warship rigging even into the new century. Although never designed for canvas, they have lengthy topmasts to elevate the W/T aerials, whose gaff appears at the main top. The topmasts are stayed to crosstrees, sailing-ship fashion, and the yards have footropes.**

ABOVE: **The rather weak original armament of the Eclipses is evident in this picture of the *Juno*. Although she carries five 152mm/6in guns it will be obvious that, from this angle, only two of them, i.e. that on the forecastle and the sponsoned weapon by the forward funnel, can bear. Fortunately, there was sufficient margin to upgrade the six waist 119mm/4.7in guns to 152mm/6in ordnance.**

Eclipse class

The long run of Apollos and Astraeas was criticized endlessly for its light armament although, in fairness, the ships were designed as inexpensive trade protection cruisers rather than combatants. As is usual, however, the advantages offered by a larger type became obvious and, even before the completion of the Astraeas, the larger Eclipses were being laid down.

These answered the critics in mounting five 152mm/6in guns. One of them was installed on the raised forecastle which was added to improve seakeeping. This was flanked by a further pair firing forward along facets at upper-deck level. Two more 152mm/6in guns were sided on the quarterdeck. In the waist, six 119mm/4.7in guns alternated with 12pdr weapons. In 1902 the 119mm/4.7in guns were upgraded to 152mm/6in ordnance, for a respectable total of 11. This followed the design of the Highflyer class derivatives, equipped with eleven 152mm/6in QF guns from the outset.

Single, open mountings such as these made for poor layouts, the Eclipses being able to command a six-gun broadside with, axially, just two bearing aft and three, theoretically, forward.

Despite a unit cost half as large again as that of an Apollo, the Eclipses were criticized for having no greater speed. Their heavier protection contributed toward a significantly greater draught, seen as inhibiting their versatility. However, they did have greater endurance and were better armed.

Unfortunately the class was always compared with the Elswick-designed cruisers, but, as was usual for minor fleets, they were untested by real action and battle damage, enjoying long and uneventful careers. Although the Admiralty view was that the Elswick ships had inferior survivability, they nonetheless boasted speeds of better than 23 knots and firepower including combinations of 203mm/8in and 152mm/6in weapons on similar dimensions and displacement.

Still able to provide useful second-line service during World War I, the class disappeared in the course of the huge cull of warships in the early 1920s.

LEFT: **Venus in a wartime guise with her larger 152mm/6in waist guns in evidence. Note the addition of the spotting top. Initially a unit of the 11th Cruiser Squadron in Irish waters, she moved during 1915 to the Red Sea and the Persian Gulf before transferring with three sisters to the East Indies Station.**

Eclipse class

	Built	Commissioned
Diana	Fairfield, Glasgow	1897
Dido	London & Glasgow	1898
Doris	Vickers, Barrow	1898
Eclipse	Portsmouth Dockyard	1897
Isis	London & Glasgow	1898
Juno	Vickers, Barrow	1897
Minerva	Chatham Dockyard	1897
Talbot	Devonport Dockyard	1896
Venus	Fairfield, Glasgow	1897

Eclipse (as designed)

Displacement: 5,689 tonnes/5,600 tons (normal)
Length: 110.9m/364ft (wl); 112.8m/370ft 4in (oa)
Beam: 16.5m/54ft
Draught: 7m/23ft (maximum)
Armament: 5 x 152mm/6in QF and 6 x 119mm/4.7in QF guns; 3 x 457mm/18in torpedo tubes
Machinery: Inverted, 3-cylinder, triple-expansion engines, 8 boilers, 2 shafts
Power: 7,308kW/9,800ihp for 20 knots
Endurance: 1,016 tonnes/1,000 tons (coal) for 12,964km/7,000nm at 10 knots
Protection: 38–76mm/1.5–3in (protective deck)
Complement: 420

LEFT: **Although less than 20 years old at the outbreak of World War I the then-colossal pair, *Powerful* (seen here) and *Terrible* played no active part, appearing vulnerable in any perceived role. Both were reduced to a training role post-war. Note the hull discontinuity caused by the double-level casemate.** ABOVE: **Her impressive size and the achievements of her "naval brigade" made the *Terrible* familiar to the public through numerous depictions. This one, in her later grey livery, shows her detail accurately and well. Note the characteristic funnel grouping.**

Powerful class

The great Russian cruisers *Rurik* and *Rossia* took from 1891 to 1898 to build. Their potential as commerce destroyers, although greatly exaggerated, resulted in the British Admiralty's equally massive response, the two Powerfuls, completed within the same timeframe.

Although the two Russians proved to be capable of only about 18 and 20 knots, respectively, the two British ships were designed for 22, a speed exceeded by both. This, together with the requirement to safely carry up to 3,048 tonnes/3,000 tons of coal in order to give them unprecedented range ("Why?" asked critics, pointing out that Great Britain, unlike Russia, was blessed with a worldwide network of coaling stations) resulted in an enormous hull, for which the required power demanded 48 of the new Belleville water-tube boilers, located in eight separate spaces.

Over 30.5m/100ft longer than a contemporary battleship, a Powerful demanded over 80 more crewmen. By any yardstick, they were expensive to operate. By contemporary critics they were excoriated because, as protected cruisers, they could not be included in a line of battle. This common but dangerous line of thought, equating size to battle worthiness, culminated in the total discrediting of both armoured and battlecruisers.

Their relatively light armament featured double-decked casemates for the first time, housing the twelve, later sixteen, 152mm/6in secondary weapons. This introduced the unhealthy trend of locating half the secondary armament at middle-deck level, too low to be of use in adverse conditions.

Temperamental, unreliable and expensive, both were non-operational by 1914. *Terrible*, however, under the command of Percy Scott, "father" of Royal Naval gunnery, had made her mark ashore. Superbly organized, her naval brigade made invaluable contributions in both the South African (Boer) War in 1899 and at the Boxer Rebellion of 1900.

Powerful class

	Built	Commissioned
Powerful	Vickers, Barrow	1898
Terrible	Thomson, Clydebank	1898

Terrible (as rearmed in 1903)

Displacement: 14,529 tonnes/14,300 tons (normal); 19,203 tonnes/18,900 tons (full load)
Length: 152.3m/500ft (bp); 163.9m/538ft
Beam: 21.6m/71ft
Draught: 9.4m/31ft (maximum)
Armament: 2 x 234mm/9.2in and 16 x 152mm/6in QF guns; 4 x 457mm/18in torpedo tubes
Machinery: 4-cylinder, triple-expansion engines, 48 boilers, 2 shafts
Power: 18,642kW/25,000ihp for 22 knots
Endurance: 3,048 tonnes/3,000 tons (coal) and 406 tonnes/400 tons (oil) for 12,964km/7,000nm at 14 knots
Protection: 76–152mm/3–6in (protective deck); 51–152mm/2–6in (casemates)
Complement: 895

LEFT: **Not a flattering picture of *Powerful*, but one that emphasizes her enormous, machinery-packed length. Note how, excepting the single 234mm/9.2in guns at either end, the weather deck is clear of armament, all secondary and tertiary guns being casemated.**

LEFT: **A rather nice depiction of** *Alabama* **under manoeuvring canvas only. She is cleared for action as her nemesis approaches. Her battle ensign is, correctly, the famous "Stars and Bars", the Confederacy's first national flag. Semmes' decision to duel with the** *Kearsarge* **was noble, but foolhardy.** ABOVE: **Little more than a fragile, if fast, armed merchantman, the** *Alabama* **was successful as long as she struck suddenly and moved quickly on, avoiding armed confrontation. Her tactics were thus those of successful raiders ever since.**

Alabama and *Trenton*

Waging war on the maritime commerce of an opponent can be very effective for the weaker adversary. For the Confederacy during the American Civil War, however, it enjoyed only brief success as privateering had recently been declared illegal under international law, effectively removing the profit motive.

Most famous of the raiders was the *Alabama*, a fast, three-masted, screw ship-sloop built in Great Britain by Laird of Birkenhead. Under her resourceful commander, Raphael Semmes, she roamed worldwide, claiming 69 prizes between August 1862 and June 1864. Seeking to rectify mechanical problems, Semmes entered the French Port of Cherbourg. Here his ship was blockaded, then sunk by the Union warship *Kearsarge*.

The *Alabama* and her fellow raiders did not affect the outcome of the war but had considerable impact on naval thought. Several navies subsequently built large cruisers, both as raiders and raider-antidotes.

Laid down in 1875, the wooden screw corvette *Trenton* was among the first American cruisers to adopt a, later-standard, "city" name. For a decade, her typical peacetime cruiser routine saw commissions in the Mediterranean, the Far East and South America.

She was refitting in New York when news came of deteriorating relationships between American, British and German officials engaged in seeking concessions in the Pacific territory of Samoa. The American consul in the capital, Apia, requested American warship presence to counteract that of three Germans already there. In March 1889 the *Trenton* duly arrived, rendezvousing with the screw sloop *Vandalia* and *Nipsic*. Also present was the British cruiser *Calliope*.

With little warning, the ships were embayed by hurricane-force winds, only the *Calliope* managing to fight her way to the relative safety of open water. The remainder were sunk or stranded, the *Trenton* and *Vandalia* being wrecked with the loss of 49 lives. The shock loss of these and the German ships led to a rapid agreement for a tripartite condominium.

Alabama

Built: Laird, Birkenhead
Commissioned: August 24, 1862
Displacement: 1,066 tonnes/1,050 tons (normal)
Length: 67m/220ft (wl)
Beam: 9.6m/31ft 8in
Draught: 5.4m/17ft 8in (normal)
Armament: 1 x 110lb, 1 x 68pdr and 6 x 32pdr guns
Machinery: Steam reciprocating engine
Speed: 13 knots
Complement: 145

Trenton

Built: New York Navy Yard
Commissioned: February 14, 1877
Displacement: 3,860 tonnes/3,800 tons (normal)
Length: 77.1m 253ft (wl)
Beam: 14.6m/48ft
Draught: 6.2m/20ft 6in (normal)
Armament: 11 x 203mm/8in MLR and 2 x 20pdr BLR
Machinery: Steam reciprocating engine
Power: 2,313kW/3,100ihp
Speed: 14 knots
Complement: 477

LEFT: **Although referred to as a "corvette", the** *Trenton* **carried most of her armament below deck. On the upper deck, right forward, she had a pair of breech-loading chase guns. Like the big 203mm/8in muzzle-loader, right aft, these were mounted on racers, enabling them to be fired on the beam as well.**

LEFT: The Union's response to the fast Confederate raiders was a group of wood-built frigates in which the designer, Benjamin Isherwood, sacrificed everything for speed. Although capable of a then world record speed of 18 knots, they burned too much fuel for their limited bunker capacity.

ABOVE: The launch of the *Madawaska* in 1865. Like the Union Navy's monitors, these large cruisers were given indigenous Indian names. During the time of the Civil War, there was considerable pride engendered in the "New" Navy, but this quickly evaporated in the expensive rehabilitation after hostilities ceased.

Wampanoag

The success of the *Alabama* and others as commerce raiders stimulated the Union Government to build a series of what were intended to be "super cruisers", capable of both hunting down commerce raiders or, if needs be, acting in a similar role.

The seven ships, commenced in 1863, are loosely referred to as the Wampanoag class, after the lead ship, but they were of various designs and sizes. All were completed after the Civil War had finished and one not at all.

The concept centred upon speed. To destroy merchant shipping, they had to catch it, so they were relatively lightly armed and devoid of any protective feature other than strategically located coal bunkers. On meeting any hostile warship, they were to use their speed to decline action.

Created by a noted clipper designer, the *Wampanoag*'s lines were fine, her hull long, both for potential speed and to accommodate the boilers and machinery, whose combined weight absorbed 1,219 tonnes/1,200 tons of the ship's 4,283 tonnes/4,215 tons displacement and, indeed, almost exactly half her length.

The ship's length was considerable in relation to its depth. Built in wood, the hull lacked longitudinal and torsional stiffness and, although its structure was augmented by metal plates, braces and ties, it worked badly.

She was, however, fast, achieving a reported near-18 knots maximum, and averaging 16.7 knots over a 38-hour trial. Her narrow-gutted hull permitted inadequate bunker space, a situation not improved by her equally inadequate auxiliary sailing rig. Chase fire, an important factor in pursuit, was also lacking owing to the fine lines.

The actual menace posed by large raiders was over-estimated, but could not be ignored, the British Admiralty responding with the large iron frigates *Inconstant* and *Shah*.

Renamed *Florida* in 1869, the *Wampanoag* was reduced to extended reserve status, thence serving in auxiliary roles until her disposal in 1885.

LEFT: Probably originally equipped with a bowsprit, the *Wampanoag* was considerably altered later in life to make her less expensive to run. She was also renamed *Florida*. With her considerable length, relative lack of depth and heavy point loading, her wooden hull worked badly and was destined for a short existence, however well maintained.

Wampanoag (as designed)

Built: New York Navy Yard
Commissioned: September 17, 1867
Displacement: 4,283 tonnes/4,215 tons (normal)
Length: 108.1m/355ft (wl)
Beam: 13.8m/45ft 2in
Draught: 5.8m/19ft (normal)
Armament: 10 x 203mm/8in, 2 x 100pdr, 2 x 24pdr and 1 x 60pdr pivot gun
Machinery: Steam reciprocating engines, 1 shaft
Power: 2,313kW/3,100ihp
Speed: About 18 knots
Protection: None
Complement: Unknown

LEFT: **The authorization of the "ABCD Squadron" in 1883 marked the foundation of the "modern" American Navy. Designed to a handy size, they were large enough to be employed independently yet not of a scale that would be difficult to justify to a hostile Treasury. The *Atlanta* had considerably less freeboard than suggested here and later landed her heavy brig sailing rig.**

The "ABCD Squadron"

Although it marked the beginning of what was known as the New Navy, the "ABCD Squadron" reflected the United States' then design inexperience by being obsolescent on completion. The nation was firmly opposed to the creation of a battle fleet, but the Naval Advisory Board, itself exposed to partisan argument and attack from the various naval support bureaux, recognized the requirement for cruisers to "show the flag", representing American interests abroad and, in time of war, to conduct operations against enemy commerce.

In practice, war could be envisioned only against Great Britain, whose maritime strength was overwhelming. What few distant coaling stations were available to American ships would probably rapidly be denied them by the British, so sailing rig remained essential to endurance, underlined by the fact that American propulsion machinery design was still inferior to that of Europe.

Approved in 1883, the squadron comprised the 3,048 tonne/3,000-ton sisters *Atlanta* and *Boston*, the 4,572 tonne/4,500-ton *Chicago* and the unarmoured "despatch boat" *Dolphin*. All three cruisers were constructed of steel, with a partial 38mm/1.5in protective deck.

Although available ordnance included a newly introduced 152mm/6in QF (or RF ["rapid fire"] in American parlance) the heavier projectile of the older 203mm/8in BL was preferred. This being a heavy weapon for smaller ships the Atlantas had to accept the weight-saving of low-freeboard fore-and-afterdecks in order to mount a single barrel at either end. The larger *Chicago* mounted four such, located in prominent, sided sponsons, whence they commanded a measure of end-on fire without interfering with the heavy, three-masted barque rig, which was greatly reduced in an 1898 modernization.

Only the *Chicago* was twin-screwed, but her original machinery, itself replaced by 1898, was archaic and, being of high profile, vulnerable to damage.

The *Atlanta* was stricken in 1912, the others serving in auxiliary roles throughout World War I.

The "ABCD Squadron"

	Built	Commissioned
Atlanta	Roach, Chester, Pa.	July 19, 1886
Boston	Roach, Chester, Pa.	May 2, 1887
Chicago	Roach, Chester, Pa.	April 17, 1889
Dolphin	Roach, Chester, Pa.	December 8, 1885

Chicago (as built)

Displacement: 4,572 tonnes/4,500 tons (normal)
Length: 99m/325ft (wl); 101.9m/334ft 4in (oa)
Beam: 14.7m/48ft 3in
Draught: 6.1m/20ft 2in (normal)
Armament: 4 x 203mm/8in BL, 8 x 152mm/6in QF and 2 x 127mm/5in QF guns
Machinery: 2-cylinder, compound, overhead beam engines, 14 boilers, 2 shafts
Power: 3,730kW/5,000ihp for 14 knots
Endurance: 1,168 tonnes/1,150 tons (coal) for 11,112km/6,000nm at 10 knots
Protection: 38mm/1.5in (protective deck over machinery only)
Complement: 300

ABOVE: **Considerably larger than the Atlantas, the *Chicago* was completed with a three-masted barque rig, that was removed in an 1898 modernization. Note how her four 203mm/8in breech-loaders are located in conspicuous sponsons to avoid interference with the sailing rig. Her broadside secondary armament is carried very low. Explosive shells made open gundecks such as this very vulnerable.**

LEFT: **Seen coaling at Malta during her delivery voyage, the *Naniwa* is painted in a livery not dissimilar to that of the Royal Navy. There would be several changes. Note how the two 26cm/10.2in guns are mounted on barbettes with no real overhead protection. Light shields would be added later.**

Naniwa class

The two Naniwas were members of the extended Elswick group of protected cruisers derived from the generic *Esmeralda*, completed in 1884. The American cruiser *Charleston* was also built to a closely related design.

William White, then working for Armstrong, modified George Rendel's original concept by increasing freeboard, enabling the full-length protective deck to be arched to above the (normal) waterline. Damage to much of its area would therefore, in theory, cause less flooding below. A further safety feature, by no means universal at that time, was the provision of a double bottom, extending from the forward to the after magazine space.

The extra freeboard, besides improving seakeeping, also increased the command of the two 26cm/10.2in guns, mounted singly in barbettes, forward and aft. Three sponsons along each side at upper deck level carried 15cm/5.9in guns. All were specified by

the Japanese to come from the German firm of Krupp. During 1900 the 15cm/5.9in weapons were replaced by Armstrong-built 152mm/6in QF guns; then, in 1902, the 26cm/10.2in guns were likewise replaced.

Although the machinery was of the low-profile, but relatively inefficient horizontally reciprocating type, the *Naniwa*'s trial speed of 18.77 knots placed her among the fastest of contemporary cruisers.

Both saw service in the Sino-Japanese and Russo-Japanese wars. Action at the Yalu and at Tsushima saw both survive considerable damage, and both were involved in the sinking of the Russian *Rurik*. Contemporary reports spoke well of their robustness and general performance, although their stability range was questionable.

The *Naniwa* was wrecked in June 1912, while the *Takachiho*, by then reduced to auxiliary duties as a transport and minelayer, was torpedoed and sunk

ABOVE: **The *Naniwa* seen here after the conclusion of the war with Russia in a new "tropical" colour scheme. By now the ship had been rearmed with a uniform eight 152mm/6in guns from Armstrong. The centreline guns have open shields, to be proved vulnerable at Tsushima, the broadside weapons are here trained outboard.**

in the course of the seizure of the German enclave and base of Tsingtao in October 1914, early in World War I.

Naniwa class

	Built	Commissioned
Naniwa	Armstrong, Elswick	December 1, 1885
Takachiho	Armstrong, Elswick	March 26, 1886

Naniwa (as built)

Displacement: 3,784 tonnes/3,725 tons (normal)
Length: 91.4m/300ft (bp); 97.5m/320ft (oa)
Beam: 14m/46ft
Draught: 5.6m/18ft 6in (normal)
Armament: 2 x 26cm/10.2in and 6 x 15cm/5.9in guns; 4 x 356mm/14in torpedo tubes
Machinery: Horizontal compound (double-expansion) engines, 6 boilers, 2 shafts
Power: 5,294kW/7,100ihp for 18 knots
Endurance: 812 tonnes/800 tons (coal) for 16,668km/9,000nm at 13 knots
Protection: 51–76mm/2–3in (protective deck)
Complement: 340

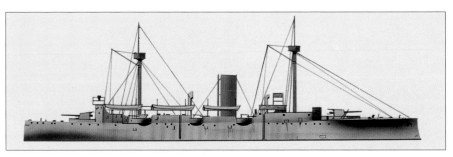

ABOVE: **Elswick gave the Naniwas a generous freeboard. This not only improved seakeeping but allowed the guns to be mounted higher. Internally, it permitted the centre of the vaulted protective deck and its openings to be above normal waterline, a great advantage if damaged in action.**

Unebi

Japan was keen to acquire expertise from the West sufficient to establish a domestic and independent warship-building capability. Commodore Matthew Perry's expedition and the ensuing 1854 Treaty of Kanagawa gave the United States an initial advantage as a source of that expertise, an advantage lost in 1861, when the Americans descended into a self-absorbing civil war.

The Dutch had enjoyed a small, but continuous presence in Japan's closed society but now found themselves elbowed aside by more ruthless French and British interests. The latter quickly had naval advisors on the spot and was making arrangements to train Japanese naval officers in Britain. The French, however, had the more immediate material success. Between 1865 and 1876 they created the major dockyard at Yokosuka from scratch, trained a largely local workforce, and then appointed the noted constructor Emile Bertin as superintendent to teach the Japanese the arts of steel shipbuilding.

Although Elswick won the order for the two Naniwas, the French built the protected cruiser *Unebi* over the same timescale. The British pair mounted, typically, a single large-calibre gun on the centreline at either end. The French opted for four, rather smaller 24cm/9.5in weapons, which demanded four large, sided sponsons. These, in turn, required the extravagant tumblehome typical of contemporary French ships.

In contrast to the Naniwas, with their light, "military" masts, the *Unebi* was given a heavy three-masted barque rig. Despite this, she had far finer proportions (L/B of 7.53, compared with a Naniwa's 6.52). Not only did she have a more archaic appearance but she also had an inferior endurance, her sailing rig being hardly auxiliary.

For the long delivery voyage, the Naniwas had the advantage of the network of British coaling stations. Less fortunate, the *Unebi* relied more on sail. In October 1887 she disappeared, still engaged on her maiden trip.

TOP: **Although launched a year after the Naniwas, the *Unebi*, with her heavy rig, looks anything but contemporary with them. Seen here in a French port prior to delivery, she has sails bent on to the yards but appears to have her bowsprit run in. Note the exaggerated ram bow.** ABOVE: **Standing rigging required that the *Unebi*'s main armament was sponson mounted. This governed hull configuration, and the effect of the tumblehome would be to reduce stability as the ship heeled under a press of sail.**

Unebi

Built: Soc. des Forges et Chantiers, le Havre
Commissioned: December 3, 1886
Displacement: 3,688 tonnes/3,630 tons (normal)
Length: 97.9m/321ft 6in (bp)
Beam: 13m/42ft 10in
Draught: 5.7m/18ft.9in (normal)
Armament: 4 x 24cm/9.5in BL and 6 x 15cm/5.9in BL guns; 4 x 381mm/15in torpedo tubes
Machinery: 3-cylinder, horizontal, triple-expansion engines, 6 boilers, 2 shafts
Power: 4,476kW/6,000ihp for 16 knots
Endurance: 10,371km/5,600nm at 10 knots
Protection: 51–76mm/2–3in (protective deck)
Complement: 280

Itsukushima class

Despite the unexplained disappearance of the le Havre-built *Unebi* while on her delivery voyage, the Japanese quickly ordered a further pair of protected cruisers from France. However, the latter's shipbuilding industry had been greatly retarded by government policies, and the only yard able to accept the order was Forges et Chantiers de la Mediterranée, which was the company that owned the nation's largest military gun manufacturer, Canet.

The result demonstrated the intimate and interconnected nature of the industry at that time, for the ships were designed by Emile Bertin (newly appointed head of Yokosuka Navy Yard), while the ships' primary weapons came from Canet (whose eponymous founder had learned his trade at Armstrong) and their secondary weapons from Armstrong, whose small, quick-firing guns were superior to the French product.

With no concession to elegance, the ships carried a single 32cm/12.6in gun which, on a displacement of 4,282 tonnes/4,215 tons, was so disproportionate as almost to warrant the term "monitor". The lead ship,

ABOVE: **With their single 32cm/12.6in Canet gun, the three Itsukushimas were, perhaps, as much monitor as cruiser. Of idiosyncratic French design, they had minimal superstructure, dominated by a lofty, stiff tripod mast bearing spotting tops. Excepting a single 119mm/4.7in gun right aft, the remaining armament was all broadside-mounted aft of amidships, crew accommodation being concentrated forward.**

Itsukushima, had a high-freeboard hull, with a full-width deckhouse that ran for 60 per cent of the ship's after length. The single, primary weapon was mounted forward on a shallow barbette, with the secondary guns mounted within and on the deckhouse. A miniscule bridge structure was located immediately before the single funnel. Abaft the funnel was a single, oversized tripod mast.

The second unit, *Matsushima*, had her 32cm/12.6in gun located aft. Consequently, she was more built-up forward and, aft, was one level lower. The third ship, *Hashidate*, was Japan's first-ever domestically built armoured ship. She was a copy of the *Itsukushima* and took six years to build.

Both French-built units survived quite severe action damage during the war with China, the main criticism being

applied to the secondary broadside batteries, whose guns were not separately screened. *Matsushima* was lost by magazine explosion in 1908, probably due to unstable cordite.

Itsukushima class

	Built	Commissioned
Hashidate	Yokosuka Navy Yard	June 1894
Itsukushima	Soc. des Forges et Ch. de la Mediterranée, la Seyne	August 1891
Matsushima	Soc. des Forges et Ch. de la Mediterranée, la Seyne	March 1891

Itsukushima class (as built)

Displacement: 4,282 tonnes/4,215 tons (normal)
Length: 89.8m 294ft 11in (bp); 99m/325ft (oa)
Beam: 15.5m/51ft
Draught: 6.3m/20ft 8in (mean)
Armament: 1 x 32cm/12.6in and 11 x 119mm/4.7in QF guns; 4 x 381mm/15in torpedo tubes
Machinery: 3-cylinder, horizontal, triple-expansion engines, 6 boilers, 2 shafts
Power: 4,028kW/5,400ihp for 16.5 knots
Endurance: 690 tonnes/680 tons (coal) for 11,112km/6,000nm at 10 knots
Protection: 38mm/1.5in (protective deck); 305mm/12in (turret)
Complement: 430

Yoshino

Being a successful series, constructed for numerous flags, the "Elswick Cruiser", although varying considerably in detail according to customer specification, was of a general form that was continuously improved. When, therefore, the Japanese sought tenders for a 4267-tonne/4,200-ton vessel, Armstrong only had to modify the form of the *Nueve de Julio*, just laid down to Argentinian account.

The Japanese were already developing the strategy of using cruiser forces as earlier fleets would use battle squadrons. Units such as the Itsukushimas, with their heavy guns, would form the slower, core force, while others such as the *Yoshino*, incorporating speed with an all-quick-firing armament, would constitute a fast wing, scouting, reporting and herding an opponent into the maw of the heavy artillery. (The Imperial Japanese Navy was still using coherent cruiser groups with devastating effect as late as 1942–43.)

Laid down in 1892, *Yoshino* continued the Elswick preference for raised forecastle and poop, separated by an open waist with high bulwarks, sections of which could be lowered to expose the broadside armament. Four 152mm/6in QF guns were carried, one each forward, aft, and two in sided sponsons, allowing them firing arcs from ahead to 60 degrees abaft the beam. Fighting tops, with light guns and searchlights, were a feature.

TOP LEFT: **Typically Elswick in appearance, the** *Yoshino* **makes a fine show under full power. The critical eye, however, would note how wet she is forward, even in a flat calm, while the wave form, with its deep hollow does not look very efficient.** TOP RIGHT: **Elswick had a reputation for plenty of guns, but note how the 47mm/1.85in weapons, here with their apertures open, are so low as to be unusable at speed, as in the picture to the left. The sponson of the starboard wing 152mm/6in gun can be seen in line with the forward funnel.** ABOVE: **This full, starboard-side view of the** *Yoshino* **gives a good idea of the layout of a contemporary light cruiser, with raised forecastle and poop, and an open waist from which the secondary armament fires through broadside apertures. The rudimentary navigating bridges, with plenty of glazing, are uncomfortably close to the main armament. The volume of coal smoke was inevitably related to speed.**

Like the Argentinian, the *Yoshino* incorporated an unusually thick protective deck and, of higher power, was briefly the world's fastest cruiser. Expected to be opposed by enemy torpedo boats and destroyers, she received an unusually large number (22) of 3pdr QF guns located, inter alia, in the bridge structure, mast fighting tops and, near uselessly, at lower-deck level.

The *Yoshino* played a notable role (against Armstrong-built Chinese ships) at the Yalu in 1894 but, during operations against the Russians outside Port Arthur in 1904, she sank following a collision, confirming Admiralty suspicions regarding the survivability of Elswick cruisers.

Yoshino

Built: Armstrong, Elswick
Commissioned: July 1893
Displacement: 4,247 tonnes/4,180 tons (normal)
Length: 109.7m/360ft (bp); 118.2m/388ft (oa)
Beam: 14.2m/46ft 6in
Draught: 5.2m/17ft (normal)
Armament: 4 x 152mm/6in QF and 8 x 119mm/4.7in QF guns; 5 x 457mm/18in torpedo tubes
Machinery: 4-cylinder, triple-expansion engines, 12 boilers, 2 shafts
Power: 11,745kW/15,750ihp for 22.5 knots
Endurance: 1,026 tonnes/1,010 tons (coal) for 16,668km/9,000nm at 10 knots
Protection: 44–114mm/1.75–4.5in (protective deck)
Complement: 375

LEFT: **On much the same specification as that of the *Yoshino*, the Japanese wanted to upgrade the main armament to a pair of 203mm/8in weapons on the *Kasagi* (shown here) and *Chitose*. Their American builders wisely increased length and beam to accommodate them. The canvas was very much a "get-you-home" addition.**

Takasago and Kasagi class

Expanding to meet the demands of the war against China, the Japanese Navy acquired the Elswick-built *Esmeralda* from Chile in 1894. Now ten years of age, she displaced only 2,327 tonnes/2,290 tons but had a full protective deck and an over-ambitious armament of a 29.4-tonne/29-ton, 254mm/10in gun at either end. This, and six 152mm/6in secondary weapons, left no margin for raised forecastle and poop. Renamed *Izumi*, she was valued for her big guns but, although influential in her day, she was a poor seaboat and was quickly reduced to auxiliary duties.

Following the war, the Japanese embarked on a replacement and expansion programme. Armstrong benefited through a contract to build an improved *Yoshino*, while two American

yards received orders for near-copies, reputedly in recognition of their having remained neutral during the recent war with China.

The seakeeping qualities of the *Yoshino* had not been above criticism and for the new ship, named *Takasago*, Armstrong were required to replace four 152mm/6in guns with two 203mm/8in weapons, and eight 119mm/4.7in QF guns with ten. This represented an increase in topside weight from 44.7 tonnes/44 tons to 51.8 tonnes/51 tons. On a hull of the same length, Armstrong compensated with an extra 0.3m/1ft of beam. Although still fast, the *Takasago* was a heavy roller. Inadequate subdivision resulted in her rapid foundering on being mined in 1904, although, at that date, damage control procedures were rudimentary.

The two American yards, building the *Kasagi* and *Chitose*, were allowed some flexibility in interpretation of the basic specification. Although obliged to retain the same scale of protection and armament as the *Takasago*, both opted for longer and beamier hulls. This resulted in (normal) displacements being increased by about 762 tonnes/750 tons and 610 tonnes/600 tons respectively. Their installed power was reduced, as was endurance and maximum speed, by nearly one knot. By not being designed to such tight margins, however, the two were probably the better ships.

Takasago and Kasagi class

	Built	Commissioned
Taksago	Armstrong, Low Walker	April 1898
Chitose	Union Ironworks, San Francisco	March 1899
Kasagi	Cramp, Philadelphia	December 1898

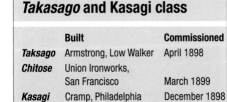

ABOVE: **The early "peacetime" livery of Japanese warships tends to conceal hull detail while the white-painted topside detail merges with a pale background. Despite her diminutive size, the *Takasago* was sufficiently protected to resist 203mm/8in gunfire but note how, due to stability considerations, the fighting tops are carried low.** LEFT: **When work was light, Armstrong would lay down a speculative cruiser, in this case a sister to the *Takasago*. The Japanese did not purchase her, however, and she became the Chilean *Chacabuco*. Note her boats are in the water and the boat boom rigged.**

Takasago (as built)

Displacement: 4,226 tonnes/4,160 tons (normal); 5,344 tonnes/5,260 tons (full load)
Length: 109.7m/360ft (bp); 118.2m/388ft (oa)
Beam: 14.2m/46ft 6in
Draught: 6.2m/20ft 6in (full load)
Armament: 2 x 203mm/8in guns, 10 x 119mm/4.7in QF, and 10 x 76mm/3in (12pdr) QF guns; 5 x 457mm/18in torpedo tubes
Machinery: 4-cylinder, vertical, triple-expansion engines, 8 boilers, 2 shafts
Power: 11,745kW/15,750ihp for 22.5 knots
Endurance: 1,041 tonnes/1,025 tons (coal) for 10,186km/5,500nm at 10 knots
Protection: 64–114mm/2.5–4.5in (protective deck)
Complement: 425

Azuma

The Sino-Japanese War of 1894–95 proved to the Japanese that discipline, practised manoeuvre and overwhelming firepower were essential to sea supremacy. As a result, the naval academy and the fleet itself were subject to considerable and urgent expansion. The thoroughness with which this was undertaken was apparent a decade later, when Japanese squadrons trounced those of the Russians, propelling their nation into the front rank of world naval powers, and consequent national rivalries.

The 1896–97 post-war naval acquisition programme had attracted considerable funding, of which little could be absorbed by the nascent domestic shipbuilding industry.

Armoured cruisers commended themselves particularly to the Japanese who used them rather as a squadron of fast Second Class battleships. Whether for speed of delivery, or to evaluate the relative quality of national construction techniques, is not clear, but the orders for six armoured cruisers of about 10,160 tonnes/10,000 tons displacement were split between Great Britain (*Asama* and *Tokiwa*, *Izumo* and *Iwate* from Armstrong at Elswick), Germany (*Yakumo* from AG Vulcan, Stettin) and the French-built *Azuma*.

Identical specifications governed speed, protection and armament, the latter introducing twin 203mm/8in BL turrets forward and aft. Perhaps the most distinctive feature of the *Azuma* was her lack of "Frenchness", there being no hint

TOP: **Of the six armoured cruisers built in Europe at the turn of the century to Japanese account, the only French-sourced ship, *Azuma*, could be identified by her unequally spaced funnels. Originally, as here, the funnels were half-cased, later being replaced by three slender, higher funnels and lighter masting.** ABOVE: **Effectively the Second Class battleships of their day, the armoured cruisers carried their twelve 152mm/6in secondary armament on two levels, eight in casemates, four in open mountings. By twinning the four 203mm/8in guns of the primary armament in turrets, space was saved but at the cost of a lower rate of fire.**

of the customary exaggerated ram bow profile, pronounced tumblehome or substantial, sponsoned gun positions. Only in the unequal funnel spacing could her likely origin be suspected.

Protection was capital-ship style, with a complete waterline belt of Harvey nickel steel, 178mm/7in amidships tapering to 89mm/3.5in at either end. Between the limits of the 203mm/8in magazines a 127mm/5in belt extended one level further upward to protect the underside of the 152mm/6in secondary casemates. The protective deck was of 76mm/3in plate.

Prominent during the Russo-Japanese War, all six armoured cruisers survived until the end of World War II, latterly in non-combatant roles.

Azuma (as built)

Built: Soc. des Chantiers de la Loire, St. Nazaire
Commissioned: July 1900
Displacement: 9,428 tonnes/9,280 tons (normal); 10,130 tonnes/9,950 tons (full load)
Length: 131.5m/431ft 6in (bp); 137.8m/452ft 5in (oa)
Beam: 18.1m/59ft 3in
Draught: 8.5m/28ft (full load)
Armament: 4 x 203mm/8in BL (2x2), 12 x 152mm/6in QF (12x1) and 12 x 76mm/3in QF (12x1) guns; 5 x 457mm/18in torpedo tubes
Machinery: 4-cylinder, triple-expansion engines, 24 boilers, 2 shafts
Power: 13,422kW/18,000ihp for 21 knots
Endurance: 1,219 tonnes/1,200 tons (coal) for 12,964km/7,000nm at 10 knots
Protection: 89–178mm/3.5–7in (belt); 76mm/3in (protective deck); 160mm/6.3in (turrets)
Complement: 720

LEFT: **Much influenced by the British "Towns", the Chikumas' distinctive bow profile set them apart. Note how the adoption of stockless, or close-stowing, anchors reduced greatly the foredeck clutter. The *Hirado*'s two very lofty masts were to elevate W/T aerials to gain range in the Pacific. The mast on the far left belongs to another ship.**

Chikuma class

It was a measure of the progress being made by the Japanese shipbuilding industry that two of the three Chikumas could be contracted out to private yards. Although experience relied heavily on the still-completing Tones, the new ships were greatly influenced by the Royal Navy's Weymouth class. Nearly 30m/100ft longer than a Tone, a Chikuma had no increase in beam and, with a 50 per cent increase in installed power, could make 26 knots, an improvement of about 3 knots. All were fitted with steam turbines but, for evaluation purposes, these were of different types. This resulted in the *Yahagi* having four shafts, the others two.

Like the British Towns, the Chikumas adopted a uniform 152mm/6in main armament. With a raised forecastle and poop hull form, they mounted a centreline gun at either end, their remaining six being sided in the waist. Four of these were slightly sponsoned to theoretically allow axial fire, although this was inhibited in practice by the effect of blast over-pressure on adjacent structures.

Care was taken over the ships' appearance, the stem having less curvature than that of the Tones, and with the latter's unusual stern profile replaced by a western-style "cruiser" stern. Of elegant proportions, the four funnels stood nearly vertical, complementing the lofty masts. The latter were necessary to extend radio transmission ranges over the vast Pacific Ocean.

Sixteen boilers were distributed over four adjacent boiler rooms, each of which was exhausted by one funnel. The spaces were roofed by the protective deck, of which the horizontal, axial section was some 45.7cm/18in above the waterline, the thickened slopes abutting the shell plating some 1m/3ft below it. Subdivided coal bunkers both covered and flanked the machinery spaces as added protection.

All were reduced to auxiliary status before World War II, the *Hirado* and *Yahagi* being scrapped only in 1947.

Chikuma class

	Built	Commissioned
Chikuma	Sasebo Navy Yard	May 17, 1912
Hirado	Kawasaki, Kobe	June 17, 1912
Yahagi	Mitsubishi, Nagasaki	July 27, 1912

Chikuma (as built)

Displacement: 4,470 tonnes/4,400 tons (standard); 5,120 tonnes/5,040 tons (full load)
Length: 134m/440ft (bp); 144.7m/475ft (oa)
Beam: 14.2m/46ft 8n
Draught: 5.1m/16ft 8in (mean)
Armament: 8 x 152mm/6in QF and 4 x 76mm/3in QF guns; 3 x 457mm/18in torpedo tubes
Machinery: Direct-drive steam turbines, 16 boilers, 2 shafts
Power: 16,778kW/22,500shp for 26 knots
Endurance: 1,148 tonnes/1,130 tons (coal) and 305 tonnes/300 tons (oil) for 18,520km/10,000nm at 10 knots
Protection: 22–57mm/0.88–2.25in (protective deck)
Complement: 430

LEFT: **Otherwise identical, the *Yahagi* had four, rather than two, shafts. The 16 boilers could burn either coal or oil. Coal, however, comprised about 80 per cent of the bunkers, probably because of its value as protection, although they had both vertical belt and protective deck. The Chikumas were Japan's first steam turbine cruisers.**

Chiyoda

The loss of the brand-new *Unebi* in 1887 came as a profound shock to the developing Japanese Navy. Although further orders were still placed in France, that for the *Chiyoda*, the *Unebi*'s replacement, went to Clydebank. Larger warships for the Royal Navy were by now being designed without sailing rig but the Japanese, with differing priorities, again specified it. The ability to proceed under sail still greatly increased cruising endurance, while teaching further mariners the art. Where the *Unebi* had a heavy barque rig, however, the *Chiyoda* had a lighter, mainly fore-and-aft barquetine rig. The three lower masts were, nonetheless, capped with substantial fighting tops, in which rapid-fire automatic weapons were mounted. These, together with the rig, were removed in 1902, when light topmasts with W/T gaff were substituted.

Shorter, but with the same beam, the *Chiyoda* would not have had to resist

the *Unebi*'s press of sail. Lacking the latter's French tumblehome, her waterplanes would have been fuller offering greater resistance to heeling. An unknown with respect to the *Unebi* at the time of her sinking was the degree of depletion of her coal bunkers, and its effect on her stability.

A critical element in the *Unebi*'s stability also had to be her relatively heavy armament. Four Krupp 24cm/9.5in guns were located at upper deck level, a combined weight of 77.2 tonnes/76 tons even without their sponsons. Also mounted at the same height were seven 15cm/5.9in weapons, representing a further 28.4 tonnes/28 tons.

Reportedly, the Japanese wanted to burden the *Chiyoda* with 32cm/ 12.6in French-built Canets, to achieve commonality with the new Itsukushimas. At 39.6 tonnes/39 tons apiece, such weapons were grossly out of scale on a 2,439-tonne/2,400-ton

ABOVE LEFT: **The liner-like proportions of the** *Chiyoda*'s **hull indicate her status as a training ship. Her final seven years or so were spent as a submarine depot ship, a role suited to her internal capacity.** ABOVE: **Later a common feature of British-built cruisers, the knuckle was unusual at this early date. The large catting davit shows that she still retains old-style stocked anchors.**

vessel, and Brown's wisely opted for a uniform armament of ten 119mm/ 4.7in QF guns, a total weight of only 20.3 tonnes/20 tons, 80 per cent of which was borne on a level lower than in the *Unebi*.

Chiyoda

Built: Brown, Clydebank
Commissioned: December 1890
Displacement: 2,439 tonnes/2,400 tons (normal)
Length: 91.4m/300ft (bp); 94.4m/310ft (oa)
Beam: 12.8m/42ft
Draught: 4.3m/14ft (normal)
Armament: 10 x 119mm/4.7in QF guns;
  3 x 457mm/18in torpedo tubes
Machinery: Vertical, triple-expansion engines,
  6 boilers, 2 shafts
Power: 4,178kW/5,600ihp for 18 knots
Endurance: 427 tonnes/420 tons (coal) for
  14,816km/8,000nm at 10 knots
Protection: 114mm/4.5in belt; 25–38mm/1–1.5in
  (protective deck)
Complement: 350

LEFT: **Note how the rigging differs in each of the pictures of Chiyoda. The short lower masts and very light topmasts indicate that sailing under canvas was never a serious proposition. The heavy tops were removed in the 1902 updating.**

LEFT: **The *Marco Polo* makes an impressive sight as she negotiates the swing bridge to enter the inner port at Taranto. Note the very large fighting tops, each carrying two 37mm/1.46in guns. The port side catting davit is swung out, ready to release an emergency anchor.**

Marco Polo

During the late 1880s, British constructors reached the conclusion that, for cruisers, "protected" was superior to "armoured". Before the improved Harvey and Krupp armour plate became available, protection in any realistic thickness was thought to be simply too heavy to cover an adequate area of the hull. On a limited displacement, a thick armoured belt was necessarily shallow and, with the ship in full load condition (or overweight), the belt could easily be submerged and of little use as intended. The 5,690-tonne/ 5,600-ton Orlandos were thus the last Royal Navy armoured cruisers until construction of the type was resumed in the late 1890s with the 12,193-tonne/ 12,000-ton Cressys.

Bucking the above trend, however, the Italian *Marco Polo* was a "one-off", an example of a small armoured cruiser (4,572 tonnes/4,500 tons), laid down in 1890 and completed in 1894. She thus bears comparison with contemporary British protected cruisers. The seven Astraeas, completed 1894–95, displaced only 224 tonnes/220 tons less, were 1.8m/6ft shorter, but 38cm/15in greater in the beam. Although more generously proportioned, the British ships could nonetheless make 19.5 knots on 6,711kW/ 9,000ihp where the Italian was good for only 17 knots with 7,460kW/10,000ihp. "Superiority" was thus a straight trade-off between, on the one hand, speed and, on the other, protection/firepower. Here, the *Marco Polo* was the better.

Both had a 51mm/2in protective deck, the Italian having a 100mm/3.9in belt in addition. Where an Astraea mounted two 152mm/6in and eight 119mm/4.7in guns, the *Marco Polo* had six and ten respectively, in similar disposition.

Obsolete by World War I, the Astraeas served only on distant stations or in auxiliary roles. Likewise, the *Marco Polo* saw no real action and, later in the war, was relegated to troop transportation. Stripped of her belt armour she served successively under the names of *Cortellazzo*, *Europa* and *Volta* before being scrapped in 1922.

Marco Polo

Built: Cantiere di Castellammare di Stabia
Commissioned: July 21, 1894
Displacement: 4,572 tonnes/4,500 tons (normal); 4,917 tonnes/4,840 tons (full load)
Length: 99.7m/327ft 3in (bp); 106m/348ft (oa)
Beam: 14.7m/48ft 3in
Draught: 6.2m/20ft 4in (full load)
Armament: 6 x 152mm/6in and 10 x 119mm/4.7in guns; 5 x 450mm/17.7in torpedo tubes
Machinery: Vertical, triple-expansion engines, 4 boilers, 2 shafts
Power: 7,460kW/10,000ihp for 17 knots
Endurance: 620 tonnes/610 tons (coal) for 10,742km/5,800nm at 10 knots
Protection: 100mm/3.9in (belt); 51mm/2in (protective deck)
Complement: 394

ABOVE: **Seen here at La Spezia in January 1898, the *Marco Polo* is about to depart on her first deployment to the Far East. She had been serving as flagship of the "flying division". Note the low waist, with two 152mm/6in and three 119mm/4.7in guns in shields firing over a high bulwark on either side.**

Giovanni Bausan class

For navies accustomed to slow ironclads, with heavy sailing rigs and broadside armament, George Rendel's design for the Chilean *Esmeralda* appeared nothing short of revolutionary. Offering a combination of speed, protection and hitting power on a relatively modest displacement, the "Elswick cruiser" promised to be a comparatively inexpensive solution to the needs of many fleets.

Armstrong sold the concept to the Italians directly from the drawing board, the *Esmeralda* herself not yet having been launched when the slightly longer *Bausan* was laid down.

Not surprisingly, the two were very similar, although the Italian differed externally in having a prominent gooseneck boat crane fitted in lieu of the more usual boat derrick. Where the *Esmeralda* had British-style open fighting tops for the location of light automatic weapons, the *Bausan* had enclosed tub-like tops.

The armament, a major selling point, was similar, with a 254mm/10in breech-loading gun, mounted in an open-backed gunhouse atop a barbette, at both ends. In place of the Chilean's six 152mm/6in

ABOVE: **Where the *Marco Polo* (opposite) has raised forward and end sections and a low waist, the *Bausan* has a raised centre section with relatively low freeboard forward and aft, giving her a "hogged" appearance. The big cutter is being rigged under the boat crane and hammocks are being aired forward.**

BL guns, the Italian substituted continental-pattern 15cm/5.9in weapons, later replaced. They were sided similarly along the raised central superstructure deck, located on shallow sponsons to increase their arcs.

Although she exhibited the common Elswick failing of inadequate freeboard, a shortcoming ever more evident as ships gathered weight in the course of their careers, the *Bausan* was received enthusiastically as the Italian Navy's first protected cruiser. She was followed by four near-sisters, built between three domestic yards.

During the late 19th century they supported the fleet during the acquisition of Italian territory in North Africa and along the Red Sea coast. In 1912 there was a brief war with Turkey. By 1914, all of the class had been relegated to auxiliary or training roles, their armaments reduced in varying degrees.

Giovanni Bausan class

	Built	Commissioned
Giovanni Bausan	Armstrong, Elswick	May 10, 1885
Etna	Cantiere di Castellammare di Stabia	December 3, 1887
Stromboli	Venice Navy Yard	March 21, 1888
Vesuvio	Orlando, Livorno	March 16, 1888
Ettore Fieramosca	Orlando, Livorno	November 16, 1889

Giovanni Bausan (as designed)

Displacement: 3,121 tonnes/3,072 tons (normal); 3,322 tonnes/3,270 tons (full load)
Length: 84.1m/276ft 1in (bp); 89.3m/293ft 2in (oa)
Beam: 12.8m/42ft
Draught: 5.9m/19ft 4in (full load)
Armament: 2 x 254mm/10in BL and 6 x 15cm/5.9in BL guns; 3 x 356mm/14in torpedo tubes
Machinery: Horizontal compound (double-expansion) engines, 4 boilers, 2 shafts
Power: 4,827kW/6,470ihp for 17 knots
Endurance: 559 tonnes/550 tons (coal) for 9,260km/5,000nm at 10 knots
Protection: 38mm/1.5in (protective deck)
Complement: 267

LEFT: **The American Wampanoag-class raiders bought about a British response in large, Inconstant-type frigates. Despite the vulnerability of these to smaller, but armoured, ships, the French followed suit with the two Tourvilles and the similar *Duguay-Trouin*. Note the tumblehome and the prominent sponsons housing 19cm/7.5in breech-loaders.**

Tourville class

The threat posed to commerce by the American Wampanoags resulted in the British building large frigates such as the *Inconstant*. Because these needed to be fast, they had long unarmoured hulls, and endurance was provided by a full sailing rig allowing them to operate on distant stations.

Finally, to subdue an enemy raider, once apprehended, a powerful armament was necessary. The resulting, very expensive warships were still, however, not able to engage smaller, but armoured warships.

Although much criticized, the type was also thought appropriate for the French Navy. Delayed by the Franco-Prussian War, the *Tourville* and *Duquesne* were funded under the 1872 Programme, followed by the smaller *Duguay-Trouin*. Like the British, the French found such ships too expensive to build and operate in any number.

All were of composite construction (i.e. wood on iron-frames) and the main armament of the Tourvilles comprised seven 19cm/7.5in breech-loading guns.

All were located on the upper deck, the chase gun being mounted axially to fire through the stem from a cramped location directly beneath the bowsprit. The remaining six were sided in sponsons, which permitted greater firing arcs while positioning them outside the mass of standing rigging.

One level down, on the middle deck, fourteen 14cm/5.5in BL guns were placed conventionally to fire on the broadside. In contrast to the old, pure sailing ships, the heavier guns were mounted at the higher level, while the scope for the middle-deck, broadside guns to run in or recoil was limited by the centreline casings that enclosed the boiler uptakes. These would also have impeded gun crews in serving their guns efficiently.

Such "transitional" designs illustrate the difficulties faced by designers in reconciling conflicting requirements of machinery, armament and sailing rig.

ABOVE: **_Amiral Duperré_ was an 11,278-tonne/ 11,100-ton armoured ship, launched in 1879. She was designed around four 34cm/13.5in breech-loaders. These were mounted singly on open barbettes with shields. Two of these are visible, sided forward of the bridge; the others were on the centreline, further aft. Sixteen 14cm/5.5in weapons were also carried, 14 of them on the broadside.**

Tourville class

	Built	Commissioned
Duquesne	At. et Ch. de la Gironde, Bordeaux	1878
Tourville	At. et Ch. de la Mediterranée, La Seyne	1878
Duguay-Trouin	At. et Ch. de la Manche, Cherbourg	1879

Tourville

Displacement: 5,563 tonnes/5,476 tons (normal)
Length: 101.6m/333ft 5in (wl)
Beam: 15.3m/50ft 3in
Draught: 7.7m/25ft 4in (normal)
Armament: 7 x 19cm/7.5in BL and 14 x 14cm/ 5.5in BL guns
Machinery: Steam reciprocating, 1 shaft
Power: 5,595kW/7,500ihp for 17 knots
Bunker: 813 tonnes/800 tons (coal)
Protection: None
Complement: 550

LEFT: **Of only half the displacement of the _Duperré_, the _Vauban_ and _Duguesclin_ (shown) were given the same layout of armament but with 24cm/9.5in breech-loaders. Again barbette-mounted, these were protected by round cupolas, clearly visible in the picture. _Duguesclin_ was completed in 1884 with a heavy brig rig and long bowsprit. Only the larger apertures in the side are gun ports.**

Dupuy de Lôme

The earliest ironclads were just that – wooden warships hung with vertical plate to keep out enemy shot. Within a couple of decades, however, concepts had advanced to include protective deck systems and the limiting of armour to the maximum thickness of plate over the minimum of vital areas. No one method was ideal; each having its adherents and detractors.

In line with the philosophy of the in-vogue Jeune École movement, the French Navy planned a new cruiser/commerce destroyer. Recent experiments, carried out against an old ironclad, had shown that the effect of a hail of fire from the new, small-calibre quick-firers could disable a warship as surely as heavy shot piercing her armour.

The new ship, a one-off, reflected this. Most commerce raiders were fast, but unprotected, intended to decline action with warships. The Dupuy de Lôme was slower, but intended to stand her ground.

Named after one of France's most influential constructors, she was an extraordinary looking vessel, flush-decked with high freeboard and an elongated plough bow. On a relatively modest displacement, the French were able to clad her entire above-water hull area in 100mm/3.9in plate. Internally, there was a 38mm/1.5in vaulted protective deck, covered with a cellular level, and with a splinter deck below it. Machinery was kept compact and below the armour by adopting low-height machinery with triple-screw propulsion.

ABOVE: At the time the ultimate in "fierce face" warships, the *Dupuy de Lôme*'s hull was protected over its complete area to main deck level. The single 194mm/7.64in gun, flanked by single 164.7mm/6.48in weapons, is visible at either end, as are the amidships 164.7mm/6.48in guns. Despite her overall weight, she had also massive tower masts.

A long, continuous superstructure deck was terminated in a short forecastle. Both forward and aft there were three individually turreted 164.7mm/6.48in guns. Amidships, single turreted 194mm/7.64in guns projected out on sponsons on both sides.

As with many innovative ships, the Dupuy de Lôme was never tested in action, but started a fashion in armoured cruisers to which Great Britain was eventually obliged to subscribe. The contemporary Edgar-class protected cruisers were considered to be the French ship's equal.

ABOVE: The extraordinary bow form was not designed as a ram but rather, with the elongated stern, a means of increasing waterline length in order to improve hydrodynamic efficiency. The *Dupuy de Lôme* is seen here with her original three funnels and her wetness is evident.

Dupuy de Lôme

Built: Brest Naval Dockyard
Commissioned: 1892
Displacement: 6,513 tonnes/6,410 tons (normal)
Length: 114.2m/375ft (wl)
Beam: 15.7m/51ft 6in
Draught: 7.2m/23ft 6in (normal)
Armament: 2 x 194mm/7.64in BL and 6 x 164.7mm/6.48in BL guns; 4 x 356mm/14in torpedo tubes
Machinery: Steam reciprocating, 3 shafts
Power: 10,440kW/14,000ihp for 19.5 knots
Bunkers: 914 tonnes/900 tons (coal)
Protection: 100mm/3.9in (sides); 38mm/1.5in (protective deck)
Complement: 515

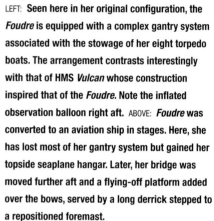

LEFT: **Seen here in her original configuration, the** *Foudre* **is equipped with a complex gantry system associated with the stowage of her eight torpedo boats. The arrangement contrasts interestingly with that of HMS** *Vulcan* **whose construction inspired that of the** *Foudre***. Note the inflated observation balloon right aft.** ABOVE: *Foudre* **was converted to an aviation ship in stages. Here, she has lost most of her gantry system but gained her topside seaplane hangar. Later, her bridge was moved further aft and a flying-off platform added over the bows, served by a long derrick stepped to a repositioned foremast.**

Foudre

A French response to the British cruiser *Vulcan*, the *Foudre* was launched in October 1895. Described as a "torpedo depot ship", she was built with a light conventional armament, her main offensive power being vested in eight torpedo boats. These were 18.3m/60ft in length, displacing 14.2 tonnes/14 tons, and were stowed topside, beneath a complex gantry designed for positioning on deck, their setting afloat and their recovery.

For lightness, the boats were to have been constructed of aluminium, but a prototype deteriorated so rapidly in contact with salt water that all were built in steel.

At her after end the *Foudre* had a facility for operating gas-filled, tethered observation balloons, a precursor of her eventual role. Like the British, the French found the "torpedo depot ship" impractical but, unsuitable for conversion to a conventional cruiser, the *Foudre* became initially a repair ship and then an ocean minelayer in 1910. She had, however, retained her original extensive workshop facilities, and these resulted in her being selected to become the French Navy's first aviation ship.

During 1911, all torpedo boat arrangements were stripped out, the ship's three distinctive, close-spaced funnels raised, and a garage-like hangar installed aft. This work was completed in March 1912, 17 months after Eugene Ely's pioneering flight from an American warship.

The *Foudre*'s hangar was built to accommodate seaplanes, to be flown from the water. In 1914 this was supplemented by a take-off platform erected over the ship's foredeck. Despite the ship's rather inadequate speed of 19.5 knots, this platform saw the French Navy's first-ever shipboard take-off in May 1914.

With the take-off platform removed in favour of further seaplane facilities, the *Foudre* joined British aviation ships for operations in support of the Dardanelles campaign. Subsequently, however, she proved to be more useful as a fleet repair ship. She was scrapped in 1922, much altered from her original configuration.

LEFT: **A couple of years after** *Foudre*'s **completion, she was equipped with facilities for stowing, inflating and towing an observation balloon, to extend her visual range prior to the launching of her torpedo boats. The latter being unsuccessful, the ship was relegated to auxiliary roles for several years prior to her conversion to an aviation ship.**

Foudre

Built: At. et Ch. de la Gironde, Bordeaux
Commissioned: 1896
Displacement: 6,065 tonnes/5,970 tons (normal); 6,188 tonnes/6,090 tons (full load)
Length: 115.9m/380ft 6in (wl); 118.9m/390ft 4in (oa)
Beam: 20.2m/66ft 2in
Draught: 5.3m/17ft 6in (normal)
Armament: 8 x 100mm/3.9in and 4 x 65mm/2.56in guns
Machinery: Vertical, triple-expansion engines, 24 boilers, 2 shafts
Power: 8,579kW/11,500ihp for 19.5 knots
Endurance: 853 tonnes/840 tons (coal) for 11,112km/6,000nm at 10 knots
Protection: 100mm/3.9in (protective deck)
Complement: 430

Stosch and Geier classes

LEFT: **Having limited naval heritage, the Germans named many ships after military heroes, the *Gneisenau* being an example. Despite her solid appearance, she was wood-sheathed on an iron frame. The class was designed to carry sixteen 15cm/5.9in breech-loaders on the broadside but, in service, the armament varied considerably.**

Following German unification, General (later Admiral) Albrecht von Stosch oversaw the transition of the Royal Prussian Navy into the Imperial German Navy. Until 1888 the service was administered by the army, and Stosch established many of its institutions.

Although its early armoured vessels were either built in Great Britain, or depended upon British design and components, less sophisticated warships were constructed domestically. Among these was a class of six Kreuzerfregatten, launched 1877–79 and named after military notables, including Stosch.

The ships were of composite construction, with zinc-sheathed wood on iron framing. All were ship rigged, with armament carried on the broadside. With considerable endurance, the class was comparable with the British *Comus*, and

contributed usefully to Germany's many colonial acquisitions of 1884–85. These included South-West and East Africa, Togo and Cameroon, New Guinea, the Bismarck Archipelago and the Marshall Islands. In later obsolescence the ships served as training and accommodation vessels, the *Gneisenau* being lost in 1900.

The empire established, the German Navy built a series of Stationskreuzer, equivalent in form and function to British corvettes. Smaller than the Kreuzerfregatten, and typified by the six Bird class, they were steel-built and sheathed in wood to upper deck level. To reduce fouling this was overlaid in muntzmetal. They were given a lighter, three-masted barquentine rig but, by 1914, this had been reduced to a handier, two-masted brig rig. Serving as a mining hulk, *Seeadler* blew up in 1917.

Typical of corvettes, they featured a raised forecastle and poop, and an open waist. They carried eight 10.5cm/4.1in guns, two each forward and aft, with four sided in the waist.

Obsolescent by 1914 some were still serving on distant stations. The *Geier* left East Africa, sailing to the western Pacific (and taking a prize) before entering American Honolulu for internment. The *Cormoran*, refitting at Tsingtao, transferred her guns and crew to an auxiliary raider.

Stosch and Geier classes

	Built	Commissioned
Bismarck	Norddeutscher Schiffbau AG, Kiel	1878
Blücher	Norddeutscher Schiffbau AG, Kiel	1878
Gneisenau	Danzig Dockyard	1880
Moltke	Danzig Dockyard	1878
Stein	AG Vulcan, Stettin	1880
Stosch	AG Vulcan, Stettin	1878
Bussard	Danzig Dockyard	1890
Condor	Blohm & Voss, Hamburg	1892
Cormoran	Danzig Dockyard	1893
Falke	Kiel Dockyard	1891
Geier	Wilhelmshaven Dockyard	1895
Seeadler	Danzig Dockyard	1892

Stosch class

Displacement: 2,565 tonnes/2,525 tons to 3,139 tonnes/3,090 tons (normal)
Length: 72.2m/237ft (wl); 82.3m/270ft (oa)
Beam: 13.7m/45ft
Draught: 5.5m/18ft 2in (normal)
Armament: 10 x 15cm/5.9in BL and 2 x 8.8cm/3.46in QF guns; 1 x torpedo tube
Machinery: 3-cylinder, single-expansion reciprocating engine, 4 boilers, 1 shaft
Power: 1,900kW/2,550ihp for 13 knots
Endurance: 325 tonnes/320 tons (coal) for 3,611km/1,950nm at 10 knots
Protection: None
Complement: 410

RIGHT: **With an easily manageable barquentine rig, twin-shaft and triple-expansion steam propulsion, the Geier class were useful colonial sloops, carrying a designed eight 10.5cm/4.1in guns. The *Seeadler*, seen here, gave her name to the magnificent natural harbour in the Admiralty Islands, strategically important during World War II, during the reconquest of New Guinea.**

LEFT: **A rather dramatic, but accurate, depiction of the *Victoria Louise* as completed, with three funnels and a heavy forward "battle mast". The design and armament layout was sound, being refined through successive classes until World War I. The "plough" bow profile was a characteristic of German armoured cruisers.**

Kaiserin Augusta and Victoria Louise class

Kaiser Wilhelm's ambitions in *Weltpolitik* resulted in frequent demands to increase the size of his fleet. Envious of the Royal Navy, he was all too aware that it could afford to out-build him at any time. His navy needed modern cruisers, yet limited budgets were biased toward capital ship construction. Where the British could build various types of cruiser, the Germans therefore sought to construct a multi-purpose ship, versatile enough to work with the fleet, on colonial duties or in commerce protection.

Launched in 1892, the one-off *Kaiserin Augusta* was, despite her 6,147-tonne/6,050-ton displacement, classed as a Kreuzerkorvette. A protected cruiser, she followed the example of the French *Dupuy de Lôme* in adopting triple-screw propulsion. Again, this was to decrease the bulk of individual engines in order to house them below armour.

The ship was capable of over 21 knots, but her four 15cm/5.9in guns were rather restricted in being located in sided casemates, forward and aft. Eight 10.5cm/4.1in weapons were sided in sponsoned casemates in the waist.

The *Kaiserin Augusta*'s slender hull proved to be weak, requiring extensive remedial structural stiffening. Her successors, the five-strong Victoria Louise class, were shorter, beamier and deeper in the hull. Altogether more capable, they paid the price in being 3 knots slower.

A single 21cm/8.2in gun was carried forward and aft, with eight 15cm/5.9in guns in casemates, four of them at middle-deck level, too low to be of any real use. Later weight reduction saw two 15cm/5.9in guns landed, the three funnels reduced to two (only half-cased) and the heavy tubular foremast reduced to a light pole. Their high profile caused marked leeway.

By 1914 all five were reduced to accommodation ships and all, except the *Victoria Louise*, were scrapped by about 1921. The exception served until 1923 as the mercantile *Flora Sommerfeld* at a time when merchant tonnage was scarce.

Kaiserin Augusta and Victoria Louise class

	Built	Commissioned
Kaiserin Augusta	Germania, Kiel	1892
Freya	Danzig Dockyard	1898
Hansa	AG Vulcan, Stettin	1898
Hertha	AG Vulcan, Stettin	1898
Victoria Louise	AG Weser, Bremen	1898
Vineta	Danzig Dockyard	1899

Victoria Louise class (as built)

Displacement: 5,750 tonnes/5,660 tons (normal); 6,595 tonnes/6,491 tons (full load)
Length: 109.1m/358ft 2in (wl); 110.6m/363ft 1in (oa)
Beam: 17.4m/57ft 1in
Draught: 6.9m/22ft 8in (mean)
Armament: 2 x 21cm/8.3in, 8 x 15cm/5.9in and 10 x 8.8cm/3.46in guns; 3 x 450mm/17.7in torpedo tubes
Machinery: 4-cylinder, triple-expansion engines, 18 boilers, 3 shafts
Power: 7,460kW/10,000ihp (for 18 knots)
Endurance: 965 tonnes/950 tons (coal) for 6,852km/3,700nm at 10 knots
Protection: 40–100mm/1.57–3.9in (protective deck)
Complement: 440

ABOVE: **Bearing the prestigious name of *Kaiserin Augusta*, Germany's first armoured cruiser proved less than successful, her long, shallow hull lacking stiffness. She mounted a dozen 15cm/5.9in guns, none of them on the centreline, with two firing aft through the unusually configured stern. During World War I she acted as a gunnery training ship. She was the first triple-screwed ship in the Imperial fleet.**

LEFT: **The** *Prinz Heinrich* **was an improved** *Fürst Bismarck,* **both of them being one-offs in the development of the best balance of qualities for an armoured cruiser. With reduced protection and only two heavy guns she was, therefore, faster. The arrangement of the secondary armament, amidships, was innovative.**

ABOVE: **Compared with** *Prinz Heinrich,* **the** *Fürst Bismarck* **(seen here) had cylindrical battle masts and was one deck lower amidships. Her secondary 15cm/5.9in turrets are more scattered, necessitating a greater weight of armour for the same scale of protection. Note how coal smoke disperses rapidly.**

Fürst Bismarck, Prinz Heinrich and Prinz Adalbert class

The *Victoria Louise* was reckoned a Second Class (or "Overseas") cruiser and thought too light for fleet work. The *Fürst Bismarck*, laid down in 1896 was, therefore, armoured with both belt and protective deck (100–200mm/ 3.9–7.87in and 50mm/2in respectively). Considerably larger at 10,862 tonnes/ 10,690 tons, she nonetheless retained her predecessors' excellent seakeeping and manoeuvring characteristics, with high-freeboard forecastle, cutaway keel and triple shafts. Twin 24cm/9.4in turrets were located forward and aft, and ten 15cm/5.9in guns were distributed on three levels in a mixture of casemates and single turrets.

In terms of fighting power, the *Fürst Bismarck* was a great step forward but her speed of only 18 knots left her no margin over that of the capital ships with which she was intended to operate.

With a reduced specification, therefore, the *Prinz Heinrich* was laid

down in 1898. Distinguishable through her extra level amidships and slender, pole masts (in place of the *Fürst Bismarck*'s cylindrical structures), she had a single 24cm/9.4in gun at either end and ten 15cm/5.9in weapons. Her major dimensions were much the same but her belt thickness was halved. Her displacement was reduced by some 1,626 tonnes/1,600 tons and, with installed power increased by about 11 per cent, she showed an improved speed of 20 knots.

Two years later, the two Prinz Adalberts showed further refinement on a hull whose dimensions were still limited by existing facilities. On a slightly increased displacement, twin 21cm/8.2cm gun turrets were located forward and aft, the protective deck was thickened and power was increased by a further 13 per cent. The same number of boilers was provided but these were now arranged in three spaces, necessitating a third funnel.

Both Prinz Adalberts became war casualties in the Baltic. The others, having served as school ships were scrapped in 1919–20.

Fürst Bismarck, Prinz Heinrich and Prinz Adalbert class

	Built	Commissioned
Fürst Bismarck	Kiel Dockyard	1900
Prinz Heinrich	Kiel Dockyard	1902
Friedrich Carl	Blohm & Voss, Hamburg	1903
Prinz Adalbert	Kiel Dockyard	1904

Prinz Adalbert (as built)

Displacement: 9,235 tonnes/9,090 tons (normal); 10,033 tonnes/9,875 tons (full load)
Length: 124.9m/410ft (wl); 126.5m/415ft 3in (oa)
Beam: 19.6m/64ft 4in
Draught: 7.8m/25ft 7in (normal)
Armament: 4 x 21cm/8.3in (2x2), 10 x 15cm/5.9in (10x1) and 12 x 8.8cm/3.46in (12x1); 4 x 450mm/17.7in torpedo tubes (4x1)
Machinery: 3-cylinder, triple-expansion engines, 14 boilers, 3 shafts
Power: 12,677kW/17,000ihp for 20.5 knots
Endurance: 1,635 tonnes/1,610 tons (coal) and 180 tonnes/177 tons (oil) for 12,500km/6,750nm at 10 knots
Protection: 80–100mm/3.15–3.9in (belt), 40–80mm/1.57–3.15in (protective deck); 30–150mm/1.18–5.9in (turrets)
Complement: 528

LEFT: **Following on quickly, the two Prinz Adalberts increased displacement to combine the best features of their two predecessors. Existing dockyard facilities prevented any significant increase in dimensions but a revised boiler arrangement permitted an improved speed. The increased number of searchlights is due to the German Navy's advocation of night engagements.**

Roon class

Laid down in 1902–03, the *Roon* and *Yorck* (sometimes rendered *York*) were the last of a group of six Grosser Kreuzer that were tightly defined by length, the first of which was the *Fürst Bismarck*. Largely repeats of the *Prinz Adalbert*, they were only about 1.3m/4ft 3in longer but were able to accommodate two further boilers. Sixteen were now divided between four spaces, each with a funnel. They were given a further 0.5m/1ft 7in in beam but this was compensated with a thinner protective deck in order to realize 21 knots. Armament was essentially similar in both scale and layout.

By this time, the Imperial German Navy had developed a distinctive national style with a general air of purpose; masts and funnels were strongly vertical, the freeboard generous, and possessing an unmistakeable profile with its pronounced ram bow and "cruiser" stern. Triple-shaft propulsion was retained for, although the resulting machinery was heavier, it was of lower

profile. Power transmitted per shaft was also less, permitting small-diameter propellers. This was a point of some significance as German ships had, perforce, to operate continually in very shallow water.

It says much for the pace of naval development, forced along by the "Dreadnought effect", that these fine cruisers should, by 1914, be deemed second-line units. The *Yorck* was, however, involved in the support of a battlecruiser bombardment of Great Yarmouth in November 1914. On her return to the Jade, she blundered into a "friendly" minefield. Striking two mines, she capsized, sinking with loss of 336 crew members.

Previously active against the Russian Baltic Fleet, the *Roon* was disarmed during 1916 with the intention of converting her to carry and operate a reported 8–10 seaplanes. For this service a replacement armament of just six 15cm/5.9in guns was planned. The project was never progressed and the ship was scrapped in 1920.

ABOVE LEFT: **Shipping a total of 16 boilers in four spaces, the *Roon* and *Yorck* (see here) added a fourth funnel. Their retention of reciprocating machinery required triple shafts and made for considerable vibration at higher speeds. The half-cased funnels, a weight-saving measure, became something of a German cruiser trademark.** ABOVE: **This impression of *Yorck* emphasizes her generous freeboard and rounded sheer strake. Note the twin 21cm/8.3in turret and the armoured conning tower immediately above it. The speed with which she capsized on being mined was a severe blow to morale.**

Roon class

	Built	Commissioned
Roon	Kiel Dockyard	1906
Yorck	Blohm & Voss, Hamburg	1905

Roon class

Displacement: 9,682 tonnes/9,530 tons (normal); 10,434 tonnes/10,270 tons (full load)

Length: 127.3m/417ft 10in (wl); 127.8m/419ft 6in (oa)

Beam: 20.2m/66ft 4in

Draught: 7.8m/25ft 5in (mean)

Armament: 4 x 21cm/8.3in (2x2) and 10 x 15cm/5.9in (10x1) and 14 x 8.8cm/3.46in (14x1) guns; 4 x 450mm/17.7in torpedo tubes (4x1)

Machinery: 3-cylinder, triple-expansion engines, 16 boilers, 3 shafts

Power: 14.168kW/19,000ihp for 21 knots

Endurance: 1,595 tonnes/1,570 tons (coal) and 211 tonnes/207 tons (oil) for 7,778km/4,200nm at 12 knots

Protection: 80–100mm/3.15–3.9in (belt); 40–60mm/1.57–2.4in (protective deck); 30–150mm/1.18–5.9in (turrets)

Complement: 550

ABOVE: **The Roons, of which the nameship is seen here, were the last to mount the upper tier of secondary weapons in turrets. This feature differentiates them clearly from the pair of Scharnhorsts, that followed. Already dated by 1914, she was destined for conversion to a seaplane carrier, but the work was never completed. The mainly coal-fired boilers were fitted with auxiliary oil sprayers.**

Minin, Vladimir Monomakh and Pamyat Azova

The 1880s were a period of strained relationships between Russia and Great Britain, and as a result the former's naval developments were of particular interest to the Royal Navy. Two prototype "belted cruisers", the 4,674-tonne/4,600-ton *General Admiral* and *Gerzog Edinburgski* had been launched in 1873–75 followed, three years later, by the greatly improved *Minin*.

Where the earlier ships were of the central-citadel type, with six large pivot guns firing over a low, reinforced parapet, the *Minin* mounted four 203mm/8in weapons, Russian-built breech-loaders in prominent sponsons, enabling two to bear forward and two aft. Of the twelve 152mm/6in weapons, eight fired on the broadside, two forward and two aft. The *Minin* had been planned originally as a turret ship but the disastrous sinking of the British *Captain* caused a redesign. Batteries on all three ships were unprotected, but all ships had a full-length 152mm/6in or 178mm/7in waterline belt.

The *Vladimir Monomakh* of 1882 was an improved *Minin*. Of much the same size, she repeated the armament layout but was constructed of steel rather than iron. Forty per cent more power required twin screws and produced a further 3 knots. Obsolete at Tsushima in 1905, she was sunk while escorting the fleet's transports.

Launched in 1887, the *Pamyat Azova* was a further development, refined for speed. Despite her longer and finer hull (115m/377ft x 15.2m/50ft compared with the *Monomakh*'s 90.4m/296.5ft x 15.8m/52ft), she was of little more displacement. Her belt was of 229mm/9in plate but

TOP LEFT: Originally fitted with a heavy ship rig, the *Minin* later had her tophamper lightened to a barque rig, as here. Despite the rather disparaging comments of those who had visited her, the *Minin*'s "big frigate" format worried a British Admiralty responsible for trade protection. TOP RIGHT: In comparison with the 13-knot, single-screw *Minin*, the *Pamyat Azova* was a relative flyer, with twin screws driving her at 18 knots. Less heavily but still adequately armed, she would have posed the greater menace being more able to decline engagement. Her armour belt was very shallow, probably submerged in the ship's deep condition. ABOVE: Although slightly the smaller, the *Vladimir Monomakh* was an improved *Minin*. She carried a deep full-length belt of slightly thinner armour but her more powerful machinery drove her twin shafts for an extra 2.5 knots. All her secondary weapons fired on the broadside, only her prominently sponsoned 203mm/8in guns enjoying axial fire. The sponsons appear vulnerable to damage by slamming.

shallow and terminating short of bow and stern. It was backed by a largely flat 64mm/2.5in protective deck. Only two 203mm/8in guns were carried, with power increased by over 50 per cent to give 18 knots.

Reduced to depot ship status, she was torpedoed and sunk in the course of the attack on Kronstadt by British Coastal Motor Boats (CMBs) in August 1919.

General Admiral, Gerzog Edinburgski, Minin, Vladimir Monomakh and Pamyat Azova

	Built	Commissioned
General Admiral	Baltic Yard, St. Petersburg	1876
Gerzog Edinburgski	Baltic Yard, St. Petersburg	1878
Minin	Baltic Yard, St. Petersburg	1881
Vladimir Monomakh	Baltic Yard, St. Petersburg	1885
Pamyat Azova	Baltic Yard, St. Petersburg	1891

Minin

Displacement: 5,845 tonnes/5,740 tons (normal); 6,250 tonnes/6,140 tons (full load)
Length: 90.9m/298ft 6in (bp)
Beam: 15m/49ft 3in
Draught: 7.7m/25ft 3in (normal)
Armament: 4 x 203mm/8in BL and 12 x 152mm/6in BL guns
Machinery: Steam reciprocating engine, 1 shaft
Power: 4,476kW/6,000ihp for 13.5 knots
Bunkers: 1,222 tonnes/1,200 tons (coal)
Protection: 178mm/7in (full length belt)
Complement: 450

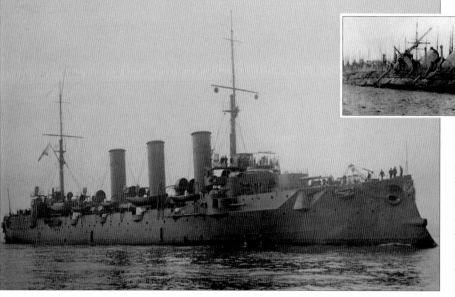

LEFT: Completed in 1902, the Stettin-built *Bogatyr* was particularly interesting in pre-dating Germany's own first "modern" class of protected cruiser, the five Bremens of 1904–05. She was very much larger, however, and carried 152mm/6in guns that German cruisers did not get until 1915. She also mounted twin turrets forward and aft. ABOVE: Longer but more lightly built and armed than the *Bogatyr*, the *Oleg* was built in St. Petersburg. Operating after the Revolution under the Bolshevik banner, she was anchored under the guns of the fortress of Kronstadt when torpedoed and sunk by a British Coastal Motor Boat (CMB) based nearby in modern-day Finland.

Bogatyr

During the late 1890s the Russian Navy, having concentrated on the acquisition of large armoured cruisers, was deficient in smaller, protected cruisers. In 1898 a common specification was sent to six builders resulting in contracts for the three best competing designs. In addition to the *Bogatyr,* from AG Vulcan, Krupp built the *Askold* and Cramp (Philadelphia) the *Varyag*.

Of the three, the *Bogatyr* was shortest but beamiest. Her protective deck was of 51mm/2in plate, compared with the others' 76mm/3in, but her funnel uptakes were better protected. Where her competitors' twelve 152mm/6in guns were largely in open mountings protected only by shields, the *Bogatyr* housed four guns in twin turrets and four in casemates, with only the remaining four in open mountings. This refinement increased displacement considerably but the contract speed was still attained comfortably.

The advantages of protection for gun crews were proven conclusively in the course of the Russo-Japanese War, when reports spoke constantly of those serving open mountings being scythed down by hails of splinters, and crushed by falling rigging.

Being attached to the Vladivostok squadron, the *Bogatyr* was spared the debacle of Tsushima, although it is noteworthy that, of the six Russian protected cruisers present, only one, the oldest, was sunk. Three of these, however, sought internment at Manila.

From the outset of World War I, Russian and German naval forces contested the Baltic. The *Bogatyr*'s minelaying capacity was well-utilized, but her most telling contribution to the war came as early as August 26, 1914. When the German cruiser *Magdeburg* was stranded on the Estonian coast, the timely arrival of the *Bogatyr* and another cruiser obliged the former's crew to blow up their ship. In their haste, they neglected to destroy their code books. These quickly found their way into British hands and subsequently proved to be of inestimable value, the fact of their compromise being kept secret.

ABOVE: The *Bogatyr* as delivered, and probably painted for Black Sea service. Note that, in contrast to the World War I picture (above), she carries light anti-torpedo nets and more complex masting. Her hull has both raised forecastle and poop, each carrying a twin 152mm/6in turret flanked by a single, casemated 152mm/6in gun at a lower level.

Bogatyr (as built)

Built: AG Vulcan, Stettin
Commissioned: 1901
Displacement: 6,751 tonnes/6,645 tons (normal)
Length: 127m/416ft 9in (bp)
Beam: 16.6m/54ft 6in
Draught: 6.3m/20ft 9in mean
Armament: 12 x 152mm/6in (2x2/8x1) and
12 x 76mm/3in (12x1) guns; 6 x 450mm/17.7in
torpedo tubes (6x1)
Machinery: Triple-expansion reciprocating engines,
2 shafts
Power: 15,100kW/20,250ihp for 24 knots
Bunkers: 1,118 tonnes/1,100 tons (coal)
Protection: 51mm/2in (protective deck);
89–127mm/3.5–5in (turrets)
Complement: 580

Rurik

The first of three large, domestically constructed cruisers, the *Rurik* combined firepower with, for the day, considerable speed. The potential of such ships for commerce raiding concerned the British Admiralty to the extent that it produced the two Powerfuls. These were large enough to operate in Far Eastern waters, but great length was the key parameter for all such ships, influencing maximum practicable speed and the volume within which the necessary machinery had to be accommodated. Also a factor in displacement, it thus influenced the limits of armour.

For extended endurance, the *Rurik* was given a heavy barque rig whose windage, even without sails spread, influenced both speed and ship motion. Because of the standing rigging, the ship's four 203mm/8in guns were mounted in sided sponsons, two forward, two aft. They shared the upper deck with six 119mm/4.7in QF guns which, likewise, were protected only by shields. On the main deck, the secondary armament comprised sixteen 152mm/6in QF weapons of which twelve were mounted in an open, broadside battery, devoid of any screens between the weapons.

About the waterline the *Rurik* had a thick, but shallow, composite belt backed by a flat protective deck. It was to penetrate such belts that larger British cruisers carried a pair of 234mm/9.2in guns. In practice, this was too few.

ABOVE: **Although her size commanded much respect, the *Rurik* shows her vulnerability in the huge expanse of unprotected hull. Her shallow belt extended from the forward embrasure as far aft as the mizzen mast but, on full load displacement, it barely extended above the the waterline, a very common failing.**

When inspected by the foreign technical press in 1895, the *Rurik* impressed with her firepower but also with the sheer vulnerability of her gunnery positions. Their dismissal of the ship as something of a "paper tiger" proved to be warranted. At the Battle of Ulsan in August 1904 she, as the smallest of the three Russian cruisers, attracted the heaviest Japanese fire. Holed aft, beyond the limit of the belt, her steering flat was flooded, with water penetrating progressively forward. With nearly 500 dead and wounded, her topsides a ruin, she was finally scuttled.

ABOVE: **In dark livery, the odd cross-section of the *Rurik*'s centre body is here well caught by the light. Reminiscent of "turret" merchant ships, the upper hull has been reduced in beam, to both reduce topweight and to improve the arcs of fire of her still essentially broadside armament.**

Rurik

Built: Baltic Yard, St. Petersburg
Commissioned: 1895
Displacement: 11,122 tonnes/10,923 tons (normal)
Length: 120.8m/396ft 6in (bp)
Beam: 20.4m/67ft
Draught: 7.9m/26ft (normal)
Armament: 4 x 203mm/8in BL, 16 x 152mm/6in QF and 6 x 119mm/4.7in QF guns
Machinery: Steam reciprocating engines, 2 shafts
Power: 9,880kW/13,250ihp for 18.5 knots
Bunkers: 2,032 tonnes/2,000 tons (coal)
Protection: 127–254mm/5–10in (composite armour belt); 64mm/2.5in (protective deck)
Complement: 770

Rossia and *Gromoboi*

Built as improved Ruriks, the *Rossia* and the *Gromoboi* were, likewise, designed to operate as long-endurance raiders. To this end, they could stow an enormous 2,540 tonnes/2,500 tons of coal, sufficient to steam from St. Petersburg to Vladivostock without refuelling. They were also built with a three-masted, barquentine sailing rig, an encumbrance later replaced with two orthodox masts. Again, however, its legacy was to oblige the ships' four 203mm/8in guns to be located in sponsons to avoid standing rigging.

Near, but not exact, sisters, they were some 1,219 tonnes/1,200 tons greater than the *Rurik*. They carried a similar scale of armament but, being considerably longer, were able to arrange it more safely. Of the two, the *Rossia*'s layout was the weaker, showing little improvement on that of the *Rurik*. In order to increase the training arcs of the sponsoned 203mm/8in guns, the ship's

sides were given considerable tumblehome. They were pierced with five 152mm/6in gun-ports per side. Her belt was as shallow as the *Rurik*'s.

Completed two years later, the *Gromoboi* (whose odd-sounding name means Thunderer) was greatly improved in having armour extended to upper deck level over that length of the sides that included the gun positions. Six 152mm/6in guns, individually casemated, fired on each broadside. Those farthest forward and aft shared two-storey casemates with the 203mm/8in weapons. To compensate for her extended vertical protection, the *Gromoboi* had a thinner protective deck.

Triple-screw ships, they never achieved their intended 20 knots although, at the Battle of Ulsan, in which the *Rurik* was lost, they survived only by out-running the pursuing Japanese armoured cruisers. Each ship received two dozen and more hits and, while their

ABOVE: The *Gromoboi* differed from the *Rossia* in the double-level casemates abreast the bridge, the upper housing a 203mm/8in gun, the lower one the twelve main deck 152mm/6in weapons. Her original three-masted rig is more decorative than functional.

armour was nowhere pierced, the carnage on the unprotected upper levels was appalling. Being based at Vladivostock, neither was at Tsushima.

Rossia and *Gromoboi*

	Built	Commissioned
Gromoboi	Baltic Yard, St. Petersburg	1900
Rossia	Baltic Yard, St. Petersburg	1898

Rossia (as built)

Displacement: 12,325 tonnes/12,130 tons (normal)
Length: 143.8m/472ft (wl); 146.2m/480ft (oa)
Beam: 20.9m/68ft 6in
Draught: 8m/26ft 3in (normal)
Armament: 4 x 203mm/8in, 16 x 152mm/6in QF and 6 x 119mm/4.7in QF guns; 6 x 450mm/17.7in torpedo tubes
Machinery: Vertical, triple-expansion engines, 32 boilers, 3 shafts
Power: 10,812kW/14,500ihp for 19 knots
Endurance: 2,545 tonnes/2,500 tons (coal) for 35,188km/19,000nm at 10 knots
Protection: 102–203mm/4–8in (belt), 64mm/2.5in (protective deck)
Complement: 725

LEFT : **Originally rigged like her near-sister *Gromoboi*, the *Rossia* was greatly improved in appearance by alterations effected when repairing heavy damage sustained during the war with Japan. She is seen here attending the 1911 Coronation review at Spithead. Note the elaborate configuration of her hull to improve firing arcs.**

LEFT: **Spain's imperial interests in 1896 included such important and widely separated territories as Cuba and the Philippines, fully justifying the construction of cruisers such as the three Oquendos. The *Infanta Maria Teresa*, seen here, was Cervera's flagship at the disastrous battle off Santiago de Cuba, July 3, 1898.**

Almirante Oquendo class

Launched from 1890, the three Oquendos were, for their size, heavily armed and armoured. They were, however, badly designed. Their belt, at an impressive 300mm/11.8in in thickness, was so heavy that it was limited to only about 1.7m/5ft 7in in depth, over two-thirds the hull length. It was roofed by a flat, protective deck which, raised to cover the engine crowns, sloped only at either end, towards bow and stern.

The hull had a flush upper deck, into which, forward and aft, was recessed a 270mm/10.5in barbette. These each supported a 28cm/11in breech-loading gun, covered by a shallow, dome-shaped cupola of only 76mm/3in thickness.

Between the two barbettes, the central section of the ships was ringed by deep, but unarmoured, bulwarks. Behind were located ten 14cm/5.5in guns. Six of these fired broadside,

through ports; the other four were sponsored for axial fire.

One level below, the middle deck housed a battery of quick-firers, both 57mm/2.24in Nordenfelts and 37mm/1.46in Hotchkiss. Firing through small, shuttered ports, these occupied a largely open-plan internal space.

Probably to save weight, both upper and middle decks were of wood planking laid directly on to the ships' beams, without steel underlay. This was a critically weak feature, but the Oquendos were designed before the Battle of the Yalu (1894) reminded the naval world of the hazards of fire.

During the short Spanish-American War of 1898, all three Oquendos, together with the Italian-built *Cristobal Colon*, were blockaded by a more powerful American squadron in the bottle-necked Santiago de Cuba. Ordered to break out,

the Spanish were destroyed piecemeal in a long pursuit. Ravaged by fire, their deck burned away, their armour unpierced but their unprotected topsides wrecked, each in turn was run aground to prevent further useless loss of life.

Almirante Oquendo class

	Built	Commissioned
Almirante Oquendo	Anglo-Spanish Shipbuilding Co, Bilbao	1892
Infanta Maria Teresa	Anglo-Spanish Shipbuilding Co, Bilbao	1891
Viscaya	Anglo-Spanish Shipbuilding Co, Bilbao	1893

LEFT: **Both gutted by fire but with their armour intact, the *Oquendo* (seen here) and the *Maria Teresa* were put ashore just a mile from each other. Far too much wood had been incorporated into their structure. Note the huge 28cm/11in Honoria gun, located on a 254mm/10in thick barbette and protected with a 76mm/3in cupola.**

Almirante Oquendo

Displacement: 7,010 tonnes/6,900 tons (normal)
Length: 103.6m 340ft (oa)
Beam: 19.8m/65ft
Draught: 6.6m/21ft 6in (normal)
Armament: 2 x 28cm/11in BL and 10 x 14cm/5.5in BL guns; 8 x 356mm/14in torpedo tubes
Machinery: Vertical, triple-expansion engines, 2 shafts
Power: 9,694kW/13,000ihp for 20 knots
Protection: 305mm/12in (partial belt); 51–76mm/2–3in (protective deck); 267mm/10.5in (barbettes)
Complement: 460

LEFT: **The mercantile-style counter stern of the *Reina Regente* was structurally weaker than the more usual, rounded "cruiser" stern, and exposed the rudder more readily to damage.** BELOW: **The low-freeboard forward and after ends of the design were, presumably, a weight-saving measure, but probably resulted in a higher centre of gravity.**

Reina Regente class

The Oquendo-class armoured cruisers were built by an Anglo-Spanish company, and their not un-British character may well have been further influenced by the three Reina Regentes, built shortly before. Somewhat smaller protected cruisers, these were launched between 1887 and 1893. Armstrong, at Elswick, had lobbied hard for the contract but their proposal was not accepted. (It wasn't wasted effort, being used as the basis for the design of the USS *Baltimore*). The specified armament for the preferred design by Thomson, on Clydebank, may also have been influenced by Armstrong's reputation for "plenty of guns". This, while displacing only 5,029 tonnes/4,950 tons, carried four 24cm/9.5in and six 12cm/4.72in guns.

Like the Oquendos, the Reina Regentes were flush-decked, and mounted all significant armament at upper-deck level. All guns were on open mountings, protected by shields. The 24cm/9.5in weapons were sided, forward and aft. The high amidships bulkhead was given a feature, broken by gun-ports through which the 12cm/4.72in and 6pdr guns fired in broadside.

Only the lead ship was British-built, the other pair was of domestic construction. The design was orthodox, with a full-length, vaulted protective deck. The only unusual feature was that the ram bow was complemented by a mercantile-style counter stern.

The *Reina Regente* disappeared, with all aboard (reportedly 402) on or about March 10, 1895, apparently foundering through stress of weather south-east of Cape Trafalgar. An official inquiry reached the conclusion that, while running light on bunkers and stores, she was rendered unstable by virtue of her heavy armament.

Although relatively new ships her two sisters were retained in home waters during the 1898 war with the United States. They were regarded as being too "defective in design and speed" to allow them to be despatched to Cuba.

A replacement cruiser, unarmoured but carrying the name *Reina Regente* was completed in 1908.

Reina Regente class

	Built	Commissioned
Alfonso XIII	Ferrol Dockyard	1893
Lepanto	Cartagena Dockyard	1895
Reina Regente	Thomson, Clydebank	1888

Reina Regente (as built)

Displacement: 5,029 tonnes/4,950 tons (normal)
Length: 97m/318ft 6in (oa)
Beam: 15.4m/50ft 6in
Draught: 6.1m/20ft (normal)
Armament: 4 x 24cm/9.5in Bland 6 x 12cm/4.72in QF guns; 5 x 350mm/14in torpedo tubes
Machinery: Vertical, triple-expansion engines, 2 shafts
Power: 8,579kW/11,500ihp for 20 knots
Bunkers: 1,118 tonnes/1,100 tons (coal)
Protection: 75–120mm/2.95–4.7in (protective deck)
Complement: 275

ABOVE: **The *Alfonso XIII* clearly shows the major design drawback of all guns, primary and secondary, being carried in open mountings, exposing their crews to blast and fragments.**

LEFT: **Seen dressed overall for, presumably, a royal visit, the *Emperador Carlos V* was, by a considerable margin, the largest cruiser in the Spanish Navy, 15.2m/50ft longer than the solitary battleship, *Pelayo*.** ABOVE: **The design of the 28cm/11in Honoria gun mountings exposed a considerable amount of the 450mm/17.5in barbette, theoretically immune to the largest guns then at sea. The ship's belt, however, was proof against only cruiser gunfire.**

Emperador Carlos V

Launched in 1895, some four years after the *Oquendo*, the *Carlos V* (*Carlos Quinto*) made an interesting comparison. The former was an armoured cruiser, with a shallow, 305mm/12in belt and a 58mm/2.3in protective deck, while the latter, a protected cruiser, had no belt as such but a deck of up to 152mm/6in thick. Carrying similar armaments, and both powered for 20 knots, the protected cruiser was the heavier by some 2,134 tonnes/2,100 tons. One reason was that the *Carlos V* was about 12.2m/40ft longer, as was the central, high-bulwarked redoubt. Unarmoured on the earlier ships, both the bulwark and the middle-deck plating below it were of 51mm/2in plate. Six 14cm/5.5in QF guns fired through ports in the bulwark. Two

more, together with four 10cm/3.9in guns, fired through middle deck ports. The upper deck 14cm/5.5in weapons were in open mountings with shields.

The protective deck on the Oquendos was largely flat, but that on the *Carlos V* sloped from above to well below the waterline. Above and below it were deep coal bunkers, which flanked the machinery and boiler spaces.

Except for her disappointingly low maximum speed, the *Carlos V* should have made a better fighting ship than the Oquendos, although all were plagued by unreliable ammunition. It is perhaps fortunate that her qualities were never tested in the war in the United States.

With the commencement of hostilities, she was first ordered to raid commerce on the US Eastern Seaboard. However,

this was quickly changed to head eastward with auxiliaries to reinforce the Philippines. Countermanded again, she was then ordered to return to home waters to meet the threat posed by a rumoured American squadron. This confusion illustrates the difficulty of meeting worldwide commitments with an inadequate navy.

Following the war with the United States, her peaceful seagoing career lasted until 1927, following which she served for five years as an accommodation ship before being scrapped.

Emperador Carlos V

Built: Cadiz Dockyard
Commissioned: 1897
Displacement: 9,398 tonnes/9,250 tons (normal); 10,058 tonnes/9.900 tons (full load)
Length: 115.8m/380ft (bp); 123.3m/404ft 8in (oa)
Beam: 20.4m/67ft
Draught: 8.7m/28ft 6in (full load)
Armament: 2 x 28cm/11in, 8 x 14cm/5.5in and 4 x 10cm/3.9in guns; 2 x 350mm/14in torpedo tubes
Machinery: 4-cylinder, triple-expansion engines, 12 boilers, 2 shafts
Power: 13,800kW/18,500ihp for 20 knots
Bunkers: 2,082 tonnes/2,050 tons (coal)
Protection: 64–152mm/2.5–6in (protective deck); 51mm/2in (upper sides – partial); 254mm/10in barbettes
Complement: 555

ABOVE: **Note how the ship's proportions are enhanced by terminating the black hull paint at upper deck level. The white central battery comprised eight 14cm/5.5in guns of French manufacture.**

LEFT: **Laying to a mooring buoy, the *Kaiser Franz Josef I* shows her barbette-mounted 24cm/9.5in guns to advantage. The side-casemated 15cm/5.9in weapons were carried too low to be of practical use.** BELOW: **Equivalent in size and protection to a contemporary British Astraea, the *Franz Josef I* carried a much heavier-calibre armament. By 1914 they were obsolescent.**

Kaiser Franz Josef I class

In August 1914 the dual monarchy of Austria-Hungary possessed the world's eighth-largest fleet. On the last day of October 1918 its ships hauled down their colours and the service ceased to exist. Despite having Europe's third-largest population, the empire claimed no foreign territory, so that a blue-water navy was always hard to justify when what was really required was an adequate defence force to protect the long eastern coastline of the Adriatic.

Under Wilhelm von Tegetthoff, the victor of Lissa, the navy had achieved direction but, following his premature death in 1871, its fortunes lapsed under the lacklustre Sterneck, and it built little of note.

Two protected cruisers, *Kaiser Franz Josef I* and *Kaiserin Elisabeth* were launched in 1889–90. Although small, they were built with single 24cm/9.5in

guns in barbettes forward and aft. Of their six 15cm/5.9in weapons, two were sided in open mountings on upper-deck sponsons and the remainder in casemates at middle-deck level, their barrels a bare three metres above the (normal) waterline.

Both were modernized in 1904–06, losing their oversized guns (and being demoted from "Grosser" to "Kleiner Kreuzer"). In their place, two further 15cm/5.9in pieces were acquired. These were 40-calibre Skodas, superior to the others, which were of the older, 35-calibre Krupp design. Both ships had their funnels raised considerably.

Together with a handful of minor German warships, the *Kaiserin Elisabeth* found herself in the beleaguered German enclave at Tsingtao in 1914. During the three-month siege, her two best guns

and some smaller pieces, together with 120 men, were landed to assist in defence. Unable to escape, the ship was scuttled a few days before the base capitulated to an Anglo-Japanese force.

The *Kaiser Franz Josef I* was restricted to local defence at Cattaro (now Kotor). Ceded to France in 1919, she sank while under tow.

Kaiser Franz Josef I class

	Built	Commissioned
Kaiser Franz Josef I	Stabilimento Tecnico Triestino, Trieste	July 2, 1890
Kaiserin Elisabeth	Pola Dockyard	November 24, 1892

Kaiser Franz Josef I (as built)

Displacement: 4,115 tonnes/4,050 tons (normal)
Length: 98m/321ft 8in (bp); 103.8m/340ft 9in (oa)
Beam: 14.8m/48ft 7in
Draught: 5.6m/18ft 4in (normal)
Armament: 2 x 24cm/9.5in and 6 x 15cm/5.9in guns; 4 x 450mm/17.7in torpedo tubes
Machinery: Horizontal, triple-expansion engines, 4 boilers, 2 shafts
Power: 6,341kW/8,500ihp for 19 knots
Endurance: 671 tonnes/660 tons (coal) for 5,926km/3,200nm at 10 knots
Protection: 57mm/2.2in (protective deck)
Complement: 435

ABOVE: **Seen in a 20th-century overall grey paint scheme, the *Kaiserin Elisabeth* could be differentiated by her foremast, crossed with two yards. She was unfortunate in being caught and destroyed at Tsingtao in 1914.**

LEFT: **All three pictures on this page show the ship in her original state, prior to her 1910 rebuilding and rearming. The deep forward facets and all sponsoned casemates would be removed.**
ABOVE: **The massive tubular "battlemasts" were also exchanged for light poles in order to reduce topweight, but nothing was done to improve the inadequate forward freeboard.**

Kaiserin und Königen Maria Theresia

Because Austria-Hungary was an empire encompassing a dual monarchy, Maria Theresia was both Empress and Queen, accounting for the unwieldly name borne by an armoured cruiser launched in 1893. Interestingly, the name, as generally written, would have appeared even more ungainly, for the standard abbreviation for both "Kaiserin und Königen" and the warship prefix of *"Kaiserlich und Königlich"* (i.e. Imperial and Royal) was "KuK". The name would thus be rendered *KuK KuK Maria Theresia.*

The belt armour fronting the protective deck was very shallow. A considerable amount of 100mm/3.9in plate was applied to the levels above it, in the areas of the forward and aft barbettes and casemates, as well as the amidships casemates. There were also transverse bulkheads of the same thickness enclosing what was referred to as a "citadel". Topside weight was further increased by two lofty "battlemasts", heavy tubular structures.

As built, the ship carried a 24cm/9.5in gun on the barbettes at either end. Of the eight 15cm/5.9in weapons, four were mounted in protruding casemates, and four in open mountings atop the citadel.

During 1909 the 24cm/9.5in guns and heavy barbettes were removed in favour of two 19cm/7.5in pieces in enclosed gunhouses. Further weight was saved by replacing the battlemasts with light poles. The 15cm/5.9in armament was relocated to accommodate sixteen 4.7cm/1.85in QF guns within and atop the citadel.

These fired 1.5kg/3.3lb projectiles and were for repelling torpedo craft.

Making only 19.35 knots on her initial trials nearly 20 years earlier, the *KuK Maria Theresia* was, by 1914, slower than even the fleet's remaining pre-Dreadnoughts. She was first based at Sebenico (now Sibenik) in a coastal defence role. By 1917, she was at Pola (now Pula), acting as accommodation ship for the crews of its growing German submarine flotilla. She was scrapped in 1920 following an undistinguished career.

Kaiserin und Königen Maria Theresia (as built)

Built: Stabilimento Tecnico Triestino, Trieste
Commissioned: March 24, 1895
Displacement: 5,202 tonnes/5,120 tons (normal)
Length: 106.7m/350ft 3in (bp); 114m/374ft 2in (wl)
Beam: 16.2m/53ft 2in
Draught: 6.5m/21ft 4in (normal)
Armament: 2 x 24cm/9.5in BL and
   8 x 15cm/5.9in QF guns;
   4 x 450mm/17.7in torpedo tubes
Machinery: Horizontal, triple-expansion engines,
   10 boilers, 2 shafts
Power: 7,274kW/9,750ihp for 19 knots
Endurance: 752 tonnes/740 tons (coal) for
   6,482km/3,500nm at 10 knots
Protection: 100mm/3.9in (citadel sides);
   57mm/2.2in (protective deck)
Complement: 485

ABOVE: **Another picture of the ship in her original paint scheme, the white area of which emphasized the height of the unarmoured central superstructure. The barbette-mounted main-calibre guns were later exchanged for lighter weapons in round mountings.**

LEFT: **The imposing appearance of the *Kaiser Karl VI* belies her displacement of less than 7,112 tonnes/7,000 tons. Her single 24cm/9.5in guns, forward and aft, were less effective than they looked as only two barrels, without proper fire control, were insufficient to sustain accurate fire at extended ranges.** BELOW LEFT: **At about 20 knots, the wave profile created by the *Sankt Georg* indicates a rather inefficient hull form. The sponsoned secondary and tertiary armament must have been the cause of much wetness in heavy weather. The permanent awnings amidships were presumably to cool the machinery spaces.**

Kaiser Karl VI and Sankt Georg

An improved version of the *KuK Maria Theresia*, the *Kaiser Karl VI* was laid down the year after the former's commissioning. For a further 5m/16ft 5in in length she could carry the same armament as well as accommodate an extra 33 per cent boiler capacity, enabling her to comfortably exceed her designed 20-knot speed.

Less bulky topside than her predecessor, the *Karl VI* carried her two 24cm/9.5in guns in turrets, rather than barbettes. A retrograde step was to locate all 15cm/5.9in secondary armament at middle-deck level. All were accommodated in armoured casemates, with two each firing axially forward and aft along facets in the hull. The others were paired amidships in extraordinarily large, sponsoned casemates which must have pounded severely in poor conditions.

Upon the *Karl VI*'s completion she, too, was followed by an improved derivative. Identifiable by her three thicker funnels, the *Sankt Georg* (St. George) was longer by a further 3m/9ft 10in, also well exceeding her contract speed. Her belt armour was thinned by 10mm/0.4in and protective deck thickened by 5mm/0.2in.

Although the disposition of the armament was similar, its power was considerably enhanced at the expense of introducing a third major calibre. The two 24cm/9.5in guns were now sited in a twin turret forward, the after turret accommodating a single 19cm/7.5in. Four 15cm/5.9in weapons fired axially forward and aft, as before, but the large sponsoned amidships casemates now housed two more 19cm/7.5in barrels per side. A greater proportion of the

Sankt Georg's firepower was thus carried very close to the waterline. While unsatisfactory for oceanic operations, it was probably justifiable in the more benign conditions to be expected in the Adriatic.

Neither ship saw significant action, probably contributing to their crews being in the forefront of the fleet mutiny of spring 1918. Both were scrapped in 1920.

Kaiser Karl VI and Sankt Georg

	Built	Commissioned
Kaiser Karl VI	Stabilimento Tecnico Triestino, Trieste	May 23, 1900
Sankt Georg	Pola Dockyard	July 21, 1905

Sankt Georg (as built)

Displacement: 7,315 tonnes/7,185 tons (normal); 7,555 tonnes/7,420 tons (full load)
Length: 117m/384ft (bp); 122m/400ft 6in (wl)
Beam: 18.8m/61ft 9in
Draught: 6.5m/21ft 4in (normal)
Armament: 2 x 24cm/9.5in (1x2), 5 x 19cm/7.5in (5x2) guns and 4 x 15cm/5.9in (4x1) guns; 2 x 450mm/17.7in torpedo tubes
Machinery: Vertical, triple-expansion engines, 12 boilers, 2 shafts
Power: 11,372kW/15,250ihp for 22 knots
Endurance: 804 tonnes/790 tons (coal) for 8,334km/4,500nm at 10 knots
Protection: 210mm/8.25in (belt); 65mm/2.5in (protective deck); 210mm/8.25in (turrets); 135–150mm/5.3–5.9in (casemates)
Complement: 630

LEFT: **Much of the long, lean hull of the *Admiral Spaun* is devoted to no less than 16 boilers. Unlike her improved derivatives, she had four shafts, their turbines located between the aftermost funnel and the mainmast. Note how little impact the ship's seven 10cm/3.9in guns have on her overall appearance.**

Admiral Spaun and Zenta class

Designed to carry seven tubes, the three Zenta-class "torpedo cruisers" were of a size, and contemporary with, the British Pelorus class. They carried eight 12cm/4.72in guns to the British ships' eight 102mm/4in, at the cost of a slightly beamier form and about a half-knot in speed. One centreline gun was carried forward and aft, with three on either side in the waist, mounted inside shutters. A sailplan was included.

Modernization saw the turtleback forecastle given a more orthodox sheer strake, while the waist guns were lowered one level, with a spardeck above. The masting was reduced and five torpedo tubes landed. One of these had fired through the stern, the profile of which was modified.

The eight British scout cruisers, commissioned in 1905 were influential

but, although fast, lacked size and endurance. Intended to undertake a similar role, the *Admiral Spaun* was somewhat larger. Her boilers developed 50 per cent more power and, being later, the ship had the benefit of steam turbines, with their greatly superior power-to-weight ratio. Capable of 27 knots, the *Spaun* and her three improved derivatives were heavily used during the sea war in the Adriatic.

All the type were badly under-armed, with guns of only 10cm/3.9in calibre. There was a wartime intention to upgrade the battery to five 15cm/5.9in guns but they could not be taken out of service long enough to effect the improvement.

The older *Spaun* was scrapped in 1920 but the three derivative were assimilated into the French and Italian

fleets. The *Novarra* became the French *Thionville*, the *Helgoland* and *Saida* the Italian *Brindisi* and *Venezia* respectively.

Admiral Spaun and Zenta class

	Built	Commissioned
Aspern	Pola Dockyard	May 29, 1900
Szigetvar	Pola Dockyard	September 30, 1901
Zenta	Pola Dockyard	May 28, 1899
Admiral Spaun	Pola Dockyard	November 15, 1914
Helgoland	Ganz & Danubius, Fiume	August 29, 1914
Novarra	Ganz & Danubius, Fiume	January 10, 1915
Saida	Cantiere Naval Triestino, Monfalcone	August 1, 1914

Improved Spaun class (as built)

Displacement: 3,592 tonnes/3,535 tons (normal); 4,491 tonnes/4,420 tons (full load)
Length: 125.2m 411ft (bp); 130.6m/428ft 8in (wl)
Beam: 12.8m/42ft
Draught: 5.3m/17ft 3in (full load)
Armament: 9 x 10cm/3.9in guns; 6 x 450mm/17.7in torpedo tubes
Machinery: Direct-drive steam turbines, 16 boilers, 2 shafts
Power: 19,090kW/25,600shp for 27 knots
Endurance: 865 tonnes/850 tons (coal) for 2,963km/1,600nm at 24 knots
Protection: 60mm/2.4in (partial belt); 20mm/0.8in (protective deck)
Complement: 330

ABOVE: **The distinction of firing the opening shots of World War I in the Adriatic fell to the *Szigetvar* (shown here) and her sister, *Zenta*. Her war ended ignominiously with mutiny, downgrading as obsolete to an accommodation hulk, cession to Great Britain as reparation and immediate scrapping in Italy.**

Directory of Cruisers

World War I

Traditional cruisers and their roles were greatly affected by World War I for, although British maritime superiority was assured by the Grand Fleet, the actual outcome of the conflict came to depend upon the defence of trade against an entirely unpredicted submarine threat.

In the early days, British cruisers proved highly vulnerable to U-boat attack but, for the Germans, employment of regular cruisers as commerce raiders proved a wasted resource, they being superseded by cheaper and more effective auxiliary raiders.

Where Germany's few modern armoured cruisers were deployed in distant operations, they proved doughty opponents, but those British examples closely integrated with the battle fleet fared badly by being brought within range of hostile capital ships.

Emerging supreme from war experience were the fleet cruisers typified by the "Towns" of both sides and the British "C" class. Fast and well-armed, they dominated war-emergency building programmes, proving to be tough and well able to absorb punishment.

LEFT: Commenced during 1896 as a speculative venture, Armstrong at Elswick sold the *Asama* and her sister, *Tokiwa*, to Japan in the following year. Note the early cylindrical, twin 203mm/8in turrets, two-level 152mm/6in casemates and anti-torpedo nets.

LEFT: Completed in 1900, the Second Class protected cruiser *Highflyer* remains linked to the sailing navy through her complex masting, the old-style fidded topmasts being supported by crosstrees and futtock shrouds. Although at anchor, she is wearing no jack and her forward end has apparently been "cleared".
BELOW: Shorter and beamier than the Highflyers, the four Arrogant type were designed for great manoeuvrability, being among the last ships intended to deliberately ram opponents. For this function they had strengthened bows and twin rudders. The *Gladiator* is seen here as a new ship. Their original mixed armament was changed to a uniform 152mm/6in during 1903–04.

Arrogant and Highflyer classes

Both classes were categorized as "Second Class cruisers". All four Arrogants were laid down in Royal Dockyards during 1895–96 and were among the last ships designed to use their rams tactically. For this, good manoeuvrability was essential, the ships being designed with a length-on-beam (L/B) ratio of only 5.6, with pronounced cut-ups and large rudder area.

Three funnels and a forest of ventilators defined the extent of the boiler spaces and the normal use of natural draught. The lofty masts included topmasts, fidded and braced, still in sailing-ship fashion. Both were crossed by a pair of yards, and supported fighting tops equipped with small quick-firing Maxim guns.

Following criticisms of inadequate armament, their six waist 119mm/4.7in guns were upgraded to 152mm/6in weapons in about 1903–04, making a total of ten 152mm/6in guns.

Of the class, *Vindictive* earned fame on the Zeebrugge and Ostend raids of 1918. The *Gladiator*, ironically, was sunk by collision in the Solent during 1908.

Ordered under the 1896–97 Estimates, the three Highflyers were essentially three-funnelled Eclipses. At 9.1m/30ft longer than the Arrogants, and with L/B increased to about 6.5, they could make nearly 2 knots more on the same power. Like the Arrogants, they exchanged their six waist 119mm/4.7in guns for 152mm/6in ordnance to give a total of eleven, only six of which could fire in broadside.

Being "protected", the two classes had full-length, vaulted armoured decks, increased in height in way of the tall engine assemblies. Deep wing coal bunkers served as side protection in lieu of an armoured belt. As was then common, the bottoms were wood sheathed and coppered to reduce fouling.

The *Hermes* was the first Royal Navy ship to be adapted (1913) for the carriage and operation of seaplanes. On August 26, 1914, her sister, *Highflyer*, entered territorial waters to sink the 13,950grt NDL liner *Kaiser Wilhelm der Grosse*, which was operating as an armed raider.

Arrogant and Highflyer classes

	Built	Commissioned
Arrogant	Devonport Dockyard	1898–99
Furious	Devonport Dockyard	1898–99
Gladiator	Portsmouth Dockyard	1898–99
Vindictive	Chatham Dockyard	1898–99
Hermes	Fairfield, Glasgow	1900–01
Highflyer	Fairfield, Glasgow	1900–01
Hyacinth	London & Glasgow	1900–01

Highflyer class (as built)

Displacement: 5,740 tonnes/5,650 tons (standard)
Length: 106.6m/350ft (bp); 113.6m/373ft (oa)
Beam: 16.5m/54ft
Draught: 6.4m/21ft (normal)
Armament: 5 x 152mm/6in (5x1), 6 x 119mm/4.7in (6x1) and 9 x 12pdr (9x1) guns; 2 x 457mm/18in torpedo tubes (fixed, submerged) (2x1)
Machinery: 2 sets 4-cylinder vertical, triple-expansion engines, 18 boilers, 2 shafts
Power: 7,460kW/10,000ihp, 19.5 knots
Endurance: 584 tonnes/575 tons (coal) for 10,186km/5,500nm at 10 knots
Protection: 36–76mm/1.5–3in (protective deck)
Complement: 457

Topaze class

All major fleets, from time to time, produced so-called "scout cruisers", but the results were rarely successful. In the period under consideration this was because these necessarily small ships could not incorporate the machinery required for the stipulated speed. Their nemesis, large armoured cruisers, were littler slower and were able to maintain speed in conditions that would slow a scout cruiser.

During 1903–04 the British Admiralty launched four pairs of very small scouts, which would prove to be more appropriate as destroyer leaders, and the quartet of Topaze-class ships (known as Gems), which, slightly larger, proved to be the starting point for the "fleet (or light) cruiser".

Rated as "Third Class cruisers", the four were given a very light, 102mm/4in armament and as high a power as was possible on the displacement. Thus where, for instance, the earlier Highflyers were given about 1.77ihp/ton displacement, the *Topaze* could boast nearer 4.33ihp/ton. The resulting speed advantage, however, was little better than 2 knots, an insufficient margin for an effective scout.

The recently patented Parsons steam turbine had, meanwhile, been applied with some success, first commercially, then by the Admiralty for comparative trials in destroyers. It was now decided that comparison would be scaled-up to cruiser size, and the Topaze-class *Amethyst* would thus be the first major warship to be turbine-driven. Compared with triple-expansion machinery, the turbine offered vibration-free running and greater compactness (although the latter virtue was offset by the need to have separate turbines for cruising and for high-speed use, and ideally, for going astern).

Amethyst proved successful, not only being about 1.3 knots faster than her fastest sister, but burning only two-thirds the fuel. By 1914, however, they had been superseded by turbine-driven classes, beginning with the Boadiceas, the first true light cruisers.

Topaze class

	Built	Commissioned
Amethyst	Armstrong, Elswick	1904–05
Diamond	Laird, Birkenhead	1904–05
Sapphire	Palmer, Jarrow	1904–05
Topaze	Laird, Birkenhead	1904–05

ABOVE: **It will be noticed from the pictures above that the Gems adopted the new-style stockless anchor. While this greatly simplified getting under way, the forecastle party of the *Diamond* appear to be catting the port anchor. All surviving World War I, the Gems were scrapped in 1920–21.**

Amethyst

Displacement: 3,048 tonnes/3,000 tons (normal)
Length: 109.7m/360ft (bp); 113.8m/373ft 6in (oa)
Beam: 12.2m/40ft
Draught: 4.4m/14ft 6in
Armament: 12 x 102mm/4in (12x1) and 8 x 3pdr (8x1) guns; 2 x 457mm/18in torpedo tubes (2x1)
Machinery: Direct-drive steam turbines, 10 boilers, 3 shafts
Power: 7,308kW/9,800shp for 21.8 knots (trials 23.6 knots)
Bunkers: 305 tonnes/300 tons (coal)
Protection: 25–50mm/1–2in (protective deck)
Complement: 300

Blake, Crescent and Edgar classes

Rated First Class cruisers, these were products of the 1889 Naval Defence Act. Earlier cruisers, incorporating both belt and protective deck, had grown over-large, with little or no speed advantage over contemporary battleships. By dispensing with heavy belt armour, the two Blakes could accommodate more powerful machinery.

Occupying nearly two-thirds of the ships' length, machinery and boilers were designed to develop 14,914kW/20,000shp for 22 knots. Four triple-expansion, inverted-cylinder engines, each in its own compartment, were coupled in pairs to drive the two shafts. Unfortunately, the big double-ended boilers gave problems under forced draught conditions and the ships were usually limited to only 11,186kW/15,000shp and 20.5 knots.

Their armament followed the layout adopted for capital ships, with the main-calibre guns mounted forward and aft, and the secondary battery sided in the waist, both in open mounts on the upper deck and in newly adopted casemates at main deck level. The forward 234mm/9.2in gun was located on a short forecastle deck.

Otherwise generally well-regarded, the pair attracted criticism with respect to their near half-million pound unit cost. About 25 per cent cost saving was therefore effected in the following Edgars. Although obviously related, they were of about 1,676 tonnes/1,650 tons less displacement and more lightly protected. Shorter by about 4.6m/15ft, they were

ABOVE: **In order to improve their speed over their predecessors', the two Blakes were considerably increased in size in order to accommodate the necessary machinery. They dispensed with a side belt but shipped a powerful single 234mm/9.2in gun at either end. The *Blake*'s 152mm/6in guns are carried at a good height.**

also finer and, in addition to their lack of forecastle, this adversely affected their heavy-weather performance in early service on the Northern Blockade. They nevertheless acquitted themselves well during the 1915 Dardanelles campaign, for which they were suited and where weather conditions were benign.

Perhaps already uncertain of the Edgars' low forward freeboard, the designer incorporated a low forecastle in two further ships (*Crescent* and *Royal Arthur*) and, interestingly, suppressed the forward 234mm/9.2in gun in favour of a pair of sided 152mm/6in weapons.

Blake, Crescent and Edgar classes

	Built	Commissioned
Blake	Chatham Dockyard	February 2, 1892
Blenheim	Thames Ironworks, Blackwall	May 26, 1894
Edgar	Devonport Dockyard	March 2, 1891
Endymion	Earle, Hull	May 26, 1894
Gibraltar	Napier, Glasgow	November 1, 1894
Grafton	Thames Ironworks, Blackwall	October 18, 1894
Hawke	Chatham Dockyard	May 16, 1893
St. George	Earle, Hull	October 25, 1894
Theseus	Thames Ironworks, Blackwall	January 14, 1896
Crescent	Portsmouth Dockyard	February 22, 1894
Royal Arthur	Portsmouth Dockyard	March 2, 1893

Edgar (as built)

Displacement: 7,468 tonnes/7,350 tons (normal)

Length: 109.7m/360ft (bp), 113.3m/371ft 9in (oa)

Beam: 18.3m/60ft

Draught: 7.2m/23ft 9in (normal)

Armament: 2 x 234mm/9.2in (2x1), 10 x 152mm/6in (10x1) and 12 x 6pdr (12x1) guns; 4 x 457mm/18in torpedo tubes (4x1)

Machinery: 2 sets inverted, triple-expansion engines, 5 boilers, 2 shafts

Power: 8,950kW/12,000ihp for 20.5 knots

Endurance: 864 tonnes/850 tons (coal) for 5,556km/3,000nm at 18 knots

Protection: 127mm/5in (protective deck); 152mm/6in (casemates)

Complement: 545

LEFT: **Four Edgars were greatly modified for the 1915 Dardanelles campaign. The *Endymion*, stemmed in a Malta dry dock, shows her enormous bulges and the gallows added to allow her to tackle defensive nets in mine- and submarine-infested waters. Her original ram bow is also in evidence.**

LEFT: **The concept of small "scouts" was never a very sound one, but the building of four pairs to a loose specification provided a useful contribution to later cruiser design. The *Foresight* was one of the pair from Fairfield, the only ones to have a short, raised poop. Note the outsize anchor and W/T gaff.**

The 1904 Scouts

Planning for a naval war focused on the North Sea, the Admiralty issued a broad specification in May 1902 for a new type of small cruiser, lightly armed but fast, suitable for watching enemy ports as well as leading a large destroyer flotilla of the time.

Unusually, the Admiralty solicited individual designs, for ships of under 3,048 tonnes/3,000 tons, from six shipbuilders. Those from four – Armstrong, Fairfield, Laird and Vickers – were accepted, and each firm was contracted to build a pair of ships for comparative trials. Broad statistics of those built are shown in the table below.

Externally, the Armstrong design stood out by virtue of its four funnels, the remainder having only three. All had a raised forecastle to improve seakeeping,

that of the Vickers ships having curved, "turtle-deck" sheer strakes. All featured a single lofty mast to facilitate radio communication. Originally, the first-of-class bore the name *Eddystone*, but the Admiralty renamed all as listed below.

Although the Admiralty had stipulated reciprocating machinery rather then steam turbines, all achieved the required 25 knots. Informed opinion, however, found "£275,000" hard to justify for such small ships, with an armament of only 12pdr guns and with limited endurance.

As if to underline the truth of this, Armstrong, the favoured firm, almost immediately went on to build two near-repeats for Brazil. Turbine-driven, they were 1.5 knots faster and were armed with ten 119mm/4.7in guns. Not surprisingly, then, as the war widened from the North

Sea, the bulk of the group were rearmed with nine 102mm/4in ordnance. Acting as convoy escorts, beyond their envisaged roles, the Armstrong-built ships were, by 1918, each carrying one or two 152mm/6in guns in addition to the remaining 102mm/4in weapons.

1904 Scouts

	Built	Commissioned
Adventure	Armstrong, Elswick	November 6, 1905
Attentive	Armstrong, Elswick	February 7, 1905
Foresight	Fairfield, Glasgow	1905–06
Forward	Fairfield, Glasgow	1905–06
Pathfinder	Laird, Birkenhead	1905–06
Patrol	Laird, Birkenhead	1905–06
Sentinel	Vickers, Barrow	1905–06
Skirmisher	Vickers, Barrow	1905–06

Armstrong vessels (as built)

Displacement: 2,682 tonnes/2,640 tons (normal); 2,957 tonnes/2,910 tons (full load)
Length: 113.9m/374ft (bp); 120.3m/395ft (oa)
Beam: 11.7m/38ft 3in
Draught: 3.7m/12ft 3in (normal)
Armament: 10 x 12pdr (10x1) and 8 x 3pdr (8x1) guns; 2 x 457mm/18in torpedo tubes (2x1)
Machinery: 2 sets vertical, triple-expansion engines, 12 boilers, 2 shafts
Power: 11,819kW/15.850ihp (max) for 25 knots
Endurance: 458 tonnes/450 tons (coal) for 5,556km/3,000nm at 10 knots
Protection: 18–50mm/0.7–2in (protective deck)
Complement: 286

	Displacement (tonnes/tons)	Length (bp) (m/ft)	Beam	Power (kW/ihp)	Trials speed (knots)
Armstrong	2,682/2,640	114.3/375	11.7m/38ft 3in	11,819/15,850	25.42
Fairfield	2,906/2,860	111.3/365	11.9m39ft 2in	11,186/15,000	25.16
Laird	2,947/2,900	112.8/370	11.8m/38ft 9in	12,267/16,450	25.06
Vickers	2,926/2,880	109.7/360	12.2m/40ft	13,050/17,500	25.07

LEFT: **Vickers' contribution included *Skirmisher*, here undergoing builder's trials. She has the general appearance of a large destroyer and it was with the larger, later destroyers, such as the Rivers, that the scouts mainly worked. Their use as leaders declined as successive classes of destroyer became faster.**

LEFT: **Although they resembled the armoured cruisers that followed with their four funnels, the eight Diadems had no side belt, while their forward and after centreline mountings were twin 152mm/6in guns in shields. They were criticized for their light armament but were reckoned to perform well. This is *Niobe*.** ABOVE: **The Diadems were no longer front-line units by 1914. The *Niobe* (left) spent much of the war as a depot ship in Halifax, Nova Scotia. Her sister *Amphitrite*, here seen in the disruptive paint scheme ("camouflage") usually seen on duty, was an Atlantic convoy escort before being converted to a minelayer in 1917.**

Diadem and Monmouth classes

Launched 1898–1900, the eight-ship Diadem class was of an intermediate size between the 14,428 tonne/14,200 ton Powerfuls of 1895 and the 9,297 tonne/9,150 ton *Blakes* of 1890. Protected cruisers, they were ordered in two groups. Where earlier classes had been given single 234mm/9.2in guns at either end (weapons virtually useless in the absence of proper fire control), the Diadems had a homogeneous armament of sixteen 152mm/6in guns. Four of these were paired in open mountings, forward and aft. The remainder were in casemates, four at the upper deck level and eight on the main deck. Apart from the last being located too low to be of use in any sort of sea, the whole layout was typical of its day in permitting only ten guns of sixteen to fire in broadside. The main deck guns were relocated to the upper deck in 1916.

Much controversy at this time attended the design and choice of boilers. Thus, the first group (*Andromeda*, *Argonaut*, *Europa* and *Niobe*) could generate 12,304kW/16,500ihp for 20.5 knots, while the second, with improved steam conditions, developed 13,423kW/18,000ihp for an extra quarter knot.

The Diadems were imposing in their appearance but they were much criticized for their lack of vertical protection. Improving steels enabled the following, and very similar, Cressys to be given both belt and protective deck. The German *Fürst Bismarck*, contemporary with the *Diadem*, was superior for on a displacement some 508 tonnes/500 tons less, she combined a 50mm/2in deck with a belt of up to 200mm/7.8in. Her armament also comprised four 24cm/9.5in guns and twelve 15cm/5.9in guns, of which only four were at main deck level.

ABOVE: **The *Andromeda* prior to World War I. Because of their imposing size, they could be employed as station flagships, the flag officer enjoying the privilege of the secluded sternwalk. Note the after bridge, and how close to the water the lowest casemates are located.** RIGHT: **The *Andromeda* as built. One contributory factor to half the armament being set so uselessly low is apparent here, the substantial mass of the torpedo net being stowed on a shelf in line with the deck above. Reduced to a training hulk in 1913, she was not scrapped until 1956.**

By 1914 the Diadems were obsolete, although at least three undertook Atlantic patrols. *Amphitrite* and *Ariadne* landed most of their armament in their conversion to large minelayers, in which role the latter was torpedoed and sunk.

Provided for in the 1898 to 1900 Estimates, the ten Monmouths, or "Counties", were answers to the French Klébers. Of very similar dimensions to the Diadems they mounted two fewer guns but were fitted with both belt and protective deck, and installed power that should have been sufficient for 23 knots. Several failed to attain contract speed until fitted with redesigned propellers. Controversy still surrounded boiler design and some of the class were therefore fitted with 24 boilers of Babcock and Wilcox design, others with 31 Bellevilles units.

Their belt was of 102mm/4in plate, tapering to 50mm/2in at either extremity, where it was closed off with a 76mm/3in transverse bulkhead. Vertically, it extended over the lower and main decks, forming a box roofed by the 30mm/1.2in main deck and floored with the vaulted protective deck.

A new departure was to mount the forward and after centreline 152mm/6in guns in paired, electrically operated turrets. As with the propulsion machinery, these could cause trouble and were cramped.

As with most contemporary British armoured cruisers, the Monmouths had generous freeboard, and their seakeeping was considered excellent. This, however, was slightly offset by their fine entry, necessary to achieve the design speed.

Of the ten, *Bedford* was lost by stranding in 1910, but the remainder of the class proved valuable during World War I. The nameship, poorly manned and exercised, was sunk with all hands at Coronel in 1914. Two of her sisters, however, were in the squadron that avenged her loss at the Falklands shortly afterwards. Of these, the *Kent*, which had made only

21.7 knots on her original trials, burned wooden furniture to boost power and to overhaul the fleeing *Nürnberg*. In the process of pursuing and sinking the fugitive, the *Kent* suffered nearly forty 10.5cm/4.1in hits. These caused little but cosmetic damage, the crew suffering only four fatalities.

ABOVE: **Popularly known as the County class, the Monmouths were designed as a smaller and more economical type of armoured cruiser, to be deployed either with the battle fleet or on trade protection. Although elderly, the class was heavily used during World War I. *Donegal*, seen here, was scrapped in 1920.**

ABOVE: **The Monmouths' belt armour was dimensioned to resist 15cm/5.9in shellfire but the nameship was sunk at Coronel by heavier 21cm/8.3in projectiles. In the ensuing battle off the Falklands the *Kent*, seen here, absorbed no less than 38 hits, from the *Nürnberg*'s 10.5cm/4.1in guns. Her superior protection and heavier firepower inevitably resulted in the German's destruction.**

ABOVE: **This view of the *Berwick* clearly shows the twin 152mm/6in forward turret, the first such mounting on British cruisers and not known for their reliability. The complexity and vulnerability of the W/T rigging is apparent. Riding to two anchors, the ship is using a mooring swivel to prevent crossed cables, or "foul hawse".**

Diadem and Monmouth classes

	Built	Commissioned
Andromeda	Pembroke Dockyard	1900
Argonaut	Fairfield, Glasgow	1900
Europa	Brown, Clydebank	1899
Niobe	Vickers, Barrow	1899
Amphitrite	Vickers, Barrow	1900
Ariadne	Brown, Clydebank	1900
Diadem	Fairfield, Glasgow	1899
Spartiate	Pembroke Dockyard	1902
Bedford	Fairfield, Glasgow	1903
Berwick	Beardmore, Glasgow	1903
Cornwall	Pembroke Dockyard	1905
Cumberland	London & Glasgow	1904
Donegal	Fairfield, Glasgow	1903
Essex	Pembroke Dockyard	1903
Kent	Portsmouth Dockyard	1903
Lancaster	Armstrong, Elswick	1904
Monmouth	London & Glasgow	1903
Suffolk	Portsmouth Dockyard	1904

Later Monmouths (as built)

Displacement: 10,159 tonnes/9,900 tons (normal)
Length: 134m/440ft (bp); 141.2m/463ft 6in (oa)
Beam: 20.2m/66ft 4in
Draught: 7.5m/24ft 6in (normal)
Armament: 14 x 152mm/6in (2x2/10x1) and 10 x 12pdr (10x1) guns; 2 x fixed submerged 457mm/18in torpedo tubes
Machinery: 2 sets vertical, triple-expansion engines, 31 boilers, 2 shafts
Power: 16,405kW/22,000ihp for 23 knots
Bunkers: 1,788 tonnes/1,760 tons (coal)
Protection: 50–102mm/2–4in (belt); 18–50mm/0.75–2in (protective deck); 100–127mm/4–5in (turrets)
Complement: 500

Cressy, Drake and Devonshire classes

Developments in the manufacturing of armour plate, first by Harvey (1891), and then by Krupp (1895), had a significant effect on warship design. During the previous decade, "compound" armour comprised a hard steel face plate hot-rolled on to a tough iron back plate. Harvey's process "cemented" or face-hardened the outer surface of a homogeneous steel plate. Krupp went further by incorporating small quantities of elements that improved the plate's resistance to penetration or to shattering.

In round figures, Harvey had one-and-a-half times and Krupp twice the stopping power of compound armour. For the designer this meant that the same level of protection could be provided at only half the weight. An alternative was to provide a belt in addition to an armoured deck, signalling the return of the armoured cruiser.

The first result was the Cressy type, upgraded Diadems that readopted the 234mm/9.2in ordnance at either end, had a thinner (50–76mm/2–3in against 64–102mm/2.5–4in) protective deck but had a 152mm/6in belt of Krupp steel, 3.5m/11ft 6in in depth. Long in manufacture, armour plate was expensive and, where a Diadem cost £582,000, a Cressy cost £780,000.

ABOVE LEFT: **The six Cressys were effectively Diadems redesigned with a belt. This was possible because of the introduction of Krupp "cemented" (surface hardened) armour which had higher resistance to penetration. This picture shows the *Sutlej*. Note the size of the forward 234mm/9.2in gun in its fully enclosed turret.** ABOVE: **The side belt of the Cressys came no higher than the lower edge of the lower gun casemates, leaving a vast, unprotected acreage, well depicted in this picture of *Aboukir*. In the event, she was simply despatched by submarine torpedo, a form of attack that post-dated her designer's experience.**

Ironically, for the three ships lost, these improvements availed them nothing. Just seven weeks after the outbreak of war, with submarine warfare an unknown quantity to either side, the *Aboukir*, *Cressy* and *Hogue* were despatched by one U-boat with four torpedoes. For the ship designer, it posed a new set of problems, for the thickest of armour was no defence against torpedoes, designed to strike below it.

If the Cressys are viewed as a response to the successful Italian Garibaldis and to the French *Montcalm*, their successors, the Drakes, were designed with the French *Jeanne d'Arc* in mind. This required a 2-knot improvement in speed, necessitating a 43 per cent increase in power, a 14 per cent

ABOVE: **Although having four funnels, the Devonshires (the nameship seen here) were improved Monmouths rather than improved Drakes (opposite). Their shorter funnels gave them a less-stately, more business-like appearance. Note the three forward-firing, fully enclosed 191mm/7.5in guns, with a higher rate of fire than a 234mm/9.2in weapon, and harder hitting than a 152mm/6in gun.**

ABOVE: **In profile, the British armoured cruisers became difficult to differentiate. The Devonshires (*Roxburgh* seen here) were the first to have 191mm/7.5in turrets flanking the bridge, but retained the two-level 152mm/6in casemates abreast the mainmast. Note the adoption of distinguishing funnel bands, although all were later given disruptive paint schemes.**

increase in length and a 35 per cent increase in cost. The result was imposing, but so large that considerable effort was made to reduce their profile and target area.

By virtue of making all 152mm/6in gun casemates double-tiered, the Drakes carried 16 secondary weapons against the Cressys' 12. Also, where the latter's belt terminated below the bridge in a 127mm/5in transverse bulkhead, that of the *Drake* was continued right to the bows at a reduced thickness of 50mm/2in, as flooding forward quickly reduced stability.

They were among the first British warships to incorporate wood treated to reduce fire risk and to have their coal bunkers, an important part of the ships' protective system, subdivided to minimize the effect of a torpedo rather than shellfire. Again, a touch of irony is added by the "fire-proofing" for, at Coronel, the Drake-class *Good Hope* was sunk by German gunfire and was, by their account, "already burning from fore to aft, presenting the unique spectacle of a sheet of flame upon a sea lashed by the tempest".

If the Cressys and Drakes represented a response to the perceived threat posed by foreign contemporaries, the Monmouths were a more moderate design aimed at the actual responsibility of commerce protection. A Monmouth was two-thirds the cost of a Drake, so it is not surprising that this otherwise maligned class of ten should have been extended by an improved batch. These were the Devonshires, a more heavily armed class of six laid down in 1902.

Although resembling Drakes, Devonshires were considerably smaller at 10,923 tonnes/10,750 tons. They were 3.1m/10ft longer than Monmouths, 0.6m/2ft greater in beam, and they were similarly powered and therefore a little slower. The belt was thickened by 50 per cent, and four 191mm/7.5in guns added, two centreline singles, forward and aft, and two more, turreted, in place of the previous forward casemates. One of two lost was the *Hampshire*, carrying Lord Kitchener.

TOP: **Not so obvious in this depiction, the four Drakes were identifiable by their four two-level casemates on each side, housing a formidable secondary armament (on paper, at least) of sixteen 152mm/6in guns. Note how the Victorian livery allowed for considerable flexibility in paint schemes.**
ABOVE: **The lack of a white upper strake on the *Leviathan* (top) as compared with the *Aboukir* (opposite) resulted from a reduction in freeboard, a conscious effort being made by designers to reduce the large overall target area of the ship. One result was to lower the lower casemates still further. At Coronel, the ill-starred *Good Hope*, seen here, was unable to use any of her lower 152mm/6in guns.**

ABOVE: ***Hogue*, seen here, was another of the Cressys. Their large number of 152mm/6in quick-firers were intended to smother an opponent, to reduce his capability to respond. The large 234mm/9.2in gun at either end was there to inflict the final, armour-piercing blow. With only two guns and no proper fire control, however, the 234mm/9.2in ordnance was inaccurate.**

Cressy, Drake and Devonshire classes

	Built	Commissioned
Aboukir	Fairfield, Glasgow	1902
Bacchante	Brown, Clydebank	1902
Cressy	Fairfield, Glasgow	1901
Euryalus	Vickers, Barrow	1904
Hogue	Vickers, Barrow	1902
Sutlej	Brown, Clydebank	1902
Drake	Pembroke Dockyard	1902
Good Hope	Fairfield, Glasgow	1902
King Alfred	Vickers, Barrow	1903
Leviathan	Brown, Clydebank	1903
Antrim	Brown, Clydebank	1905
Argyll	Scott, Greenock	1906
Carnarvon	Beardmore, Glasgow	1905
Devonshire	Chatham Dockyard	1905
Hampshire	Armstrong, Elswick	1905
Roxburgh	London & Glasgow	1905

Drake class

Displacement: 14,326 tonnes/14,100 tons (normal)
Length: 152.3m/500ft (bp); 161.3m/529ft 6in (oa)
Beam: 21.6m/71ft
Draught: 8.2m/27ft (mean)
Armament: 2 x 234mm/9.2in (2x1), 16 x 152mm/6in (16x1) and 12 x 12pdr (12x1) guns; 2 x fixed 457mm/18in torpedo tubes (2x1)
Power: 23,490kW/31,500ihp for 23 knots
Endurance: 1,270 tonnes/1,250 tons (coal) for 6,019km/3,250nm at 19 knots
Protection: 76–152mm/3–6in (belt); 50–76mm/2–3in (deck); 127–152mm/5–6in (turrets and casemates)
Complement: 900

LEFT: **The two Black Princes (*Duke of Edinburgh* shown here) virtually qualified as Second Class battleships. The great length necessary to accommodate machinery for 23 knots gave them a beam sufficient to mount four 234mm/9.2in wing turrets in the waist. Compared with these, her casemated 152mm/6in weapons look insignificant.**

Black Prince, Warrior and Minotaur classes

By 1902, the prestige of the armoured cruiser was soaring. Big, powerful, expensive, looking every inch a warship, she was proposed by some, who were forgetting what she was designed for, to be suitable for laying in a line of battle. Effectively a Second Class battleship, she was to develop even further under Watts, the newly appointed Director of Naval Construction (DNC).

At the time of the changeover in DNC, the Devonshires were introducing the 191mm/7.5in gun as the armoured cruiser's primary weapon. The Board of Admiralty, however, considered it too light for ships of this size, and, for the following class, required not only the 234mm/9.2in gun but six of them to be disposed in single turrets in the "hexagonal" layout then much in favour. Despite the Cressys having already demonstrated that a casemated, main deck battery of 152mm/6in secondary guns was unworkable in any sea, it was to be retained as easier to control. Too late to rectify, the Monmouths' 102mm/4in belt had been shown in tests to be unable to stop a 152mm/6in shell, so a minimum of 152mm/6in over vital areas was specified.

Although water-tube boilers were by now becoming generally accepted, the Admiralty insisted on including a proportion of the old cylindrical type, as being more economical at cruising speeds. This mix affected the overall length although, compared with the Drakes, the next pair (*Black Prince* and *Duke of Edinburgh*) were 7.3m/24ft shorter but 0.76m/2.5ft greater in the beam.

In order that the forward 234mm/9.2in wing turrets, mounted at upper deck level, could fire ahead, the forecastle was narrow and facetted, allowing the sea to sweep the upper deck along its length. One level below was the broadside 152mm/6in battery which, predictably, proved to be so ineffectual that, having survived Jutland, the *Duke of Edinburgh* had her guns relocated to the upper deck and the casemates plated over.

The situation was rectified in what should have been the final four of the class but which, on account of differences, became known as the Warriors. These used the same hull and had six 234mm/9.2in guns in the same hexagonal layout but, in place of the casemated 152mm/6in battery, had four 191mm/7.5in weapons arranged in single turrets at upper deck level, two per side.

In terms of firepower, speed and protection, British armoured cruisers compared well with their foreign contemporaries until, as the Warriors were all reaching launch stage, there were reports that the US Navy was progressing from the mixed 203mm/8in and 152mm/6in armament of the Pennsylvanias to 254mm/10in and 178mm/7in guns in the four new Tennessees (also known as Washingtons). Used by only two ships in the Royal Navy, the 254mm/10in gun was not

LEFT: **Last of the three classes depicted on these pages, the Minotaurs carried the majority of their armament quite low. Casemates were dispensed with in favour of single turrets, the forbidding row of five 191mm/7.5in guns along either side being their distinguishing feature. The *Defence*, shown here, was lost with all hands at Jutland, having come within range of the enemy battle line.**

favoured and, as the penetrative power of the reliable 234mm/9.2in projectile was only slightly inferior, this calibre was retained for the final trio of armoured cruisers, the Minotaurs. In these, the hexagonal layout was abandoned. Only four 234mm/9.2in guns were carried, but in twin turrets located on the forecastle and quarter deck. Along the waist at upper-deck level were no less than five single 191mm/7.5in turrets per side. They also had an all-water tube boiler outfit.

Despite a further increase in physical size and displacement, the Minotaurs could have only the same scale of protection and their massive dispersed armament, with its separate requirements for safe ammunition paths, resulted in a somewhat congested design. A 17 per cent increase in installed power was also required to give the same speed.

Bristling with armament, the armoured cruiser had been progressed as far as was possible. The Minotaurs were completed in 1908, the same year in which the British themselves made the type obsolete with the entry into service of the *Invincible*, first of the battlecruisers.

ABOVE: **An excellent picture of the Warrior-class *Natal* shows an armament midway between the *Black Prince* and the *Warrior*. The single 234mm/ 9.2in gun at either end is flanked by two more, making six in total. The 152mm/6in casemated guns have been replaced by turreted 191mm/7.5in guns, two on either side. The *Natal* was destroyed in 1915 at Cromarty by a magazine explosion.**

Black Prince, Warrior and Minotaur classes

	Built	Commissioned
Black Prince	Thames Ironworks, Blackwall	January 1906
Duke of Edinburgh	Pembroke Dockyard	March 1906
Achilles	Armstrong, Elswick	March 1907
Cochrane	Fairfield, Glasgow	February 1907
Natal	Vickers, Barrow	1907
Warrior	Pembroke Dockyard	1907
Defence	Pembroke Dockyard	April 1908
Minotaur	Devonport Dockyard	March 1908
Shannon	Chatham Dockyard	March 1908

Minotaur class

Displacement: 14,834 tonnes/14,600 tons (normal); 16,400 tonnes/16,100 tons (full load)

Length: 149.3m/490ft (bp); 158.1m/519ft (oa)

Beam: 22.7m/74ft 6in

Draught: 7.9m/26ft (normal)

Armament: 4 x 234mm/9.2in (2x2), 10 x 191mm/7.5in (10x1) and 16 x 12pdr guns; 5 x 457mm/18in fixed torpedo tubes

Machinery: 2 sets vertical, triple-expansion engines, 23 boilers, 2 shafts

Power: 20,134kW/27,000ihp for 23 knots

Endurance: 1,018 tonnes/1,000 tons (coal) and 763 tonnes/750 tons (oil) for 15,093km/8,150nm at 10 knots

Protection: 76–152mm/3–6in (belt); 38–50mm/1.5–2in (protective deck), 178–203mm/7–8in (turrets)

Complement: 755

ABOVE: **Having received 21 hits at Jutland, 15 of them from major-calibre projectiles, the *Warrior* slowly foundered while under tow. Hampered by their limited speed – all were powered by reciprocating machinery – armoured cruisers proved deficient in their major role of opposed reconnaissance.**

LEFT: **The Boadiceas and closely similar Actives of 1909–13 were the forerunners of the numerous Town classes. Their design was possible through the adoption of the steam turbine, itself compact but also requiring fewer engine room staff, hence less accommodation. The *Blanche* was attached to the Grand Fleet's 4th Battle Squadron.**

Boadicea, Active and "Town" classes

Already regarded by the Royal Navy as a developing threat at the turn of the century, the German Navy began to commission a series of what the British classed as "Third Class cruisers". Between 1900 and 1904 ten of these steadily improved vessels were completed. Although generally stated to be unarmoured they had a thin protective deck and mounted ten 10.5cm/4.1in guns that totally outclassed the much-criticized 12pdr of the four pairs of British scout cruisers launched in 1904.

Germany then increased the size slightly and, at a rate of about two per year, began building their derived "Town"-class cruisers. Also carrying ten 10.5cm/4.1in guns, and with thicker protection, these steadily increased in displacement in order to incorporate more powerful machinery which, by 1908, drove

them at up to 24 knots. Except for their triple-expansion machinery, these were a superior type to which the Royal Navy had no direct equivalent. Britain's first response was the three Boadiceas, launched in 1908–09. Although their turbines gave them a knot or so advantage, both of their six 102mm/4in guns and their protection were inferior.

They were followed in 1911–12 by the three very similar Actives, which mounted ten 102mm/4in guns apiece. Although there appears to be no reason why the Boadiceas should not have been similarly upgunned, only the *Blonde* was rearmed.

Both the Boadicea and Active classes were primarily destroyer leaders. Their 14.1kg/31lb, 102mm/4in projectiles were inadequate even to stop a destroyer and, for working directly with the battle fleet, there was a requirement for an equally fast vessel, but somewhat larger both to retain a margin over the battle fleet, even in poor weather conditions, and to carry the more potent 152mm/6in gun.

With the need recognized in good time, the first group of British "Towns" began to be launched in 1909. In the first five, the Bristols, ten waist-mounted 102mm/4in guns were supplemented by a single 152mm/6in forward and aft in a dual-calibre layout that mirrored that of contemporary armoured cruisers, complete with difficult fire control.

The Bristols were the first of four groups of "Towns" that represented the beginning of a divergent line of development, i.e. "fleet cruisers" aimed specifically at offensive reconnaissance. Their main characteristics are shown below.

ABOVE: **The Southampton-class ships, the Australian-flagged *Melbourne* (seen here) and *Sydney* both served with the Royal Navy for much of World War I. Slightly finer-lined than the Birminghams, which followed, they carried only one forecastle gun and were the first with the new-profile bow.**

	Launched	Displacement tonnes/tons	Armament	Dimensions m/ft
Bristol (x5)	1909–10	4,877/4,800	2 x 152mm/6in; 10 x 102mm/4in	138 x 14.4/453 x 47
Weymouth (x4)	1910–11	5,334/5,250	8 x 152mm/6in	137 x 14.8/450 x 48.5
Southampton (x7)	1911–12	5,487/5,400	8 x 152mm/6in	137 x 14.9/450 x 48.8
Birmingham (x3)	1913	5,527/5,440	9 x 152mm/6in; 1 x 76mm/3in	139.2 x 15.2/456.8 x 50

Three more Southamptons (*Brisbane*, *Melbourne* and *Sydney*) and the Birmingham-class *Adelaide* served with the Royal Australian Navy, both the *Adelaide* and *Brisbane* being home-built. Completed late, *Adelaide* differed in detail.

Although all of these groups were of pre-war construction, their protection evolved to meet the perceived threat. Thus the first two had protective decks, the third was double-skinned by way of machinery spaces, while the Birminghams added a full-length belt capable of stopping a 10.5cm/4.1in projectile.

The "Towns" were very heavily used throughout World War I, during which period the only two losses (*Falmouth* and *Nottingham*) were due to submarine torpedo. Several, particularly *Southampton* and the broadly similar *Chester*, survived severe damage by gunfire. *Chester*, and her sister *Birkenhead*, were being built to Greek account when taken over by the Royal Navy. Their main difference lay in their 140mm/5.5in armament, whose 37.6kg/83lb shells were more easily handled than the 45.4kg/100lb, 152mm/6in projectile.

In the course of the war most had their foremast converted to a tripod to reduce vibration in the fire control top. The "Towns", specifically *Weymouth*, were the first Royal Navy light cruisers to be fitted with flying-off platforms for fighter aircraft.

ABOVE LEFT: **A forecastle view of the Bristol-class *Glasgow*. Escaping from the debacle of Coronel in November 1914, the ship gained revenge shortly afterward, assisting in sinking the *Leipzig* at the Falklands and, later, the *Dresden*. Note the heavy, cast shield of the 152mm/6in gun.** ABOVE: **The five Bristols (*Newcastle* seen here) were the first of the Towns, being considerably stretched, four-shaft Actives. They were alone in having a short forecastle and mixed armament, with 102mm/4in secondaries.**

"Town" classes

	Built	Commissioned
Bristol	Brown, Clydebank	1910
Glasgow	Fairfield, Glasgow	1910
Gloucester	Beardmore, Glasgow	1910
Liverpool	Vickers, Barrow	1910
Newcastle	Armstrong, Elswick	1910
Dartmouth	Vickers, Barrow	1911
Falmouth	Beardmore, Glasgow	1911
Weymouth	Armstrong, Elswick	1911
Yarmouth	London & Glasgow	1912
Chatham	Chatham Dockyard	1912
Dublin	Beardmore, Glasgow	1913
Southampton	Brown, Clydebank	1913
Brisbane	Cockatoo, Sydney	1915
Melbourne	Cammell Laird, Birkenhead	1913
Sydney	London & Glasgow	1913
Birmingham	Armstrong, Elswick	1914
Lowestoft	Chatham Dockyard	1914
Nottingham	Pembroke Dockyard	1914
Adelaide	Cockatoo, Sydney	1922

ABOVE: **Serving alongside the Italian Navy in the Adriatic, a weather-worn *Weymouth* enters Grand Harbour, Malta. Closely following the Bristols, the four Weymouths carried eight 152mm/6in guns, three forward, one aft, and two on either side in the waist, protected by high bulwarks. Note the stump mainmast.**

Birmingham class

Displacement: 5,527 tonnes/5,440 tons (normal)
Length: 131.9m/430ft (bp), 139.2m/456ft 9in (oa)
Beam: 15.1m/49ft 6in
Draught: 4.8m/15ft 10in (normal)
Armament: 9 x 152mm/6in guns (9x1);
  2 x 533mm/21in fixed torpedo tubes (2x1)
Machinery: Direct-drive steam turbines,
  12 boilers, 2 shafts
Power: 18,643kW/25,000shp for 25 knots
Bunkers: 1,184 tonnes/1,165 tons (coal);
  239 tonnes/235 tons (oil)
Protection: 50–76mm/2–3in (belt); 38mm/1.5in
  (protective deck)
Complement: 435

Arethusa and C-classes

Smaller than the "Towns", the Arethusas continued the line of development begun with the Boadicea and Active groups. Larger than the scouts, fast enough to act as destroyer leaders, and with a 76mm/3in belt capable of stopping a 10.5cm/4.1in shell at close range, they proved effective. They were intended to support the battle fleet by leading destroyer attacks against that of the enemy, while also acting to break-up any similar attack on his part. To fulfill this role they were fitted with a dual-calibre armament of rapid-firing 102mm/4in to deal with destroyers and a few 152mm/6in to deter the attentions of any cruiser covering them.

Comparatively small, however, these ships were lively, making them poor gun platforms and causing difficulty with the manual loading of 45.4kg/100lb, 152mm/6in shells. Metacentric height and, to some extent, stability, therefore had to be deliberately reduced to increase roll period and steadiness. The general adoption of oil-firing contributed to the problem, as oil tanks tended to be carried lower than coal bunkers, lowering the centre of gravity and increasing stiffness.

A large increase in installed power gave them a sea speed of 27 knots, which could be comfortably exceeded. Commodore Tyrwhitt, taking over the new *Arethusa* in 1914, wrote enthusiastically: "She's a regular flyer and a ripper ..." With the

ABOVE: **As long as a Town, but considerably narrower, the C-class cruisers were essentially slightly enlarged Arethusas. Extremely successful, the type developed quickly through several sub-types. *Champion* belonged to the two-funnelled Cambrian class.**

ship heavily damaged at the Heligoland Bight, he temporarily wore his flag in the Town-class *Lowestoft*. "[She was] a size larger than the *Arethusa*", he commented, "but slower and rather too big for my job ... We destroyer folk have ways and customs which are quite unknown to the big ships." Obviously, the Admiralty had it about right.

Following on were the six Carolines, first of the successful C-class which, in half-a-dozen variants, eventually ran to 28 ships. Two further Carolines (*Calliope* and *Champion*) were used to trial different arrangements of gearing.

ABOVE: **Gunnery practice with the 152mm/6in ordnance on *Champion*'s forecastle under the watchful eye of the "Chief GI" (gunnery instructor). Note the light gun shield, compared with those on the Towns, the bridge-wing semaphores and the canvas-screened chart table.**

ABOVE: **The Caledon type, completed in 1917, was given an all-centreline armament of five 152mm/6in guns. This broadside by *Calypso* shows how they were disposed. Sturdy tripod masts allowed vibration-free observation and spotting. Tall mainmasts were not required for North Sea operations.**

The Carolines carried eight 102mm/4in guns, sided in the waist and on the forecastle deck. Contrary to historical precedent, the two 152mm/6in weapons were in centreline, in a superfiring disposition, pointing aft. By 1918, the forecastle 102mm/4in gun had mostly been exchanged for additional 152mm/6in ordnance.

Where the Carolines inherited the eight-boiler and three funnel arrangement of the Arethusas, the six follow-on Cambrians benefited from improved technology having only six boilers and two funnels. They were, otherwise, repeats.

In 1916, Armstrong completed the *Centaur* and *Concord*. Incorporating material assembled from deferred Turkish warships, they differed in mounting an all-centreline armament of five 152mm/6in guns. They also had two high-angle (HA) 76mm/3in weapons and a fire control top. The latter necessitated a substantial tripod mainmast, which was eventually fitted to all.

The four Caledons of 1917 were repeats on slightly enlarged hulls, followed by the five Ceres type. These had their bridge structure moved a little further aft in order to permit a second 152mm/6in gun to be located to superfire the forecastle weapon. With increasing topside weight, beam was increased by 0.46m/1ft 6in to improve stability.

The final group, five Carlisles, were similar but, in order to reduce wetness, increased forward freeboard with the so-called "trawler bow".

From 1934 the surviving thirteen Cs were slated for conversion to anti-aircraft cruisers. *Coventry* and *Curlew* were duly rebuilt as prototypes in 1935–36. Lack of funds and priority then slowed the programme until it was overtaken by World War II. Only nine were eventually converted. Their armament varied, with differing mixes of single and twin 102mm/4in high-angle (HA) and multiple 2pdr pompoms, together with the requisite directors and early radar. Five were sunk during World War II, three of them, ironically, by aircraft.

BELOW: **Nine later C-class were converted to anti-aircraft cruisers. The *Curacoa*, see here, is carrying eight high-angle 102mm/4in in twin mountings, and a pompom. Note the two directors, full radar outfit and tripod mainmast.**

ABOVE: **Still fitted with a light-pole foremast, the 1915-built *Cleopatra* belongs to the early, three-funnelled Caroline group. During a Harwich Force operation in 1916, she rammed an enemy destroyer, cutting her in two. In such close-fought encounters, the ships' 76mm/3in side belt proved its worth.**

Carlisle group (as built)

Displacement: 4,760 tonnes/4,685 tons (normal); 5,338 tonnes/5,254 tons (full load)
Length: 129.5m/425ft (bp); 137.5m/451ft 6in (oa)
Beam: 13.3m/43ft 6in
Draught: 4.4m/14ft 6in (normal)
Armament: 5 x 152mm/6in (5x1) and 2 x 76mm/3in HA (2x1) guns; 8 x 533mm/21in torpedo tubes (4x2)
Machinery: Geared steam turbines, 6 boilers, 2 shafts
Power: 22,371kW/30,000shp for 28 knots
Endurance: 950 tonnes/935 tons (oil) for 10,927km/5,900nm at 10 knots
Protection: 38–76mm/1.5–3in (belt); 25mm/1in (partial protective deck)
Complement: 330

Arethusa and C-classes

	Built	Commisssioned
Arethusa	Chatham Dockyard	August 11, 1914
Aurora	Devonport Dockyard	September 5, 1914
Galatea	Beardmore, Glasgow	December 10, 1914
Inconstant	Beardmore, Glasgow	January 4, 1915
Penelope	Vickers, Barrow	December 10, 1914
Phaeton	Vickers, Barrow	February 3, 1915
Royalist	Beardmore, Glasgow	March 21, 1915
Undaunted	Fairfield, Glasgow	August 29, 1914
Caroline	Cammell Laird, Birkenhead	December 4, 1914
Carysfort	Pembroke Dockyard	June 8, 1915
Cleopatra	Devonport Dockyard	June 1, 1915
Comus	Swan Hunter, Tyne	May 21, 1915
Conquest	Chatham Dockyard	June 1, 1915
Cordelia	Pembroke Dockyard	January 3, 1915
Calliope	Chatham Dockyard	June 15, 1915
Champion	Hawthorn Leslie, Tyne	December 20, 1915
Cambrian	Pembroke Dockyard	May 31, 1916
Canterbury	Brown, Clydebank	May 9, 1916
Castor	Cammell Laird, Birkenhead	November 12, 1915
Constance	Cammell Laird, Birkenhead	January 26, 1916
Centaur	Vickers, Barrow	August 16, 1916
Concord	Vickers, Barrow	December 18, 1916
Caledon	Cammell Laird, Birkenhead	March 6, 1917
Calypso	Hawthorn Leslie, Tyne	June 21, 1917
Carradoc	Scotts, Greenock	June 15, 1917
Cassandra	Vickers, Barrow	June 29, 1917
Cardiff	Fairfield, Glasgow	June 25, 1917
Ceres	Brown, Clydebank	June 1, 1917
Coventry	Swan Hunter, Tyne	February 21, 1918
Curacoa	Pembroke Dockyard	February 18, 1918
Curlew	Vickers, Barrow	December 14, 1917
Cairo	Cammell Laird, Birkenhead	October 14, 1919
Calcutta	Vickers, Barrow	August 10, 1919
Capetown	Cammell Laird, Birkenhead	April 10, 1922
Carlisle	Fairfield, Glasgow	November 16, 1918
Colombo	Fairfield, Glasgow	June 18, 1919

LEFT: **A little larger but otherwise very similar to the late C-type, the D-type** *Dauntless* **here clearly shows the differences. Superfiring single 152mm/6in at both ends are supplemented by two more on the centreline, before and abaft the funnels. Two quadruple torpedo tube mountings replace four triples.**

D-class

Unlike the British, the Germans upgraded light cruiser gun calibre in one step, without any mixed-calibre armaments. As early as 1914, the two Regensburgs introduced an all-15cm/5.9in armament and, although the layout meant that only five of their seven weapons could fire in broadside, this out-classed the early British C-class.

In the D-class, therefore, the British produced a stretched C-type; its extra 6.1m/20ft permitted an extra centreline 152mm/6in gun. In profile, a "D" appeared very similar to a Carlisle but with a larger gap between forefunnel and bridge, where the extra gun was located on the centreline.

In reality, however, both bridge and funnels had been moved aft. Set about 12.2m/40ft further from the bows, the bridge experienced less violent vertical motion while its one-level extra height made it dryer. Extra protection and the substitution of triple for twin torpedo

tubes necessitated a 0.6m/2ft increase in beam. As the same C-class machinery was to be fitted, speed loss was minimized by optimizing shaft speed and propeller design.

Conventional bows were fitted to the first group of three (*Danae, Dauntless* and *Dragon*), with the last five taking the unlovely "trawler" bow to further reduce wetness. Four further ships were cancelled at close of hostilities.

A 1936 proposal to rearm all eight as AA cruisers (but with twin 114mm/4.5in HA guns as opposed to the Cs' 102mm/4in armament) came to nothing. However, a one-off conversion was undertaken on the *Delhi* during 1941, in order to allow the Royal Navy to evaluate the US Navy's then-new 127mm/5in 38 weapon, of which five single mountings were fitted. They were not adopted.

Where the C-class AA conversions proved useful both in home and Mediterranean waters, the unconverted

Ds had limited potential during World War II, not least because of their endurance. Only *Dunedin* was lost.

D-class

	Built	Commissioned
Danae	Armstrong, High Walker	June 22, 1918
Dauntless	Palmers, Tyne	December 2, 1918
Dragon	Scotts, Greenock	August 16, 1918
Delhi	Armstrong, High Walker	June 7, 1919
Despatch	Fairfield, Glasgow	June 30, 1922
Diomede	Vickers, Barrow	October 7, 1922
Dunedin	Armstrong, High Walker	October 20, 1919
Durban	Scotts, Greenock	October 31, 1921

D-class

Displacement: 5,233 tonnes/5,150 tons (normal); 5,893 tonnes/5,800 tons (full load)
Length: 135.6m/445ft (bp); 143.9m/472ft 6in (oa)
Beam: 14.2m/46ft 6in
Draught: 4.6m/15ft (normal)
Armament: 6 x 152mm/6in (6x1); 2 x 76mm/3in HA (2x1) and 2 x 2pdr pompom (2x1) guns; 12 x 533mm/21in torpedo tubes (4x3)
Machinery: Geared steam turbines, 6 boilers, 2 shafts
Power: 29,828kW/40,000shp for 29 knots
Endurance: 1,077 tonnes/1,060 tons oil for 12,408km/6,700nm at 10 knots
Protection: 38–76mm/1.5–3in (belt); 25mm/1in (partial protective deck)
Complement: 450

LEFT: **At speed in North Sea conditions, smaller cruisers could be very wet. For this reason, the final six C-class ships (Carlisle type), and five of the eight completed Ds, were given so-called "trawler" bows. These significantly increased forward freeboard but did nothing for the ships' appearance.** *Durban* **is seen here.**

FAR LEFT: **In response to rumours that the enemy was constructing extra-fast cruisers, the Department of Naval Construction rapidly produced a stretched D-class cruiser with two sets of machinery. The extra length of the resulting E-class (*Enterprise* seen here) also permitted a seventh gun, 16 torpedo tubes, and an aircraft to be carried.**

ABOVE: **Abaft the funnels the E-class, seen here on *Emerald*, carried a revolving platform from which, wind-over-deck permitting, a biplane fighter/reconnaissance aircraft such as the Fairey Flycatcher could simply lift off. Note that the mainmast is offset to port to accommodate this.**

E-class

Developed directly from the D-class, the Es thus harked back to the Arethusas yet, in the case of the *Enterprise*, also looked forward to the cruisers of World War II by dint of being fitted with a prototype of the later-standardized 152mm/6in twin turret.

The class's origins lay in an urgent response to the rumoured new, high-speed German cruisers which were believed to be nearing completion. These turned out to be no more than the Brummers which were completed in 1916 in some secrecy but capable of an unexceptional 28 knots.

The Admiralty's demand for a 34-knot cruiser was quickly realized by the considerable extrapolation of a D-type. Tests indicated that a hull of 20 per cent greater length and marginally increased L/B ratio (9.82 against 9.57) could make 33 knots light with 59,656kW/80,000shp.

This was achieved by incorporating two sets of machinery being built for the new destroyer-leaders. Externally, this arrangement resulted in a return to three funnels, set battlecruiser-style with a pronounced gap between the second and third.

Although large and fast, the Es, of which only two were ever completed, and those long after the war, were armed with seven 152mm/6in guns. *Emerald* mounted her two forward weapons as superimposed singles, the *Enterprise* in the prototype twin turret.

Completed with four triple torpedo tube mountings, both ships were soon given quadruples. Their 16 tubes constituted the largest such armament of any British warship.

Between the mainmast and after funnel, as built, there was a revolving, flying-off platform for a float plane. During the 1930s a catapult was substituted, causing the mainmast to be relocated forward of the after funnel. The funnels were also increased in height.

With World War II and a proliferation of personnel and electronics, the forecastle deck was extended aft and the masts converted to tripods.

E-class

	Built	Commissioned
Emerald	Armstrong, High Walker	January 14, 1926
Enterprise	Brown, Clydebank	March 31, 1926
Euphrates	Fairfield, Glasgow	Cancelled

Emerald (as built)

Displacement: 8,636 tonnes/8,500 tons (normal); 9,602 tonnes/9,450 ton (full load)
Length: 163m/535ft (bp); 173.6m/570ft (oa)
Beam: 16.6m/54ft 6in
Draught: 5m/16ft 6in (normal)
Armament: 7 x 152mm/6in guns (7x1), 2 x 102mm/4in HA and 2 x 2pdr pompom guns; 12 x 533mm/21in torpedo tubes (4x3)
Machinery: Geared steam turbines, 8 boilers, 4 shafts
Power: 59,656kW/80,000shp for 33 knots
Endurance: 757 tonnes/745 tons (oil) for 14,816km/8,000nm at 15 knots
Protection: 38–76mm/1.5–3in (belt); 50mm/1in (partial protective deck)
Complement: 560

LEFT: **Because of their size and range, the two E-class were much employed between the wars in the Indian Ocean and the Far East. *Enterprise* is seen here in those stations' usual colour scheme of white hull and buff funnels. The knuckle became a feature of British cruiser design.**

LEFT: **Apparently attending a 1930s Kiel Navy Week (note the German K-class cruisers), the *Frobisher* is in a festive mood. All her boats are swung out but not lowered, her liberty men going ashore in a German naval launch. Note how the anchor is catted prior to securing to the buoy.** ABOVE: ***Frobisher* is seen here with early World War II modifications. She now mounts only five main-calibre weapons but has gained high-angle armament and modern directors. Note the light tripod mainmast, radar outfit and disruptive paint scheme.**

Hawkins class

Construction of true "cruisers", built to operate independently, effectively halted in the Royal Navy when the first battlecruiser ran trials in 1908, making obsolete the current line of large cruiser development. From 1907, however, the burgeoning German Navy had been building an evolving line of "Town"-class cruisers which could, and would, be pre-positioned on distant stations in order to operate against commerce in war. Intelligence suggested that these ships would be complemented by larger cruisers with improved all-round capability, including larger-calibre guns. From 1912, therefore, the Admiralty conducted studies for a range of counters with varying combinations of size, speed, armament – and cost. Gun calibre had to be balanced against rate of fire and the 191mm/7.5in gun – used until 1908 for armoured cruisers – emerged favourite.

As the rumoured German ships turned out to be just that, the British "reply"

never materialized. With war in 1914, however, the cruiser problem proved very real. The first wave of commerce-raiding German cruisers was dealt with comparatively quickly, but the Admiralty was sufficiently concerned in 1915 about a resumption to re-examine the studies.

The Board's required combination of qualities demanded a displacement approaching 10,160 tonnes/10,000 tons, with a price tag that saw just four ordered, with a fifth some months later. Known officially as "Improved Birminghams" (a title so tenuously true as to suggest deliberate obfuscation to conceal their true function), the Hawkins class carried seven 191mm/7.5 guns, five on the centreline, two sided in the waist. Different in concept to smaller "fleet" cruisers, they carried only six torpedo tubes, two fixed, and four trainable. For extended endurance, cruising turbines were fitted, while four of the twelve boilers were coal-fired. As the reported enemy threat again failed

to materialize, most of the class were completed post-war. The fifth ship, *Cavendish*, was renamed *Vindictive* and completed as an aircraft carrier.

Hawkins class

	Built	Commissioned
Cavendish	Harland & Wolff, Belfast	September 21, 1918
Effingham	Portsmouth Dockyard	July 10, 1925
Frobisher	Devonport Dockyard	September 20, 1924
Hawkins	Chatham Dockyard	July 23, 1919
Raleigh	Beardmore, Glasgow	February 17, 1920

Hawkins class (as designed)

Displacement: 10,465 tonnes/10,300 tons (normal); 12,575 tonnes/12,350 tons (full load)
Length: 172.1m/565ft (bp); 184.3m/605ft
Beam: 17.7m/58ft
Draught: 5.3m/17ft 3in (normal)
Armament: 7 x 191mm/7.5in (7x1), 10 x 76mm/3in (10x1) and 2 x 2pdr pompom (2x2) guns; 6 x 533mm/21in torpedo tubes (2x2, 2x1)
Machinery: Geared steam turbines, 12 boilers, 4 shafts
Power: 44,742kW/60,000shp for 30 knots
Bunkers: 1,504 tonnes/1,480 tons (oil); 874 tonnes/860 tons (coal)
Protection: 38–76mm/1.5–3in (belt); 25–38mm/1–1.5in (partial protective deck)
Complement: 665

RIGHT: **Seen between the wars in Far East colours, the *Hawkins* shows the typically under-armed appearance of the class. Only the *Effingham* was fully modernized, losing the after funnel with its prominent searchlight towers and gaining an all-152mm/6in armament.**

New York (CA.2) and *Brooklyn* (CA.3)

American big-ship design of the late 19th century exhibited both foreign influence and strong individualism. Authorized in 1888, the armoured cruiser *New York* was required to operate both as a unit of a battle squadron and as a commerce destroyer. Good protection and armament were thus required to be allied to speed and endurance.

On a high-freeboard hull whose forward and after ends showed considerable French influence, six 203mm/8in guns were disposed in a twin, centreline turret forward and aft, and single wing mountings under shields in the waist. To reduce weight, barbettes projected down only one deck, but with smaller-diameter armoured tubes continuing down to the handling spaces.

Unusually, each of the two shafts was driven by two steam reciprocating engines working in tandem. Individual engines could thus be built lower and, therefore, more easily protected. For economic cruising, the leading unit could be disconnected, but a drawback, exposed in action, was that the ship had to be stopped to recouple it.

While only 76mm/3in on the flat, the *New York*'s protective deck slopes were 152mm/6in thick. Above it was a "cellular", or closely subdivided deck. The belt, at only 102mm/4in, was relatively light, but ran full length.

ABOVE: **Best-remembered for wearing Schley's flag at the Battle of Santiago in 1898, the *Brooklyn* (CA.3) showed considerable German influence, not least in the masting and the bow and stern profiles. Clearly visible is the pronounced tumblehome, which enabled the wing turrets to bear axially.**

To free the name for a new battleship, she was renamed *Saratoga* in 1911. As this name, in turn, was required for a new battlecruiser, she was further renamed *Rochester* in 1917, under which name she existed until 1938.

The *Brooklyn*, which followed some four years later from the same yard, took the design further. A better-protected and most imposing vessel, with commanding freeboard and height of funnels, she showed increasing German influence, including tubular "battlemasts". A forecastle was added to further improve seakeeping, and the 203mm/8in gun wing mountings were twinned. To improve their potential for axial fire they were located, French-style, on armoured sponsons projecting from hull sides with pronounced tumblehome.

New York (CA.2) and Brooklyn (CA.3)

	Built	Commissioned
Brooklyn (CA.3)	Cramp, Philadelphia	December 1, 1896
New York (CA.2)	Cramp, Philadelphia	August 1, 1893

Brooklyn (as built)

Displacement: 9,363 tonnes/9,215 tons (normal); 10,232 tonnes/10,070 tons (full load)
Length: 122m/400ft 6in (wl); 122.6m/402ft 6in (oa)
Beam: 19.7m/64ft 9in
Draught: 7.3m/24ft (normal)
Armament: 8 x 203mm/8in (4x2); 12 x 127mm/5in (12x1); 5 x 457mm/18in fixed torpedo tubes (5x1)
Machinery: 4 vertical steam reciprocating engines, 7 boilers, 2 shafts
Power: 11,931kW/16,000ihp for 20 knots
Endurance: 914 tonnes/900 tons (coal) for 9,445km/5,100nm at 10 knots
Protection: 76–203mm/3–8in (belt); 76–152mm/3–6in (protective deck); 156–203mm/6.5–8in (barbettes)
Complement: 560

ABOVE: **Earlier than the *Brooklyn*, the *New York* (CA.2) was slightly smaller but better protected. Because of only a moderate tumblehome, however, she could only accommodate single 203mm/8in guns in the waist, and these in vulnerable open mountings. The larger casemated guns were of 102mm/4in calibre.**

LEFT: *California* (CA.6) of 1904 seen here in Pacific Fleet colours. In terms of protection, as well as the effectiveness of their new-pattern 203mm/8in guns, these heavy cruisers were rated the equivalent of older battleships, hence their "state" names. Note the mix of stockless and close-stowing anchors.

BELOW: Recognizing the impracticalities of aircraft taking-off from warships, the US Navy was a pioneer of shipboard catapults. The *West Virginia* (CA.5), renamed *Huntington* in 1916, was the second to be fitted with a quarterdeck catapult, together with a kite-balloon facility.

Pennsylvania class (CA.4–9)

Victory over Spain in the war of 1898 gave the United States responsibility for significant territorial acquisition in the Caribbean and the western Pacific. Deficient in ships with the necessary endurance, however, the US Navy benefited from congressional approval for naval expansion. This included armoured cruisers, a type then of universal interest, being as large as contemporary battleships but trading armament for speed. Protection, due to Harvey armour, was not significantly sacrificed.

With limited practical experience upon which to draw, the designers of the six Pennsylvanias showed considerable technical boldness. Completed from 1905, they bear comparison with the contemporary British Duke of Edinburghs. Of a similar length, but slightly finer, the Americans displaced about 1,016 tonnes/1,000 tons more. Protection was on a very similar scale but, where the British shipped a primary battery of six 234mm/9.2in guns, the Americans, very satisfied with four 203mm/8in weapons, mounted them in twin turrets on the centerline forward

and aft. Ten 152mm/6in quick-firing (QF) guns, five per side, were located behind armour in a main-deck broadside battery. Four more of the weapons were mounted at the corners of the citadel at upper-deck level.

The prestige attached to these ships is indicated by the "state" names that were bestowed. Although somewhat under-armed, they were looked upon as Second Class battleships, to the extent that most eventually received a battleship-style cage foremast.

During World War I, however, all were renamed with more conventional "city" names. In 1918, the *San Diego* (ex-*California*) betrayed the basic frailty of the design by succumbing to a single mine.

Early in the application of aviation to its battle fleet, the US Navy used the *Huntington* (ex-*West Virginia*) in experiments with seaplane catapults and aerostats. None of the class was ever proved in action and, following some service as auxiliaries, the five survivors were scrapped in 1930–32, by which time they were totally obsolete.

Pennsylvania class (as built)

Displacement: 14,070 tonnes/13,850 tons (normal); 15,576 tonnes/15,330 tons (full load)
Length: 152.9m/502ft (wl); 153.5m/503ft 11in (oa)
Beam: 21.2m/69ft 7in
Draught: 7.3m/24ft (normal)
Armament: 4 x 203mm/8in (2x2), 14 x 152mm/6in (14x1) and 18 x 76mm/3in (18x1) guns; 2 x 457mm/18in fixed torpedo tubes (2x1)
Machinery: 2 vertical, triple-expansion engines, 30 boilers, 2 shafts
Power: 17,150kW/23,000ihp for 22 knots
Bunkers: 914 tonnes/900 tons (coal – normal), 2,032 tonnes/2,000 tons (coal – maximum)
Protection: 89–152mm/3.5–6in (belt); 38–102mm/1.5–4in (protective deck); 38–156mm/1.5–6.5in (turrets)
Complement: 825

Pennsylvania class (CA.4–9)

	Built	Commissioned
California (CA.6) (*San Diego*, 1914)	Union Ironworks, San Francisco	August 1, 1907
Colorado (CA.7) (*Pueblo*, 1916)	Cramp, Philadelphia	January 19, 1905
Maryland (CA.8) (*Frederick*, 1916)	Newport News	April 18, 1905
Pennsylvania (CA.4) (*Pittsburgh*, 1912)	Cramp, Philadelphia	March 9, 1905
South Dakota (CA.9) (*Huron*, 1920)	Union Ironworks, San Francisco	January 27, 1908
West Virginia (CA.5) (*Huntington*, 1916)	Newport News	February 23, 1905

Tennessee class (CA.10–13)

In order to achieve a desired establishment of ten modern armoured cruisers, the US Navy followed the Pennsylvanias with the four similar Tennessees, Concerned at tendencies of growth in successive classes, Congress imposed a 14,733-tonne/14,500-ton displacement limit. However, as they were to be equipped with far-weightier 254mm/10in gun twin turrets in place of the *Pennsylvania*'s 203mm/8in ordnance, and speed was to remain the same, there would have to be compromise. Improved boiler technology helped by allowing 16 boilers in place of the earlier 30. Space could thus be utilized more economically in terms of areas to be protected.

A greater proportion of the available displacement was devoted to armour although, except on casemates and turrets (strictly, gunhouses), it tended to be spread farther and more thinly. Thus, the belt was more extensive, but 25mm/1in was shaved from its maximum thickness. For the protective deck, slopes and flat were also reduced in weight. The upper-deck 76mm/3in battery, previously unprotected, received 51mm/2in armour.

The rule of thumb for capital ships was that the belt should have a thickness equal to the calibre of the main armament, and we see here, in the armoured cruiser, a warship far better able to inflict punishment than to absorb it.

With the 1917 entry of the United States into World War I, all the big cruisers were heavily involved in the escort of Atlantic convoys. For this protracted, generally low-speed duty the ships had not only to fill all available coal bunkers for a capacity of 2,032 tonnes/2,000 tons, but also to carry half as much again as deck cargo. Their consequent increased draught made the secondary 152mm/6in battery unworkable. Most guns were thus removed and their embrasures plated over.

Wrecked during 1916, the hull of the *Memphis* (ex-*Tennessee*) survived until 1937, while the *Seattle* (ex-*Washington*) served as an auxiliary until 1946.

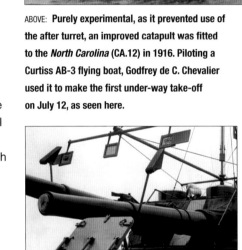

ABOVE: **Purely experimental, as it prevented use of the after turret, an improved catapult was fitted to the *North Carolina* (CA.12) in 1916. Piloting a Curtiss AB-3 flying boat, Godfrey de C. Chevalier used it to make the first under-way take-off on July 12, as seen here.**

ABOVE: **An interesting view of the after 254mm/10in gun turret of the *Washington* (CA.11). Firing is being simulated with an optical aid, rigged temporarily. Three screens are aligned with the sighting hoods, and shielded mirrors are attached to each gun barrel. Note the tompion, or plug, fitted to the gun muzzle.**

ABOVE: **Although superficially similar, the Tennessees could be distinguished from the Pennsylvanias by their much larger 254mm/10in gun turrets and more complex bridge structure. All except the *Maryland* of the Pennsylvania class received battleship-style cage foremasts before World War I.**

Tennessee class (CA.10–13)

	Built	Commissioned
Montana (CA.13) (*Missoula*, 1920)	Newport News	July 21, 1908
North Carolina (CA.12) (*Charlotte*, 1920)	Newport News	May 7, 1908
Tennessee (CA.10) (*Memphis*, 1916)	Cramp, Philadelphia	July 17, 1906
Washington (CA.11) (*Seattle*, 1916)	New York Shipbuilding	August 7, 1906

Tennessee class (as built)

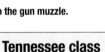

Displacement: 14,733 tonnes/14,500 tons (normal); 16,125 tonnes/15,870 tons (full load)

Length: 152.9m/502ft (wl); 153.7m/504ft 5in (oa)

Beam: 22.2m/72ft 11in

Armament: 4 x 254mm/10in (2x2); 16 x 152mm/6in (16x1); 22 x 76mm/3in (22x1); 4 x 533mm/21in fixed torpedo tubes (4x1)

Machinery: 2 vertical, triple-expansion engines, 16 boilers, 2 shafts

Power: 17,150kW/23,000ihp

Bunkers: 914 tonnes/900 ton (coal – normal); 2,032 tonnes/2,000 tons (maximum)

Protection: 51–127mm/2–5in (belt); 25–89mm/1–3.5in (protective deck); 51–229mm/2–9in (turrets)

Complement: 855

LEFT: **The US Navy's Cruiser 2 was the *Charleston*, whose Elswick design was similar to that of the Japanese *Naniwa*. Designed to carry two 254mm/10in guns, the Americans preferred 203mm/8in ordnance but, due to their lack of availability, initially fitted twin 152mm/6in weapons. The *Charleston* never carried sailing rig.**

Newark and *Charleston* (Cruisers 1 & 2)

Toward the close of the 1880s the US Navy embarked on an expansion program which taxed its resources to such an extent that, to act as the design basis for a group of protected cruisers, plans for the Japanese *Naniwa* were purchased from Armstrong at Elswick.

The *Newark*, which became Cruiser 1 of the so-called New Navy, was a typical late-Victorian warship, whose inefficient machinery needed to be backed up by a full sailing rig to confer any reasonable standard of endurance. Her heavy three-masted rig, the last aboard any American

warship, precluded centerline armament, so all twelve 152mm/6in guns were mounted broadside. Four each side were sited in projecting sponsons to give an element of near-axial fire.

Although the rig was in contravention of the wishes of the General Board, it gave the ship considerable "presence", and she was fitted as a flagship, with extra accommodation below a raised poop deck.

Modernization in 1898 saw the sailing rig removed and all 152mm/6in guns replaced by newer models. Sold out in 1913, she acted as a quarantine hulk until 1926.

Her only sister, *San Francisco* (Cruiser 5), was rearmed with modern 127mm/5in weapons in 1910 and converted for minelaying, serving during World War I and then as an auxiliary through to 1939.

The *Charleston* (Cruiser 2) was a further, but slightly smaller, variation on the design. From the outset she was fitted with two light pole masts with fighting tops. This rig permitted a single 203mm/8in gun to be located on the centerline, forward and aft, with six 152mm/6in guns mounted broadside in sponsons. As the major weapons were delivered late, the ship carried a temporary armament of four further 152mm/6in guns. Her machinery was of an already obsolete compound, or double-expansion design. She was lost by grounding during 1899.

ABOVE: **The last US warship designed with sail, the *Newark*, or Cruiser 1, is seen here prior to 1898, when the rig was reduced. The twelve 152mm/6in guns are all on the broadside, eight of them in distinctive, open-sided sponsons to give a degree of near-axial fire.**

Newark, *San Francisco* and *Charleston* (Cruisers 1, 2 & 5)

	Built	Commissioned
***Newark* (Cruiser 1)**	Cramp, Philadelphia	February 2, 1891
***San Francisco* (Cruiser 5)**	Union Ironworks, San Francisco	November 15, 1890
***Charleston* (Cruiser 2)**	Union Ironworks, San Francisco	December 26, 1889

Newark (as completed)

Displacement: 4,149 tonnes/4,083 tons (normal)
Length: 94.4m/310ft (wl); 99.8m/327ft 7in (oa)
Beam: 15m/49ft 2in
Draught: 5.7m/18ft 9in (normal)
Armament: 12 x 152mm/6in (12x1) guns;
　6 x 356mm/14in torpedo tubes
Machinery: Steam, triple-expansion engines,
　4 boilers, 2 shafts
Power: 6,339kW/8,500ihp for 18 knots
Endurance: 864 tonnes/850 tons (coal) for
　15,371km/8,300nm at 10 knots
Protection: 51–76mm/2–3in (protective deck);
　51mm/2in (casemates)
Complement: 384

Baltimore and *Philadelphia* (Cruisers 3 & 4)

Built in parallel with the three previous cruisers were two others of much the same size and capability. These, too, had their basis in an Elswick design. The 5,029-tonne/4,950-ton Spanish protected cruiser *Reina Regente* was launched in 1887, for which Armstrong had unsuccessfully tendered. However, their proposed design was well-gunned and superior to the *Charleston* in carrying four 240mm/9.5in guns (sided both forward and aft) and six 120mm/4.72in guns in broadside sponsoned casemates. Duly acquired, the design was translated by Cramp into the *Baltimore* (Cruiser 3), with a mix of 203mm/8in and 152mm/6in guns on the same layout.

With several variations of cruiser on virtually the same displacement, it is evident that the General Board was experimenting to find the type best-suited to its needs. Thus, built on the same hull dimensions, the *Philadelphia* (Cruiser 4) had a uniform armament of twelve 152mm/6in guns. Her layout comprised two sided 152mm/6in guns forward and aft, with four broadside guns on each side, of which the farthest forward and farthest aft were prominently sponsoned for the purpose of providing a degree of near-axial chase fire.

The arrangement aboard the *Baltimore* was obviously less than satisfactory for, following her active involvement in the war against Spain, it was modified to that of the *Philadelphia*.

Both ships were obsolete by 1910 but, where the *Philadelphia* embarked on a new career alternating as a receiving ship and prison hulk that lasted until 1927, the *Baltimore* was reprieved to be converted during 1913–14 into a

minelayer, armed with just four 127mm/5in guns. Involvement in laying the 70,263 mines comprising the great Northern mine barrage was followed by long service as an auxiliary until her final disposal in 1942.

TOP: **An enormous freeboard and a forest of ventilators marked the very similar *Baltimore* and *Philadelphia* (Cruisers 3 and 4 respectively). *Baltimore*'s four 203mm/8in guns are sponsoned on forecastle and poop, and the 152mm/6in secondary armament in the waist. Note the very small bridge structure and the token fighting tops.**
LEFT: **A nice sketch of the *Philadelphia* under construction. Note the continuous longitudinals and intercostal transverse members. The fitter is working in what will be the double bottom. The inset shows the vaulted framing that supports the protective deck.** BELOW LEFT: **Her jack struck, the *Philadelphia* is under way, but with hammock covers still airing and the accommodation ladder down. She differed from the *Baltimore* by having a homogeneous 152mm/6in armament. Note the personnel on the open navigating bridge with the armoured conning tower beneath.**

Baltimore and *Philadelphia* (Cruisers 3 & 4)

	Built	Commissioned
Baltimore (Cruiser 3)	Cramp, Philadelphia	January 7, 1890
Philadelphia (Cruiser 4)	Cramp, Philadelphia	July 28, 1890

Baltimore (as built)

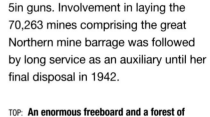

Displacement: 4,470 tonnes/4,400 tons (normal); 4,677 tonnes/4,593 tons (full load)
Length: 99.8m/327ft 6in (wl); 102.1m/335ft (oa)
Beam: 14.8m/48ft 6in
Draught: 5.9m/19ft 6in (normal)
Armament: 4 x 203mm/8in (4x1) and 6 x 152mm/6in (6x1) guns; 5 x 356mm/14in torpedo tubes (5x1)
Power: 8,020kW/10,750ihp for 19 knots
Endurance: 864 tonnes/850 tons (coal) for 13,334km/7,200nm at 10 knots
Protection: 64–102mm/2.5–4in (protective deck); 51mm/2in (casemates)
Complement: 345

Olympia (Cruiser 6)

Approved in 1890, the Second Class protected cruiser *Olympia* was conceived with an eye to commerce raiding, with a consequent high speed and long endurance.

Four 203mm/8in guns were again favoured for their penetrative power, but the weight of two twin armoured "barbette turrets" was significant to the ship's design. A 102mm/4in secondary battery was proposed to compensate for this extra weight but was rejected as being too light. Weapons of 152mm/6in, on the other hand, with projectiles of over three times the weight, were considered to have too low a rate of fire. The 127mm/5in weapon that was adopted as a compromise proved to be so satisfactory that it has remained a standard calibre to

the present day. All ten 127mm/5in guns were located in armoured casemates in a superstructure configured to permit a measure of chase fire.

On a four-hour speed trial, the *Olympia*'s "vertical-inverted, direct-acting, triple-expansion engines" developed a reported 12,593kW/17,363ihp for a speed of 21.69 knots against a service maximum of 20 knots.

The ship gained fame as the flagship of Commodore Dewey in the rout of the Spanish squadron at Manila on May 1, 1898. As with the *Baltimore*, however, the 203mm/8in pieces did not perform as well as expected in action and, in a 1901–03 modernization, the ship landed one turret, together with her four torpedo tubes, of which she had one

ABOVE: **An early picture of *Olympia*, showing her original three fighting tops, the lower ones serving as searchlight platforms. Her two twin 203mm/8in gun turrets were superior to those originally planned and the turret armour was only 76mm/3in thick to reduce weight.**

fixed in both bow and stern and one trainable on either side in the waist.

After this date, *Olympia*'s main employment was in sea training for midshipmen. By World War I, her value was limited, but she received a uniform armament of ten 127mm/5in guns. Her early fame saw her retained long after her useful life had expired and, after long years as a static auxiliary, she was sold out in 1957 to be restored to her original appearance as a museum ship.

ABOVE: **Honoured for her role as flagship at the 1898 Battle of Manila, the *Olympia* (Cruiser 6) survives in perpetuity as a museum ship. Unusually, side decks run the length of the central superstructure, which houses the 127mm/5in secondary armament. Two of her fighting tops have been removed.**

Olympia (as built)

Built: Union Ironworks, San Francisco
Commissioned: February 5, 1895
Displacement: 5,588 tonnes/5,500 tons (normal); 6,005 tonnes/5,910 tons (full load)
Length: 103.3m/339ft (wl); 104.8m/344ft 1in (oa)
Beam: 16.2m/53ft
Draught: 6.6m/21ft 6in (normal)
Armament: 4 x 203mm/8in (2x2) and 10 x 127mm/5in (10x1) guns; 4 x 457mm/18in torpedo tubes
Machinery: Steam, triple-expansion engines, 4 boilers, 2 shafts
Power: 10,070kW/13,500ihp for 20 knots
Endurance: 1,168 tonnes/1,150 tons (coal) for 25,000km/13,500nm at 10 knots
Protection: 51–121mm/2–4.75in (protective deck); 89–114mm/3.5–4.5in (turrets)
Complement: 420

Cincinnati class (Cruisers 7 & 8)

Described as "scout cruisers", the two Cincinnatis, completed in 1894, were contemporary with the British Apollo-class equivalents. Their superstructure, minimized to reduce profile, comprised little more than a two-level bridge, a single pole mast and two lofty funnels. Mainmasts, stump and full-height, were added later to spread W/T aerials.

One 152mm/6in gun was carried on the foredeck, while ten 127mm/5in weapons were disposed, four each side in casemates and two sided on the quarterdeck. At main deck level, the casemated pieces could have been of little use with any sea running. Two were later removed and the forward gun replaced by a further 127mm/5in.

Four torpedo tubes (one visible in the stem above the waterline) were included, although fitting of all appears doubtful. They launched the Howell torpedo, being adopted as the US Navy's standard. Engine-less and trackless, the weapon derived its propulsive energy from a heavy flywheel, run up to high speed before launch. The gyroscopic action of the flywheel maintained trim, while a heavy pendulum detected course changes and corrected them through a rod attachment with the rudders. The Howell torpedo reportedly carried a 43.5kg/96lb warhead some 365.8m/400yds at 25 knots.

As scouts, the ships' modest speed was against them, but they spent busy lives, spanning two maritime wars. In that against Spain, the *Raleigh* was present at the Manila action, while her sister participated in the blockade of Cuba. Typical of cruisers of their time, they were involved in policing operations, quelling unrest in Haiti, Nicaragua, Guatemala, San Domingo (now the Dominican Republic) and Panama. *Cincinnati* assisted in the aftermath of two natural disasters – the 1903 Mont Pelée eruption in Martinique and the 1917 San José earthquake in Guatemala. Employed in second-line operations during World War I, both were sold for scrapping in 1921.

ABOVE LEFT: **Although only capable of a moderate 19 knots, the *Cincinnati* and the *Raleigh* (seen here) were built as scout cruisers. A single 152mm/6in gun is located on the foredeck, with eight of her ten 127mm/5in guns in casemates. Freeboard is good for a ship of her size.** ABOVE: **On April 27, 1898, in the course of the blockade of Cuba, the *Cincinnati* and *New York* exchanged fire with the shore batteries covering the port of Matanzas. Note how upper-deck gun crews are completely unprotected from blast and fragments.**

Cincinnati class (Cruisers 7 & 8)

	Built	Commissioned
Cincinnati (Cruiser 7)	Brooklyn Navy Yard	June 16, 1894
Raleigh (Cruiser 8)	Norfolk Navy Yard	April 17, 1894

Cincinnati class (Cruisers 7 & 8)

Displacement: 3,373 tonnes/3,320 tons (normal); 3,698 tonnes/3,640 tons (full load)
Length: 91.4m/300ft (wl); 93.3m/306ft 2in (oa)
Beam: 12.8m/42ft
Draught: 5.5m/18ft (normal)
Armament: 1 x 152mm/6in and 10 x 127mm/5in (10x1) guns; 4 x 356mm/14in torpedo tubes
Machinery: Steam, triple-expansion engines, 2 shafts
Power: 7,460kW/10,000ihp for 19 knots
Endurance: 565 tonnes/556 tons (coal) for 16,020km/8,650nm at 10 knots
Protection: 12.7–51mm/0.5–2in (protective deck)
Complement: 310

ABOVE: **With her very lofty funnels, *Cincinnati* (Cruiser 7) appears newly completed. Two, more solid, masts were quickly added shortly thereafter. In 1918 the mainmast was reduced to a stub sufficient to support the W/T aerials. By then, the bow torpedo tube had also been removed.**

LEFT: **With her two relatively short funnels, symmetrically disposed masts and line of boats, the *Minneapolis* (Cruiser 13) could pass muster at a distance or in poor visibility as a passenger liner, a considerable advantage if operating as a commerce raider. She never served as such.**

Columbia class (Cruisers 12 & 13)

Civil war experience of blockade running and commerce-raiding made a lasting impression on American naval thought, reflected in the building of the two Columbias. These were to be fast enough to catch the fastest of transatlantic passenger liners while being fitted with bunkers sufficient for protracted operations.

At a time when American cruisers were powered for, at most, 20 knots, these were designed for 22.5 knots although only officially for 21. Hydrodynamic laws being what they are, this apparently modest increase in speed demanded an enormous increase in power. Inevitably, this solution lay in a long hull of which

much (in this case, 53 per cent of waterline length) was devoted to boilers and machinery.

The required 15,658kW/21,000ihp was, for the first time, transmitted via three shafts, apparently due to limitations in shaft, rather than propeller manufacture. The three vertical reciprocating engines occupied separate spaces, those driving the wing shafts being side by side, divided by a longitudinal bulkhead, and ahead of the centerline unit. For extended endurance, or maintenance, one or other unit could be shut down.

The height of these "cathedral" engines was such that they projected

through the protective deck, their tops requiring protection by an armoured glacis. An odd feature of the design was that it was intended to utilize three funnels, but *Columbia* had four and *Minneapolis* two.

The nameship made 22.8 knots on trials in 1894 (but the Cunard Line *Lucania*, in the same year, made an Atlantic crossing at an average 22 knots).

As built, the armament included two 152mm/6in chase guns on the foredeck and one 203mm/8in gun on the afterdeck to deter pursuers. This was later exchanged for two further 152mm/6in weapons.

The Columbias probably influenced the decision to build the two British Powerfuls and the French *Chateurenault*, respectively launched and laid down in 1895.

LEFT: **Designed as a commerce destroyer, *Columbia* (Cruiser 12) was unusual in having a single 203mm/8in gun on her afterdeck to deter pursuit. Two 152mm/6in guns on the foredeck were sufficient to tackle her intended quarry. Note the very tall masts for long-range W/T reception.**

Columbia class (as built)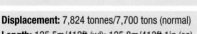

Displacement: 7,824 tonnes/7,700 tons (normal)
Length: 125.5m/412ft (wl); 125.8m/413ft 1in (oa)
Beam: 17.7m/58ft 2in
Draught: 6.9m/22ft 6in (normal)
Armament: 1 x 203mm/8in, 2 x 152mm/6in (2x1), and 8 x 102mm/4in (8x1) guns; 4 x 356mm/14in torpedo tubes (4x1)
Machinery: 3 steam, triple-expansion engines, 10 boilers, 3 shafts
Power: 15,658kW/21,000ihp for 22.5 knots
Endurance: 2,164 tonnes/2,130 tons (coal) for 47,226km/25,500nm at 10 knots
Protection: 38–64mm/1.5–2.5in (protective deck)
Complement: 465

Columbia class (Cruisers 12 & 13)

	Built	Commissioned
Columbia (Cruiser 12)	Cramp, Philadelphia	April 23, 1894
Minneapolis (Cruiser 13)	Cramp, Philadelphia	December 13, 1894

Denver class (Cruisers 14–19)

The six Denvers resulted directly from the war against Spain, in which American success brought territorial commitments as far apart as the western Pacific and the Caribbean. Combat experience exposed the shortage of modern fighting ships, resulting in programmes for large armoured vessels, but the need to police the acquired territories required small cruisers of a type new to the US Navy.

"Cruising vessels" in the classic sense, the Denvers had no real equivalent in the British Royal Navy, although the concept was close to that of the masted-cruisers of a decade earlier still to be found on distant stations. Better described by their later categorization of "gunboats", the Denvers were usually termed "peace cruisers", an accurate description.

Never designed to fight a serious action with other ships, they were unarmoured except for a "protective deck" amidships, that had 64mm/2.5in plate only on the slopes. They were, nonetheless, well-armed, completing

with ten 127mm/5in guns. Eight of these were casemated at main deck level, with only six bearing on the broadside. None was fitted with a shield.

Where a corvette-style hull – with forecastle, poop and an open waist – might have been expected, the Denvers were flush-decked. This gave not only more spacious accommodation, necessary for duties in tropical waters, but also provided emergency troop quarters, utilized when a cruiser was summoned to quell local unrest.

They were powered for only 16.5 knots, their twin shafts giving some redundancy in the event of damage being incurred in isolated regions. Their counter sterns and lofty, but greatly

ABOVE: **Usually described as "peace cruisers", the Denvers were later in their careers reclassified "gunboats". The *Cleveland* (Cruiser 19), (later CL.21) is seen here with her original ten 127mm/5in guns. After World War I, the forward two casemates were plated-in and two of their guns relocated to the upper deck.** LEFT: **Despite her small size, *Des Moines* (Cruiser 15) served in theatres as diverse as Canada, the Caribbean, North Russia, the Mediterranean and West Africa.**

raked, funnels and masts – to say nothing of their tropical paint scheme – gave them a rather yacht-like air.

Their armament was later reduced to eight 127mm/5in guns and one 76mm/3in HA weapon. These small vessels proved to be very useful and they subsequently lasted (except for the wrecked *Tacoma*) until the 1930s.

Denver class (as built)

Displacement: 3,251 tonnes/3,200 tons (normal); 3,810 tonnes/3,750 tons (full load)
Length: 89m/292ft (wl); 94.1m/308ft 10in (oa)
Beam: 13.4m/44ft
Draught: 4.8m/15ft 9in (normal)
Armament: 10 x 127mm/5in (10x1) guns
Machinery: 2 steam, triple-expansion engines, 6 boilers, 2 shafts
Power: 3,730kW/5,000ihp for 16.5 knots
Endurance: 738 tonnes/725 tons (coal) for 4,075km/2,200nm at 10 knots
Protection: 64mm/2.5in (slopes in way of machinery spaces)
Complement: 330

Denver class (Cruisers 14–19)

	Built	Commissioned
Chattanooga (Cruiser 16)	Crescent Shipyard, Elizabethport, NJ	October 11, 1904
Cleveland (Cruiser 19)	Bath Iron Works, Maine	November 2, 1903
Denver (Cruiser 14)	Neafie and Levy, Philadelphia	May 17, 1904
Des Moines (Cruiser 15)	Fore River, Quincy, Massachusetts	March 5, 1904
Galveston (Cruiser 17)	Trigg, Richmond, Virginia	February 15, 1905
Tacoma (Cruiser 18)	Union Ironworks, San Francisco	January 30, 1904

LEFT: **A pristine *Charleston* (Cruiser 22) enters dry dock at Bremerton Navy Yard, Washington State. A general air of cheerful anticipation indicates that this is a homecoming. Note how the ship is being warped into the dock, the lines maintaining her alignment as she is hauled in by winch.** ABOVE: **In assisting the salvage of a submarine, stranded at Eureka, California, the *Milwaukee* (Cruiser 21) herself went ashore. Seen here in January 1917, she proved impossible to refloat and became a total loss. She still wears her ensign and grey, wartime livery.**

St. Louis class (Cruisers 20–22)

Authorized as 8,128-tonne/8,000-ton diminutives of the then-building Pennsylvania/Tennessee classes, the St. Louis trio only succeeded in attracting criticism as being "poor relations". Preliminary studies soon showed that the considerable size limitation would limit speed if armament and protection were to be provided to the expected standard. This would place the ships at a disadvantage compared with some foreign cruisers, and with the large armed-liners expected to be used as commerce raiders.

The first sacrifice had to be the deletion of any 203mm/8in guns in favour of an all-152mm/6in armament. A waterline belt was deemed indispensable in addition to a protective deck but, in order to confer adequate endurance, large bunkers were required, further increasing the deep displacement.

Obliged to compromise, Congress grudgingly accepted the need to increase designed displacement to 9,856 tonnes/9,700 tons. For their part, the Navy had to agree a slightly disappointing 22-knot speed and protection reduced to the point where

ABOVE: **Although having imposing looks, the three St. Louis-class ships were criticized for their light 152mm/6in armament. They were classed as "semi-armoured cruisers", yet later took "CA" (heavy cruiser) identifiers. The *St. Louis* (Cruiser 20), seen here, became CA.18.**

the resulting ships were described as "semi-armoured".

The 102mm/4in belt was both shallow and short, the same plate thickness also covering the eight 152mm/6in guns of the casemated main deck battery. The four weapons mounted in the superstructure at upper deck level were also protected by 102mm/4in face plates. A single unshielded centerline 152mm/6in gun was mounted both forward and aft. The lack of turrets in these positions provided a useful means of differentiating the ships from the larger armoured cruisers which, superficially, looked very similar. The protective deck

was pared down to 51mm/2in in the flat and 76mm/3in on the slopes.

The *Milwaukee* was lost by stranding in 1917 but her sisters, renumbered CA.18 (*St. Louis*) and CA.19 (*Charleston*) served until the 1930 cull of obsolete cruisers, with the entry into service of the "treaty cruisers".

St. Louis class (Cruisers 20–22)

	Built	Commissioned
Charleston (Cruiser 22)	Newport News, Virginia	October 17, 1905
Milwaukee (Cruiser 21)	Union Ironworks, San Francisco	December 10, 1906
St. Louis (Cruiser 20)	Neafie & Levy, Philadelphia	August 18, 1906

St. Louis class (as built)

Displacement: 9,856 tonnes/9,700 tons (normal); 11,136 tonnes/10,960 tons (full load)
Length: 129.2m/424ft (wl); 129.9m/426ft 6in (oa)
Beam: 20.1m/66ft
Draught: 6.9m/22ft 6in (normal)
Armament: 14 x 152mm/6in (14x1) and 18 x 76mm/3in (18x1) guns
Machinery: 2 steam, triple-expansion engines, 16 boilers, 2 shafts
Power: 15,660kW/21,000ihp for 22 knots
Bunkers: 1,524 tonnes/1,500 tons (coal)
Protection: 203mm/4in (partial belt); 51–76mm/ 2–3in (protective deck)
Complement: 565

Montgomery class (Cruisers 9–11)

As one of the varied "ABCD Squadron" the *Dolphin* had been designed to operate against commerce but, too small to qualify as a true cruiser, she spent her life as a "peace cruiser", or gunboat.

The concept of *guerre de course* (war against commerce) remained attractive, not least through continuing French enthusiasm for it, and it was now proposed that the US Navy build three simple and inexpensive 2,000-tonne/ 1,968-ton vessels for this purpose. Congress required small hulls, in order to minimize initial cost, but proposed to use the latest technology to realize a speed of 18 knots. The two are not easily compatible, as a longer hull is more easily driven, and will reduce operational fuel costs as well as being a better sea-boat. As no builder would commit himself to an 18-knot contract speed, the requirement was reduced to 17 knots with a bonus for any improvement on this, the *Montgomery* exceeding 19 knots.

The design was very tight; plate thicknesses were defined to sixteenths of an inch (1.6mm), yet the light displacement still grew by about 10 per cent. There was no weight margin for protection, reliance being placed totally on the stopping power of coal bunkers flanking the machinery spaces. Two masts were stepped; neither was crossed but they were capable of spreading a full sail plan in order to increase cruising endurance. Nevertheless, the ships were generally regarded as gunboats.

Their designed armament – a single 152mm/6in gun forward and aft, together with eight casemated broadside 127mm/5in guns and six Howell torpedo tubes – proved to be over-ambitious, the ships being very tender. Armament was thus reduced to nine or ten 127mm/5in and only two torpedo tubes.

Obsolete, the *Detroit* was sold out in 1911. Her sisters served throughout

World War I, although *Marblehead* was renamed *Anniston* in 1918 to release the name for the new CL.12 scout cruiser.

Montgomery class (Cruisers 9–11)

	Built	Commissioned
Detroit (Cruiser 10)	Columbian Iron Works, Baltimore	July 20, 1894
Marblehead (Cruiser 11)	City Point Iron Works, Boston	April 2, 1894
Montgomery (Cruiser 9)	Columbian Iron Works, Baltimore	June 21, 1894

Montgomery class (as designed)

Displacement: 2,235 tonnes/2,200 tons (normal); 2,449 tonnes/2,410 tons (full load)
Length: 78.3m/257ft (wl); 82.1m/269ft 6in (oa)
Beam: 11.3m/37ft
Draight: 4.4m/14ft 6in (normal)
Armament: 2 x 152mm/6in (2x1) and 8 x 127mm/5in (8x1); 6 x 356mm/14in torpedo tubes (6x1)
Machinery: 2 steam triple-expansion engines, 2 shafts
Power: 4,030kW/5,400ihp for 18 knots
Endurance: 5,926km/3,200nm at 10 knots
Protection: None
Complement: 275

LEFT: **Before the advent of air reconnaissance, scout cruisers were an essential means of determining enemy disposition. This view of** *Chester*, **which took the designator CL.1, first of the new "light cruiser" sequence, clearly shows her high freeboard and small silhouette.**

Chester class (CL.1–3)

Completed in 1908, the three Chester-class scout cruisers trialled the new technologies of steam turbine propulsion and radio. They were authorized in 1904, when four pairs of experimental British scouts were fitting out. While recognizing the latter's potential, the Americans thought them too small for ocean work (they were designed primarily for North Sea operations). Their own ships were, therefore, given 16 per cent greater waterline length at a cost of 25 per cent greater displacement. The British design improved seaworthiness by using a raised forecastle and poop, linked by

a lower, open waist, whereas the US approach featured a short forecastle of exceptionally high freeboard. Profile was minimized with four fairly short funnels and very little superstructure. Two very lofty masts spread the aerials for the essential radio communication. The overall appearance made little concession to grace.

The class was used to evaluate the relative merits of steam turbines and reciprocating machinery. *Birmingham* was thus conventionally powered, while *Chester* and *Salem* received Parsons and Curtis turbines, respectively. Against a contract requirement for 24 knots

Birmingham made about 24.3 knots. *Chester* and *Salem* made about 26.5 and 26 knots respectively against an anticipated 25. The General Board, however, held endurance to be of equal value to speed.

Not intended to engage anything larger than a destroyer, the ships had only vertical (i.e. short-range) protection and a projected armament of 76mm/3in guns. These were later upgraded to 127mm/5in when foreign equivalents appeared.

Birmingham's high forecastle was utilized for Eugene Ely's historic first-ever aircraft ascent from a warship's deck in November 1910. *Chester* was renamed *York* in 1928 in order to release the name for a new "treaty cruiser". All three were discarded during 1930.

ABOVE: **An early American steam turbine warship, the** *Salem* **(CL.3) consumed enormous quantities of coal at her full speed of 24 knots. The regular and dirty task of "coaling ship" could be alleviated somewhat by mechanized facilities such as this one at Newport, Rhode Island.**

Chester class (CL.1–3)

	Built	Commissioned
Birmingham (CL.2)	Fore River, Quincy, Massachusetts	April 11, 1908
Chester (CL.1)	Bath Iron Works, Maine	April 25, 1908
Salem (CL.3)	Fore River, Quincy, Massachusetts	August 1, 1908

Chester (as built)

Displacement: 3,897 tonnes/3,835 tons (normal); 5,004 tonnes/4,925 tons (full load)
Length: 128m/420ft (wl); 128.9m/423ft 3in (oa)
Beam: 14.3m/47ft 1in
Draught: 5.1m/16ft 9in (normal)
Armament: 2 x 127mm/5in (2x1) and 6 x 76mm/3in (6x1) guns; 2 x 533mm/21in torpedo tubes (2x1)
Machinery: Direct-drive steam turbines, 12 boilers, 4 shafts
Power: 11,931kW/16,000shp for 25 knots
Endurance: 1,271 tonnes/1,250 tons (coal) for about 9,260km/5,000nm at 10 knots
Protection: 51mm/2in (belt in way of machinery spaces)
Complement: 360

LEFT: **Attending what appears to be a British Naval Review (she wears a British courtesy ensign), the *Suma* shows obvious similarities with Elswick-designed cruisers.**
BELOW: **The slightly later *Akashi* shows differences in masting and bow decoration. The dark ribband is carried at sheer strake level, giving the illusion of greater freeboard.**

Suma class

Delivered shortly before the Sino-Japanese War of 1894–95, the Elswick-built cruiser *Yoshino* created a considerable impression, underlined by the rapid acquisition of the *Esmeralda* (renamed *Izumi*) from the same yard.

The Japanese, keen to develop domestic expertise, and with these Armstrong-designed exemplars soon to be commissioned, produced a generally similar diminutive in the *Suma*. The first all-Japanese product of this type, she mounted a 152mm/6in gun forward and aft, and six 119mm/4.7in guns in slightly sponsoned openings at main deck level. She was given generous freeboard, but her builders were insufficiently vigorous in weight control, and sea trials during 1896 showed her to be tender, with inadequate stability. Modifications were required, and these were incorporated also in her sister, *Akashi*, still a year from launch.

This small modern cruiser force marked the end of piecemeal acquisition and the beginning of a coherent fighting fleet that would gain respect as the Imperial Japanese Navy.

In an era punctuated by unrest, the two ships led useful lives. In the course of the 1900 Boxer Rebellion the *Suma*, as part of a multinational force, landed Japanese marines to assist in the occupation of Tientsin. Both ships participated in the limited Japanese success of the Battle of the Yellow Sea during the Russo-Japanese War of 1904–05. Just four days later the *Akashi* received heavy mine damage at the Battle of Ulsan.

By World War I both ships were obsolete but in response to British requests for assistance in escorting Mediterranean convoys, the *Akashi* operated from Malta during 1917

as leader of two Japanese destroyer flotillas, in accordance with the terms of the Anglo-Japanese Alliance.

Both ships were demilitarized early in the 1920s, the *Suma* being scrapped in 1928 and her sister being expended as a target (ironically to air-dropped torpedoes) in 1930.

Suma class

	Built	Commissioned
Akashi	Yokosuka Navy Yard	March 30, 1899
Suma	Yokosuka Navy Yard	December 2, 1896

Suma class

Displacement: 2,753 tonnes/2,710 tons (normal)
Length: 89.9m/295ft 3in (bp); 93.4m/306ft 8in (wl)
Beam: 12.2m/40ft 1in (*Suma*); 12.7m/41ft 8in (*Akashi*)
Draught: 4.7m/15ft 5in (mean)
Armament: 2 x 152mm/6in (2x1) and 6 x 119mm/4.7in (6x1) guns; 2 x 380mm/15in torpedo tubes (2x1)
Machinery: Vertical, triple-expansion engines, 8 boilers, 2 shafts
Power: 6,263kW/8,400ihp for 20 knots
Endurance: 610 tonnes/600 tons (coal) for 22,224km/12,000nm at 10 knots
Protection: 25mm/1in (protective deck, on flats); 50mm/2in (protective deck, on slopes)
Complement: 295

ABOVE: **Compared with those of the *Suma*, the *Akashi*'s high waist bulwarks give the ship the appearance of a flush deck. In fact, she has a raised forecastle and poop.**

Niitaka and Otowa classes

During the period 1892–99, over which Yokosuka built the two 2,743-tonne/2,700-ton Sumas, three more larger protected cruisers were purchased abroad – the 4,226-tonne/4,160-ton *Takasago* from Elswick and the 4,877-tonne/4,800-ton Kasagis from the United States.

Laid down in Japan in 1901 was the *Tsushima*, first of the two 3,455-tonne/3,400-ton Niitaka class, smaller and better-suited to home yards still acquiring the skills of modern warship construction. Their building span, 1901–04, made them exact contemporaries with the British Topaze class which, except in armament and speed, they closely resembled. The latter were finer-lined and faster, but were built with an all-102mm/4in armament. Japanese ships at this time were less integrated into fleet work and more likely to be engaged in independent operations so, despite their modest displacement, the Niitakas were given six 152mm/6in

guns. All were in open shields, four being located in sponsons to improve axial fire. Ten open 76mm/3in quick-firers were also shipped to deter destroyer attack.

From a distance, the two appeared to be flush-decked, but actually they had a raised forecastle and poop, linked by an open waist with high bulwarks.

The slightly smaller *Otowa,* third of the group, was built within the same timeframe. Her hull was obviously refined for, on a modest increase in power, she was credited with an extra knot of speed. Her armament was completely different, comprising two 152mm/6in, six 119mm/4.7in and four 76mm/3in guns, much in line with the British *Amethyst* as rearmed. Her three funnels were taller, thinner and more widely spaced.

Otowa was wrecked in home waters in July 1917; the *Niitaka*, with great loss of life, on the Kamchatka Peninsula in August 1922. By 1936 the lone *Tsushima* had

ABOVE: **Slightly better protected than *Niitaka* and *Tsushima*, the *Otowa*, shown here, differed in detail, such as having thinner funnels and a repositioned foremast. In appearance and armament disposition, these resembled British Third Class cruisers.**

been reduced to static harbour training, in which role she remained when destroyed in 1944 by air attack at Kure.

Niitaka and Otowa classes

	Built	Commissioned
Niitaka	Yokosuka Navy Yard	January 27, 1904
Tsushima	Kure Navy Yard	February 14, 1904
Otowa	Yokosuka Navy Yard	September 6, 1904

Niitaka class

Displacement: 3,413 tonnes/3,360 tons (normal); 3,780 tonnes/3,720 tons (full load)
Length: 102m/334ft 8in (bp); 103.4m/339ft 3in (wl)
Beam: 13.4m/44ft 1in
Draught: 4.9m/16ft 2in (normal)
Armament: 6 x 152mm/6in (6x1) and 10 x 76mm/3in (10x1) guns
Machinery: Vertical, triple-expansion engines, 16 boilers, 2 shafts
Power: 7,010kW/9,400ihp for 20 knots
Endurance: 610 tonnes/600 tons (coal) for 7,408km/4,000nm at 10 knots
Protection: 38–64mm/1.5–2.5in (protective deck)
Complement: 320

LEFT: **The *Niitaka*, shown here, and the *Tsushima* were sisters.**

LEFT: **Small design differences – a clipper, or "swan" bow profile, and gently raked funnels and masts – greatly enhanced the appearance of the** *Tone.* ABOVE: *Mogami* **and** *Yodo* **were slightly larger, near-sisters of** *Tone. Mogami* **reverted to a more severe aspect, lacking the** *Tone*'s **pleasing symmetry.**

Tone, *Mogami* and *Yodo*

The Anglo-Japanese Alliance of 1902 exposed the growing Japanese Navy to strong British influence, and the typically British gun layout of the *Otowa* was repeated on the *Tone*, launched in 1904, a month after the *Otowa*'s entry into service.

Often described as "yacht-like", the *Tone* demonstrated that the generally austere appearance of warships could be considerably softened without affecting fighting qualities. Nearly 12m/39ft 4in longer than her predecessor, the *Tone* was classified as a Second Class protected cruiser and was given an exaggerated clipper bow and a modified counter stern. These were set off by three nicely proportioned funnels raked at a graceful angle, as were the lofty, light masts, necessary for increasing the range of the low-powered radio of the time.

The *Tone* was the last Japanese cruiser to be powered by reciprocating steam machinery, which proved to be bulky. The ship's increased length was required to accommodate the additional 50 per cent in installed power necessary for an extra two knots. It gave an open waist of length sufficient to mount four 119mm/4.7in guns per side. Two more 119mm/4.7in guns flanked the bridge structure.

Discarded in 1931, the *Tone* was sunk as an aerial target in 1933. This action clearly demonstrated the growing Japanese interest in the possibilities offered by air attack on warships.

Completed in 1908, the *Mogami* and *Yodo* were near-sisters. Very small protected cruisers, they were better rated as dispatch vessels or gunboats. Like the *Tone*, the *Yodo* was fitted with a clipper bow and a full mercantile-style counter stern. She had two widely spaced funnels and standard reciprocating engines. Her running mate *Mogami* was given Parsons-type steam turbines and,

with two extra boilers, carried three funnels. Her appearance was closer to that of a contemporary British scout, with a straight stem and "cruiser" stern.

Mogami was scrapped in 1931, her name passing to a new light cruiser. *Yodo* was converted for survey work and survived World War II.

Tone, *Mogami* and *Yodo*

	Built	Commissioned
Tone	Sasebo Navy Yard	May 15, 1910
Mogami	Mitsubishi, Nagasaki	September 16, 1908
Yodo	Kawasaki, Kobe	April 8, 1908

Tone (as built)

Displacement: 4,165 tonnes/4,100 tons (normal); 4,979 tonnes/4,900 tons (full load)
Length: 109.6m/359ft 10in (bp); 113.7m/373ft 4in (wl)
Beam: 14.3m/46ft 11in
Draught: 5.1m/16ft 9in (normal)
Armament: 2 x 152mm/6in (2x1) and 10 x 119mm/4.7in (10x1) guns; 3 x 457mm/18in torpedo tubes (3x1)
Machinery: Vertical, triple-expansion engines, 16 boilers, 2 shafts
Power: 11,190kW/15,000ihp for 23 knots
Endurance: 345 tonnes/340 tons (coal) and 77 tonnes/76 tons (oil) for 6,667km/3,600nm at 10 knots
Protection: 38–76mm/1.5–3in (protective deck)
Complement: 180

LEFT: **In appearance,** *Yodo* **was a two-funnelled, single-masted repeat of** *Tone.* **Note the very generous freeboard and the unusual, slightly convex flare.**

Asama class

Early in 1896, Armstrong laid down the armoured cruiser *O'Higgins* for Chile. The company was so confident of the design, into which it had put so much work, that it laid down two further, speculative keels. These were reserved by the Japanese, who were seeking six of the type quickly. They incorporated significant alterations at any early stage, and the final products differed considerably. Far more protection was worked into what became the Asamas, increasing displacement by some 1,626 tonnes/1,600 tons and necessitating over 1m/3ft 4in extra beam. The finer-lined Chilean vessel had no less than 30 boilers to generate the 11,931kW/ 16,000ihp required for 21 knots. These resulted in three very imposing funnels. The Japanese, with fewer boilers of a different type, required only two, but each handsomely exceeded the contract speed, bettering 23 knots on trials.

An unusual feature for the period was the housing of the four 203mm/8in guns in twin turrets (more correctly, gunhouses), one forward, one aft.

Fourteen 152mm/6in weapons were fitted, four in open shields in the waist, the remainder in casemates. Six casemates were located at main deck level, too low to be of much practical use.

The ships were completed in the old livery of the Imperial Japanese Navy – black hull, white upperworks, black funnels with white identification bands. A somewhat forbidding scheme, it was abandoned for all-grey paintwork in 1903, soon after the Royal Navy changed from its handsome Victorian livery.

Both ships had long lives and saw considerable action. During the Russo-Japanese War, *Asama* served at Chemulpo and the Yellow Sea, and *Tokiwa* at Port Arthur and Ulsan. Both were extensively damaged at Tsushima. During World War I, by contrast, both saw much activity but no action. With the general disarmament of the 1920s, they were downgraded to coastal defence and training, but *Tokiwa*, converted for minelaying, served actively during World War II. Both survived but were scrapped during 1947.

ABOVE LEFT: **A veteran of Tsushima, the *Asama* is pictured in an early aerial view. She is in grey livery, with her original armament and probably wears the flag of a rear admiral. Note how the light emphasizes the tumblehome amidships.**
ABOVE: **An impressive early view of *Tokiwa*, laying to anchor and dressed overall. The bulge in the stem accommodates the outboard end of a capped torpedo tube. While still serving as a training ship, *Tokiwa*, with other venerable Japanese warships, was sunk in shallow water by American aircraft in August 1945, and was scrapped in 1947.**

Asama class

	Built	Commissioned
Asama	Armstrong Whitworth, Elswick	February 8, 1899
Tokiwa	Armstrong Whitworth, Elswick	April 18, 1899

Asama (as built)

Displacement: 9,825 tonnes/9,670 tons (normal); 10,668 tonnes/10,500 tons (full load)
Length: 124.3m/408ft (bp); 134.7m/442ft (oa)
Beam: 20.4m/67ft
Draught: 7.5m/24ft 6in
Armament: 4 x 203mm/8in (2x2) and 14 x 152mm/6in (14x1) guns; 5 x 457mm/18in torpedo tubes (5x1)
Machinery: Vertical, triple-expansion engines, 12 boilers, 2 shafts
Power: 13,423kW/18,000ihp for 22 knots
Endurance: 1,422 tonnes/1,400 tons (coal) for 18,520km/10,000nm at 10 knots
Protection: 89–178mm/3.5–7in (belt); 51mm/2in (protective deck); 152mm/6in (turrets)
Complement: 700

LEFT: **Seen in an early paint scheme, the *Asama* still has her heavy fighting tops and anti-torpedo nets. Despite her battleship-like appearance, the turreted guns were only of 203mm/8in calibre with 152mm/6in ordnance in the casemates and waist. She was badly damaged on two occasions by stranding.**

LEFT: **Seen later in her career, *Iwate* has had her anti-torpedo nets removed and has only small fire-control platforms on her masts. Her secondary armament has also been reduced.** BELOW: **In obsolescence, the *Iwate* made 16 overseas cruises as a cadet training ship. Although reboilered, she retained coal firing.**

Idzumo class

The Japanese requirement for six new armoured cruisers resulted in Armstrong receiving a repeat *Asama* order. Armoured cruisers at this time had so inflated a reputation that they were held to be worthy of laying in a line of battle. The advisability of doing this depended much upon the quality of the opposition, the Japanese getting away with it against the Russians.

Not surprisingly, the new ships (*Idzumo* is sometimes rendered *Izumo*) followed the *Asama* design closely, the major difference being in the latter's dated cylindrical boilers being supplanted by Bellevilles. These large water-tube units had seen early problems but had been used successfully by Armstrong in the Chilean *O'Higgins*. More efficient, but individually of lower output, 24 Bellevilles were required. Less

demanding of space, however, they enabled the Idzumos to be marginally shorter than the Asamas despite a necessary reversion to the three-funnelled *O'Higgins* arrangement.

As the new boiler outfit was also considerably lighter, a greater proportion of the ships' displacement could be devoted to protection, a weight redistribution which, in turn, led to an extra 0.5m/1ft 6in in beam. The designed displacement was the same, as was the armament, except for the deletion of the torpedo tube let into the ship's stems (in the Asamas this fitting had attracted its own 152mm/6in armour cladding).

Both ships received extensive damage at the Battle of Ulsan (1904) and again at Tsushima (1905) but proved well able to absorb it. Following a relatively uneventful World War I (although *Iwate*

assisted in the capture of the German enclave and naval base of Tsingtao) both were downgraded to coastal defence ships. During the 1930s they were reboilered for reduced power, their armament also being greatly reduced. Used for training during World War II, they were sunk at Kure in shallow water in 1945.

LEFT: **This impression of the *Idzumo* (often rendered *Izumo*), shows the ship with fighting tops and full armament. During the early 1920s, all the Japanese armoured cruisers landed their lower casemated 152mm/6in guns.**

Idzumo class

	Built	Commissioned
Idzumo	Armstrong Whitworth, Elswick	September 6, 1900
Iwate	Armstrong Whitworth, Elswick	February 22, 1901

Idzumo (as built)

Displacement: 9,906 tonnes/9,750 tons (normal); 10,435 tonnes/10,270 tons (full load)
Length: 121.9m/400ft (bp); 132.5m/434ft 10in (oa)
Beam: 20.9m/68ft 6in
Draught: 7.3m/24ft (normal)
Armament: 4 x 203mm/8in (2x2), 14 x 152mm/6in (14x1) and 12 x 76mm/3in (12x1) guns; 4 x 457mm/18in torpedo tubes (4x1)
Machinery: Vertical, triple-expansion engines, 24 boilers, 2 shafts
Power: 10,817kW/14,500ihp for 20.75 knots
Endurance: 1,575 tonnes/1,550 tons (coal) for 12,964km/7,000nm at 10knots
Protection: 76–178mm/3–7in (belt); 64mm/2.5in (protective deck); 152mm/6in (turrets)
Complement: 680

ABOVE LEFT: **Seen at about the beginning of World War I, the *Yakumo* has gained masthead fire-control platforms, but retains her anti-torpedo nets.**
ABOVE: **Aerial views of earlier ships are unusual, but valuable in giving a clear view of the mass of topside detail then common. Note the great height of the light W/T topmast extensions.**

Yakumo and *Azuma*

The final pair of armoured cruisers acquired by Japan following the war with China is interesting in that one each was built in France and Germany, affording a useful comparison with their Elswick running mates.

With identical armament specifications, both ships, like the Elswicks, carried four 203mm/8in guns in twin centerline turrets. There were two fewer 152mm/6in weapons, but eight of them were located at upper deck level (four casemated and four in open shields) and only four in casemates on the main deck, where they were of limited use.

As with the second pair of Elswick vessels, both were specified with 24 Belleville boilers. In the German-built *Yakumo*, these were grouped in adjacent spaces, resulting in three symmetrically spaced funnels. The French-built *Azuma*, in contrast, enhanced survivability by separating boiler rooms with a machinery

space. This necessitated a hull some 5.5m/18ft greater in length and unevenly spaced funnels.

Both thickness of protection and endurance were also to be the same and, as displacement was not fixed, national characteristics asserted themselves. The German was the shorter, beamier and slower, reflecting the requirement for shallower-draught designs, and the philosophy that a capacity for absorbing hard knocks rated as a higher priority than providing an extra knot of speed.

The careers of each paralleled those of the four Elswick boats. Extensively and effectively employed during the Russo-Japanese War, they spent most of World War I uneventfully in the Pacific. Both were re-rated for coastal defence during the 1920s but, where the *Yakumo* was reboilered for lower power and partial oil-firing, the *Azuma* was not,

being reduced to harbour service in 1941. Rearmed virtually as an anti-aircraft cruiser, the *Yakumo* survived hostilities to be used post-war to repatriate Japanese garrisons. She, and the bomb-damaged *Azuma,* were both scrapped during 1946.

Yakumo and *Azuma*

	Built	Commissioned
Azuma	Soc. Des Ch. De la Loire, St. Nazaire	July 17, 1900
Yakumo	AG Vulcan, Stettin	June 7, 1900

Yakumo (as built)

Displacement: 9,891 tonnes/9,735 tons (normal); 10,455 tonnes/10,290 tons (full load)
Length: 124.6m/408ft 11in (bp); 132.2m/434ft (oa)
Beam: 19.5m/64ft
Draught: 7.2m/23ft 8in (normal)
Armament: 4 x 203mm/8in (2x2), 12 x 152mm/6in (12x1) and 12 x 76mm/3in (12x1) guns; 5 x 457mm/18in torpedo tubes (5x1)
Machinery: Vertical, triple-expansion engines, 24 boilers, 2 shafts
Power: 11,560kW/15,500ihp for 20 knots
Endurance: 1,320 tonnes/1,300 tons (coal) for 12,964km/7,000nm at 10 knots
Protection: 89–178mm/3.5–7in (belt), 64mm/2.5in (protective deck); 152mm/6in (turrets)
Complement: 725

ABOVE: **Although constructed to the same specification, the German-built *Yakumo* (above) and the French-built *Azuma* show clear external differences due to preferences in national style.**

Kasuga class

Having used armoured cruisers to good effect against the Chinese, the Japanese acquired more as friction built up, shortly afterward, with Russia. Already having built in Britain, France and Germany, they now looked to Italy,

Beginning in 1894 the Italian Navy had sought to build a new type, designed to suit its requirements. Purchasers, however, were readily available, the first four hulls going to Argentina, the fifth to Spain. The Italians then built three to their own account before Argentina ordered two more. These were laid down in 1902 as the *Mitra* and *Roca* but launched as *Rivadavia* and *Moreno* respectively. At this stage, ownership passed to the Japanese, the ships completing as *Kasuga* and *Nisshin*.

Italian fashion in major warships was to have two groups of boiler rooms separated by the machinery space. This resulted in two funnels with exceptionally wide spacing, and with minimal superstructure set around them. Dead amidships rose a single powerful mast, creating a symmetrical, double-ended effect from which it was difficult to estimate the ship's heading.

The somewhat ad hoc nature of the acquisition was reflected in the *Kasuga* being built with a single 254mm/10in gun turret forward and a twin 203mm/ 8in gun turret aft, her sister having two twin 203mm/8in mountings. Both had fourteen 152mm/6in guns, of which ten were casemated at main deck level. Of limited use, these were later landed.

Delivered early in 1904, both ships were able to play significant roles against the Russian fleet at both the Yellow Sea and Tsushima. Both ships received 12 more modern boilers in 1914 and, following World War I, had their

152mm/6in secondary batteries replaced by more advanced weapons. By the 1930s both had been reduced to training duties and, in 1936, *Nisshin* was expended as a target. *Kasuga* was scrapped following World War II.

Kasuga class

	Built	Commissioned
Kasuga	Ansaldo, Sestri Ponente	December 20, 1903
Nisshin	Ansaldo, Sestri Ponente	January 17, 1904

Kasuga (as built)

Displacement: 7,783 tonnes/7,660 tons (normal), 8,621 tonnes/8,485 tons (full load)

Length: 104.8m/344ft (bp); 111.5m/366ft (wl)

Beam: 18.7m/61ft 4in

Draught: 7.4m/24ft 3in (normal)

Armament: 1 x 254mm/10in gun, 2 x 203mm/8in (1x2), 14 x 152mm/6in (14x1) and 10 x 76mm/3in (10x1) guns; 4 x 457mm/18in torpedo tubes (4x1)

Machinery: Vertical, triple-expansion engines, 8 boilers, 2 shafts

Power: 11,040kW/14,800ihp for 20 knots

Endurance: 1,209 tonnes/1,190 tons (coal) for 10,186km/5,500nm at 10 knots

Protection: 76–150mm/3–5.9in (belt); 20–35mm/0.8–1.4in (protective deck); 120–150mm/4.5–5.9in (turrets)

Complement: 550

LEFT: **Armoured cruisers such as *Kasuga* were affected by the 1922 Washington Treaty, following which she was partially disarmed to serve out her career as a training ship, being scrapped in 1948.**

Tsukuba and Kurama classes

TOP: **The exceptionally uncluttered appearance of the *Tsukuba* contrives to give an impression of fragility. The housing of the anti-torpedo nets is particularly neat.** ABOVE: **In reality an elegant ship, the *Satsuma* had a broadside weight of about 94 per cent that of the British *Dreadnought*. Lacking the latter's steam turbine machinery, however, she was significantly slower.**

Determined to achieve total independence in warship production the Japanese had their first naval constructor of note, Lt (later Vice-Admiral) Kondo Motoki, qualify at the Royal Naval College, Greenwich. His first major projects were the four Tsukuba and Kuramas and the two Satsuma-class battleships, to which they bore a distinct "family resemblance".

Although ordered in 1904, the two Tsukubas were not completed until 1908, by which time the British had introduced the *Dreadnought* and the battlecruiser (still referred to as a "large armoured cruiser"). These had also exploited the advantages of steam turbine propulsion and primary oil-firing.

Kondo's initial enterprise was thus dated even before completion, with the problem compounded further by the *Dreadnought* being brought to builders' trials in the proverbial "year and a day", a construction time setting a benchmark against which Japan's new-found expertise would be tested.

Not surprisingly, Kondo specified an armament disposition that echoed contemporary Western practice, i.e. large-calibre weapons in centerline turrets forward and aft, with medium-calibre guns sided on two levels in casemates and open shields.

By way of comparison, at the time of the Tsukubas' laying-down the French were building the *Michelet* and *Rénan* with four 194mm/7.64in and twelve 164.7mm/6.48in guns apiece, while the British were completing the Devonshires (four 191mm/7.5in and six 152mm/6in guns). Kondo, however, decreed four 305mm/12in, twelve 152mm/6in and twelve 119mm/4.7in guns. Here, he was profiting from experience in war, choosing big guns for their penetrative power, medium calibre for shredding an opponent above his armour, and minor calibre sufficient to stop destroyers.

Battleships, he believed, should dominate from a distance and, with the Satsumas, he nearly trumped the *Dreadnought* in specifying no less than sixteen 305mm/12in guns. Only lack of finance saw the ships completed with a mixed armament of four 305mm/12in and twelve 254mm/10in guns.

ABOVE: **Completed slightly earlier than her otherwise identical sister *Kurama*, *Ibuki* was given pole masts. With optical fire-control instruments now being located in the tops, the vibration could prove unacceptable.**

As *Satsuma*'s sister, *Aki* acquired steam turbine propulsion by virtue of being laid down a year later, as did *Ibuki*, the second ship of the Tsukubas' follow-on pair. The Tsukubas' heavy main battery was paid-for in speed, which was only 20.5 knots, compared with the 22–23 knots of the aforementioned French and British ships. (To refer to the Tsukuba quartette as "battlecruisers", as they later were, was to totally misrepresent the term.)

The later *Kurama* and *Ibuki* were of rather higher power to realize 21.25 and 22.5 knots respectively. Their extra steam plant, fitted with oil sprayers in addition to coal firing, required more space, increasing overall length by 10.7m/35ft. Beam was increased by only a negligible amount, but room was found for four twin 203mm/8in turrets, which complemented the two twin 305mm/12in mountings in a "hexagonal" layout.

Japanese-designed ships of this era had a sort of fragile elegance that belied the determined manner in which they were fought. With their three funnels and lofty masts (*Kurama* had tripods) the latter pair were, perhaps marginally the more handsome, but all looked good at speed.

All, of course, were completed well after hostilities with Russia but, early in World War I, British and Australian naval forces were assisted by a Japanese squadron comprising *Tsukuba*, *Kurama* and the earlier *Asama* in the search for von Spee's fugitive force. No encounter resulted, but it would be most interesting to war-game the likely outcome of such a clash, the opposing forces being better balanced.

Shortly before, the *Ibuki* had been sharing convoy escort with the Australian cruiser *Sydney*, but it was the latter that had the good fortune to be detached, resulting in the detection and destruction of the German raider *Emden*.

Designed with insufficient experience, constructed too hastily, the four (and, indeed, the Satsumas) were not judged to be successful. *Tsukuba* blew up in 1917, while the remainder were scrapped by 1924, a consequence of Washington Treaty limitations.

ABOVE: *Ikoma*'s crew "man ship" for a fleet review at Kiel. Her five large searchlights, strategically located, indicate a continuing interest in night engagements. The lack of canvas dodgers around them give *Ikoma* a more open appearance than that of her sister. BELOW: At speed, *Ibuki* shows an elegant profile. With mixed armaments and only 20–22 knots' speed, the four were never the battlecruisers that they were labelled.

BELOW: A fine picture of *Kurama*, with her heavy tripod masts. Note the large twin 203mm/8in turrets in the waist and the triangular day-shape hoists, probably indicating rudder angle.

Tsukuba and Kurama classes

	Built	Commissioned
Ikoma	Kure Naval Yard	March 24, 1908
Tsukuba	Kure Naval Yard	January 14, 1907
Ibuki	Kure Naval Yard	November 1, 1909
Kurama	Yokosuka Naval Yard	February 28, 1911

Kurama (as built)

Displacement: 14,875 tonnes/14,640 tons (normal); 15,850 tonnes/15,600 tons (full load)
Length: 136.8m/449ft (bp); 147.8m/485ft (oa)
Beam: 22.9m/75ft 4in
Draught: 7.9m/26ft 1in (normal)
Armament: 4 x 305mm/12in (2x2), 8 x 203mm/8in (4x2) and 14 x 119mm/4.7in (14x1) guns; 3 x 457mm/18in torpedo tubes (3x1)
Machinery: Vertical, triple-expansion engines, 28 boilers, 2 shafts
Power: 16,778kW/22,500ihp for 21.25 knots
Bunkers: 2,032 tonnes/2,000 tons (coal) and 218 tonnes/215 tons (oil)
Protection: 152–178mm/6–7in (belt); 51mm/2in (protective deck); 152–178mm/6–7in (turrets)
Complement: 845

LEFT: The *Pisani* laying at Genoa. Note how the armoured area amidships is devoid of scuttles and how the tubular masts are stiff enough to obviate the need for standing rigging, which would inhibit upper-deck guns. ABOVE: As she appeared during World War I, *Pisani* has landed her mainmast and had the foremast considerably reduced. The lower fighting top is now a searchlight platform and a pair of canvas windsails augments the ventilation amidships.

Vettor Pisani class

Italy's first armoured cruiser (although reckoned a "Third Class battleship") was the 4,572-tonne/4,500-ton *Marco Polo*, completed in 1894. Although given a forecastle and poop, she appeared to have a flush-deck at first glance because a wide central deckhouse ran the length of the waist. Of her six 152mm/6in guns, one was carried on both forecastle and poop, with two sided at either end of the waist and able to fire to within 30 degrees of the axis. Two casemated 119mm/4.7in guns gave axial fire from either end, with six more in open shields firing broadside from the waist.

Five years later the Italian Navy returned to the same yard for the *Vettor Pisani*, one of two "Second Class battleships". Twelve 152mm/6in guns were carried but only four were sided at upper deck level, the remaining eight being casemated on the low-freeboard middle deck. There was a forecastle but no poop. Chase fire was limited to a single axial 119mm/4.7in weapon and two 152mm/6in guns sided at upper deck level but not able to bear within 15 degrees of the axis. Two 152mm/6in and one 119mm/4.7in guns could bear directly aft across the quarterdeck.

The Pisanis' profile differed from that of the *Marco Polo* largely in the widely spaced funnels. These resulted from interposing the machinery space between two pairs of boiler rooms. Stout, tubular "military masts" with fighting tops also replaced the pole masts of the *Marco Polo*.

By World War I the cruisers were obsolete and were designated for operations in support of the military. These were considerable, involving the supply and evacuation of the Serbian Army from Albania, and supporting Italian expeditionary forces in Albania and Macedonia. In 1917 both *Marco Polo* and *Carlo Alberto* were stripped for conversion to troop transports, being renamed *Cortellazzo* and *Zenson* respectively. All three were scrapped by 1922, at a time of general clear-out of obsolete and superfluous war-built tonnage.

ABOVE: **Arriving for a foreign port visit, the *Alberto* has "manned ship", is lowering the accommodation ladder and has put the pinnace overside with the boat derrick.**

Vettor Pisani class

	Built	Commissioned
Marco Polo	Cantiere di Castellammare di Stabia	July 21, 1894
Carlo Alberto	La Spezia Navy Yard	May 1, 1898
Vettor Pisani	Cantiere di Castellammare di Stabia	April 1, 1898

Vettor Pisani (as built)

Displacement: 6,827 tonnes/6,720 tons (normal); 7,358 tonnes/7,242 tons (full load)
Length: 99m/325ft (bp); 105.7m/347ft (oa)
Beam: 18m/59ft 1in
Draught: 7m/23ft (normal)
Armament: 12 x 152mm/6in (12x1), 6 x 119mm/4.7in (6x1) and 2 x 75mm/2.95in guns; 5 x 450mm/17.7in torpedo tubes (5x1)
Machinery: Vertical, triple-expansion engines, 8 boilers, 2 shafts
Power: 9,694kW/13,000ihp for 19 knots
Endurance: 998 tonnes/982 tons (coal) and 120 tonnes/118 tons (oil) for 11,112km/6,000nm at 10 knots
Protection: 110–150mm/4.3–5.9in (belt); 37mm/1.5in (protective deck); 150mm/5.9in (casemates)
Complement: 504

Garibaldi class

Notable for their symmetry of profile, the Garibaldis were a heavier type of armoured cruiser than the Pisanis and, built later, answered critics of the latter's light armament. They were to be capable of laying in a line of battle, yet have the flexibility necessary to conduct independent missions. This resulted in a strange assortment of weapons, with a single 254mm/10in gun turreted forward and two 203mm/8in aft. Of fourteen 152mm/6in guns, two were sided in open shields abreast each funnel, with the remaining ten casemated at main deck level, creating useful ventilation ports.

They were apparently designed to an "ideal" weight distribution, whereby 40 per cent of normal displacement was allocated to the bare hull, 25 per cent to added protection, 20 per cent to propulsion and 15 per cent to armament. The result certainly looked right, the high-freeboard, flush-decked hull looking well in the handsome black and buff livery that pre-dated the universal grey.

The 254mm/10in gun fired a 198kg/436lb projectile, compared with the 113kg/249lb shell of the 203mm/8in weapon which had a higher rate of fire. Probably the best test of this peculiar combination came with Japanese experience at Tsushima. The two Garibaldis fought in the battle line, the *Kasuga* with one 254mm/10in and two

203mm/8in guns, the *Nisshin* with two twin 203mm/8in mountings. That the Japanese subsequently retained the 254mm/10in weapon appears to indicate that fire-control complications were not insurmountable.

Having constructed five of the class to foreign account before taking on their own, the Italians found these reliable workhorses. Their involvement in the 1911 war against Turkey did not test them unduly and World War I was spent largely in the Adriatic where, in 1915, the *Garibaldi* fell victim to an Austrian

submarine. The surviving pair was relegated to training duties post-war, the *Varese* being discarded in 1923 and the newer *Ferruccio* in 1930.

LEFT: **At anchor on a windless day, the *Ferruccio* is shown to advantage by the hazy sun. She appears to be painted in a relatively pale livery of uniform shade. As her broadside armament is missing she is probably acting as a training ship (1924–29).**

Garibaldi (as built)

Displacement: 7,467 tonnes/7,350 tons (normal); 8,230 tonnes/8,100 tons (full load)
Length: 104.9m/344ft 2in (bp); 111.8m/366ft 10in (oa)
Beam: 18.2m/59ft 9in
Draught: 6.9m/22ft 8in (normal)
Armament: 1 x 254mm/10in; 2 x 203mm/8in (1x2), 14 x 152mm/6in (14x1) and 10 x 76mm/3in; 4 x 450mm/17.7in torpedo tubes (4x1)
Machinery: Vertical, triple-expansion engines, 24 boilers, 2 shafts
Power: 10,444kW/14,000ihp for 19.5 knots
Endurance: 1,219 tonnes/1,200 tons (coal) for 17,224km/9,300nm at 10 knots
Protection: 80–150mm/3.1–5.9in (belt); 38mm/1.5in (protective deck); 140–150mm/5.5–5.9in (turrets)
Complement: 550

Garibaldi class

	Built	Commissioned
Francesco Ferruccio	Venice Navy Yard	September 1, 1905
Giuseppe Garibaldi	Ansaldo, Genoa	January 1, 1901
Varese	Orlando, Livorno	April 5, 1901

Piemonte, Lombardia and *Calabria*

Being built speculatively by Armstrong, the *Piemonte* was acquired by the Italian Navy in 1888. The Elswick cruisers enjoyed a reputation for being faster and more heavily armed than Royal Navy equivalents. This was sometimes achieved through design short-cuts, such as restricted bunker space and the use of fast-running, reciprocating machinery which, while more compact, was also more prone to mechanical problems. Speed also depended upon fine hull forms, which could detract from stability. With a length-on-breadth (L/B) ratio of about 8.42, *Piemonte* was not unduly fine but still compared with 7.34 for contemporary British *Apollos*.

The ship was over-gunned when purchased, four of her six 152mm/6in guns being sided in large sponsons which, in so small a ship, created wetness. Both guns and sponsons were soon removed. With reduced armament, *Piemonte* was well thought of, but remained a one-off.

In 1888 the Italians also laid down the *Lombardia*, first of a domestically designed class. Four knots inferior to the Elswick ship, these had a comfortable L/B ratio of only 7.05, better able to accommodate their four 152mm/6in and six 119mm/4.7in guns. Known as "*Regioni*", the class varied considerably in detail. Deeper in the hull, they incorporated a cellular level above the protective deck, a feature lacking in *Piemonte*.

The Italian Navy had acquired the Armstrong-built *Dogali* a few years earlier and she, rather than the *Piemonte*, accounted for a distinct "family resemblance".

Calabria was a single-funnelled variant with a three-masted sailing rig. Intended for protracted colonial duties she was, like many of her British equivalents, wood-sheathed for comfort and for resistance to fouling.

Obsolete in a new century, the class found employment as submarine/seaplane tenders or as minelayers.

ABOVE: **Still lacking her armament, *Calabria* is seen here running trials in May 1897. The only single-funnelled variant of the "*Regioni*", she has her schooner-rig canvas bent and awnings furled along her length on the centreline. Note the half-cased funnel.**

Piemonte and Lombardia and Calabria classes

	Built	Commissioned
Piemonte	Armstrong, Elswick	August 8, 1889
Calabria	La Spezia Navy Yard	July 12, 1897
Elba	Cantiere di Castellammare de Stabia	December 1, 1895
Etruria	Orlando, Livorno	July 11, 1894
Liguria	Ansaldo, Genoa	December 1, 1894
Lombardia	Cantiere de Castellammare de Stabia	February 16, 1893
Puglia	Taranto Navy Yard	May 26, 1901
Umbria	Orlando, Livorno	February 16, 1894

Lombardia (as built)

Displacement: 2,428 tonnes/2,390 tons (normal); 2,844 tonnes/2,800 tons (full load)

Length: 80m/262ft 7in (bp); 84.8m/278ft 4in (oa)

Beam: 12m/39ft 4in

Draught: 4.6m/15ft 1in (normal)

Armament: 4 x 152mm/6in (4x1), 6 x 119mm/4.7in (6x1), and 8 x 57mm/2.2in (8x1) guns; 3 x 450mm/17.7in torpedo tubes (3x1)

Machinery: Horizontal, triple-expansion engines, 4 boilers, 2 shafts

Power: 5,222kW/7,000ihp for 17.5 knots

Endurance: 467 tonnes/460 tons (coal) for 7,408km/4,000nm at 10 knots

Protection: 50mm/2in (protective deck)

Complement: 257

ABOVE: **A high bulwark surrounded the extent of the armament of the *Etruria*. At either end, sided 152mm/6in guns are clearly visible, while the positions of the three starboard-side 119mm/4.7in weapons are nicely picked out by the oblique light. Note the old-fashioned tops and fidded topmasts.**

Goito class

ABOVE: **The stern profile of individual ships of the class (this is the *Goito*) varied depending on whether the stern torpedo tube was located internally or on deck.**

The late 1880s saw the full flowering of the French Navy's *"Jeune École"* movement, which believed that overwhelming numbers of small, torpedo-armed craft could offset the strength of the Royal Navy and also that of the Italians; the latter viewed as the "principal enemy" astride the route to and from French interests in the Levant.

Exercises showed, however, that such small craft were so slowed by a chop that they were vulnerable to larger vessels which, while not necessarily faster, could maintain speed in the conditions.

In addition to guns, these larger craft could, themselves carry torpedoes. The first British attempt, four 533-tonne/525-ton Grasshoppers of 1896, were too small, but these were immediately followed by fourteen 747-tonne/735-ton Gossamers. These, known as "torpedo gunboats", probably inspired the four Italian Goitos. Elevated to "torpedo cruisers", three were authorized in

1885 and a further one in 1887. Their designer, the great Benedetto Brin, here experimented, so that they differed very considerably.

Like their British equivalents, all carried five 356mm/14in torpedo tubes but the requirement for 18 knots resulted in differing solutions. Two were twin-screwed, the two-funnelled *Goito* making her contracted speed but the single-funnelled *Confienza* being slower by 1 knot. Both of the others were triple-screwed, the centerline shaft extending beneath and beyond the rudder blade. The *Montebello* alone had three tall, unevenly spaced funnels of exaggerated rake. She also had triple-expansion engines, against the remainder's old-fashioned double-expansion, or "compound" machinery.

Where the British ships carried one or two 119mm/4.7in guns, these were difficult to lay in poor conditions and the Italians, more realistically opted for 57mm/2.2in weapons, except in the *Confienza*.

The type proved an evolutionary dead-end in both navies as torpedo craft themselves developed into "torpedo boat destroyers". Only *Goito* and *Montebello* lasted long enough to see service during World War I.

Goito class

	Built	Commissioned
Confienza	La Spezia Navy Yard	April 11, 1890
Goito	Cantiere di Castellammare di Stabia	February 16, 1888
Montebello	La Spezia Navy Yard	January 21, 1889
Monzambano	La Spezia Navy Yard	August 11, 1889

Goito (as built)

Displacement: 856 tonnes/842 tons (normal); 1,062 tonnes/1,045 tons (full load)
Length: 70m/229ft 9in (bp); 73.4m/240ft 11in (oa)
Beam: 7.9m/25ft 11in
Draught: 3.4m/11ft 8in (normal)
Armament: 4 x 57mm/2.2in guns (4x1) and 5 x 37mm/1.46in (5x1) guns; 5 x 356mm/14in torpedo tubes (5x1)
Machinery: Three vertical compound engines, 6 boilers, 3 shafts
Power: 1,954kW/2,620ihp for 18 knots
Endurance: 180 tonnes/177 tons (coal) for 1,852km/1,000nm for 10 knots
Protection: 25–40mm/1–1.6in (protective deck)
Complement: 107

LEFT: **The *Monzambano* combines a low-freeboard forward end with a torpedo-boat-style turtledeck. The extreme rake of funnels and masts gives the illusion of a list.**

Quarto and Bixio and Aquila classes

Early scouts of the Italian Navy had struggled to reach 22 knots but, with the development of the steam turbine and oil-firing, authorization was given in 1909 for a new-style prototype in which protection and weight of armament would be subordinated to speed. The resulting *Quarto* proved to be capable of 28 knots on a displacement of some 3,271 tonnes/3,220 tons, carrying a light armament of six 119mm/4.7in guns and two torpedo tubes. This compared with the contemporary British Boadiceas (3,404 tonnes/ 3,350 tons, 26 knots, six or ten 102mm/4in guns, two torpedo tubes) and the German Kolbergs (4,430 tonnes/4,360 tons, 25.5 knots, twelve 10.5cm/4.1in, two torpedo tubes). With a 50mm/2in protective deck, the Kolbergs were heavier all round but the *Quarto*, with a 40mm/1.6in deck, compared very favourably with the largely unprotected Boadiceas.

ABOVE: **Despite their extra funnel, the *Bixio* and *Marsala* (seen here) were of lower installed power, and slower than the *Quarto* prototype. The funnel caps were distinctive. As scout cruisers, they have high-mounted lookouts and topmasts for long-range radio communication.**

The *Quarto* had four sets of direct-drive Parsons steam turbines, although only two shafts were required to transmit the full thrust via small-diameter, high-revving propellers. For years she was among the fastest ships in the Italian Navy, operating usually as a destroyer leader. She was able to carry a deck-load of 200 mines and, for a period in the late 1920s, added a small Macchi floatplane. She was discarded early in 1939.

Built in parallel with the *Quarto*, the two Bixios provided a useful comparison. Both types had a raised forecastle, but the Bixios carried their flare further aft, adopting a characteristic

ABOVE: **During World War I, the *Bixio* and *Marsala* could be differentiated by the positions of their searchlights. These flanked the third funnel of the *Bixio* (seen here) and the fourth funnel of the *Marsala* (above right).**

ABOVE: ***Marsala*, with her searchlights in their original location above the bridge. She is approaching a berth with her starboard anchor "a'cockbill", ready for instant release in the event of a misjudgement in manoeuvring.**

rising knuckle to avoid excessive width at forecastle deck level. The *Quarto*'s ten boilers required three low, evenly spaced funnels (rather reminiscent of Japanese practice) but the Bixios' 14 boilers resulted in four funnels. These were unevenly spaced as boiler and turbine spaces were alternated. The two waist guns were sided, and the superstructure was arranged capital-ship-style to allow them to fire across the deck.

The Bixios had American-designed Curtiss turbines. At full speed, these turned the propellers at 435rpm, compared with the *Quarto*'s 575rpm. This allowed a more efficient design of propeller, although three shafts were required. Nonetheless, the pair failed to reach their expected speed. Both had left the service by the end of the 1920s.

An unwritten rule of ship design is that successive classes will increase in size. The Aquilas, however, bucked this trend. Being smaller, they retained their categorization of "*esploratori*", being closer to a super-destroyer than to a light cruiser. Departure from the norm was due to this four-ship class having been originally ordered to Romanian account. They were already under construction in 1914 when, after some prevarication, Italy decided to enter the war in support of the Western Alliance. The ships were therefore requisitioned for the Italian Navy.

In just the three years since the laying down of the Bixios, marine engineering had advanced considerably. Steam conditions were greatly improved, while gearing reduced shaft speed, further raising the efficiency of propellers whose design was now better understood. The Aquilas, while somewhat smaller, thus disposed of over 29,840kW/40,000shp on two shafts, all being able to exceed their designed speed of 36.5 knots.

Their "cruiser" status depended largely upon their three 152mm/6in guns, but these were later reduced to four or five 119mm/4.7in weapons. As with most Italian warships, they were fitted for minelaying.

ABOVE: **A wartime picture of *Aquila* at speed, her seaboat swung out for immediate use. At full speed, the endurance was poor, being limited to a little over 10 hours' steaming.**

Following their service during World War I, two (*Nibbio* and *Sparviero*) were eventually purchased by the Romanians, becoming the *Marasesti* and *Marasti* respectively. As such they lasted until the 1960s. With Italy's involvement in the Spanish Civil War, the *Aquila* and *Falco* were among various warships transferred to the Spanish Nationalist Navy, many retaining their Italian crews. Acquired permanently, they served under Spanish colours until the late 1940s.

ABOVE: ***Quarto*'s three regularly spaced funnels were reminiscent of those in Japanese scout cruisers. Turbine driven, she was commissioned in 1912, starting a trend to speed, allied to light construction. She is reputed to have maintained her speed until her disposal in 1938. Her relative longevity was due to an iconic status.**

ABOVE: **The light, fluffy smoke of the *Bixio* betrays the fact that she is still, primarily, a coal-burner. Her three superstructure blocks were configured dreadnought-style to allow the two waist guns, at least in theory, to fire across the ship.**

Quarto and Bixio and Aquila classes

	Built	Commissioned
Quarto	Venice Navy Yard	May 11, 1912
Marsala	Cantiere di Castellammare di Stabia	August 4, 1914
Nino Bixio	Cantiere di Castellammare di Stabia	May 5, 1914
Aquila	Pattison, Naples	February 8, 1917
Falco	Pattison, Naples	February 20, 1920
Nibbio	Pattison, Naples	May 15, 1918
Sparviero	Pattison, Naples	July 15, 1917

Quarto (as built)

Displacement: 3,271 tonnes/3,220 tons (normal); 3,434 tonnes/3,380 tons (full load)

Length: 126m/413ft 7in (bp); 104.2m/342ft (oa)

Beam: 12.9m/42ft 4in

Draught: 4m/13ft 2in (normal)

Armament: 6 x 119mm/4.7in (6x1) and 6 x 76mm 3in (6x1) guns; 2 x 450mm/17.7in torpedo tubes (2x1)

Machinery: Direct-drive steam turbines, 10 boilers, 2 shafts

Power: 18,643kW/25,000shp for 28 knots

Endurance: 478 tonnes/470 tons (coal) and 51 tonnes/50 tons (oil) for 2,592km/1,400nm at 12 knots

Protection: 40mm/1.6in (protective deck)

Complement: 320

LEFT: **Termed "Second Class battleships", the** *Pisa* **and** *Amalfi* **were completed with only a mainmast. By 1918 the** *Pisa* **had received a light foremast, which greatly improved her appearance, as seen here. Note the difference in size between the 254mm/10in main battery guns and the sided 191mm/7.5in weapons.**

ABOVE: **A third unit of this type was the Greek** *Averoff*, **completed by Orlando in 1910. She could be recognized by her British-style tripod masts. Less apparent was the reduction of her main battery calibre from 254mm/10in to 234mm/9.2in.**

Pisa class

During 1901–03 the four Cuniberti-designed small battleships of the Regina Elena class were laid down. While not espousing Cuniberti's own ideas on the all-big-gun capital ship, they would prove to be remarkably successful on their limited, 13,005-tonne/12,800-ton displacement. Even before their launch, two similar-looking diminutives were commenced. Only some 4m/13ft 1in shorter, these were designed as armoured cruisers. Twin 254mm/10in turrets required single 305mm/12in guns at either end, and four twin 191mm/7.5in guns replaced six twin 203mm/8in weapons as secondary armament. Although the belt was thinned, horizontal protection was improved. With smaller displacement on much the same dimensions, and equipped with machinery of the same power, the Pisas were good for an additional 2 knots.

Other than to closely resemble their line-of-battle colleagues, it is not easy to explain the building of the Pisas when, over exactly the same period, the Italians built the two San Giorgios. Of almost identical size, armament power and speed, these were of entirely different layout, the boiler spaces and their three funnels being closely grouped in the Pisas but in two widely spaced blocks in the San Giorgios.

Both Pisas were completed with a single, heavy mast, stepped abaft the funnels but, by 1918, the nameship had gained a light foremast, which she retained following her 1921 reclassification as a coastal defence and training ship in which roles she served until 1937. During the late 1920s she carried a Macchi floatplane on the after superstructure but, with no catapult, its operation was cumbersome.

Her sister, *Amalfi*, was not so fortunate. On July 7, 1915, just six weeks after Italy's entry into the war, she was covering a sweep into the upper Adriatic when she was torpedoed and sunk by a German-crewed "Austrian" submarine, with the loss of 66 of her crew. Germany was not yet at war with Italy, but was operating coastal submarines from Pola.

Pisa class

	Built	Commissioned
Amalfi	Cantiere Odero, Genoa	September 1, 1909
Pisa	Cantiere Orlando, Livorno	September 1, 1909

Pisa (as built)

Displacement: 9,810 tonnes/9,655 tons (normal); 10,577 tonnes/10,410 tons (full load)

Length: 130m/426ft 9in (bp); 140.5m/461ft 2in (oa)

Beam: 21.1m/69ft 2in

Draught: 7.1m/23ft 4in (normal)

Armament: 4 x 254mm/10in (2x2), 8 x 191mm/7.5in (4x2) and 16 x 76mm/3in (16x1) guns; 3 x 450mm/17.7in torpedo tubes (3x1)

Machinery: Vertical, triple-expansion engines, 22 boilers, 2 shafts

Power: 14,914kW/20,000ihp for 23 knots

Endurance: 1,555 tonnes/1,530 tons (coal) and 71 tonnes/70 tons (oil) for 4,900km/2,650nm at 12 knots

Protection: 76–203mm/3–8in (belt); 51mm/2in (protective deck); 38–178mm/1.5–7in (turrets)

Complement: 680

LEFT: **The launch of the** *Amalfi* **in 1905. Ten years later she became the Italian Navy's first major loss of World War I. Supporting a destroyer sweep in the upper Adriatic, she was sunk by a locally assembled German UB submarine working from Pola.**

FAR LEFT: **If British warships on the whole exhibited a certain restrained elegance, those of the French at the turn of the century subscribed to the "fierce-face" school. Though small and relatively weakly armed, the armoured cruiser *Bruix* has a magnificently aggressive air.**

ABOVE: **This nice representation of the *Amiral Charner* sits her solidly in the water, clearly emphasizing the extreme tumblehome and sponsoned casemates so characteristic of contemporary French design. The steam pinnace in the foreground appears to be taking liberties with the Regulations for the Prevention of Collisions at Sea.**

Amiral Charner class and *Pothuau*

In 1893, a decade before Britain again began commissioning armoured cruisers, the French completed the one-off *Dupuy de Lôme.* Apparently certain of her success, they were already launching a further class of four, the smaller Amiral Charners.

Where the *Dupuy de Lôme* had a high freeboard hull, fully clad in 100mm/3.9in armour and using exaggerated tumblehome to facilitate axial fire, the Charners adopted what was effectively a shallow hull with lighter armour, the upper hull being a narrow, lightly built superstructure with side decks to accommodate six single 140mm/5.5in

turrets. Unlike the earlier ship, they carried their two 191mm/7.5in guns on the centerline, rather than sided in the waist. They retained the "fierce-face" ram bow, a feature that must have been a considerable impediment in a head sea, as the forward waterplane area decreased rapidly with its immersion.

The *Chanzy* was lost by stranding in 1907 and the *Charner* by submarine torpedo in 1916. The remaining pair were stricken following World War I.

The *Pothuau* was laid down in 1893 as a further one-off, being a closer copy of the *Dupuy de Lôme* in overall shape and depth of protection, but with her

armament disposed more in accord with that of the Charners. She carried ten 138.6mm/5.45in guns to the Charners' six and, lacking the *Dupuy de Lôme*'s marked tumblehome, depended upon sponsoned casemates.

A feature of the contemporary French cruisers was the long, continuous superstructure, which appeared to be part of the hull.

None of these armoured cruisers was ever used in the commerce raiding role for which they had been intended. *Pothuau* had light pole masts rather than the heavy "military masts" of the earlier ships. Late in World War I she lost her mainmast in favour of a kite balloon facility. She was scrapped in 1929.

ABOVE: **Bows of extreme shape, such as this one, tended to make a ship bury her nose in a head sea. *Pothuau*'s bridge does, therefore, appear very well forward.**

Charner class and *Pothuau*

	Built	Commissioned
Amiral Charner	Rochefort Dockyard	1895
Bruix	Rochefort Dockyard	1896
Chanzy	At. et. Ch. de la Gironde, Bordeaux	1896
Latouche-Treville	At. et Ch. de la Seine, le Havre	1895
Pothuau	At.et Ch. de la Seine, le Havre	1896

Pothuau (as built)

Displacement: 5,466 tonnes/5,380 tons (normal)
Length: 109.7m/360ft (wl); 112.9m/370ft 8in (oa)
Beam: 15m/49ft 3in
Draught: 6.5m/21ft 4in (normal)
Armament: 2 x 194mm/7.64in (2x1) and
  10 x 138.6mm/5.45in (10x1) guns
Machinery: Horizontal, triple-expansion engines,
  16 boilers, 2 shafts
Power: 7,758kW/10,400ihp for 19 knots
Endurance: 648 tonnes/638 tons (coal) for
  8,334km/4,500nm at 10 knots
Protection: 35–60mm/1.4–2.4in (belt);
  35–85mm/1.4–3.4in (protective deck);
  180mm/7.1in (turrets)
Complement: 455

Jeanne d'Arc

First to be laid down (although not the first to be completed), *Jeanne d'Arc* initiated a series of imposing, multi-funnelled French cruisers, mostly armoured, that were absolutely distinctive. All were characterized by a high-freeboard hull, a long continuous superstructure, and funnels set in two widely separated groups, the boiler spaces being likewise grouped and separated by machinery spaces. Preceding classes had been fitted with horizontal, triple-expansion engines (low in height and not extending through the protective deck) but, starting with the *Jeanne d'Arc*, the more efficient vertical type was installed.

The ship was designed by the noted constructor Émile Bertin as a prototype response to large contemporary British protected cruisers, but he failed in his attempt to achieve a significantly superior speed. Three propellers were required and it is probable that the water flow over them was less than ideal. It is reported that, despite the machinery developing about 746kW/1,000ihp more than required by contract, the ship's trial speeds did not exceed 21.75 knots against a designed 23. The proposed remedial measure of reducing the area of the bilge keels was not likely to have made a great deal of difference. Like the two British Powerfuls that preceded her, she was a prodigious eater of coal.

The *Jeanne d'Arc*'s forecastle was fully armour-clad but, from the bridge aft, the belt was two decks deep, bounded above and below by protective decks. The resulting "box" was closely subdivided and, in theory, greatly limited flooding due to action damage.

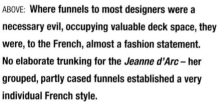

ABOVE: **Where funnels to most designers were a necessary evil, occupying valuable deck space, they were, to the French, almost a fashion statement. No elaborate trunking for the *Jeanne d'Arc* – her grouped, partly cased funnels established a very individual French style.**

A single 194mm/7.64in turret was located at either end. On the long forecastle deck, two 138.6mm/5.45in turrets were sided forward, and two aft. Ten more 138.6mm/5.45in guns were carried at a good height in casemates and sponsons at upper deck level.

Throughout the 1920s, the ship was used for training and she was not scrapped until 1934.

LEFT: **Although of more than twice the displacement of *Pothuau*, the *Jeanne d'Arc* mounted only four more secondary guns. Her extra size and length were the cost of a further 4 knots. The considerable freeboard favoured by French designers saw their ships carry secondary weapons at a useful height.**

Jeanne d'Arc

Built: Toulon Dockyard
Commissioned: 1903
Displacement: 11,329 tonnes/11,150 tons (normal)
Length: 145.4m/477ft 3in (oa)
Beam: 19.4m/63ft 9in
Draught: 8.1m/26ft 5in (normal)
Armament: 2 x 194mm/7.64in (2x1) and
  14 x 138.6mm/5.45in (14x1) guns;
  2 x 450mm/17.7in torpedo tubes (2x1)
Machinery: Vertical, triple-expansion engines,
  48 boilers, 3 shafts
Power: 20,880kW/28,000ihp for 21.5 knots
Endurance: 2,032 tonnes/2,000 tons (coal) for
  25,000km/13,500nm at 10 knots
Protection: 150mm/5.9in (belt); 75mm/2.95in
  (forecastle); 50mm/1.97in (protective deck);
  200mm/7.87in (turrets)
Complement: 625

LEFT: The *Marseillaise* here shows clearly many French characteristics. Note the widely spaced funnel groups and double-curvature stem profile, the large-diameter military mast and the relatively shallow turrets atop their barbettes. Even the anchor profile and its semi-recessed housing are unique to French design. ABOVE: Still new, the *Montcalm* is seen here in 1902. The large, rectangular ventilator amidships, above the machinery space, is typical. Note how the steam pipes exit at the tops of the funnels and how, due to the pronounced tumblehome, davits are seated on the shell plating.

Kléber, Gueydon and Aube classes

Three years or more before the *Jeanne d'Arc* ran trials to prove Bertin's armoured cruiser concept, the French commenced work on two related classes, each of three ships, the 7,824-tonne/7,700-ton Klébers and the 9,662-tonne/9,510-ton Gueydons. All were powered for a realistic 21 knots but, again, their triple-shaft propulsion caused problems, not least with poor manoeuvrability and weak hull scantlings. Having fewer boilers, both classes required "only" two pairs of funnels. While their profiles were similar, the smaller Klébers could be distinguished by their two pole masts, the larger vessels having a heavier, "military" type foremast and bulkier bridge structure.

The Klébers had a homogeneous main armament of eight 164.7mm/6.48in guns in four twin turrets. Two of these were mounted centerline on the very long forecastle deck; the others were sided in the waist at upper deck level. They were designed for colonial duties and their lower hulls were wood and copper-sheathed to retard fouling. Their belt was shallow, decreasing in height from forward to aft.

More heavily protected and armed, the Gueydons copied the *Jeanne d'Arc*'s 194mm/7.6in armament at either end, but adopted the 164.7mm/6.48in gun as secondary calibre in place of 138.6mm/5.45in weapon, with only eight (rather than fourteen) being carried, in casemates. These were located on the upper deck, all but the forward pair laying above an unprotected middle deck and thus vulnerable to splinter damage from below.

The five-ship Amiral Aube class were improved Gueydons. Only slightly increased in dimensions, they nonetheless displaced a further 914 tonnes/900 tons, due mainly to a modified and better-protected layout for the secondary armament. Four of the 164.7mm/6.48in guns were now housed in single turrets at forecastle-deck level. These were fitted with armoured trunks. Two more were casemated at upper-deck level and two on the middle deck.

Kléber, Gueydon and Aube classes

	Built	Commissioned
Desaix	Penhoët, St. Nazaire	1904
Dupleix	Rochefort Dockyard	1903
Kléber	Chantiers de la Gironde, Bordeaux	1903
Dupetit-Thouars	Toulon Dockyard	1903
Gueydon	Lorient Dockyard	1902
Montcalm	Forges et Chantiers de la Méditerranée, la Seyne	1901
Amiral Aube	Penhoët, St. Nazaire	1904
Condé	Lorient Dockyard	1904
Gloire	Lorient Dockyard	1904
Marseillaise	Brest Dockyard	1903
Sully	Forges et Chantiers de la Méditerranée, la Seyne	1903

Gueydon class (as built)

Displacement: 9,662 tonnes/9,510 tons (normal)
Length: 137.9m/452ft 8in (wl); 139.8m/459ft (oa)
Beam: 19.4m/63ft 8in
Draught: 7.5m/24ft 6in (normal)
Armament: 2 x 194mm/7.6in (2x1) and
    8 x 164.7mm/6.48in (8x1) guns;
    2 x 450mm/17.7in torpedo tubes (2x1)
Machinery: Vertical, triple-expansion engines,
    20 boilers, 3 shafts
Power: 14,914kW/20,000ihp for 21 knots
Endurance: 1,625 tonnes/1,600 tons (coal) and
    51 tonnes/50 tons (oil) for 18,520km/10,000nm
    at 10 knots
Protection: 60–150mm/2.4–5.9in (belt);
    50mm/1.97in (protective deck); 200mm/7.87in
    (turrets)
Complement: 590

LEFT: **This splendid view of** *Michelet* **clearly shows several features in the development of the French armoured cruiser. All secondary guns bar four are disposed in single, sided turrets. The bridge structure is a compact mass and the extent of the armoured belt is clearly defined.** ABOVE: **The brooding presence of the** *Michelet* **dominates a North African port in this simple but effective impression. A half-sister of the Gambetta class, she had her armament reduced in the hope of remedying a chronic lack of speed, a common problem with reciprocating machinery.**

Gambetta and Michelet classes

The French armoured cruiser program continued apace, with the *Léon Gambetta*, first of a new and larger type, actually laid down before the last of the preceding Aubes. With an additional 8m/26ft 3in more in length and a further 2,185 tonnes/2,150 tons displacement, a Gambetta carried twice the firepower, more powerful machinery to maintain her predecessors' 22 knots, and greatly improved horizontal protection.

The greater armament was possible through the adoption of twin turrets. This approach was not universally popular as they are concentrated assets, while a pair of guns had a slower rate of fire than two separate singles. The Gambetta trio thus mounted a twin 194mm/7.64in turret on the centerline at either end, the forward one on the long forecastle deck, the after on the upper deck. Also at forecastle deck

level were three twin 164.7mm/6.48in guns per side. Again, only four secondary weapons were casemated, the forward pair at upper deck level, the after pair on the main deck, as in the Aubes. Although still bearing a strong "family likeness", their funnels were shorter, without the unusual caps.

The vertical protection scheme followed that of the Aubes, but the belt was tied to horizontal protective decks at its upper and lower edges. The space thus enclosed was closely subdivided, much of it coal-filled. This offered further protection but proved very difficult to work on those occasions when the bunkers were actually needed.

A fourth-of-class, *Jules Michelet*, carried a lighter 12-gun secondary battery. This was disposed in four single turrets along either side of the long

forecastle deck, with four casemated as before. The ship carried 20 improved boilers against the *Gambetta*'s 28. The additional 1,119kW/1,500ihp allowed her to achieve 23.2 knots on trials.

The *Gambetta* and *Hugo* carried conventional boat cranes abreast the forward funnels, and the *Ferry* and *Michelet* distinctive gooseneck cranes.

Gambetta and Michelet classes

	Built	**Commissioned**
Jules Ferry	Cherbourg Dockyard	1906
Léon Gambetta	Brest Dockyard	1903
Victor Hugo	Lorient Dockyard	1906
Jules Michelet	Lorient Dockyard	1908

Gambetta (as built)

Displacement: 12,751 tonnes/12,550 tons (normal)
Length: 148m/485ft 10in (bp)
Beam: 21.4m/70ft 3in
Draught: 8.2m/26ft 11in
Armament: 4 x 194mm/7.64in (2x2) and
  16 x 164.7mm/6.48in (6x2/4x1) guns;
  4 x 450mm/17.7in torpedo tubes (4x1)
Machinery: 4-cylinder, vertical, triple-expansion
  engines, 28 boilers, 3 shafts
Power: 20,507kW/27,500ihp for 22 knots
Endurance: 2,133 tonnes/2,100 tons (coal) for
  22,224km/12,000nm at 10 knots
Protection: 90–170mm/3.5–6.7in (belt);
  20–35mm/0.79–1.38in and
  45–65mm/1.77–2.55in (protective decks);
  140–200mm/5.5–7.87in (turrets)
Complement: 730

ABOVE: **Compared with the one-off** *Michelet*, **the Gambetta-class** *Jules Ferry* **is more cramped by having 12 of her 16 secondary guns mounted in sided twin turrets. There was a wide variation in funnel caps and boat cranes. The high freeboard allowed them to maintain speed.**

LEFT: **The splendidly named Waldeck-Rousseau class had a uniform armament of 194mm/7.64in guns, disposed mainly in twin and single turrets. One of the four located in casemates can be seen here, suffering the usual problem of being too close to the waterline. The ship is *Edgar Quinet*.**

Renan and Rousseau class

Built over the same time span as the *Michelet*, the larger *Ernest Renan* was not so much an evolution as an alternative type. She was intended to be the first of three with an extra 9m/29ft 6in length to accommodate no less than 40 Niclausse large-tube boilers (as opposed to the 20 less reliable small-tube du Temple type in the *Michelet*). The objective was to develop the 27,600kW/37,000ihp necessary for 23 knots. (It might be noted that a British Minotaur, of the same size and displacement, could make 23 knots on 20,142kW/27,000ihp.)

Reverting to six funnels, the *Renan* was an imposing ship, armed identically with the *Michelet*, with the variation that the tertiary, anti-torpedo boat battery was increased from twenty-two 47mm/1.85in guns to a more potent

sixteen 65mm/2.6in weapons. Protection, otherwise similar, was improved with the addition of a 150mm/5.9in transverse bulkhead, closing off the after end of the armoured "box".

The further two units, *Edgar Quinet* and *Waldeck-Rousseau*, suffered the usual fate of ships that grew to a size where the armament no longer appeared to be sufficient. Primary and secondary batteries were therefore, combined into a single calibre, 194mm/7.64in, of which there were 14 guns. These were disposed in a twin turret forward and aft, three single turrets along both sides in the waist, and four in casemates. Of these, the aftermost pair was located very low, at main deck level.

Completed in 1910, this pair was the ultimate expression of French armoured

cruiser design. The type had already been abandoned elsewhere, made obsolete by the battlecruiser, to say nothing of the steam turbine and oil-fired boilers.

Despite their obsolescence, all three lasted until the 1930s, the *Rousseau* serving as Far East flagship until 1936.

Renan and Rousseau class

	Built	Commissioned
Ernest Renan	Penhoët, St. Nazaire	1908
Edgar Quinet	Brest Dockyard	1910
Waldeck-Rousseau	Lorient Dockyard	1910

Rousseau (as built)

Displacement: 14,072 tonnes/13,850 tons (full load)
Length: 156.9m/515ft (bp); 159m/521ft 11in (oa)
Beam: 21.4m/70ft 3in
Draught: 8.4m/27ft 6in (full load)
Armament: 14 x 194mm/7.64in (2x2/10x1) guns; 2 x 450mm/17.7in torpedo tubes (2x1)
Machinery: 4-cylinder, vertical, triple-expansion engines, 40 boilers, 3 shafts
Power: 27,590kW/37,000ihp for 23 knots
Endurance: 2,337 tonnes/2,300 tons (coal) for 18,520km/10,000nm at 10 knots
Complement: 840

RIGHT: **The *Renan*, seen here, could be easily differentiated through her boat cranes, situated amidships. In the Rousseaus, they flanked the forward funnel group.**

LEFT: **The extraordinary hull form of the *d'Entrecasteaux* is clearly visible in this picture. From the exaggerated bow to the counter, the curvature changes twice from convex to concave. The huge central casemate is virtually a battery in itself. She existed until 1938, latterly in the role of training ship.**

Friant and d'Entrecasteaux classes

Small, protected cruisers were built in considerable numbers by the late-Victorian Royal Navy for colonial duties, largely superseding sail-assisted sloops and corvettes. With fewer colonial interests, France had little requirement for such ships, and there are few examples. The five Friants are, therefore, interesting exceptions, bearing comparison with a contemporary British Apollo or the German *Gefion* which latter type was developed much further. Like these, the three surviving Friants were obsolete by 1914 and saw active service only because of the emergency.

Even by French standards, the line of the bow was exaggerated, less a ram than an expression of national identity. The resulting very short forecastle deck saw the muzzle of the 40-calibre, 164.7mm/6.48in forward-gun almost reach to the jackstaff. Six of these guns were carried, four of them in deep sponsons. These were supported on the pronounced tumblehome and must have made for wet ships. The double row of large, rectangular ports ensured good ventilation in tropical conditions.

The contemporary *d'Entrecasteaux* doubled the Friants' displacement, and demanded a further half-set of boilers for the required 19 knots (which she never achieved). Tacked-on abaft the machinery space, these resulted in a third funnel, located well aft.

She was armed after the style of a British *Edgar*, with a centerline 240mm/9.5in gun at both end and twelve 138.6mm/5.45in secondary weapons. Two of these were carried in open mountings on either side of the waist. One level below was four casemates per side.

Extended by World War I, her life continued in a long training role, first under the Belgian flag, then the Polish. She was finally scrapped in 1938.

ABOVE: **Designed for service in tropical climates, the Friants were given a double row of large square ports, uninterrupted by a side belt as these were protected cruisers. By the end of World War I, with reduced machinery and a single funnel, she served as a submarine depot ship.**

Friant and d'Entrecasteaux classes

	Built	Commissioned
Bugeaud	Cherbourg Dockyard	1898
Cassard	Cherbourg Dockyard	1895
Chasseloup-Laubat	Cherbourg Dockyard	1898
d'Assas	Penhoët, St. Nazaire	1895
du Chayla	Cherbourg Dockyard	1897
Friant	Brest Dockyard	1895
d'Entrecasteaux	Forges et Ch. de la Méditerranée, la Seyne	1898

Friant (as built)

Displacement: 3,800 tonnes/3,740 tons (normal); 4,075 tonnes/4,000 tons (full load)
Length: 94m/308ft 6in (bp); 100m/328ft 3in (oa)
Beam: 13m/42ft 8in
Draught: 6.4m/21ft (normal)
Armament: 6 x 164.7mm/6.48in (6x1) and 4 x 100mm/4in (4x1) guns; 2 x 450mm/17.7in torpedo tubes (2x1)
Machinery: Vertical, triple-expansion engines, 2 shafts
Power: 7,460kW/10,000ihp for 19 knots
Endurance: 696 tonnes/685 tons (coal) for 11,112km/6,000nm at 10 knots
Protection: 80mm/3.15in (protective deck)
Complement: 376

LEFT: **Capable of 23 knots, the *Chateaurenault* was designed as a commerce raider, a role assisted by her symmetrical, four-funnelled profile which, at a distance, resembled that of a passenger liner. Her pale paint scheme is made to look even less warlike through the addition of a narrow, dark ribband.**

ABOVE: **In regular warship livery the *Chateaurenault*'s armament is more apparent. During World War I she was used for trooping, and it was while acting in this capacity that she was torpedoed and and sunk off Cephalonia in December 1917.**

Chateaurenault and *Jurien de la Gravière*

Like the US Navy *Columbia*, the *Chateaurenault* was designed specifically as a commerce destroyer, and given something of a mercantile appearance. That of the American was not convincing but the Frenchman adopted a straight stem and a merchant ship's counter stern. Her four plain funnels were half-cased and elegantly raked. However, like the *Columbia*, she was betrayed from a distance by the foremast being located with the bridge structure rather than on the foredeck.

Her 23-knot speed required a troublesome triple-shaft arrangement.

While she achieved contract speed, she was prone to vibration that upset gun-laying. Like the *Guichen* that followed, *Chateaurenault* was considered something of a failure and was serving as a troop transport when sunk by an Austrian submarine late in 1917.

The protected cruiser *Jurien de la Gravière* also imitated the appearance of an armoured cruiser of considerably greater capability. With her two lofty pole masts, she closely resembled the Kléber-class cruisers which were still under construction but, where she carried a similar primary battery of eight

164.7mm/6.48in guns, she had nothing else larger than a 47mm/1.85in gun.

She was also designed for war against commerce. Longer but narrower in the beam, her finer hull packed the same power as a Kléber, but her planned 23 knots was difficult to attain, although it was still of concern to the British. It was reported by the French themselves that her boilers "gave an infinity of trouble", being prone to leaks and difficult to stoke. They doubted that she could maintain 20 knots for three hours, while she consumed so much fuel that her actual range was probably only half that officially claimed. She was stricken from the active list in 1922.

ABOVE: **The impressively named *Jurien de la Gravière* had the general appearance of an armoured cruiser, but lacked vertical protection. She never achieved her designed speed.**

Chateaurenault and *Jurien de la Gravière*

	Built	Commissioned
Chateaurenault	Forges et Ch. de la Méditeranée, la Seyne	1900
Jurien de la Gravière	Lorient Dockyard	1901

Chateaurenault (as built)

Displacement: 8,230 tonnes/8,100 tons (normal)
Length: 134.9m/442ft 10in (bp); 140m/459ft 7in (oa)
Beam: 18m/59ft 2in
Draught: 7.5m/24ft 7in (normal)
Armament: 2 x 164.7mm/6.48in (2x1) and 6 x 138.6mm/5.45in (6x1) guns
Machinery: 4-cylinder, vertical, triple-expansion engines, 28 boilers, 3 shafts
Power: 17,900kW/24,000ihp for 23 knots
Endurance: 2,134 tonnes/2,100 tons (coal) for 13,890km/7,500nm at 12 knots
Protection: 60–100mm/2.4–3.9in (protective deck)
Complement: 605

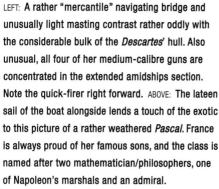

LEFT: **A rather "mercantile" navigating bridge and unusually light masting contrast rather oddly with the considerable bulk of the** *Descartes'* **hull. Also unusual, all four of her medium-calibre guns are concentrated in the extended amidships section. Note the quick-firer right forward.** ABOVE: **The lateen sail of the boat alongside lends a touch of the exotic to this picture of a rather weathered** *Pascal.* **France is always proud of her famous sons, and the class is named after two mathematician/philosophers, one of Napoleon's marshals and an admiral.**

Guichen and Descartes class

The *Guichen* and *Jurien de la Gravière* are often paired because they were both designed as commerce destroyers and resembled armoured cruisers. However, there were considerable differences between the former pair and *Guichen* whose resemblance to an armoured cruiser was far less convincing. Her hull was devoid of much of the clutter typical of larger ships, its double tier of rectangular ports emphasizing its exaggerated tumblehome.

The *Guichen* was laid down in 1895, two years before *de la Gravière*, but was completed one year after, in 1902, nearly seven years in the building. She was 4m/13ft 1in shorter but 1.7m/5ft 7in greater in the beam. Despite this extra portliness, she was still powered for 23 knots. This demanded over 40 per cent greater installed power.

Her displacement was almost half as much again, derived from no less than 36 boilers and a heavier protective deck. Her armament, however, was lighter. No more practical than *de la Gravière,* the *Guichen* was, likewise, discarded in 1922.

Predating the *Guichen* were the Descartes, a class of four 4,115-tonne/4,050-ton protected cruisers. They were of a similar size but inferior to the contemporary British Astraeas. Only three out of eight of the latter class survived to see active service during World War I, but only the nameship of the French class operated in the conflict, the remaining three having been hulked pre-war. Even the less-than-onerous duties of guardship to the West Indies finally proved too much for the *Descartes* and she was disarmed in 1917.

Built in different yards, the ships' individual displacement varied somewhat. Their protective deck was overlaid with a cellular level, topped by a light splinter deck. The four 164.7mm/6.48in guns were grouped in a casemated amidships redoubt. Located at main deck level, they fired axially along the tumblehome of the hull, a very characteristic feature.

Guichen and Descartes class

	Built	Commissioned
Guichen	Penhoët, St. Nazaire	1902
Catinat	Ch. de Granville, le Havre	1896
Descartes	Ch. de la Loire, Nantes	1896
Pascal	Toulon Dockyard	1897
Protet	At. et Ch. de la Gironde, Bordeaux	1898

Descartes class (as built)

Displacement: 4,115 tonnes/4,050 tons (normal)
Length: 99m/324ft 11in (bp); 101.1m/331ft 10in (oa)
Beam: 13m/42ft 8in
Draught: 6.5m/21ft 4in (normal)
Armament: 4 x 164.7mm/6.48in (4x1) and 10 x 100mm/3.9in (10x1) guns; 2 x 356mm/14in torpedo tubes (2x1)
Machinery: Triple-expansion engines, 16 boilers, 2 shafts
Power: 6,714kW/9,000ihp for 19 knots
Endurance: 676 tonnes/665 tons (coal) for 11,112km/6,000mm at 10 knots
Protection: 20–50mm/0.79–2in (protective deck)
Complement: 390

LEFT: **Berthed in the Penfeld, under the forbidding walls of Brest's chateau, the** *Guichen* **is seen undergoing mechanical maintenance (note the protective covers in way of the forward funnels). Unusually, her stem was straight and vertical, while her stern (nearest the camera) was extended.**

Surcouf class, *Lavoisier* and *d'Estrées*

Although classified as "Third Class cruisers", these interesting little ships were too small and of insufficient endurance to undertake protracted independent operations. They were designed to work as handmaidens to a fleet and its commander-in-chief, in a role that the French term "*avisos*" and the British "despatch vessels". Their nearest contemporary Royal Navy equivalent would be the Barracouta class, loosely termed "torpedo cruisers".

Stemming from several yards, the Surcoufs differed in detail and had displacements of 1,870–1,910 tonnes/1,840–1,880 tons. While given an armoured deck, with a splinter deck above, their hulls were not deep enough for a full cellular layer. Superstructure comprised little more than a miniscule bridge, set around the forefunnel. The funnels themselves were widely spaced and varied considerably in individual dimensions.

Four 138.6mm/5.45in guns were located in amidships casemates, sited over the tumblehome to permit something approaching axial fire. These projections again looked as if they would cause wetness.

The *d'Estrées* was of the same length but with 3m/9ft 10in or 33 per cent increase in beam. She was faster by 2 knots but only at the cost of 40 per cent greater installed power. Her larger deck space permitted four secondary 100mm/3.9in guns to be added. She differed in appearance from the Surcoufs, having two short funnels and lacking the exaggerated curvature of bow and stern.

The Lavoisier-class cruisers were of an intermediate 2,337-tonne/2,300-ton design falling between the Surcoufs and *d'Estrées.* They were fitted with only two 100mm/3.9in secondary guns, but carried a pair of 450mm/17.7in torpedo tubes.

The late introduction of the steam turbine into French shipbuilding brought the possibility of a class of 29-knot scout cruisers. These, the proposed ten 4,572-tonne/4,500-ton Lamotte-Picquets, were never built, due to changing priorities.

ABOVE: **High and dry, aground on a rocky shore, the *Infernet* is beyond redemption and is already being stripped. Note the damage to the port propeller and rudder. Although the screws protrude significantly from the hull, no above-water propeller guards are fitted.**

Surcouf class, *Lavoisier* and *d'Estrées*

	Built	Commissioned
Coëtlogon	Penhoët, St. Nazaire	1891
Cosmao	At. et Ch. de la Gironde, Bordeaux	1891
Forbin	Rochefort Dockyard	1890
Lalande	At. et Ch. de la Gironde, Bordeaux	1890
Surcouf	Cherboug Dockyard	1890
Troude	At. et Ch. de la Gironde, Bordeaux	1890
d'Estrées	Rochefort Dockyard	1899
Galilée	Rochefort Dockyard	1897
Lavoisier	Rochefort Dockyard	1897

Surcouf (as built)

Displacement: 1,877 tonnes/1,848 tons (normal)
Length: 95m/311ft 10in (bp)
Beam: 9m/29ft 6in
Draught: 4.7m/15ft 6in (normal)
Armament: 4 x 138.6mm/5.45in (4x1) and 9 x 47mm/1.85in (9x1); 5 x 450mm/17.7in torpedo tubes (5x1)
Machinery: Vertical, triple-expansion engines, 2 shafts
Power: 4,476kW/6,000ihp for 20 knots
Endurance: 203 tonnes/200 tons (coal) for 4,444km/2,400nm at 10 knots
Protection: 40mm/1.57in (protective deck)
Complement: 190

LEFT: *Scharnhorst* and *Gneisenau* were a near-identical pair; the latter is shown here. Easily confused with the smaller Roons, they could be differentiated by their cruiser stern and the full-depth battery amidships, accommodating two 21cm/8.2in and three 15cm/5.9in guns per side. Note boats under davits as well as crane.

Scharnhorst class and *Blücher*

As with the armoured cruisers of major foreign fleets, those of the German Navy were subject to creeping escalation in size and capability. Launched in 1906, the Scharnhorsts were the last in the line of development that had begun with the *Victoria Louise*. They were the ultimate in German armoured cruisers and, as such, bear comparison with the British Minotaurs and the French *Renan*. All were powered for 23 knots but, as with capital ships, the Germans had the lowest length/breadth ratio. Both British and French opted for an armament of four main guns (234mm/9.2in and 194mm/7.64in respectively) and a relatively large number of secondaries (ten 191mm/7.5in and twelve 164.7mm/6.48in respectively). The Scharnhorsts, however, had eight main-calibre weapons of 21cm/8.2in calibre and only six intermediate 15cm/5.9in guns. Inasmuch as this permitted a heavier volume and better control of main battery fire, this was obviously an improvement. Both weapons were reliable and capable of a very respectable range.

Following previous practice, half the main armament and all of the secondary armament were casemated within a well-protected central redoubt, which also covered the machinery. The belt, as ever, was the best compromise between thickness and area to be covered.

The two sisters differed only in minor detail and, indeed, could easily be confused with the preceding Roons. The latter, however, had a pair of 15cm/5.9in single turrets in the waist at upper deck level, where the Scharnhorsts had two 21cm/8.2in guns mounted in casemates.

Excellent ships, it was the misfortune of the Scharnhorsts to be pitted in their final action against battlecruisers, ships designed specifically as the armoured cruiser's nemesis.

In April 1906 the British laid down the first battlecruiser. Referred to as a "large armoured cruiser", she was built in great secrecy. German intelligence gleaned little beyond the fact that she was to be larger and faster, carrying a homogenous battery of 234mm/9.2in guns. The last was a deliberately misleading leak by the British to conceal her true armament of eight 305mm/12in weapons.

Although Admiral Alfred von Tirpitz was reluctant to divert funds from capital ship construction to what he considered to be reconnaissance units, he nonetheless authorized a single ship in response during 1907. As the Germans considered their 21cm/8.2in gun to be at least the equal of a British 234mm/9.2in, the new ship, to be named *Blücher*, was given 12, disposed hexagon-fashion in 16 turrets.

The Germans discovered their error too late to correct it, and the *Blücher* became a one-off – larger, faster and more

LEFT: **Von Spee's flagship *Scharnhorst* urgently resupplies at Valparaiso following the Battle of Coronel (November 1914). The battle resulted in the first defeat suffered by the Royal Navy in a century, avenged shortly afterward in the Battle of the Falklands (December 1914). Note the large, single 21cm/8.2in guns amidships and the configuration of the hull.**

expensive than a Scharnhorst, but about a knot slower and completely outgunned by an Invincible-class battlecruiser.

In appearance, she resembled the true German battlecruisers that quickly followed, but was smaller and was alone in being fitted with "gooseneck" boat cranes. She was also alone in combining a single turret forward and aft with (after 1913) a British-style tripod foremast.

Too large and too valuable to be considered just another armoured cruiser, the *Blücher* was treated by the Germans as a battlecruiser but, being less capable than her peers, she was relegated to the rear of a battle line. During the long tail chase that was the Dogger Bank action of January 1915, the *Blücher* thus became the successive target of each pursuing British battlecruiser as it crept into extreme range. Having, over three hours, absorbed an estimated 70 hits, she sank with nearly 800 of her crew. Her last, great service had been to completely divert the attention of the British, allowing her three consorts to escape.

TOP: **Although *Blücher* was a one-off armoured cruiser, she looked like a battlecruiser. Being employed as such would quickly prove to be her nemesis. Note the complex rigging for the deployment of her anti-torpedo nets, the large number of searchlights and the steam pinnace alongside.** ABOVE: **The cruelly punished *Blücher* capsizes at the Dogger Bank action in January 1915. As tail-ender of Hipper's battlecruiser line, she diverted the British sufficiently long to allow her colleagues to escape. Note the sided, amidships 21cm/8.2in guns still trained abaft the beam against her pursuers.**

Scharnhorst class and *Blücher*

	Built	Commissioned
Gneisenau	AG "Weser", Bremen	March 6, 1908
Scharnhorst	Blohm & Voss, Hamburg	October 24, 1907
Blücher	Kiel Dockyard	October 1, 1909

Scharnhorst class

Displacement: 11,806 tonnes/11,620 tons (normal); 13,230 tonnes/12,990 tons (full load)
Length: 143.8m/472ft (wl); 144.6m/474ft 8in (oa)
Beam: 216m/70ft 11in
Draught: 8.1m/26ft 7in (normal)
Armament: 8 x 21cm/8.2in (2x2/4x1) and 6 x 15cm/5.9in (6x1) guns; 4 x 450mm/17.7in torpedo tubes (4x1)
Machinery: Vertical, 3-cylinder, triple-expansion engines, 18 boilers, 3 shafts
Power: 19,388kW/26,000ihp for 22.5 knots
Endurance: 2,032 tonnes/2,000 tons (coal) for 9,445km/5,100nm at 12 knots
Protection: 8–150mm/3–6in (belt); 35–60mm/1.38–2.4in (protective deck); 30–170mm/1.18–6.7in (turrets)
Complement: 765

ABOVE: **The buff-and-white Far East livery of the *Scharnhorst* disguises the considerable freeboard that was a beneficial feature of German armoured cruisers. The radiussed forward sheer strake, not really a turtledeck, was a feature of their design. The voluminous coal smoke, inevitable at high speed, contrasts with the pristine paintwork.**

LEFT: **Defined as an "*aviso*", or despatch vessel, rather than as a light cruiser, the *Hela* was armed lightly with only 8.8cm/3.46in guns. Her exaggerated ram bow housed one of three torpedo tubes. By 1914, when she was sunk by submarine torpedo, she had been given a second funnel.**

Early light cruisers

Germany's colonial ambitions of the 1880s resulted in the building of two types of cruisers, one for "overseas" and the other for "fleet" roles. The 3,810-tonne/3,750-ton *Gefion* of 1894 was the last example of the former type prior to their being merged into a single design capable of fulfilling either purpose. Her classification of "corvette-cruiser" alluded both to her imperial duties and to her partly open waist, upon which six of her ten 10.5cm/4.1in guns were mounted. Two more were sided upon each of her raised forecastle and poop decks.

Gefion was powered for a modest 19 knots and lightly constructed, with only a 25–40mm/1–1.57in protective deck. However, her basic design was well suited for providing the basis for the Bremens of 1902 onward, themselves the beginning of a long and successful series. Confined largely to harbour service during World War I, she was sold in 1919.

Built at the same time as the *Gefion*, the *Hela* paralleled the size and functions of the contemporary French "*avisos*". Of only half the displacement of the *Gefion*, she was also very lightly protected, carrying only four 8.8cm/3.46in guns.

She did, however, provide the basic design for a further ten "fourth rate" vessels. Of the same length as the *Hela*, but 1.2–1.4m/3ft 11in–4ft 7in greater in the beam, these were (mostly) powered for 21.5 knots, were better protected and carried a similar main battery to the *Gefion*.

Attractive little ships, they were, nonetheless, ambitious for their size. Even with an increased beam they tended to be crank.

They saw considerable action, with *Ariadne* being sunk at the Heligoland Bight action, the *Frauenlob* at Jutland, and the *Undine* by submarine torpedo. *Niobe*, long-transferred, was sunk during World War II, a conflict which the *Arkona*, *Amazone* and *Medusa* managed to survive, serving until 1929–31.

Early light cruisers

	Built	Commissioned
Amazone	Germania, Kiel	November 15, 1901
Ariadne	AG. "Weser", Bremen	May 18, 1901
Arkona	AG "Weser", Bremen	May 12, 1903
Frauenlob	AG "Weser", Bremen	February 17, 1903
Gazelle	Germania, Kiel	June 15, 1901
Medusa	AG "Weser", Breman	July 26, 1901
Niobe	AG "Weser", Breman	June 25, 1900
Nymphe	Germania, Kiel	September 20, 1900
Thetis	Danzig Dockyard	September 14, 1901
Undine	Howaldtswerke, Kiel	January 5, 1904
Gefion	Schichau, Danzig	June 27, 1894
Hela	AG "Weser", Bremen	May 3, 1896

Undine (as built)

Displacement: 2,743 tonnes/2,700 tons (normal); 3,160 tonnes/3,110 tons (full load)

Length: 104.4m/342ft 8in (wl); 105m/344ft 8in (oa)

Beam: 12.3m/40ft 4in

Draught: 5.6m/18ft 5in (normal)

Armament: 10 x 10.5cm/4.1in (10x1) guns; 3 x 450mm/17.7in torpedo tubes (3x1)

Machinery: Vertical, 4-cylinder, triple-expansion engines, 8 boilers, 2 shafts

Power: 4,474kW/6,000ihp for 21.5 knots

Endurance: 713 tonnes/700 tons (coal) for 8,148km/4,400nm at 12 knots

Protection: 20–80mm/0.79–3.1in (protective deck)

Complement: 255

ABOVE: **A series of ten very similar ships, the Gazelles were the German Navy's first extended light cruiser class. The bow form and general forward clutter made them wet. The *Undine*, shown here, was a further victim of submarine attack but the remainder, with modified bows, served in the post-war fleet.**

Bremen class

Following an Imperial edict of 1903, all German light cruisers were named after cities. The first of these were the seven Bremens, heavily based on the *Gefion* prototype. Their design showed far better discipline in weight economy for, on a hull of basically the same dimensions, they showed 483 tonnes/475 tons (or over 12 per cent) less displacement. This in spite of carrying the same ten 10.5cm/4.1in guns in the same layout, and a thickened protective deck made the more effective by the incorporation of new Krupp-patent armour-grade steel.

At 19 knots, the *Gefion* had been too slow and a puzzling feature of the Bremens was that, while their installed power was increased by only 746kW/1,000ihp (about 11 per cent), their speed was increased by no less than 3 knots. One can only assume a very much improved underwater form.

The *Lübeck* differed in being the German Navy's first steam-turbine-propelled cruiser. The system was direct-drive and the ship was fitted with four, small-diameter propellers per shaft.

In profile, the *Gefion*'s "ploughshare" bow profile was replaced by an elongated "ram" bow. This proved to make the ships wet at higher speeds, and all were later modified. The *Gefion*'s vertical funnels and masts were given a rake in the Bremens. With a need to reduce topside weight, however, these were also modified, being reduced to half-casings.

Sometimes listed as a separate class, the *Danzig* and *Leipzig* varied in detail. In profile, they had vertical funnels and masts from the outset, while the foremast was stepped from the bridge structure rather than forward of it.

The *Leipzig* was sunk by gunfire at the Falklands in December 1914, while the *Bremen* was destroyed by mines in

the Baltic. *Hamburg* and *Berlin*, although hulked, and serving in the capacity of accommodation ships or depot ships, survived to be scrapped and scuttled (respectively) after World War II.

Bremen class

	Built	Commissioned
Berlin	Danzig Dockyard	April 4, 1905
Bremen	AG "Weser" Bremen	May 19, 1904
Danzig	Danzig Dockyard	December 1, 1907
Hamburg	AG "Vulcan", Stettin	March 8, 1904
Leipzig	AG "Weser", Bremen	April 20, 1906
Lübeck	AG "Vulcan", Stettin	April 26, 1905
München	AG "Weser", Bremen	January 10, 1905

Bremen (as built)

Displacement: 3,333 tonnes/3,280 tons (normal); 3,860 tonnes/3,800 tons (full load)
Length: 110.6m/363ft (wl); 111.1m/364ft 8in (oa)
Beam: 13.3m/43ft 8in
Draught: 5.5m/18ft 2in (normal)
Armament: 10 x 10.5cm/4.1in (10x1) guns; 2 x 450mm/17.7in torpedo tubes (2x1)
Machinery: Vertical, 3-cylinder, triple-expansion engines, 10 boilers, 2 shafts
Power: 7,460kW/10,000ihp for 22 knots
Endurance: 874 tonnes/860 tons (coal) for 7,871km/4,250nm at 12 knots
Protection: 20–80mm/0.79–3.1in (protective deck)
Complement: 295

LEFT: **Lead ship of a class of four, the *Königsberg* was station ship in German East Africa. Following a short raiding career conspicuously lacking in initiative, she was blockaded and finally destroyed amid the mud and jungle of the Rufiji delta. Her wreck remained until the 1960s.** ABOVE: **The *Emden* had notable success as a raider in the Indian Ocean during 1915, sinking 16 merchant ships.**

Königsberg and Dresden class

The Bremens initiated a continuous building sequence of multi-purpose light cruisers that produced, on average, two ships annually, their gradual refinement being accompanied by increasing size and displacement.

Laid down in 1905, the *Königsberg* is sometimes classified as a one-off, being the only ship with a 115.3m/378ft 6in hull. Over 4m/13ft 1in longer than a Bremen, she had reciprocating engines powered for 23 knots.

Although longer than the *Danzig*, the *Königsberg* was virtually indistinguishable except for a less protruding bow profile. Her three near-sisters had rearranged boiler and machinery spaces, resulting in asymmetrically spaced funnels. This new layout increased hull length by a further 2m/6ft 7in.

Of the three, the *Stettin* was turbine-driven and equipped with two propellers per shaft. A sister, *Stuttgart*, was

modified late in World War I to carry three seaplanes aft. Four of her ten 10.5cm/4.1in guns had to be sacrificed but she could now alternatively carry over 100 mines.

Both laid down in 1906, the *Dresden* and *Emden* readopted a three symmetrical funnel profile. The *Dresden* was also turbine-propelled, with two screws per shaft. They were also a further 1m/3ft 3in longer.

Having less cutaway on the keel profile, these classes were more directionally stable and less manoeuvrable than the Bremens, but were less tender.

Two of the class, *Emden* and *Königsberg*, became notable raiders during World War I, the former by virtue of her many successes, the latter because she holed-up in a muddy East African delta, necessitating a protracted operation to effect her destruction.

The *Nürnberg* was destroyed by gunfire at the Falklands, while her colleague, *Dresden*, escaped to spend three months as a fugitive before being run down. Cornered by British cruisers, she was scuttled in March 1915.

The final pair, *Stettin* and *Stuttgart*, were surrendered to Great Britain for demolition at the war's end.

Königsberg and Dresden class

	Built	Commissioned
Königsberg	Kiel Dockyard	April 6, 1907
Nürnberg	Kiel Dockyard	April 10, 1908
Stettin	AG "Vulcan", Stettin	October 29, 1907
Stuttgart	Danzig Dockyard	February 1, 1908
Dresden	Blohm & Voss, Hamburg	November 14, 1908
Emden	Danzig Dockyard	July 10, 1909

Emden (as built)

Displacement: 3,724 tonnes/3,665 tons (normal); 4,338 tonnes/4,270 tons (full load)
Length: 117.9m/387ft (wl); 118.3m/388ft 4in (oa)
Beam: 13.5m/44ft 4in
Draught: 5.5m/18ft 2in (normal)
Armament: 10 x 10.5cm/4.1in (10x1) guns; 2 x 450mm/17.7in torpedo tubes (2x1)
Machinery: Vertical, 3-cylinder, triple-expansion engines, 12 boilers, 2 shafts
Power: 10,066kW/13,500ihp for 23.5 knots
Endurance: 803 tonnes/790 tons (coal) for 6,945km/3,750nm at 12 knots
Protection: 20–80mm/0.79–3.1in (protective deck)
Complement: 360

LEFT: **Sole survivor of von Spee's squadron after the Falklands battle, the *Dresden* was on the run for nearly three months. Out of coal and in need of mechanical refit, she was run to ground at Mas a Tierra. Abandoned under a flag of parley, she was scuttled and already sinking as the British approached.**

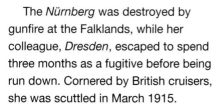

LEFT: The *Augsburg* lays to a buoy in a placid Kiel Fjord. Note how the curvature of the bow profile has become less extreme. The triangular day shapes, suspended from the mainmast, are connected to the rudder chains, moving differentially as rudder angle is applied. *Augsburg*'s rudder is here amidships.

ABOVE RIGHT: Wearing a battle ensign, the *Augsburg* engages Russian forces on the Baltic, where she saw most action. She is shown with her original 10.5cm/4.1in guns but she and the *Kolberg* were later converted to carry six 15cm/5.9in weapons, together with about 120 mines.

Kolberg class

By 1907–08, when the four Kolbergs were laid down, the Germany Navy had developed a versatile strain of light cruisers, well-adapted for fleet work, although probably less so for colonial duties where coal supplies and dockyard support could be sparse.

It was important to have a speed margin over the battle fleet, and the steam turbine promised compact and lighter machinery (and lower maintenance), with the possibility of faster cruisers without a punitive growth in size. Since the turbine's introduction by Parsons, however, the Curtiss Company and several German concerns had developed their own versions. More than their British equivalents, therefore, German cruisers became "one-off" test-beds for various types of machinery. Without reduction gearing, it was also difficult to translate developed power

into thrust, the Germans experimenting with two, even four, small-diameter propellers attached to the same relatively high-revving shaft.

Each of the four Kolbergs had turbines of different origins. The *Mainz* had two shafts, the remainder four. Powered for a full 2 knots more than the preceding Dresdens, the Kolbergs were 12m/39ft 4in longer and carried an extra pair of 10.5cm/4.1in guns. Their larger hulls were much stiffer, permitting a later upgrading of armament to include six 15cm/5.9in weapons.

The latter modification became general as the British were constructing equivalent vessels, all of which carried 152mm/6in guns. Multiple German 10.5cm/4.1in guns were highly effective in producing "smothering fire", but the British 152mm/6in possessed indisputably greater stopping-power.

All such arguments were somewhat academic for the *Köln* and *Mainz*, which were overwhelmed by the 305mm/12in gun fire of British battlecruisers at the Heligoland Bight action. Following the war, the *Augsburg* was one of many comparatively new German ships scrapped, while the *Kolberg* herself, awarded to the French as reparation, served until 1929 as the *Colmar*, one of four assuming Alsatian names.

Kolberg class

	Built	Commissioned
Augsburg	Kiel Dockyard	October 1, 1910
Kolberg	Schichau, Danzig	June 21, 1910
Köln (Cöln)	Germania, Kiel	June 16, 1911
Mainz	AG "Vulcan", Stettin	October 1, 1909

Kolberg (as built)

Displacement: 4,430 tonnes/4,360 tons (normal); 4,994 tonnes/4,915 tons (full load)

Length: 130m/426ft 9in (wl); 130.5m/428ft 4in (oa)

Beam: 14m/46ft

Draught: 5.5m/18ft (normal)

Armament: 12 x 10.5cm/4.1in (12x1) guns; 2 x 450mm/17.7in torpedo tubes (2x1)

Machinery: Direct-drive steam turbines, 15 boilers, 4 shafts

Power: 14,168kW/19,000shp for 25.5 knots

Endurance: 985 tonnes/970 tons (coal) and 117 tonnes/115 tons (oil) for 6,019km/3,250nm at 14 knots

Protection: 20–80mm/0.79–3.1in (protective deck)

Complement: 365

ABOVE: One of several German cruisers to be ceded to France and Italy, the *Kolberg* became the French *Colmar*, as seen here. Note the larger 15cm/5.9in gun, modified searchlight arrangements and a Rangefinder added atop the armoured conning tower. She served the French Navy until 1929.

LEFT: *Karlsruhe* and *Rostock* were twin-screwed, higher powered versions of the four Breslau type. Stationed in Central America in 1914, the *Karlsruhe* (shown here) acted briefly as a raider but, while still being sought by Royal Navy cruisers, was destroyed by an internal explosion. BELOW: The two Graudenzes were three-funnelled versions of the Karlsruhes but, curiously, this impression of the *Regensburg* omits the "Y" gun, possibly removed to permit a full deckload of mines. The ten 10.5cm/4.1in guns were later exchanged for seven 15cm/5.9in weapons. Ceded to France, her wreck can still be seen screening Lorient U-boat pens.

Magdeburg, Karlsruhe and Graudenz classes

By the end of the first decade of the 20th century, Britain and Germany were locked into a ruinously expensive "naval race" where rivalry in cruiser construction was no less fierce than that in dreadnoughts.

In 1909, the British laid down the *Chatham*, which repeated the eight 152mm/6in gun armament of the preceding Weymouths, increased installed power to 18,643kW/25,000shp and, for the first time, put armour into a belt rather than into a protective deck. The immediate German response was the four Magdeburgs, whose similar power required 16 boilers and four funnels. Although primarily coal-fired, they could use oil sprays for mixed firing to boost acceleration and speed.

Experimentation with machinery continued. All had steam-turbine propulsion but, where the *Strassburg* had two shafts, the *Breslau* had four and the remaining pair, three.

Although the designed armament remained twelve 10.5cm/4.1in guns, all (except *Breslau*) had exchanged them for seven 15cm/5.9in weapons by 1916. Their torpedoes were now also of a harder-hitting 500mm/19.7in calibre. They were the first to add an 18–60mm/0.71–2.4in belt to a 20–60mm/0.79–2.4in protective deck.

Increased displacement was reduced by adopting longitudinal framing in place of the earlier combination of longitudinal and transverse. A new, pleasingly raked "cruiser bow" was also introduced.

Before they were completed, four Karlsruhe and Graundenz-class ships were laid down. While a further 3.5m/11ft 6in longer, they had a uniform, twin-shaft arrangement. The Karlsruhes were higher-powered repeats of the Magdeburgs, and virtually indistinguishable from them. The Graudenz pair, however, reverted to a three-funnel layout. They also introduced superimposed after guns and four torpedo tubes of heavier 500mm/19.7in calibre.

Breslau, under the Turkish flag, was sunk in the Mediterranean. Post-war, the *Strassburg* and *Graudenz* served in the Italian Navy, the *Stralsund* and *Regensburg* with the French fleet.

Magdeburg, Karlsruhe and Graudenz classes

	Built	Commissioned
Breslau	AG "Vulcan", Stettin	May 10, 1912
Magdeburg	AG "Weser", Bremen	August 20, 1912
Stralsund	AG "Weser", Bremen	December 10, 1912
Strassburg	Wilhelmshaven Dockyard	October 9, 1912
Karlsruhe	Germania, Kiel	January 15, 1914
Rostock	Howaldstwerke, Kiel	February 5, 1914
Graudenz	Kiel Dockyard	August 10, 1914
Regensburg	AG "Weser", Bremen	January 3, 1915

Graudenz (as built)

Displacement: 4,989 tonnes/4,910 tons (normal); 6,482 tonnes/6,380 tons (full load)

Length: 139m/456ft 3in (wl); 142.7m/468ft 5in (oa)

Beam: 13.8m/45ft 4in

Draught: 5.9m/19ft 3in (normal)

Armament: 12 x 10.5cm/4.1in (12x1) and 2 x 8.8cm/3.46in (2x1) guns; 4 x 500mm/19.7in torpedo tubes (4x1)

Machinery: Direct-drive steam turbines, 12 boilers, 2 shafts

Power: 19,388kW/26,000shp for 27.5 knots

Endurance: 1,301 tonnes/1,280 tons (coal) and 381 tonnes/375 tons (oil) for 10,186km/5,500nm at 12 knots

Protection: 18–60mm/0.71–2.4in (belt); 20–60mm/0.79–2.4in (protective deck)

Complement: 367

ABOVE: The Breslau type were the first with four funnels and raked bow. The nameship appears here to be escort for the Kaiser's annual trip to Norway. Later notorious as having been transferred to Turkey in company with the battlecruiser *Goeben*, she foundered on mines early in 1918.

LEFT: **Wiesbaden** shows off her elegant, destroyer-like lines. Note the light signal yards which, being of diagonal X-form, appear asymmetric in quarter views. The toughness of the design was demonstrated at Jutland, where she absorbed tremendous punishment before sinking, most of her crew being lost.

Wiesbaden, Königsberg (II) and Köln (II) classes

The two Wiesbadens laid down in 1913 were 2.6m/8ft 6in longer than the preceding Karlsruhe and Grundenz-class ships. Designed to carry eight 15cm/5.9in guns from the outset, they had to be superimposed aft and the remainder sided. To reduce shaft speed, both had experimental hydraulic "transformers", on either shaft, with alternative propulsion by a smaller, cruising turbine equipped with reduction gearing. Their protective scheme was similar to that in the Graudenz and it proved very effective at Jutland when the Wiesbaden withstood tremendous punishment.

The succeeding quartette of Königsbergs (II) was commenced in 1914. As was customary, all were known by "ersatz" titles prior to launch, by which time, in 1915–16, they were granted names of cruisers already lost in action.

Of 151.4m/496ft 9in in length, they were given protective stowage for 200 mines, a feature that probably contributed to their tendency to trim by the stern. Their appearance differed from that of the preceding Wiesbadens in that the foremost of the three half-cased funnels was slightly longer than its partners, while two single 8.8cm/3.46in

high-angle guns were located on the centreline abaft them. The Karlsruhe (II) was the first German cruiser with turbines driving through full reduction gearing. Since the Graudenz, all carried ten coal- and two oil-fired boilers. Surrendered at the armistice, the Königsberg (II) served until 1936 as the French cruiser Metz.

The Köln (II) class, commenced in 1915, was the ultimate expression of the German World War I light cruiser. These were essentially further-enlarged repeats of the Königsbergs (II) but with eight coal- and six oil-fired boilers. Slow wartime construction saw only the Köln (II) and Dresden (II) ever completed of a projected ten vessel class. Both, together with Karlsruhe (II) were lost by scuttling at Scapa Flow in 1919. Salvaged, the Emden (II) and Nürnberg (II) were expended by the French and British respectively in tests-to-destruction.

LEFT: **This elevated view of Köln (II) arriving for internment at Scapa shows the sided layout of her open 15cm/5.9in gun mountings. Note that these later units had a lengthened forefunnel.**

Wiesbaden, Königsberg (II) and Köln (II) classes

	Built	Commissioned
Frankfurt	Kiel Dockyard	August 20, 1915
Wiesbaden	AG "Vulcan", Stettin	August 23, 1915
Emden (II)	AG "Weser", Bremen	December 16, 1916
Karlsruhe (II)	Kiel Dockyard	November 15, 1916
Königsberg (II)	AG "Weser", Bremen	August 12, 1916
Nürnberg (II)	Howaldtswerke, Kiel	February 15, 1917
Dresden (II)	Howaldtswerke, Kiel	March 28, 1918
Frauenlob (II)	Kiel Dockyard	Scrapped, incomplete
Köln (II)	Blohm & Voss, Hamburg	January 17, 1918
Leipzig (II)	AG "Weser", Bremen	Scrapped, incomplete
Magdeburg (II)	Howaldtswerke, Kiel	Scrapped, incomplete
Rostock (II)	AG "Vulcan", Stettin	Scrapped, incomplete
Wiesbaden (II)	AG "Vulcan", Stettin	Scrapped, incomplete

Plus three un-named; never launched

Köln (II) (as designed)

Displacement: 6,726 tonnes/6,620 tons (normal); 7,605 tonnes/7,485 tons (full load)
Length: 149.8m/491ft 9in (wl); 155.5m/510ft 5in (oa)
Beam: 14.2m/46ft 7in
Draught: 6.2m/20ft 4in (normal)
Armament: 8 x 15cm/5.9in (8x1) and 3 x 8.8cm/3.46in (3x1) guns; 4 x 500mm/19.7in torpedo tubes (2x2)
Machinery: Geared steam turbines, 14 boilers, 2 shafts
Power: 23,116kW/31,000shp for 27.5 knots
Endurance: 1,118 tonnes/1,100 tons (coal) and 1,067 tonnes/1,050 tons (oil) for 10,556km/5,700nm at 12 knots
Protection: 18–60mm/0.71–2.4in (belt); 20–60mm/0.79–2.4in (protective deck)
Complement: 560

Pillau and Brummer classes

In the course of the development of the German fleet cruiser there were two further pairs of ships built that did not quite fit the mould. A pair of 4,471-tonne/4,400-ton protected cruisers was laid down by Schichau in 1913 to their own design and to the account of pre-revolutionary Russia. Named *Maraviev Amurskyi* and *Admiral Nevelskoy*, they were slightly smaller than their German counterparts, and could be distinguished by their greater freeboard and vertical stem. Their three funnels were also cased to about two-thirds their height.

The two were appropriated at the outbreak of war, and their armament changed from a planned eight 13cm/5.1in and four 63mm/2.5in Russian-pattern guns to eight 15cm/5.9in and four 5.2cm/2in guns, the latter later exchanged for two 8.8cm/3.46in weapons.

Powered for 27.5 knots and capable of carrying 120 mines apiece, they were valuable acquisitions and were

commissioned into the German Navy as the *Pillau* and *Elbing* respectively. The latter was lost at Jutland and the former taken post-war by the Italians, serving until 1944 as the *Bari*.

The second pair was the *Brummer* and *Bremse*, laid down in 1915 as fast, offensive minelayers. To facilitate their operation in British waters they were deliberately profiled to resemble Arethusa-class ships, with bows of distinctive curvature, three slender funnels of equal height and masts crossed British style. Authenticity was increased through the ability to quickly strike the mainmast. Carrying their capacity load of 400 mines they were tender but, in normal trim, they were stiffer and sea-kindly.

Their main achievement was to surprise a UK-Norway convoy in October 1917 while operating together. They sank two escorting British destroyers and ten merchantmen. Just 20 months

ABOVE: **Designed to carry no less than 400 mines, the *Brummer* and *Bremse* were configured to resemble British Aurora-class cruisers. A pole mainmast could be shipped and the bow profile was more heavily curved. The pair successfully ambushed a British convoy in October 1917.**

later, both were on the bottom of Scapa Flow following the grand scuttling of the interned German fleet.

Pillau and Brummer classes

	Built	Commissioned
Elbing	Schichau, Danzig	September 4, 1915
Pillau	Schichau, Danzig	December 14, 1914
Bremse	AG "Vulcan", Stettin	July 1, 1916
Brummer	AG "Vulcan" Stettin	April 2, 1916

Brummer (as built)

Displacement: 4,455 tonnes/4,385 tons (normal); 5,949 tonnes 5,855 tons (full load)
Length: 135m/443ft 2in (wl); 140.4m/460ft 10in (oa)
Beam: 13.2m/43ft 4in
Draught: 5.9m/19ft 6in (normal)
Armament: 4 x 15cm/5.9in (4x1) and 2 x 8.8cm/3.46in (2x1) guns; 2 x 500mm/19.7in torpedo tubes (2x1)
Machinery: Geared steam turbines, 6 boilers, 2 shafts
Power: 24,608kW/33,0000shp for 28 knots
Endurance: 610 tonnes/600 tons (coal) and 1,016 tonnes/1,000 tons (oil) for 10,742km/5,800nm at 12 knots
Protection: 40mm/1.57in (belt); 150mm/4.13in (protective deck)
Complement: 310

LEFT: **Distinguishable from other German light cruisers by virtue of their vertical stems, *Pillau* and *Elbing* were being built to Russian account when taken over. Ceded to Italy in 1919, the *Pillau* was renamed *Bari*. As seen here, her funnels were reduced to two and, together with her masts, shortened.**

FAR LEFT: **The elegant lines of the German-built *Askold* pre-date those of later German light cruisers. She also incorporated both protective deck and side belts. Guns at upper deck level are of 15cm/5.9in calibre; those on the main deck are of 76mm/3in.**

ABOVE: **Seized by the Bolsheviks in 1917, the *Askold* was taken by the British in August 1918. After two years' service as a depot ship she was offered back to the Russians, but was in so deplorable a state that she was scrapped in Germany. Of her former glory, only the Imperial eagle remains here, at the stem head.**

Askold

Hitherto weak in effective, medium-sized cruisers, the Russian Navy ordered nine in the late 1890s. Three of 6,096 tonnes/6,000-tons, (*Aurora*, *Diana* and *Pallada*) came from the Admiralty Yard at St. Petersburg but, as they were powered for only 20 knots, the design for the remaining six was put out to competition. This was won by Schichau, which was commissioned to build *Bogatyr*. The same general specification was issued to other builders for the remaining five.

Krupp's Germania Yard at Kiel only had recent experience in three of the small, 2,642-tonne/2,600-ton Gazelles, and had not built a 6,096-tonne/6,000-tonne vessel since the *Kaiserin Augusta*, completed in 1892. The *Askold*, which

they launched for the Russians in March 1900, thus contained elements of that design, but considerably refined in both form and power in order to produce a then-challenging 23-knot speed.

The *Kaiserin Augusta* could make 21 knots on 10,440kW/14,000ihp but the *Askold*, although longer and narrower, would require 17,896kW/24,000ihp. To develop this power, nine licence-built Thornycroft narrow-tube boilers were grouped in five adjacent, watertight spaces, each exhausted by a funnel. These five, quite closely spaced, earned the ship the nickname of "the packet of Woodbines", among the British, with whom she worked closely in the Indian Ocean and in the Mediterranean during World War I.

The *Kaiserin Augusta*'s flush-decked hull was retained, together with the long, narrow superstructure deck, which was profiled in plan to allow one centerline and four casemated guns to fire forward. A similar arrangement gave stern fire while two further, casemated, guns fired on the beam.

Askold's protective deck was of Krupp's patented nickel-steel plate, thickened to 100mm/3.94in on the high glacis that protected the crowns of the boilers and the three engines. On trials, the ship made a very respectable 24 knots on 17,599kW/23,600ihp.

LEFT: **Seen in Tsarist colours, the *Askold* attends a French fleet review. Although fitted for anti-torpedo nets, her stowage shelf is empty. Note that the net booms appear here, in an early picture, and above at her scrapping, but not during World War I (above left).**

Askold

Built: Germania, Kiel
Commissioned: 1901
Displacement: 6,096 tonnes/6,000 tons (normal)
Length: 129.9m/426ft 6in (bp)
Beam: 15m/49ft 3in
Draught: 6.2m/20ft 3in (normal)
Armament: 12 x 152mm/6in (12x1);
　　12 x 76mm/3in (12x1) guns; 6 x 381mm/15in
　　torpedo tubes (6x1)
Machinery: Vertical, triple-expansion engines,
　　9 boilers, 3 shafts
Power: 17,896kW/24,000ihp for 23 knots
Bunkers: 1,118 tonnes/1,100 tons (coal)
Protection: 76mm/3in (protective deck)
Complement: 500

Directory of Cruisers

1918 to the Present Day

Between the wars, international treaties circumscribed cruiser numbers and introduced the concept of "heavy" and "light" cruisers. Most routinely carried aircraft for spotting and reconnaissance, together with increasing numbers of lighter weapons to meet the fast-developing menace of air attack. In commerce protection, cruisers were valued particularly in the provision of convoy defence in the face of hostile air superiority. This led directly to the introduction of the specialist category of anti-aircraft cruiser.

With war, cruiser-on-cruiser actions were confined largely to fierce exchanges in the Pacific but, in all theatres, cruisers proved invaluable for gunfire support to operations ashore. Using conference-limited designs as a starting point, the United States built extended classes of standard cruiser before 1945. Mostly mothballed during the ensuing Cold War, they proved ill-suited for conversion to guided-missile status, and fell victim to block obsolescence. Bespoke guided-missile cruisers emerged, with progressive miniaturization of electronics reducing them to the scale of large destroyer-sized escorts.

LEFT: **Although hailed as a "ship of the future" on her completion in 1964, the USS _Long Beach_ (CGN.9) proved to be an evolutionary dead-end, her nuclear power plant over-expensive, her solid-state 3-D radar over-complex, and her all-missile armament lacking in versatility.**

FAR LEFT: HMS *Kent*, probably seen here in late 1941, is considerably modified from her peacetime condition. Short tripod masts have replaced the earlier tall poles. Radars and light automatic weapons proliferate. She has not been cut down a level right aft, nor has she gained the ungainly boxy hangar, as on the *Suffolk* (right). INSET: A battle-ready *Suffolk* in 1942 has her main armament trained to cover each quadrant. Despite a good stability range, several of the class acquired so much extra top-weight that they were cut down aft and landed their torpedo tubes. Her original open bridge has been covered.

County classes (1926–29)

Following World War I, the British fleet was well served by large numbers of Town- and C-class cruisers, but these were not suitable for long-endurance, independent patrols in support of trade. With the wholesale disposal of large armoured and protected cruisers made obsolete by war, replacements were required. The design starting point for these was the new Hawkins class which was also held to be the reason why the Washington Treaty allowed future cruiser maxima to be 10,160 tonnes/10,000 tons displacement with a 203mm/8in main battery. As all five signatories immediately began building to these limits, the resulting ships became known as "treaty cruisers".

British designers, together with their foreign peers, found 10,160 tonnes/10,000 tons a tight stricture when tied to a 203mm/8in armament. To gain even inadequate levels of protection, the planned 74,570kW/100,000shp installed

ABOVE: A pre-war impression, showing *Exeter* with, incorrectly, equal-sized funnels. Neither ship was greatly modified before becoming a war casualty. Distinguished at the battle of the River Plate, the *Exeter* was lost in the Far East early in 1942. The *York* became a casualty during the 1941 battle for Crete.

ABOVE: Bedevilled both by global tonnage restrictions and tough economies, the Royal Navy built a couple of "B"-type heavy cruisers, 2,032 tonnes/2,000 tons lighter than the Counties and with two fewer guns. The *Exeter*, here, may be distinguished from the *York* by her vertical funnels and masts.

power for 33 knots had to be reduced to 59,656kW/80,000shp for 31.5 knots. This reduced machinery weight but, more importantly, it reduced the size of the associated spaces, allowing protection to be thickened.

The design of the twin 203mm/8in turret was novel, particularly in the available 65-degree elevation for a dubious anti-aircraft (AA) capability. Despite their spacious gunhouse, the weapons proved trouble prone. Considerable problems also attended the "for but not with" aircraft arrangements now required for independent cruiser activities.

The approved design was highly distinctive, the massive flush-decked hull featuring a continuous double line of scuttles that even flanked the machinery spaces, betraying a lack of side armour. High freeboard made for a more than usually spacious standard of accommodation but was, in itself, a subtle design feature that added depth to the hull, increasing longitudinal stiffness at little penalty in material weight.

With weight at so high a premium, the three funnels required by the spacing of the eight boilers could not have been welcome, particularly as they required subsequently to be significantly lengthened.

The first group of eight, known as the Kent class, were ordered under the 1924–25 Programme but, savaged by budgetary cuts, emerged as five British and two Australian units. Their design incorporated a partly internal anti-torpedo bulge which, too shallow to be effective, was omitted from the second group, the four Londons of 1925–26. This enabled the lines of the hull to be refined giving a theoretical extra three-quarters of a knot.

A final pair (the Dorsetshires) was added in 1926, with much the same characteristics but with heavier gun mountings and, like the Londons, lacking the Kent-type's torpedo tubes. Their protection was also redistributed and their fire-control arrangements improved.

Modernization during the 1930s saw some of what were popularly termed the Counties have their after end razed by

LEFT: Mechanics prepare *Suffolk*'s Walrus amphibian for catapulting. Ideally suited for its task of spotting and reconnaissance, the aircraft greatly enhanced a cruiser's capacity for area search. First flown in 1933, the Walrus was designed by R.J. Mitchell, father of the Spitfire fighter. ABOVE: *Devonshire* as completed, arriving from the Far East with paying-off pendant streamed. Note the very generous freeboard and capital-ship style sternwalk. Her aircraft is a Hawker Osprey which, in its seaplane form, was described as a fighter/reconnaissance aircraft. As a cadet training ship, *Devonshire* survived until 1954.

one deck level, saving weight sufficient to improve protection and to add a massive box hangar for aircraft.

Alone of all the groups, the *London* received an early wartime reconstruction that saw her gain a two-funnelled profile superficially similar to that of a "Crown Colony".

Although two further-improved ships (to have been named *Northumberland* and *Surrey*) were cancelled, a pair of 8,382-tonne/8,250-ton, six-gun diminutives was built. These, *York* and *Exeter,* were the first of what were hoped would be a class of fleet cruiser of a size capable of undertaking trade protection duties. With similar machinery to their larger running mates, they were fitted with only two funnels, the fatter forward one being two trunked into a single casing.

Continuously improved, particularly in fire-control, anti-aircraft armament and, eventually, electronics, the Counties performed well under wartime conditions. *Canberra, Cornwall, Dorsetshire* and both diminutives all became war casualties. Of the various international designs of "treaty cruisers", the Counties can be fairly claimed to have been given the best-balanced design.

ABOVE: Due to the outbreak of war, *London* became the only County to undergo thorough modernization. Her new layout and appearance closely followed that of a "Crown Colony", but the high freeboard was retained.

BELOW: The British 203mm/8in gun, seen here on *London*, was introduced as a direct result of the Washington Treaty. It was a 50-calibre weapon which fired a 116kg/256lb shell. Designed for a 70-degree elevation and an optimistic rate of fire of 12 rounds per minute, the mounting was overweight.

County classes (1926–29)

	Built	Commissioned
Kent	Chatham Dockyard	June 25, 1928
Australia	Brown, Clydebank	April 24, 1928
Berwick	Fairfield, Glasgow	February 15, 1928
Canberra	Brown, Clydebank	July 10, 1928
Cornwall	Devonport Dockyard	May 8, 1928
Cumberland	Vickers, Barrow	February 23, 1928
Suffolk	Portsmouth Dockyard	May 31, 1928
London	Portsmouth Dockyard	January 31,1929
Devonshire	Devonport Dockyard	March 18, 1929
Shropshire	Beardmore, Glasgow	September 12, 1929
Sussex	Hawthorn Leslie, Tyne	March 19, 1929
Dorsetshire	Portsmouth Dockyard	September 30, 1930
Norfolk	Fairfield, Glasgow	April 30, 1930

County classes (1926–29) (for later variants)

Displacement: 9,703 tonnes/9,550 tons (standard); 13,463 tonnes/13,250 tons (full load)
Length: 181.5m/595ft (bp); 192.7m/632ft 8in (oa)
Beam: 20.1m/66ft
Draught: 5.2m/17ft (standard)
Armament: 8 x 203mm/8in (4x2), 4 x 102mm/4in (4x1) guns and 4 x 2pdr pompom (4x1) guns; 8 x 533mm/21in torpedo tubes (2x4)
Machinery: Geared steam turbines, 8 boilers, 4 shafts
Power: 59,656kW/80,000shp for 32.25 knots
Endurance: 3,251 tonnes/3,200 tons (oil) for 23,150km/12,500nm at 12 knots
Protection: 25mm/1in (sides – amidships); 76–112mm/3–4.4in (magazines); 25mm/1in (turret)
Complement: 784

Leander and Improved Leander classes

Throughout the 1920s the Royal Navy was well-served by the many light cruisers of the late war's emergency programmes. By the end of the decade, however, general parameters for replacements had been drawn up, designed around an eight-gun main battery of four twin 152mm/6in turrets. The desired 31.5-knot speed and 6,000 nautical mile endurance would require machinery of 47,000kW/63,000shp and a (standard) displacement of about 7,112 tonnes/7,000 tons. With facilities for two aircraft, the proposal appeared a useful compromise for both fleet and trade protection duties. Additional incentive to build was to be provided by the forthcoming 1930 London Naval Conference, which would effectively end the "treaty cruiser" race while putting a global limit on permitted light cruiser tonnage. To construct adequate numbers of these, individual displacements would need to be minimized, assisted by the new technique of welding, obviating the weight of rivets and plate overlaps.

An innovation was to group three boiler rooms together, ahead of three adjacent machinery spaces. Although the arrangement was vulnerable to a single torpedo hit, it allowed six boilers to be exhausted via a single, trunked funnel. This large and unique feature (hated by those who had to paint it) was very much the "trademark" of the five-ship Leander class of the early 1930s. Of these, *Ajax* and *Achilles* achieved fame at the River Plate, while the *Orion* survived some of the worst damage sustained by a British cruiser.

American design practice favoured alternating boiler and machinery spaces to improve survivability, and this "unit system" was incorporated in three follow-on Leanders, or Amphions, all of which were transferred to the Royal Australian Navy. They differed externally in their two, widely spaced funnels, which resulted in cramped aircraft arrangements.

In practice, boilers could be operated at higher than designed pressures, generating power for 32.5 knots.

Leander and Improved Leander classes

	Built	Commissioned
Leander	Devonport Dockyard	March 24, 1933
Achilles	Cammell Laird, Birkenhead	October 6, 1933
Ajax	Vickers, Barrow	April 12, 1935
Neptune	Portsmouth Dockyard	February 12, 1934
Orion	Devonport Dockyard	January 18, 1934
Perth (ex-*Amphion*)	Portsmouth Dockyard	July 6, 1937
Hobart (ex-*Apollo*)	Devonport Dockyard	January 13, 1936
Sydney (ex-*Phaeton*)	Swan Hunter, Tyne	September 24, 1935

Leander class

Displacement: 7,366 tonnes/7,250 tons (standard); 9,703 tonnes/9,550 tons (full load)

Length: 159m/522ft (bp;) 168.9m/554ft 6in (oa)

Beam: 17.1m/56ft

Draught: 4.7m/15ft 6in

Armament: 8 x 152mm/6in (4x2); 4 x 102mm/4in (4x1) (later eight, 4 x 2) guns; 3 x quadruple 12.7mm/0.5in machine-guns; 8 x 533mm/21in torpedo tubes (2x4)

Machinery: Geared steam turbines, 6 boilers, 4 shafts

Power: 53,690kW/72,000shp for 32.5 knots

Endurance: 1,829 tonnes/1,800 tons (oil) for 12,964km/7,000nm at 16 knots

Protection: 25–76mm/1–3in (over machinery); 88mm/3.46in (magazines); 25mm/1in (turret roofs)

Complement: 570

ABOVE: **Of the five original Leander-class ships, the nameship and *Achilles* were operated by the Royal New Zealand Navy. *Ajax*, seen here, and *Achilles* achieved fame at the River Plate action in 1939. Pictured here post-war, *Ajax* has tripod masts and four twin 102mm/4in HA mountings, and "X" turret has been removed.**

LEFT: Seen post-war as a unit of the Mediterranean Fleet, the *Aurora* has wartime modifications – tripod masts, enhanced light armament, radar and extended bridge. She had a fine fighting record with Force "K", but was transferred to Nationalist China in 1945 as the *Chungking*. ABOVE: Small, agile and with good anti-aircraft armament, the four Arethusas were employed mainly in the Mediterranean. The *Penelope*, in her original condition, without ensign and making smoke, is seen here probably on contractors' sea trials. Dry-docked during the Malta blitz, she was so punctured by fragments as to be nicknamed "Pepperpot".

Arethusa class

At the same time as the Leander design development there was a requirement for a new class of small fleet cruiser – fast and handy enough to lead destroyers yet able to shadow unobtrusively, qualities well exhibited in the C- and D-classes. These, however, displaced under 4,064 tonnes/4,000 tons, considered insufficient for the new ships, which would require endurance adequate to operate in Far Eastern waters. Other desirable features included six 152mm/6in guns in twin turrets, a speed of at least 32 knots and minimum protection against destroyer gunfire.

The five proposals evolved for consideration nicely illustrate the compromises necessary in warship design, where the dominant qualities of speed, armament and protection can be improved only at the expense of each other. Of the five draft designs, the smallest could make 38 knots but was

entirely unprotected, while the largest embodied the required protection and armament but was of 6,909 tonnes/ 6,800 tons and could manage only 31.5 knots. An acceptable mean resulted in the 5,537-tonne/5,450-ton Arethusa design, of which the nameship was ordered under the 1931 Programme.

With machinery again disposed according to the unit system, there were two widely spaced funnels, which again constricted topside aircraft arrangements. The class was limited to only four ships, mainly because foreign fleets particularly that of the Japanese, were building large and powerful 152mm/6in cruisers which the Royal Navy needed to watch. Tonnage remaining under the London Treaty had to be devoted to these.

Much British opinion considered that the Arethusas represented "an awful lot of ship for only six guns", while the Americans thought them too small to

be of much use. The quartet nonetheless gained great credit in the Mediterranean, where the *Aurora* in particular led destroyers to considerable effect, the task for which she was intended.

The *Galatea* and *Penelope* became war losses, both to submarine torpedoes.

Arethusa class

	Built	Commissioned
Arethusa	Chatham Dockyard	May 23, 1935
Aurora	Portsmouth Dockyard	November 12, 1937
Galatea	Scotts, Greenock	August 4, 1935
Penelope	Harland & Wolff, Belfast	November 13, 1936

Arethusa class

Displacement: 5,537 tonnes/5,450 tons (standard); 7,010 tonnes/6,900 tons (full load)
Length: 146.2m/480ft (bp); 154.2m/506ft (oa)
Beam: 15.5m/51ft
Draught: 4.2m/13ft 9in
Armament: 6 x 152mm/6in (3x2), 8 x 102mm/4in (4x2) and 8 x 2pdr pompom (2x4) guns; 6 x 533mm/21in torpedo tubes (2x3)
Machinery: Geared steam turbines, 4 boilers, 4 shafts
Power: 47,724kW/64,000shp for 32.25 knots
Endurance: 1,320 tonnes/1,300 tons (oil) for 10,186km/5,500nm at 15 knots
Protection: 70mm/2.76in (over machinery); 85mm/3.35in (magazines)
Complement: 500

ABOVE: *Galatea*, seen pre-war. She has no aircraft aboard, which emphasizes the position of the after funnel, set unusually far back due to the separated boiler spaces. Like the *Penelope*, she eventually fell victim to a submarine torpedo, small cruisers proving vulnerable to hits in the machinery spaces.

Southampton and Improved Southampton classes

Japan, with some reason, felt aggrieved at what she considered inadequate tonnage quotas allocated to her at the Washington and 1930 London conferences. At the latter, global tonnage limits were agreed on for both heavy and light cruiser categories and, as few more of the former could now be built, the emphasis was now focused on ships with guns of under 155mm/6.1in calibre. British policy was to keep individual size limited in order to gain the maximum number of, what were hoped to be, inexpensive cruisers. With barely half the United Kingdom's allocation, however, Japan decided to opt for size and fighting power. To this end, she would be able to construct a dozen vessels, each of a little under 8,738 tonnes/8,600 tons displacement. In 1931, therefore, the *Mogami* was laid down, to be armed with no less than

ABOVE MIDDLE: **As designed, with four turrets, the Towns were elegant, but lacked AA defence. *Gloucester*, shown here, was destroyed by air attack in May 1941.**
ABOVE: ***Birmingham* was the only Town to lack a knuckle forward. Note, in this 1946 picture, "X" turret replaced by a quadruple 40mm/1.57in mounting, and the wartime accumulation of radars.**

five triple 155mm/6.1in turrets. Little information was released about them, but the type was also known to be fast and reasonably protected.

That the Japanese were cheating may well have been suspected but, in the absence of means of verification, both Britain and the United States were stirred to suitable response, the latter in developing the design of the 10,169-tonne/ 10,000-ton 15-gun Brooklyn class.

By mid-1933 the Japanese had four large light cruisers under construction and then, as treaty terms required, announced their intention of commencing a further four. The British Admiralty thus called for counter-proposals, all more modest than either the Japanese or American designs because their waterline length needed to be compatible with dry docks existing within the Commonwealth. This length realistically permitted only four turrets and would affect maximum speed.

It was required that the new ships be able to take on any other 152mm/6in-armed opponent. Vertical armour over magazines and machinery spaces was thus specified to be impervious to such calibre at any range, and horizontal protection to be good out to 14,630m/16,000yds, beyond which range 152mm/6in hits would be rare.

A first pair was ordered under the 1933 Programme and, at 9,246 tonnes/9,100 tons, were able to ship four triple 152mm/6in turrets and a realistic anti-aircraft (AA) battery of four 102mm/4in mountings. Fire control was initially limited by financial stricture rather than by space.

Three further units were added in each of the 1934 and 1935 Programmes. With the final trio, the rapidly growing aerial threat was acknowledged with thickened horizontal protection. Vertical armour was slightly thinned in order to spread it over a greater area but, even so, displacement increased by some 305 tonnes/300 tons, necessitating a small increase in both

LEFT: **En route to becoming a museum ship in 1992, *Belfast* shows all her post-war modifications. All surviving Towns acquired the inelegant lattice masting.** BELOW: **Completed in "Far Eastern" livery, *Southampton* is seen at her Tyneside fitting-out berth. The oblique lighting shows clearly the extent of her vertical protection.** BOTTOM: **Seen in 1946, *Liverpool* shows her wartime modifications. Her starboard anchor is catted, preparatory to the use of its cable to secure to a buoy in Malta's Grand Harbour.**

beam and installed power to maintain stability range and legend maximum speed.

With the addition of considerable wartime topweight, a major modification was the landing of "X" turret in favour of increased AA weaponry.

A final pair, commenced under the 1936 Programme, differed considerably. Restrictions on length were relaxed, enabling them to make an extra half knot on the same power. Consideration was given to fitting them with four quadruple 152mm/6in turrets, but these proved to be too complex. A major design difference was to move boilers and machinery considerably further aft, opening a considerable gap between bridge structure and fore-funnel. While this reduced smoke nuisance it did nothing for the ships' appearance. Their extra displacement allowed their after turrets to be carried one level higher, a further two twin 102mm/4in high-angle (HA) mountings to be added, and protection to be further improved.

Both types performed well under wartime conditions, with *Southampton*, *Gloucester* and *Manchester* of the original class and *Edinburgh* of the improved type becoming war casualties.

Southampton and Improved Southampton classes

	Built	Commissioned
Southampton	Brown, Clydebank	March 6, 1937
Birmingham	Devonport Dockyard	November 18, 1937
Glasgow	Scotts, Glasgow	September 9, 1937
Gloucester	Devonport Dockyard	January 17, 1939
Liverpool	Fairfield, Glasgow	November 2, 1938
Manchester	Hawthorn Leslie, Tyne	August 4, 1938
Newcastle	Vickers, Tyne	March 5, 1937
Sheffield	Vickers, Barrow	August 25, 1937
Edinburgh	Swan Hunter, Tyne	July 6, 1938
Belfast	Harland & Wolff, Belfast	August 3, 1939

Later Southampton class

Displacement: 9,754 tonnes/9,600 tons (standard); 12,852 tonnes/12,650 tons (full load)
Length: 170m/558ft (bp); 180m/591ft (oa)
Beam: 19.8m/64ft 10in
Draught: 5.33m/17ft 6in
Armament: 12 x 152mm/6in (4x3), 8 x 102mm/4in (4x2) and 8 x 2pdr pompom (2x4) guns; 6 x 533mm/21in torpedo tubes (2x3)
Machinery: Geared steam turbines, 4 boilers, 4 shafts
Power: 61,520kW/82,500shp for 32 knots
Endurance: 2,032 tonnes/2,000 tons (oil) for 14,816km/8,000nm at 16 knots
Protection: 114mm/4.5in (over machinery and magazines); 51mm/2in (turret roofs)
Complement: 700

Improved Southampton class

Displacement: 10,516 tonnes/10,350 tons (standard); 13,466 tonnes/13,250 tons (full load)
Length: 176.4m/579ft (bp); 186.9m/613ft 6in (oa)
Beam: 19.3m/63ft 4in
Draught: 5.26m/17ft 3in
Armament: 12 x 152mm/6in (4x3), 12 x 102mm/4in (4x2) and 16 x 2pdr pompom (2x8) guns; 6 x 533mm/21in torpedo tubes (2x3)
Machinery: Geared steam turbines, 4 boilers, 4 shafts
Power: 61,520kW/82,500shp for 32.5 knots
Endurance: 2,439 tonnes/2,400 tons (oil) for 18,520km/10,000nm at 16 knots
Protection: 114mm/4.5in (over machinery and magazines); 51mm/2in (turret roofs)
Complement: 785

LEFT: **HMS *Bermuda*, probably in the late 1950s. Her bridge has been enclosed in line with standards for nuclear warfare. Although comprehensive, her electronics are dated. The line of Carley floats in way of the forward funnel show that survival arrangements remain as poor as ever.**

ABOVE: ***Nigeria* was the last "Crown Colony" to retain her four triple 152mm/6in turrets, giving a more balanced profile, as originally designed. "X" turret was traditionally manned by Royal Marines, whose bandsmen may well be performing here on the turret roof.**

"Crown Colony" class

With the scheduled expiry of the 1922 Washington Treaty, limitation was carried forward with the Second London Conference of 1936. This was not a success as the dictatorships were already pushing the world toward another war, and rearmament was in the air. Japan considered herself a naval power equal to Great Britain and the United States, and withdrew when her delegates failed to persuade them to agree to parity on tonnage allocations. Italy, smarting from sanctions imposed by the League of Nations following her Ethiopian adventure, refused to sign the ensuing agreement.

Although little was gained from the conference, cruiser development was affected inasmuch as the signatories agreed to continue the moratorium on heavy cruisers (subject to a let-out clause) and that 152mm/6in ships should not exceed 8,128 tonnes/8,000 tons standard displacement. No limit was imposed on numbers although these, for the British, were circumscribed by a tight fiscal policy in time of recession.

As the international climate deteriorated, British defence budgets increased. Over a dozen proposed variations on an 8,128-tonne/8,000-ton vessel were developed for Admiralty consideration, combining the functions of fleet duty and trade protection, with anti-ship or dual-purpose anti-aircraft (AA) armament. The latter was arranged around the newly adopted 133mm/5.25in weapon selected for the contemporary Dido-class cruisers. As the Admiralty had pushed unsuccessfully for a 7,112-tonne/7,000-ton upper limit, 8,128 tonnes/8,000 tons appeared generous, allowing proposed arrangements of seven, and even eight, twin 133mm/5.25in gunhouses. Their 36.4kg/80lb projectiles compared poorly, however, with the 51kg/112lb, 152mm/6in round as a ship-stopper, and the Japanese use of the latter decided the issue.

After exhaustive consideration the Admiralty, perhaps surprisingly, opted for a Southampton's scale of armament on a displacement of some 15 per cent less. Because of this

ABOVE: **The blank side in way of the machinery spaces denotes the extent of the *Gambia*'s protection. Neither of those lost succumbed to gunfire, however; one was lost to bombing and the other to torpedo. *Gambia* was the last of class to serve in the Royal Navy, their material condition deteriorating rapidly.**

ABOVE: **Fully commissioned, *Gambia* lays in a dockyard basin as a "matey" passes with unusually purposeful stride. Elevated to the same angle, 102mm/4in and 40mm/1.57in weapons can be easily made out. *Gambia* served most of World War II under the New Zealand flag.**

similarity, the new type, to be called the Fiji class (or, generically, the "Crown Colonies"), is often assumed to have been a "no-frills" diminutive. However, despite four triple 152mm/6in turrets appearing to be somewhat ambitious on the size, the design was very carefully thought out, resulting in a more spaciously laid-out hull and a smaller crew.

A major departure, from the point of view of ship design, was the adoption of a modestly proportioned transom stern. Although immediately denounced for its somewhat utilitarian appearance if offered, at minimal penalty in weight, more internal space aft and a marginal increase in speed. From the stability angle, it also offered increased buoyancy to counter a stern trim following damage. Experience also proved it to reduce propeller-induced vibration.

By the end of 1937, when the first block of five Fijis was ordered, the provision of new cruisers was considered urgent and a further four contracts were let in the following year. All were completed after the outbreak of war and the abandonment of treaty restrictions. Additional weight, much of it located high in the ships, thus increased with each ship, eventually amounting to over 10 per cent of legend

ABOVE: **In 1957, *Nigeria* was purchased by the growing Indian Navy. Before transfer, she was given a modernization to bring her up to the standard of the latest. She finally lost "X" turret and gained lattice masts which did nothing for her appearance. She is seen here as the *Mysore* in Indian dark grey livery.**

displacement. Certain features, including wood deck sheathing, searchlights and one aircraft crane, were dispensed with, but the ninth hull, *Uganda*, and the final pair, had to lose "X" turret. Even this major step was largely offset by the enhancement of AA weaponry and the addition of torpedo tubes.

During 1944 there was a general move toward the removal of aircraft and their arrangements from cruisers. Always space-consuming and a considerable fire hazard, their passing caused little regret, their function being assumed by carrier-borne aircraft and the cruiser's own radars.

Of the 11 "Crown Colonies", only two, *Fiji* and *Trinidad* became war casualties, both by air attack. *Uganda*, *Gambia* and *Nigeria* served under the Canadian, New Zealand and Indian flags respectively. *Ceylon* and *Newfoundland* went to Peru after the war.

"Crown Colony" class

	Built	Commissioned
Fiji	Brown, Clydebank	May 5, 1940
Bermuda	Brown, Clydebank	August 21, 1942
Gambia	Swan Hunter, Tyne	February 21, 1942
Jamaica	Vickers, Barrow	June 29, 1942
Kenya	Stephens, Glasgow	September 27, 1940
Mauritius	Swan Hunter, Tyne	January 4, 1941
Nigeria	Vickers, Tyne	September 23, 1940
Trinidad	Devonport Dockyard	October 14, 1941
Uganda	Vickers, Tyne	January 13, 1943
Ceylon	Stephens, Glasgow	July 13, 1943
Newfound-land	Swan Hunter, Tyne	January 20, 1943

"Crown Colony" class

Displacement: 8,636 tonnes/8,500 tons (standard); 10,923 tonnes/10,750 tons (full load)
Length: 163.9m/538ft (bp); 169.2m/555ft 6in (oa)
Beam: 18.9m/62ft
Draught: 5m/16ft 6in (standard)
Armament: 12/9 x 152mm/6in (4x3/3x3), 8 x 102mm/4in (4x2) and 8/12 x 2pdr pompom (2x4/3x4) guns; 6 x 533mm/21in torpedo tubes
Machinery: Geared steam turbines, 4 boilers, 4 shafts
Power: 59,656kW/80,000shp for 32.25 knots
Endurance: 1,727 tonnes/1,700 tons (oil) for 14,816km/8,000nm at 16 knots
Protection: 82mm/3.23in (over machinery spaces); 88mm/3.46in (magazines sides); 51mm/1in (turret roofs)
Complement: 735

ABOVE: ***Jamaica* was the only "Crown Colony" to ship a stump mast amidships. Offset to port, and forward of the after funnel, only its top is visible here. Note how the centre 152mm/6in gun is set in to avoid mutual interference when salvo firing.**

LEFT: Prettiest of ships, the Didos were designed for the AA defence of formations and convoys. They proved to be absolutely invaluable in the confines of the Mediterranean where, in the absence of carriers, enemy air superiority was the norm. *Sirius* is seen here leaving Malta.

Dido and Improved Dido classes

The Royal Navy's C-in-C, Mediterranean, was more aware than most that his fleet operated in relatively confined waters which, even in the mid-1930s, were under most potential threat from land-based air power. Therefore, when the Admiralty favoured expending its treaty-limited cruiser tonnage on ships capable of both fleet and trade protection duties, he persisted with a case for a small design of fleet escort, capable of mounting barrage anti-aircraft (AA) fire in defence of the fleet or of convoys, against high-level bombing or torpedo aircraft.

At the outset, the case was weakened for lack of a suitable gun. Even in a dual-purpose (DP) mounting, a destroyer-type 119mm/4.7in lacked sufficient punch against surface targets. Trials with a proposed 130mm/5.1in were not progressed while the World War I 140mm/5.5in was not considered for development. Only toward the end of 1935 did a new 133mm/5.25in prototype become available, to be complemented by a high-angle (HA) mounting promising an 80-degree elevation.

On the strength of this the Board of Admiralty gave initial approval in June 1936 for a 5,385-tonne/5,300-ton cruiser with, unusually, five twin turrets. Three were located in superfiring, centreline positions forward, resulting in a comparatively lofty bridge structure. This, in turn, demanded tall funnels, raked to carry smoke clear of the bridge. Although the resulting large silhouette was criticized, it had a pleasing elegance, assisted by the low freeboard aft (another criticized feature).

The first five ships of what were known as the Dido class were ordered under the 1936 Programme. With the London Treaty of that year removing limitation on numbers of hulls, five more followed in the 1937 and 1938 Programmes. A final six were added in 1939 during the run-up to war. It was the misfortune of the class that the chosen 133mm/5.25in gun and mounting was also specified for the DP secondary armament of the new King George V-class battleships.

The resulting demand for 40 extra mountings greatly slowed delivery for the Didos, affecting both completion dates and final armament. Three of the first four cruisers completed with only four turrets apiece, while two later units, *Scylla* and *Charybdis*, were given an all 114mm/4.5in destroyer-scale armament.

The final five units were designated the Improved Dido class. Recast around a conventional, four-turret layout, they had a lower bridge, set further forward, together with lower

ABOVE LEFT: *Scylla* (seen here) and *Charybdis* lost their 133mm/5.25in turrets to new battleships and, in turn, each acquired four twin 114mm/4.5in mountings intended for the updating of D-class cruisers. Their armament was thus on a par with a Tribal-class destroyer. LEFT: *Hermione* has the full outfit of five 133mm/5.25in turrets. This was not without its problems, as the considerable weight forward of the bridge structure caused heavy pitching which resulted in structural damage. With so much topweight, stability was also a delicate issue.

ABOVE: **A deck view of *Phoebe* at an unspecified date. Note the elevation of the guns in "X" mounting. Their 36.3kg/80lb shells could be fired at elevations of up to 80 degrees but the round turrets were cramped internally.**

LEFT: **The five Improved Didos were completed to a four-turret design, which permitted automatic AA weapons to be mounted in the old "Q" position. This in turn allowed the bridge structure to be lowered and lengthened, and the funnels to be shorter. The *Diadem*'s masts appear here to have been shortened but have been doctored by the censor.** MIDDLE LEFT: **The lowered, vertical silhouette of the later ships lacked the elegance of the original Didos but the larger bridge structure permitted them to work efficiently as force flagships. Topweight problems continued and the *Royalist*, which landed her torpedo tubes in 1944, had not regained them in this post-war shot.**

funnels. These no longer needed to be raked which, while beneficial in making their heading more difficult to determine, gave them an appearance more business-like than elegant.

In practice, the original layout proved over-ambitious, the weight of the three forward mountings causing distortion and cracking under dynamic loading in a seaway. Nor was the 133mm/5.25in gun an unqualified success. When it worked without breakdown, it worked well, but it was too heavy and lacked agility for it to be a truly efficient AA weapon.

Although several Didos were serving in the Pacific by the end of 1944, the type had limited endurance and earned its keep primarily in the Mediterranean.

Due to their limited size and questionable subdivision, the Didos were vulnerable to a single torpedo hit in a machinery space. Four of the five lost were sunk by torpedo and one by the still-new German air-launched, radio-controlled glider bomb. Four (*Bonaventure*, *Hermione*, *Naiad* and *Spartan*) were lost in the Mediterranean, the *Charybdis* in the English Channel.

Dido and Improved Dido classes

	Built	Commissioned
Dido	Cammell Laird, Birkenhead	September 30, 1940
Argonaut	Cammell Laird, Birkenhead	August 8, 1942
Bonaventure	Scotts, Greenock	May 24, 1940
Charybdis	Cammell Laird, Birkenhead	December 3, 1941
Cleopatra	Hawthorn Leslie, Tyne	December 5, 1941
Euryalus	Chatham Dockyard	June 30, 1941
Hermione	Stephen, Linthouse, Glasgow	March 25, 1941
Naiad	Hawthorn Leslie, Tyne	July 24, 1940
Phoebe	Fairfield, Glasgow	September 27, 1940
Scylla	Scotts, Greenock	June 12, 1942
Sirius	Portsmouth Dockyard	May 6, 1941
Bellona	Fairfield, Glasgow	October 29, 1943
Black Prince	Harland & Wolff, Belfast	November 20, 1943
Diadem	Hawthorn Leslie, Tyne	January 6, 1944
Royalist	Scotts, Greenock	September 10, 1943
Spartan	Vickers, Barrow	August 10, 1943

ABOVE: ***Bellona* in her late World War II condition, painted in a disruptive camouflage scheme and with paravane fittings on the stem. She was used extensively in Arctic waters, where the massive accumulations of topside ice exacerbated her already tender stability.**

Dido class (with intended armament)

Displacement: 5,588 tonnes/5,500 tons (standard); 7,366 tonnes/7,250 tons (full load)
Length: 147.8m/485ft (bp); 156m/512ft (oa)
Beam: 15.4m/50ft 6in
Draught: 4.3m/14ft 3in (standard)
Armament: 10 x 133mm/5.25in (5x2) and 8 x 2pdr pompom (2x4) guns; 6 x 533mm/21in torpedo tubes (2x3)
Machinery: Geared steam turbines, 4 boilers, 4 shafts
Power: 46,233kW/62,000shp for 32.25 knots
Endurance: 1,118 tonnnes/1,100 tons (oil) for 10,186km/5,500nm at 16 knots
Protection: 76mm/3in (sides to machinery spaces and magazines); 50mm/2in (roofs to magazines)
Complement: 490

LEFT: **Despite their advanced armament, the Tigers were obsolete on completion.** *Tiger* **and** *Blake* **were thus rebuilt aft to operate and support four AS helicopters for fleet support.** *Blake*, **here exercising with an American carrier, has lost all conventional armament except her forward 152mm/6in and 76mm/3in mountings.**

Swiftsure and Tiger classes

The "Crown Colony" design was considered a success and, in interest of wartime standardization, the later, nine-gun Uganda sub-class provided the basis for two groups of near-identical follow-ons. The three Minotaurs of the 1941 Programme had their beam increased by 0.31m/1ft to compensate for additional topweight. One of them, *Bellerophon*, was completed with an extra 0.61m/2ft in the beam, effectively qualifying her to belong to the later Tiger class of the 1941 (Supplementary) and 1942 Programmes.

Minotaur was completed as the Royal Canadian Navy's *Ontario*, whereupon the first group were renamed the Swiftsure class. Of the Tigers, both the lead ship and the *Hawke* were cancelled, the earlier *Bellerophon* assuming the name *Tiger*.

For a long time, the three remaining Tigers remained incomplete. Several armament schemes were proposed for them but when, in 1954, the decision was made to proceed, it was with fully automatic, dual-purpose, 152mm/6in and 76mm/3in twin mountings. Two

152mm/6in turrets occupied "A" and "X" positions, with 76mm/3in in the "B" position and sided in the waist. Although their hulls were already upwards of ten years old and their machinery of pre-war design, the ships were extensively remodelled, with far bulkier superstructure. The considerable increase in displacement exacted a 3-knot speed penalty.

Completed slowly in an era of severe economic stricture, the Tigers came into service too late, after the guided-missile age had already begun. Their complex new weaponry had the usual teething problems but, being already obsolescent, was never really cured of them.

With the Cold War emphasis on anti-submarine warfare (ASW) the fleet required more large specialist helicopters

and the *Tiger* and *Blake* were earmarked in 1964 for conversion to Command Helicopter Cruisers, carrying four Sea Kings apiece. Unconverted, the *Lion* was scrapped in 1972.

In their original form, the Tigers were the Royal Navy's last conventional cruisers.

Swiftsure and Tiger classes

	Built	Commissioned
Swiftsure	Vickers, Tyne	June 22, 1944
Bellerophon (renamed *Tiger*)	Brown, Clydebank	March 24, 1959
Ontario (ex-*Minotaur*)	Harland & Wolff, Belfast	May 25, 1945
Tiger (renamed *Bellerophon*)	Vickers, Tyne	Cancelled
Blake	Fairfield, Glasgow	March 18, 1961
Defence (renamed *Lion*)	Scotts, Greenock	July 20, 1960
Hawke	Portsmouth Dockyard	Cancelled
Superb	Swan Hunter, Tyne	November 16, 1945

Tiger class (before conversion)

Displacement: 9,703 tonnes/9,550 tons (standard); 11,888 tonnes/11,700 tons (full load)

Length: 163.9m/538ft (bp); 169.2m/555ft 6in (oa)

Beam: 19.5m/64ft

Draught: 7m/23ft (standard)

Armament: 4 x 152mm/6in (2x2) and 6 x 76mm/3in (3x2) guns

Machinery: Geared steam turbines, 4 boilers, 4 shafts

Power: 59,636kW/80,000shp for 29.5 knots

Endurance: 1,930 tonnes/1,900 tons (oil) for 15,742km/8,500nm at 16 knots

Protection: 82mm/3.23in (over machinery spaces); 88mm/3.46in (magazine sides); 50mm/2in (turret roofs)

Complement: 750

ABOVE: **In her original configuration, the** *Tiger* **clearly shows her "Crown Colony" ancestry. A fully automatic twin 152mm/6in turret is located at either end, with a 76mm/3in twin in "B" position and two more in the waist. Emphasis is on gunnery, with a director for each mounting, height-finding and search radars.**

LEFT: The Omahas were considerably, and individually, modified in the course of the war. In this July 1942 picture, the *Cincinnati* (CL.6) has lost her upper casemated guns and her aircraft catapults. She was the first cruiser to be fitted with the large CXAM-1 air search radar. BELOW: The *Omaha* (CL.4) in her original configuration. She then had ten torpedo tubes, the portside upper deck triple mounting being just visible ahead of the mainmast. The very tall masts were for the benefit of long-range radio transmission.

Omaha class

A first impression of the Omahas is one of an overgrown version of the "four piper" destroyers that they were intended to lead. Like them, they appeared very narrow-gutted although their length-to-breadth (L/B) ratio of 9.93 was not exceptionally high. In all, they appeared to be a good compromise of what can be achieved on a limited displacement and tight cost limit. However, their endurance was less than had been hoped for, and two, rather than four, aircraft were carried.

Earlier scout cruisers, although smaller, had high freeboard hulls that were anything but discrete, but the Omahas exhibited much of the long, easy sheerline of their destroyer charges.

A requirement for maximum end-on and broadside fire resulted in a unique gun arrangement. A narrow twin 152mm/6in turret was sited on the centreline, forward and aft. Flanking them and located at the corners of the bridge and after superstructure, were double-tiered casemates, each housing a further gun. Six barrels could therefore bear either ahead or astern and eight could be presented on either beam.

The original design dedicated the low quarterdeck to a fixed centreline catapult but design developments resulted in two trainable units being fitted one level higher, abaft the funnels.

As built, the ships had ten torpedo tubes, sided triple banks on the upper deck abaft the catapults and, below, twins at main deck level. These were closed off by shutters but, like the casemated guns, these positions proved to be very wet in adverse conditions, and the twin tubes were later removed.

By World War II standards, the Omahas lacked effective anti-aircraft fire control and their subdivision was inadequate. The low after freeboard and fine run gave very little reserve buoyancy to counter stern trim induced by action damage. Used mainly in second-line duties, however, none of their number was lost.

Omaha class

	Built	Commissioned
CL.4 *Omaha*	Seattle Construction & DD Co	February 24, 1923
CL.5 *Milwaukee*	Seattle Construction & DD Co	June 20, 1923
CL.6 *Cincinnati*	Seattle Construction & DD Co	January 1, 1924
CL.7 *Raleigh*	Bethlehem Steel, Quincy	February 6, 1924
CL.8 *Detroit*	Bethlehem Steel, Quincy	July 31, 1923
CL.9 *Richmond*	Cramp, Philadelphia	July 2, 1923
CL.10 *Concord*	Cramp, Philadelphia	November 3, 1923
CL.11 *Trenton*	Cramp, Philadelphia	April 19, 1924
CL.12 *Marblehead*	Cramp, Philadelphia	September 8, 1924
CL.13 *Memphis*	Cramp, Philadelphia	February 4, 1925

Omaha class

Displacement: 7,214 tonnes/7,100 tons (standard); 7,874 tonnes/7,750 tons (full load)
Length: 167.6m/550ft (wl); 169.2m/555ft 1in (oa)
Beam: 16.9m/55ft.4in
Draught: 4.1m/13ft 6in (standard)
Armament: 12 x 152mm/6in (2x2/8x1) and 2 (later 8) x 76mm/3in (2x1) guns; 10 (later 6) x 533mm/21in torpedo tubes
Machinery: Geared steam turbines, 12 boilers, 4 shafts
Power: 67,113kW/90,000shp for 35 knots
Endurance: 1,991 tonnes/1,960 tons (oil) for 13,149km/7,100nm at 15 knots
Protection: 76mm/3in (belt); 38mm/1.5in (protective deck)
Complement: 815

LEFT: **At Pearl Harbor, the *Raleigh* (CL.7) was hit in the machinery spaces by a torpedo, then by a bomb that passed through her. She flooded to the extent that she developed negative stability but was saved initially by lashing barges alongside. Final repairs were effected in California.**

FAR LEFT: **Oldest of the American "treaty cruisers" the two Pensacolas were unique in mounting ten 203mm/8in guns in a combination of twin and triple turrets. *Salt Lake City* (CA.25) here shows her distinctive bow profile and unusual "reverse bow wave" camouflage scheme.** ABOVE LEFT: **An early picture of the Northampton-class *Augusta* (CA.31). Although she spent the war in the Atlantic and was never fully modernized, she would gain very much more tophamper, with the tripod mainmast built around the after funnel.** BELOW: **The two Indianapolis class were an improved version of the Northamptons (*Indianapolis* seen here). Note how the superstructure layout is dominated by the requirements of aircraft, most of which were subsequently removed as fire hazards. This late World War II picture shows her with improved directors.**

Pensacola, Northampton and Indianapolis classes

With the 1922 Washington Treaty unintentionally creating the 10,160-tonne/10,000-ton 203mm/8in cruiser the US Navy embarked on a programme of 16, whose construction was to parallel that of the Omahas.

As ever, design studies led to necessary compromise, it being decided to combine a ten-gun main battery, and protection against destroyer-calibre (i.e. 127mm/5in) gunfire with a conservative speed of 32 knots. The 203mm/8in guns would be disposed in four turrets with, unusually, triples superfiring twins to keep the maximum number of weapons "dry".

Although 32 knots necessitated only seven boilers, eight could be accommodated with little penalty, giving the ships marginally higher speed. Unlike British practice, designers saved weight with a relatively shallow, flush-decked hull, relying on pronounced flare and sheer to maintain dryness. An observation floatplane was deck-stowed on either side of the after funnel.

So carefully was weight controlled that standard displacement came out at only 9,246 tonnes/9,100 tons. Only two ships, *Pensacola* and *Salt Lake City*, were thus built to this design, which was immediately recast to become the six Northamptons (CA.26–31). These were greatly improved by having a long forecastle for dryness, with extra strength and accommodation space. One main battery gun was sacrificed in order to improve layout with three triple turrets. A hangar was built around the after funnel and compartmentalization greatly improved, primarily through subdivision of the previously large boiler spaces. For an extra 3m/10ft on waterline length and 0.31m/1ft on the beam, they could now also be protected to resist destroyer gunfire at beyond 7,315m/8,000yds.

Problems with weight distribution caused sufficient ship movement to make poor gun platforms. This was partially rectified in the following pair, *Portland* (CA.33) and *Indianapolis* (CA.35), which were again slightly longer and utilized nearly the full allowable displacement to improve protection and gunnery arrangements with improved turrets and directors.

Pensacola, Northampton and Indianapolis classes

	Built	Commissioned
CA.24 *Pensacola*	New York Navy Yard	February 6, 1930
CA.25 *Salt Lake City*	New York Shipbuilding	December 11, 1929
CA.26 *Northampton*	Bethlehem Steel, Quincy	May 17, 1930
CA.27 *Chester*	New York Shipbuilding	June 24, 1930
CA.28 *Louisville*	Puget Sound Navy Yard	January 15, 1931
CA.29 *Chicago*	Mare Island Navy Yard	March 9, 1931
CA.30 *Houston*	Newport News	June 17, 1930
CA.31 *Augusta*	Newport News	January 30, 1931
CA.33 *Portland*	Bethelehem Steel, Quincy	February 23, 1933
CA.35 *Indianapolis*	New York Shipbuilding	November 15, 1932

Pensacola/Salt Lake City (as designed)

Displacement: 9,246 tonnes/9,100 tons (standard); 10,821 tonnes/10,650 tons (full load)
Length: 173.6m/570ft (wl); 178.4m/585ft 6in (oa)
Beam: 19.9m/65ft 3in
Draught: 5m/16ft 3in
Armament: 10 x 203mm/8in (2x3/2x2) and 4 x 127mm/5in (4x1) guns; 6 x 533mm/21in torpedo tubes (2x3)
Machinery: Geared steam turbines, 8 boilers, 4 shafts
Power: 79,789kW/107,000shp for 32.5 knots
Endurance: 2,144 tonnes/2,110 tons (oil) for 12,964km/7,000nm at 15 knots
Protection: 62–100mm/2.44–3.94in (belt); 25mm/1in (protective deck); 37–62mm/1.46–2.44in (turrets)
Complement: 655

LEFT: The ill-fated *Quincy* (CA.39) seen here covering the initial landings on Guadalcanal in August 1942. Days later she was lost, together with her sisters *Astoria* (CA.34) and *Vincennes* (CA.44), in the disastrous night action off Savo Island. ABOVE: The *New Orleans* (CA.32) seen here soon after her completion, with very light masting and open bridge platforms. The Astorias had their aircraft arrangements moved aft into a bulky, full width superstructure block. Note the height of the catapults.

BELOW: *New Orleans* again. By the end of the war she had acquired two large directors, the after one atop a considerable new tower superstructure. A cowl was added to the forward funnel and the port catapult was landed as weight compensation for the many new automatic weapons.

Astoria class

It will already be apparent that so-called "treaty cruisers" earned their appellation of "tinclads" through favouring armament and speed over protection. The US Navy suffered unduly in this respect through the rapidity with which it implemented its planned 16-ship programme. Designers were over-diligent in their efforts to save weight, resulting in early units being completed at nearly 914 tonnes/900 tons underweight. This could have been used to improve protection but following units were so well advanced that by the time that the situation was appreciated, little could be done.

With the final group (the Astorias), therefore, fierce debate developed over whether the extra displacement should be devoted to vertical or horizontal armour, to defeat short- or long-range fire respectively. How it was finally distributed would have a considerable "knock-on" effect on the ships overall layout.

In the event, the priority of protection was increased further at the expense of survivability. To decrease the area to be protected, machinery spaces were shortened by 4.26m/14ft. This reduced the length sufficiently to make impossible the sensible earlier unit system, whereby boiler and machinery spaces alternated. Externally, this design shift was evident in the closer-spaced funnels, which displaced the catapults and aircraft hangar further aft.

A more compact superstructure also replaced the earlier heavy tripod masts. This was made possible by improvements in radio technology, where antenna lengths were being reduced. The reduced tophamper greatly increased the unobstructed firing arcs of the ships' anti-aircraft weapons.

Three of the class were lost together in the disastrous Savo Island action of August 1942. Here, in a short nocturnal action, Japanese cruisers surprised an American-Australian force. Overwhelming short-range Japanese fire easily penetrated their armour, while uncontrollable fires were started in aircraft and boat facilities as well as in ready-use ammunition stowage areas. In two cases, a single torpedo hit put all boiler spaces out of action.

Astoria class

	Built	Commissioned
CA.32 *New Orleans*	New York Navy Yard	February 15, 1934
CA.34 *Astoria*	Puget Sound Navy Yard	April 28, 1934
CA.36 *Minneapolis*	Philadelphia Navy Yard	May 19, 1934
CA.37 *Tuscaloosa*	New York Shipbuilding	August 17, 1934
CA.38 *San Francisco*	Mare Island Navy Yard	February 10, 1934
CA.39 *Quincy*	Bethlehem Steel, Quincy	June 9, 1936
CA.44 *Vincennes*	Bethlehem Steel, Quincy	February 24, 1937

Astoria class

Displacement: 10,110 tonnes/9,950 tons (standard); 12,599 tonnes/12,400 tons (full load)
Length: 176.1m/578ft (wl); 179.1m/588ft (overall)
Beam: 18.8m/61ft 9in
Draught: 5.9m/19ft 6in (standard)
Armament: 9 x 203mm/8in (3x3) and 8 x 127mm/5in (8x1) guns; 8 x 12.7mm/0.5in MG (2x4)
Machinery: Geared steam turbines, 8 boilers, 4 shafts
Power: 79,789kW/107,000shp for 32.4 knots
Endurance: 1,935 tonnes/1,900 tons (oil) for 13,150km/7,100nm at 15 knots
Protection: 76–127mm/3–5in (belt); 57mm/2.24in (protective deck); 37–203mm/1.46–8in (turrets)
Complement: 751

Wichita and Brooklyn class

The inadequate protection of the earlier 203mm/8in "treaty cruisers" was a matter of some concern to the US Navy's designers and, when the 1930 London Naval Treaty allowed a total of 145,803 tonnes/143,500 tons of 152mm/6in cruisers, the demand from the outset was for more armour. Close behind were calls for a reckonable anti-aircraft (AA) battery and for four aircraft. Its requirements being different from those of the Royal Navy, the US Navy was ready to build 10,160-tonne/10,000-ton light cruisers in order to get what it wanted.

The rather messy aircraft arrangements in amidships locations on earlier ships had limited aircraft to two but, in the new Brooklyns, the aviation facility was banished aft. On the quarterdeck, sided catapults flanked hatch access to underdeck stowage for the required four machines. Externally, the development showed in a high freeboard and handling crane, the latter becoming a distinctive feature. The new layout was a success, greatly reducing the complexity of the earlier central structure and became the basis for later classes.

ABOVE: Last of the so-called "treaty cruisers", the *Wichita* (CA.45) was effectively a Brooklyn rearmed with three triple 203mm/8in turrets and enclosed single 127mm/5in mountings. Early in her active war she spent time in the Atlantic. A British light cruiser is visible to the left and a storeship lays on the far side of *Wichita*.

ABOVE: To a dramatic backdrop of burning oil tanks, *Phoenix* (CL.46) sorties from Pearl Harbor. The number of personnel, topside suggests that the actual raid has been completed. The ship's luck held right through until 1982 when, under the Argentinian flag as *General Belgrano,* she was torpedoed by a British submarine near the Falklands' exclusion zone.

Extra space in the waist allowed four single 127mm/5in guns to be mounted in tubs along either side. To save weight, the weapons were without shields but represented a genuine dual-purpose (DP) secondary battery. As an AA weapon the newly introduced 28mm/1.1in cannon was disliked as its projectiles had to impact the target in order to detonate. In contrast, the airbursts of a 127mm/5in gun created a distinct deterrent to a would-be attacker.

Although it was far slower-firing, the 203mm/8in gun was much preferred to the 152mm/6in by the Americans, who felt the latter lacked punch. Without sufficient heavy cruisers, the US Navy assumed, however, that they would have to work in conjunction with 152mm/6in ships and that these, therefore, should be capable of resisting 203mm/8in gunfire. For compatibility, a 32.5-knot speed was still required and, to match the new Japanese Mogamis, 15 guns were also needed. To achieve anything like the required level of protection, it was obvious that the full 10,160 tonnes/10,000 tons of displacement would be necessary.

A study was undertaken to examine whether shipping four triples rather than five twin turrets would release enough weight to make a dramatic difference to the design's immunity zone. It proved not to, so the distinctive "three turrets forward" layout was adopted, a disposition similar to that of a Mogami.

To minimize the area to be protected, the boiler spaces and engine rooms were again grouped. In the final two hulls, however, improved and smaller boilers allowed the spaces again to be divided although, as the funnels retained their spacing, this involved extra under-deck ducting.

Later modifications saw the single, 25-calibre 127mm/5in guns replaced by the new, and more effective, twin 127mm/5in 38-calibre weapon.

By treaty rules, the US Navy was still one heavy cruiser below permitted strength. Although it had only limited protection against 203mm/8in gunfire, designers modified the Brooklyn hull to accept three triple turrets with the heavier gun. The gun mountings were larger and heavier than those in the Astorias so that, for the first time, barrels could be elevated individually rather than in a common sleeve.

Only one ship, the *Wichita* (CA.45) was built to this design but she proved to be influential to the long series of war-built heavy cruisers that would shortly follow.

With fully worked-up crews, the rate of fire of a Brooklyn could be phenomenal, some being credited with ten rounds per barrel per minute. At the battle in the Surigao Strait in October 1944, for instance, individual ships were firing upwards of 1,000 rounds in the space of a quarter hour.

ABOVE: **An early wartime view of *Boise* (CL.47), the ship still painted a uniform shade of grey and lacking later electronics. The after freeboard is exceptionally generous as this was the first class of American cruiser to incorporate an aircraft hangar beneath the quarterdeck.**

ABOVE: **An interesting detail of the after end of *Philadelphia*. Note the two catapults, mounted along the deck edges and flanking the hatch access to the underdeck hangar. The aircraft crane was typical of US cruisers and has a Curtiss SOC-3 Seagull scouting and observation aircraft "on the hook".**

Wichita and Brooklyn class

	Built	Commissioned
CL.40 *Brooklyn*	New York Navy Yard	September 30, 1937
CL.41 *Philadelphia*	Philadelphia Navy Yard	September 23, 1937
CL.42 *Savannah*	New York Shipbuilding	March 10, 1938
CL.43 *Nashville*	New York Shipbuilding	June 6, 1938
CL.46 *Phoenix*	New York Shipbuilding	October 3, 1938
CL.47 *Boise*	Newport News	August 12, 1938
CL.48 *Honolulu*	New York Navy Yard	June 15, 1938
CL.49 *St. Louis*	Newport News	May 19, 1939
CL.50 *Helena*	New York Navy Yard	September 18, 1939
CA.45 *Wichita*	Philadelphia Navy Yard	February 16, 1939

Brooklyn class (as built)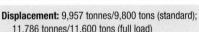

Displacement: 9,957 tonnes/9,800 tons (standard); 11,786 tonnes/11,600 tons (full load)
Length: 182.8m/600ft (wl); 185.3m/608ft 4in (oa)
Beam: 18.8m/61ft.8in
Draught: 5.9m/19ft 6in (standard)
Armament: 15 x 152mm/6in (5x3) and 8 x 127mm/5in (8x1) guns
Machinery: Geared steam turbines, 8 boilers, 4 shafts
Power: 74,600kW/100,000shp for 32.5 knots
Endurance: 2,235 tonnes/2,200 tons (oil) for 13,890km/7,500nm at 15 knots
Protection: 80–127mm/3.1–5in (belt); 50mm/2in (deck); up to 168mm/6.6in (turrets)
Complement: 870

ABOVE: **The career of the *Helena* (CL.50) was brief and eventful. Torpedoed at Pearl Harbor, she was repaired stateside and returned to the Western Pacific. She fought in a dozen, mainly nocturnal, actions before being struck by three torpedoes at the first battle of Kula Gulf.**

LEFT: **Armed with the lighter and more agile 127mm/5in 38, the American Atlanta-class cruisers were more effective AA platforms than the equivalent British Didos. *Oakland* (CL.95) belonged to the second group, which exchanged the wing 127mm/5in turrets for six more 40mm/1.57in weapons.**

Atlanta class

Although the US Navy disliked small cruisers it found, just as the British had long before, that large ships such as the 7,112-tonne/7,000-ton Omahas were not satisfactory for fleet work, lacking the necessary agility to either support or to repulse destroyer attack. The Second London Naval Conference of 1936 created a new unit displacement limit of 8,128 tonnes/8,000 tons which resulted in a new interest in smaller hulls. In 1938, a series of design studies culminated in the choice of a 6,096-tonne/6,000-ton vessel, too small to carry aircraft, but with the ability to work with and against destroyers, while covering the fleet against air attack.

Flush decked, with a long, easy sheer incorporating a British-style knuckle forward, the Atlantas had a single-calibre armament of sixteen 127mm/5in 38s. Three twin mountings were located in superfiring positions forward and aft, with a further two flanking the after superstructure. Forward of these were sided quadruple torpedo tubes. Automatic weapons, as designed, were limited to four quadruples of the unloved 28mm/1.1in cannon and six of the newly introduced 20mm/0.79in Oerlikons.

Soon classified as anti-aircraft cruisers (CLAA), the class of 11 comprised three distinct groups. The first four were followed by a second, which suppressed the two 127mm/5in waist mountings for more automatic weapons.

Inadequate stability saw most boats and their crane landed and extra ballast shipped. With the final trio, the torpedoes were omitted and the two centreline mountings at either end sited at the same level. Even splinter protection was reduced to reinvest in what eventually amounted to no less than thirty-two 40mm/1.57in and sixteen 20mm/0.79in weapons.

Additional crew to man this extensive battery and the endlessly proliferating electronics took the complement from a designed 549 to 812, with consequent overcrowding and loss of amenities.

ABOVE: **Confusingly, the sunken *Juneau* (CL.52) was replaced by a second of the name (CL.119), one of three built to a design modified to carry twenty-four 40mm/1.57in guns. Note how the centre 127mm/5in gunhouse is carried at the same height as the farthest. There are no aircraft, the afterdeck being occupied by two twin 40mm/1.57in. A quadruple mounting superfires the 127mm/5in.**

Atlanta class

	Built	Commissioned
CL.51 *Atlanta*	Federal Shipbuilding, Kearny	December 24, 1941
CL.52 *Juneau* (I)	Federal Shipbuilding, Kearny	February 14, 1942
CL.53 *San Diego*	Bethlehem Steel, Quincy	February 10, 1942
CL.54 *San Juan*	Bethlehem Steel, Quincy	February 28, 1942
CL.95 *Oakland*	Bethlehem Steel, San Francisco	July 17, 1943
CL.96 *Reno*	Bethlehem Steel, San Francisco	December 28, 1943
CL.97 *Flint*	Bethlehem Steel, San Francisco	August 31, 1944
CL.98 *Tucson*	Bethlehem Steel, San Francisco	February 3, 1945
CL.119 *Juneau* (II)	Federal Shipbuilding, Kearny	February 15, 1946
CL.120 *Spokane*	Federal Shipbuilding, Kearny	May 17, 1946
CL.121 *Fresno*	Federal Shipbuilding, Kearny	November 27, 1946

CL.51 and 52 both lost on November 13, 1942

First Atlanta group (as designed)

Displacement: 6,604 tonnes/6,500 tons (standard); 8,474 tonnes/8,340 tons (full load)

Length: 161.5m/530ft (wl); 165m/541ft 6in (oa)

Beam: 16.2m/53ft 3in

Draught: 5m/16ft 6in

Armament: 16 x 127mm/5in (8x2) guns; 8 x 533mm/21in torpedo tubes (2x4)

Machinery: Geared steam turbines, 4 boilers, 4 shafts

Power: 55,927kW/75,000shp for 32.7 knots

Endurance: 1,473 tonnes/1,450 tons (oil) for 14,816km/8,000nm at 15 knots

Protection: 28–95mm/1.1–3.75in (belt); 32mm/1.26in (deck and gunhouses)

Complement: 549

LEFT: Carrying no more 152mm/6in guns than, say, an 7,257-tonne/8,000-ton British "Crown Colony", the sheer size of the Worcesters appeared excessive. *Roanoke* is shown here. The design was no longer bound by treaty, incorporated heavy horizontal and vertical protection, and excellent subdivision. They could also maintain 32 knots.
BELOW: The ultimate US light cruisers of World War II design were completed too late to participate. *Roanoke* (CL.145) shows her twelve 152mm/6in guns, arranged in twin, fully automatic turrets. Note the fire control on its high tower, and the lack of aircraft catapults, although the crane remains.

Worcester class

Even in wartime, some concepts can take so long in development that they are doomed to obsolescence before completion. Such was the large Worcester-class light cruiser. Well before the United States entered the war they could see at first hand the deadly result of German air attack on Royal Navy ships obliged to operate beyond air cover. The Americans' 25-calibre 127mm/5in gun was ineffective against high-level bombing while its successor, the 127mm/5in 38-calibre, had yet to be proven. It was therefore decided to develop an automatic 152mm/6in dual-purpose gun. This, it was hoped, would counter not only the high-flyer but also provide rapid, smothering fire on to a surface target. The latter role, however, enjoyed a lower priority, for it was initially proposed that most of the protection be concentrated in a thickly armoured deck.

The pattern for the standard, war-built light cruiser had already been decided. This was largely based upon a pre-war design, and the new cruiser would need to be of an entirely new concept. The new design enjoyed little priority as the emergency programmes rightly consumed almost all the available manpower and material resources.

The size of what became the Worcester class escalated rapidly. Six twin 152mm/6in 47 gunhouses, disposed similarly to the layout of the late Atlanta class, and twelve twin 76mm/3in 50s (in place of the earlier thickets of 40mm/1.57in guns) required space; the resulting area, once armoured, increased displacement, and survivability required a unit-system machinery layout, which demanded length.

With the US Navy preferring weight of fire to volume it was proposed that the Worcester class be armed with the new automatic 203mm/8in gun, but the need to evaluate the 152mm/6in 47-calibre

(possibly against the new threat of anti-ship missiles) led to four of the class being ordered. By the time two had been completed, however, they had been superseded by carrier-borne and ship-launched missiles. The second pair were thus cancelled in August 1945.

Worcester class

	Built	Commissioned
CL.144 *Worcester*	New York Shipbuilding	June 26, 1948
CL.145 *Roanoke*	New York Shipbuilding	April 4, 1949
CL.146 *Vallejo*	New York Shipbuilding	Cancelled before launch
CL.147 *Gary*	New York Shipbuilding	Cancelled before launch

Worcester class

Displacement: 15,037 tonnes/14,800 tons (standard); 18,289 tonnes/18,000 tons (full load)
Length: 202.3m/664ft (wl); 207m/679ft 6in (oa)
Beam: 21.5m/70ft 8in
Draught: 6.5m/21ft 6in (standard)
Armament: 12 x 152mm/6in (6x2) and 24 x 76mm/3in (12x2) guns
Machinery: Geared steam turbines, 4 boilers, 4 shafts
Power: 89,484kW/120,000shp for 32 knots
Endurance: 2,438 tonnes/2,400 tons (oil) for 14,816km/8,000nm at 15 knots
Protection: 76–127mm/3–5in (belt); 88mm/3.46in (protective deck); 50–168mm/2–6.6in (turrets)
Complement: 1,560

LEFT: Seen separately at a distance, the *Worcester* (CL.144) could easily be confused with a late Atlanta, a distinguishing feature being the aircraft crane. The big gun tubs amidships contain twin 76mm/3in (rather than quadruple 40mm/1.57in) to defeat the kamikazes' threat. Note the large peacetime pendant numbers.

LEFT: **Even at completion, the Cleveland-class light cruisers (the nameship shown here) had a very crowded appearance, not least because of a heavy, dual-purpose secondary armament of six twin 127mm/5in 38s. By contrast, the masts at this stage seemed under-populated, with a surface search antenna at the foremast head and air search at the main.**

Cleveland and Fargo classes

Ship design is usually a process of evolution, with successful examples influencing their successors. The last of the treaty-limited Brooklyns was commissioned after the outbreak of war in Europe, but now, with all restrictions discarded, the problem for the US Navy was to produce light and heavy cruisers in the greatest number in uninterrupted programmes of series production. Both types were to be "no frills" workhorses and, with the Brooklyns having created a good impression, they became the starting point.

TOP: **An early overhead view of *Cleveland* (CL.55) emphasizes her compact superstructure, her long fine entry and generous waterplanes aft. The clear quarterdeck indicates the hangar hatch access. The starboard catapult was later removed and gun tubs added either side of the "fantail".** ABOVE: **At a little more than 10 knots, *Providence* (CL.82) moves clearly through a calm sea, with little disturbance. Weight accumulation was a concealed problem, however, for, when full power trials were eventually conducted, designed speed required over 8 per cent more power than that predicted.**

The final pair of Brooklyns had been redesigned, their machinery disposed on the unit system with alternate boiler and machinery spaces for enhanced survivability. They also received the new pattern 127mm/5in 38-calibre gun as a dual-purpose secondary weapon. Even before the war, however, the ships were showing signs of being cramped and of carrying too much topweight. As recast for the new Cleveland class the design was built around four, rather than five triple 152mm/6in turrets. The hull was maintained at the same length but was given extra beam. Right aft, the hull was given fuller sections and a distinct tumblehome in order to increase waterplane area and, thus, reserve stability. This was probably in response to criticism that the under-deck hangar was a large floodable space with considerable free surface.

Measures to increase stability were, however, soon offset by significant improvements in armament. In terms of footprint and weight, the twin 127mm/5in 38-calibre was superior to two singles. It was, nonetheless, not a trifling load for a light cruiser. Six were accommodated in the "hexagonal" layout that was to characterize the war-built cruisers, with one centreline gunhouse superfiring the 152mm/6in turrets at both ends, and others flanking the forward and after ends of the main superstructure.

The problem of topweight was, however, insidious. Automatic weapons first specified for the Brooklyns had been comparatively simple 12.7mm/0.5 machine-guns. These were later upgraded to the unsatisfactory 28mm/1.1in cannon. By the time that the first of the new Clevelands had been launched, shortly before the Pearl Harbor attack, the new twin 40mm/1.57in Bofors-pattern gun was being introduced. Where the twin 40mm/1.57in gun occupied much the same space and weight as a quadruple 28mm/1.1in weapon it was soon largely displaced by the quadruple 40mm/1.57in. Each of these required additional substructure and, with no available under-deck space, this meant elevating them, with a knock-on effect for the field of fire of neighbouring weapons and, of course, on ship stability. The process continued with the growing need to engage multiple aerial targets simultaneously, leading to a proliferation of directors which also needed to be located at points high in the superstructure.

With stability reserves so tight that planned improvements to radars had to be deferred, a major redesign of the ship was ordered during 1943. Externally, this showed in the massive single funnel, made possible by some rearrangement of machinery spaces. This permitted a shorter superstructure, in turn improving the "sky arcs" for AA weapons. All main and secondary gun mountings were lowered by small, but significant amounts. With the standard Cleveland-class programme in full flood, however, only two units (CL.106 and 107) were built to this revised specification.

Despite the shortcoming of an increasingly elderly and restrictive design, the Clevelands became the longest-ever cruiser series. About 35 could be considered eventually to have been completed, nine of them as fast light aircraft carriers (CVL). Thirteen more were cancelled, either outright or partially complete. Half a dozen were converted in about 1960 to interim guided-missile cruisers (CLG).

ABOVE: *Fargo* and *Huntington*, seen here, were the only two Clevelands to be completed to the revised, single-funnel configuration, which permitted a more compact superstructure with significant weight saving. Post-war, she served with the Mediterranean-based US Sixth Fleet. BELOW: **Even though executing a simultaneous starboard turn, *Biloxi* (CL.80) remains remarkably vertical, thus not complicating the fire-control solution. She has fired the centre gun of No.2 turret, the barrel still recovering from recoil. This late 1943 shot shows little electronic clutter topside.**

Cleveland and Fargo classes

	Commissioned		Commissioned
CL.55 *Cleveland*	June 15, 1942	CL.91 *Oklahoma City* (B)	December 22, 1944
CL.56 *Columbia*	July 24, 1942	CL.92 *Little Rock* (B)	June 17, 1945
CL.57 *Montpelier*	September 9, 1942	CL.93 *Galveston* (B)	May 28, 1958
CL.58 *Denver*	October 15, 1942	CL.94 *Youngstown*	Cancelled
CL.59 *Amsterdam* (I) (A)		CL.95 *Oakland*	July 17, 1943
CL.60 *Santa Fe*	November 24, 1942	CL. 96 *Reno*	December 28, 1943
CL.61 *Tallahassee* (I) (A)		CL.97 *Flint*	August 31, 1944
CL.62 *Birmingham*	January 29, 1943	CL.98 *Tucson*	February 3, 1945
CL.63 *Mobile*	March 24, 1943	CL.99 *Buffalo* (II) (A)	
CL.64 *Vincennes*	January 21, 1944	CL.100 *Newark* (I) (A)	
CL.65 *Pasadena*	June 8, 1944	CL.101 *Amsterdam* (II)	January 8, 1945
CL.66 *Springfield* (B)	September 9, 1944	CL.102 *Portsmouth*	June 25, 1945
CL.67 *Topeka* (B)	December 23, 1944	CL.103 *Wilkes-Barre*	July 1, 1944
CL.76 *New Haven* (I) (A)		CL.104 *Atlanta*	December 3, 1944
CL.77 *Huntington* (I) (A)		CL 105 *Dayton* (II)	January 7, 1945
CL.78 *Dayton* (I) (A)		CL.106 *Fargo* (II)	December 9, 1945
CL.79 *Wilmington* (I) (A)		CL.107 *Huntington* (II)	February 23, 1946
CL.80 *Biloxi*	August 31, 1943	CL.108 *Newark* (II)	Cancelled
CL.81 *Houston*	December 20, 1943	CL.109 *New Haven* (II)	Cancelled
CL.82 *Providence* (B)	May 15, 1945	CL.110 *Buffalo* (III)	Cancelled
CL.83 *Manchester*	October 29, 1946	CL.111 *Wilmington* (II)	Cancelled
CL.84 *Buffalo* (I)	Cancelled	CL.112 *Vallejo*	Cancelled
CL.85 *Fargo* (I) (A)		CL.113 *Helena*	Cancelled
CL.86 *Vicksburg*	June 12, 1944	CL.114	Cancelled
CL.87 *Duluth*	September 18, 1944	CL.115 *Roanoke*	Cancelled
CL.88	Cancelled	CL.116 *Tallahassee* (II)	Cancelled
CL.89 *Miami*	December 28, 1943	CL.117 *Cheyenne*	Cancelled
CL.90 *Astoria*	May 17, 1944	CL.118 *Chattanooga*	Cancelled

(A) Completed as Independence-class CVLs; (B) Later converted to CLGs

Cleveland class (improved)

Displacement: 10,313 tonnes/10,150 tons (standard); 12,090 tonnes/11,900 tons (full load)

Length: 182.8m/600ft (wl); 185.3m/608ft 4in (oa)

Beam: 19.6m/64ft 4in

Draught: 5.9m/19ft 6in (standard)

Armament: 12 x 152mm/6in (4x3), 12 x 127mm/5in (6x2) and 16 x 40mm/1.57in (4x4) guns

Machinery: Geared steam turbines, 4 boilers, 4 shafts

Power: 74,570kW/100,000shp for 32.5 knots

Endurance: 1,880 tonnes/1,850 tons (oil) for 16,205km/8,750nm at 15 knots

Protection: 88–127mm/3.46–5in (belt); 50mm/2in (protective deck); 76–152mm/3–6in (turrets)

Complement: 1,250

Baltimore and Oregon City classes

As the war-built Clevelands sprang from the Brooklyns, so did the 203mm/8in Baltimores stem from the one-off *Wichita*, herself an adapted Brooklyn. A major difference, however, was that where the Clevelands maintained the same length with a 7.7 per cent increase in beam, the latter had waterline length increased by 10.7 per cent and beam by 15 per cent. Inevitably, this resulted in a slower ship (although this was offset by more powerful machinery) but one less plagued by chronic topweight problems.

Like the *Wichita*, the *Baltimore* carried three triple 203mm/8in turrets, with a hexagonally disposed secondary dual-purpose battery of twelve 127mm/5in 38-calibre weapons housed in six twin gunhouses. Although the US Navy preferred the 203mm/8in gun to the 152mm/6in because of its superior penetration and stopping power (a typical projectile was about twice the weight) it attracted criticism because of its relatively

slow rate of fire. At this time, the Royal Navy reckoned on experienced gun crews being able to fire about six rounds per minute per 203mm/8in barrel, and eight rounds per 152mm/6in. The US Navy, however, claimed only four rounds per minute for 203mm/8in weapons. These used similar separate ammunition, i.e. the shell was loaded before the bagged firing charge. The weight of the projectile required mechanical loading, with the guns at a fixed angle of elevation. It will be apparent that the longer the firing range, and the consequent greater difference between the required elevation and the fixed loading angle, the slower the rate of fire. A fully automatic 203mm/8in gun was under development, but would require a larger ship to accommodate it (see Des Moines class).

In 1939, when the Baltimores required statistics were being argued between the General Board and the various responsible Bureaux, it would have taken considerable prescience to

forecast the extent to which each class would be burdened by the extra manpower demanded by wartime improvements. The size selected for the Baltimores was about right, but had to be defended against criticism that it would bar the ships from using many strategically located dry docks.

Itself overburdened at this time, the newly created Bureau of Ships (BuShips) passed much of the design work to Bethlehem Steel which, not surprisingly, went on to build many of the class.

Where the Baltimores would, in service, suffer the same proliferation of automatic weapons as did the Clevelands, the weight factor was less critical. Nonetheless, they too underwent a major redesign, with superstructure rearranged around a single large funnel, reducing the tophamper that restricted both director and gun performance. Only the first eight units were thus completed in the two-funnelled configuration. Of these, only the first four had characteristic

double aircraft cranes right aft. Later ships carried only two aircraft, the smaller underdeck hangar being served by a single, centreline crane.

Other than those converted, the Clevelands were discarded quickly after the war. More useful, often as peacetime flagships, the Baltimores and the single-funnelled Oregon Citys went on to give a further decade of service. Five saw conversion to interim guided-missile cruisers while one, the *Northampton* (CA.125) was totally remodelled as a new-style command cruiser.

For those still serving as heavy cruisers, the main updated features were ten twin 76mm/3in 50-calibre guns in place of the remaining quadruple 40mm/1.57in weapons, and a remodelled bridge. The US Navy preferred enclosed bridges but, for hostilities only, adopted the British-style open bridge, from which there was a better perception of the air threat.

ABOVE: **Post-war removal of catapults and aircraft gave the Baltimores a spacious quarterdeck, the crane being retained as a general-purpose utility. Space was again available for boats, most of the *Columbus*'s (CA.74) contingent here being waterborne. In 1962 the ship was recommissioned as a missile cruiser (CG.12).**

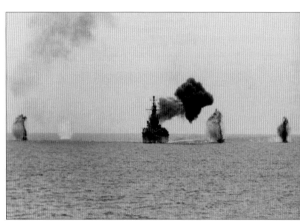

ABOVE: **The *Saint Paul* (CA.73) was the longest serving of the class, by virtue of having been considerably refitted to serve as a fleet flagship. Seen here on a bombardment detail off Vietnam, she has been neatly bracketed by shore batteries.**

Baltimore and Oregon City classes

	Commissioned			Commissioned
CA.68 *Baltimore*	April 15, 1943		CA.126 *Cambridge*	Cancelled
CA.69 *Boston* (A)	June 30, 1943		CA.127 *Bridgeport*	Cancelled
CA.70 *Canberra* (A)	October 14, 1943		CA.128 *Kansas City*	Cancelled
CA.71 *Quincy*	December 15, 1943		CA.129 *Tulsa*	Cancelled
CA.72 *Pittsburg*	October 10, 1944		CA.130 *Bremerton*	April 29, 1945
CA.73 *Saint Paul*	February 17, 1945		CA.131 *Fall River*	July 1, 1945
CA.74 *Columbus* (B)	June 8, 1945		CA.132 *Macon*	August 26, 1945
CA.75 *Helena*	September 4, 1945		CA.133 *Toledo*	October 27, 1946
CA.122 *Oregon City*	February 16, 1946		CA.135 *Los Angeles*	July 22, 1945
CA.123 *Albany* (B)	June 15, 1946		CA.136 *Chicago* (B)	January 10, 1945
CA.124 *Rochester*	December 20, 1946		CA.137 *Norfolk*	Cancelled
CA.125 *Northampton* (C)	1953		CA.138 *Scranton*	Cancelled

(A) Completed as guided-missile cruisers (CAG); (B) Completed as guided-missile cruisers (CG); (C) Completed as command cruiser (CLC)

Baltimore and Oregon City classes

Displacement: 13,920 tonnnes/13,700 tons (standard); 17,933 tonnes/17,650 tons (full load)
Length: 202.3m/664ft (wl); 205.2m/673ft (oa)
Beam: 21.6m/70ft 6in
Draught: 6.2m/20ft 6in (standard)
Armament: 9 x 203mm/8in (3x3), 12 x 127mm/5in (6x2) and 48 x 40mm/1.57in (12x4) guns
Machinery: Geared steam turbines, 4 boilers, 4 shafts
Power: 89,484kW/120,000shp for 33 knots
Endurance: 2,388 tonnes/2,350 tons (oil) for 18,520km/10,000nm at 15 knots
Protection: 102–155mm/4–6.1in (belt); 63mm/2.48in (protective deck); 76–203mm/3–8in (turrets)
Complement: 1,425

Des Moines class

Last and largest of the American gun-armed cruisers, the Des Moines were vehicles for the new 203mm/8in gun with an anticipated improvement in the rate of fire from three to seven rounds per minute. Design for both gun and ship began in May 1943 and the first vessels were expected to be available by mid-1945.

It was hoped that the new weapon might be installed in the existing Oregon City-class design, but the arrangements for the new gun prescribed that only two could be accommodated in a turret of the same size as the old triple. Although six of the new weapons could be expected to fire 42 rounds per minute against the 27 of nine of the old type, the General Board favoured a new-design, nine-gun vessel with proper weight margins for electronics and directors, together with improved resistance to bombs and torpedoes. Secondary and AA armament would remain as before.

Necessarily larger magazines required that the armour be extended for their protection, the increased space and weight forcing up hull dimensions and

displacement. Waterline length was thus increased by 11m/36ft (5.4 per cent), whereas beam was increased by 7.7 per cent. Despite this marginally greater portliness, however, the extra length permitted improvement of lines, so that the ships made much the same speed on the same power as the smaller Oregon Citys. The extra beam enabled torpedo protection to be improved, while greater displacement permitted much of the weather deck to be of 25mm/1in plate to initiate the detonation of bombs before deep penetration.

Limited to only three units, all completed post-war, the Des Moines could be distinguished from the Oregon Citys at a distance by their very tall main director towers. Aircraft, from this and other classes of cruiser, were being removed at about this time, although their conspicuous cranes were retained.

ABOVE LEFT: The *Des Moines* (CA.134) is seen here refuelling from the attack carrier *F.D. Roosevelt* (CVA.42). Pre-dating the carrier's modernization with angled deck, the picture probably dates to the late 1950s. In the absence of attendant fleet oilers, it was usual to extend the range of smaller vessels through taking oil from carriers. ABOVE: As a flagship *Newport News* (CA.148) here carries a wide-band radio antenna right forward and on No.2 turret, their key locations emphasizing their importance. The prominent bucket-shaped device at the foremast head is a TACAN aircraft beacon.

Des Moines class

	Built	Commissioned
CA.134 *Des Moines*	Bethlehem Steel, Quincy	November 16, 1948
CA.139 *Salem*	Bethlehem Steel, Quincy	May 14, 1949
CA.140 *Dallas*		Cancelled
CA.148 *Newport News*	Newport News Drydock	January 29, 194

Des Moines class

Displacement: 17,171 tonnes/16,900 tons (standard); 21,286 tonnes/20,950 tons (full load)
Length: 213.3m/700ft (wl); 218.3m/716ft 6in (oa)
Beam: 23.3m/76ft 4in
Draught: 6.7m/22ft (standard)
Armament: 9 x 203mm/8in (3x3), 12 x 127mm/5in (6x2) and 24 x 76mm/3in (12x2) guns
Machinery: Geared steam turbines, 4 boilers, 4 shafts
Power: 89,484kW/120,000shp for 32.5 knots
Endurance: 2,718 tonnes/2,675 tons (oil) for 19,446km/10,500nm at 15 knots
Protection: 102–155mm/4–6.1in (belt); 25mm/1in and 88mm/3.46in (decks); 95–203mm/3.75–8in (turrets)
Complement: 1,800

Guided-missile conversions

By the end of World War II the aircraft carrier embodied a fleet's offensive power to the extent that its defence was a first priority. In the early Cold War era, the threat from bomber and torpedo aircraft had been extended to include large, air-launched stand-off missiles. To provide the fleet with a layered anti-aircraft defence, capable of meeting the greatest threat at a safe distance, the Americans developed a family of ship-launched missiles with overlapping capability. These were the Talos, reportedly of 105km/65 miles slant range, the Terrier, of 32km/20 miles, and the Tartar, of about 16km/10 miles. It would prove difficult to convert existing flotilla ships to missile carriers (although several were), so remodelled cruisers formed the backbone of the first generation of fleet missile escorts.

Completed in 1955–56, the pioneer conversions were of the *Boston* (CA.69) and *Canberra* (CA.70) to "single enders", retaining cruiser characteristics forward and an after end reconfigured for two twin-arm Terrier systems and individual electronics.

Proceeding them, and almost simultaneous

with the construction of the *Long Beach* was the reconstruction of six light cruisers. Three, *Providence* (CL.82), *Springfield* (CL.66) and *Topeka* (CL.67), were Terrier-equipped and three, *Galveston* (CL.93), *Little Rock* (CL.92) and *Oklahoma City* (CL.91), mounted the Talos system. All were single-enders, the Terrier-ships having a bulkier associated tophamper.

The ultimate rebuilds in this very expensive programme were those of the *Albany* (CA.123), *Chicago* (CA.136) and *Columbus* (CA.74), completely reconfigured as "double-enders"; with Talos systems forward and aft, and Tartar systems sided in the waist.

Ungainly and looking every bit the conversions that they were, the cruisers had the advantage of relatively generous magazine capacity, surviving until the

ABOVE LEFT: **Of the six Clevelands converted to missile cruisers, the *Oklahoma City* (CLG.5) was one of four fitted as task force command ships. The bridge structure was extended forward at the cost of No.2 triple turret and two 127mm/5in mountings. Electronic fits varied considerably between ships.** ABOVE: *Albany* **(CG.10) was one of three heavy cruisers converted to double-ended missile ships. Here, wreathed in her own smoke, she simultaneously launches both her heavy Talos missiles and secondary Tartars. So many weapons and guidance systems resulted in a conflict for space.**

late 1970s until superseded by smaller, purpose-built "cruisers", built around later and more compact missile systems.

Guided-missile conversions

	Converted by	Recommissioned
CAG.1 *Boston*	New York Shipbuilding	November 1, 1955
CAG.2 *Canberra*	New York Shipbuilding	June 15, 1956
CLG.3 *Galveston*	Philadelphia Navy Yard	May 28, 1958
CLG.4 *Little Rock*	New York Shipbuilding	May 23, 1957
CLG.5 *Oklahoma City*	Bethlehem Steel, San Francisco	May 23, 1957
CLG.6 *Providence*	Boston Navy Yard	September 17, 1959
CLG.7 *Springfield*	Bethlehem Steel, Quincy	July 2, 1960
CLG.8 *Topeka*	New York Navy Yard	March 26, 1960
CG.10 *Albany*	Boston Navy Yard	March 11, 1962
CG.11 *Chicago*	San Francisco Navy Yard	May 2, 1964
CG.12 *Columbus*	Puget Sound Navy Yard	December 1, 1962

Albany type (as converted)

Displacement: 13,920 tonnes/13,700 tons (standard); 17,882 tonnes/17,600 tons (full load)
Length: 202.3m/664ft (wl); 205.4m/674ft 1in (oa)
Beam: 21.2m/69ft 8in
Draught: 8.2m/27ft (standard)
Armament: 4 x Talos launchers, 104 missiles (2x2) and 4 x Tartar launchers, 84 missiles (2x2); 2 x 127mm/5in guns; 1 x eight-cell ASROC AS launcher
Machinery: Geared steam turbines, 4 boilers, 4 shafts
Power: 89,484kW/120,000shp for 31.5 knots
Endurance: 14,260km/7,700nm at 20 knots (oil capacity not reported)
Protection: 102–155mm/4–6.1in (belt); 75mm/2.95in (deck); 25mm/1in (magazines)
Complement: 1,100

LEFT: **Much as originally completed, the nuclear-powered missile cruiser *Long Beach* (CGN.9) has two Terrier systems forward and one Talos system aft. Her only guns are two single 127mm/5in 38s about amidships. Designed-to-task, she is much more compact than an Albany conversion.**

Long Beach (CGN.9)

The successful introduction of the nuclear submarine in 1955 encouraged the US Navy's development of a family of nuclear reactors, suitable for the propulsion of a range of surface ships. The existing family of surface-to-air missiles (SAMs) was already threatened with replacement by the bulky new Typhon system and active consideration was being given to the deployment of strategic Regulus II/Polaris missiles by surface warships.

To combine these technologies, together with a minimum speed of 30 knots, required a cruiser-sized hull for which design work commenced in 1954. The bulk and weight of reactors and shielding pushed up dimensions and, although Typhon had been shelved in favour of curing faults in the existing systems, Talos was mandated.

The sheer space required for propulsion plant and missile magazines was instigating a massive shift in design philosophy, away from heavily armoured ships, designed to absorb punishment, towards larger, volume-critical ships, too large to armour, and intended to inflict pain from a range at which they, themselves, would escape it.

Completed in 1961 as something of a prestige ship, the *Long Beach* was first armed with a Talos system aft and two Terriers forward, and "for but not with" Regulus II/Polaris. She was also equipped (as an intended carrier escort) with sonar and ASROC stand-off anti-submarine missiles. Two 127mm/5in 38-calibre guns were added later when complaints were made that she was helpless against minor conventional attack, where guided missiles would be useless in response.

A major external feature was the enormous, square bulk of the bridge structure, clad on four sides by the panels of the electronically scanned SPS32/33 radars, integrated with the Naval Tactical Data System (NTDS). Later refits saw these removed, along with the Talos system. The Terrier missiles were superseded by standard SM-2 Extended Range missiles. Harpoon missiles added anti-surface ship capability and Tomahawk cruise missiles were installed for shore bombardment missions.

Long Beach (CGN.9)

Built: Bethlehem Steel, Quincy
Commissioned: September 9, 1961
Displacement: 15,342 tonnes/15,100 tons (standard); 17,374 tonnes/17,100 tons (full load)
Length: 219.7m/721ft 3in (oa)
Beam: 22.3m/73ft 3in
Draught: 9.5m/31ft (extreme)
Armament (as designed): 2 x Talos launchers, 80 missiles (1x2); 4 x Terrier launchers, 168 missiles (2x2); 1 x ASROC AS launcher; 2 x 127mm/5in 38 guns (2x1)
Machinery: Geared steam turbines, 2 pressurized, water-cooled reactors, 2 shafts
Power: 59,656kW/80,000shp for 30.5 knots
Endurance: Dependent upon stores and ordnance, not fuel
Protection: Not announced; some aluminium armour added retrospectively
Complement: 990

ABOVE: **Built to test advanced technologies, the *Long Beach* has been remodelled several times. Here, her Terrier systems, forward, have been replaced by Standard SM-2. Aft, her obsolete Talos has been removed, the space being taken by two Vulcan-Phalanx CIWS and two armoured Harpoon SSM launchers.**

California and Virginia classes

To complete its pioneering nuclear-propelled squadron the US Navy produced (1962–67) *Bainbridge* (CGN.25) and *Truxtun* (CGN.35), essentially modified versions of the contemporary Leahy and Belknap classes of fleet guided-missile escort.

Experience with this pair led to the slightly enlarged, flush-decked pair of Californias (completed 1974–75) and the four-ship Virginia class (1976–80). Until 1975, all were categorized as "frigates" but their size and prestigious "state" names saw them relabelled "cruisers". Neither term agrees with traditional practice but indicates the difficulty of pigeonholing newly developing types of warship.

Superficially, the two classes are very similar but the Virginias, some 4m/13ft 1in the shorter, may be distinguished by the knuckle, which was incorporated to reduce wetness on the foredeck. Both have the two-block, funnel-less profile typical of nuclear-propelled ships, and have the various elements of their all-purpose armament disposed along the centreline.

Each type has a single 127mm/5in 54-calibre gun forward and aft, their arcs limited somewhat by the twin-arm missile launchers beyond. Both launch the standard SM-1 MR surface-to-air missile (SAM) but where those on the Virginias can also launch ASROC anti-submarine (ASW) missiles, the Californias have a separate, eight-cell ASROC launcher and reload facility.

Both types have Harpoon anti-ship missiles. On the Californias these are located aft; on the Virginias, forward. A helicopter spot, without facilities, is provided right aft, but it is encumbered if armoured box launchers for Tomahawk cruise missiles are carried.

The weapons inventory is completed by AS torpedo tubes and close-in weapon systems (CIWS), mounted on the superstructure with decoy launchers and designed to destroy any incoming anti-ship missile that cannot be deflected or seduced.

It will be noted that, where nuclear propulsion has proved viable for submarines and aircraft carriers, large escorts have reverted to conventional power units.

ABOVE: In this dramatic shot, the *Arkansas* (CGN.41) is undergoing a shock test. The ship is anchored a calculated distance from a large explosive charge for the purpose of establishing the shock resistance of on-board systems.

ABOVE LEFT: The hull of the *Mississippi* (CGN.40) shows its clear derivation from that of the conventionally propelled Belknaps. The MK.26 launcher on the foredeck was designed for Standard SM-1 missiles. In this picture she lacks the Harpoon launchers forward of the bridge and the Tomahawk box launchers aft. ABOVE: The older *California* (CGN.36) presents a more squat appearance. Her after 127mm/5in gun is carried one level higher and she retains basic helicopter facilities aft. The small box forward of the bridge is a reload facility for the ASROC launchers not carried in the Virginias.

California and Virginia classes

	Built	Commissioned
CGN.36 *California*	Newport News Shipbuilding, Virginia	February 16, 1974
CGN.37 *South Carolina*	Newport News Shipbuilding, Virginia	January 25, 1975
CGN.38 *Virginia*	Newport News Shipbuilding, Virginia	September 11, 1976
CGN.39 *Texas*	Newport News Shipbuilding, Virginia	September 10, 1977
CGN.40 *Mississippi*	Newport News Shipbuilding, Virginia	August 5, 1978
CGN.41 *Arkansas*	Newport News Shipbuilding, Virginia	October 18, 1980

Virginia class (as built)

Displacement: 10,567 tonnes/10,400 tons (light); 11,481 tonnes/11,300 tons (full load)
Length: 177.8m/583ft 8in (oa)
Beam: 19.2m/63ft (oa)
Draught: 9.6m/31ft 6in (extreme)
Armament: 8 x Tomahawks SSM (2x4); 8 x Harpoon SSM (2x4); standard SM-2 MR and ASROC ASW (68 rounds total); 2 x 127mm/5in 54 guns; 2 x CIWS; 6 x 323mm/12.7in AS torpedo tubes (2x3)
Machinery: Geared steam turbines, 2 pressurized, water-cooled reactors, 2 shafts
Power: 52,200kW/70,000shp for 30-plus knots
Endurance: Not dependent upon fuel
Protection: Not announced
Complement: 620

FAR LEFT: **Despite her scruffy appearance, the** *Ooi* **seen here in the early 1920s, was a relatively new ship. Her 140mm/5.5in gun calibre was selected as having the heaviest projectile that could be manually worked by the average Japanese seaman. Her bow profile was new in Japanese warships.** ABOVE: **Slightly clearer, this picture of** *Ooi* **shows the short well at the forward end of the long, full-width, amidships deckhouse. In 1940, this deckhouse was razed and, suitably sponsored, each side deck was fitted with five quadruple 610mm/24in torpedo tube mountings.**

Tenryu, Kuma and Nagara classes

Intended to act as leaders for new destroyer flotillas, the two Tenryus, completed in 1919, closely paralleled the first group of British C-class cruisers. Lightly constructed, but belted, they had a raised forecastle but low freeboard aft. Four 140mm/5.5in guns were mounted singly along the centreline together with two triple banks of torpedo tubes, one of which was located, German-style, at the break of the forecastle. The 140mm/5.5in guns could elevate to no more than 20 degrees (improved to 30 degrees in later ships) but their 38kg/84lb ammunition was the heaviest that could be hand-loaded by the average Japanese sailor.

These and later derivatives could all lay mines, using temporary rails along either side deck. The mines were unusual in being intended for laying in the path of an advancing enemy squadron. They were thus laid in floating pairs, connected by a 100m/328ft cable. Any ship snagging the cable would draw the mines into it before being able to lose sufficient way.

Plans existed in the 1930s to convert the Tenryus to AA cruisers but dockyards were, at the time, fully employed with alternative naval work of higher priority.

As Japan's first modern light cruisers, the Tenryus were immediately succeeded by the five Kumas, improved and enlarged. Longer by some 20.4m/67ft, they bore much the same relationship to the Tenryus as a British D-class did to an early C-class. To decrease wetness, the raised forecastle was complemented by a long amidships deckhouse. Before and abaft of this light construction were four pairs of torpedo tubes, two on either beam. One spare torpedo was provided for each. Seven single 140mm/5.5in guns were carried disposed to give a broadside of six.

ABOVE: *Tenryu* (seen here) and *Tatsuta* were the first and smallest of this light cruiser series and make an interesting contrast with the British C-type ships that inspired them. The three funnels were based on a narrow, centreline "fiddley", bounded fore and aft by triple 533mm/21in torpedo tube mountings.

ABOVE: *Tenryu*'s appearance in the late 1930s. Note the four guns, all on the centreline. She has just raised anchor and is gathering way as her forecastle party direct a hose jet down the hawse pipe to clean mud from the anchor. The foremast was made a tripod in 1930.

The Imperial Japanese Navy (IJN) regarded the torpedo as a battle-winning weapon and, during the 1930s, developed the formidable 610mm/24in Type 93. Oxygen-propelled, it carried a warhead 50 per cent heavier than the contemporary 533mm/21in American or British torpedoes. It also enjoyed up to four times the range, and a higher speed. Doctrine emphasized night attack, using torpedo spreads in preference to gunfire, which would betray an attacker's position.

With this in mind, the heavy cruiser squadrons were to be accompanied by one or more Kumas, remodelled as "torpedo cruisers". However, only two (*Kitakami* and *Ooi*) of a planned three were so modified, their amidships section sponsored to give the deck space necessary to mount an astonishing five quadruple 610mm/24in torpedo banks per side. With changing war priorities, and the loss of the *Ooi*, the damaged *Kitakami* was again heavily modified to carry eight Kaiten midget submarines on deck. Transported on rails, these were launched over a reconfigured stern.

Of equal dimensions, six Nagara-class ships followed on from the Kumas. At 5,781 tonnes/5,690 tons, such ships were considered capable of undertaking scouting operations in support of a battle squadron. Following earlier experiment with the *Kitakami* they were equipped with an aircraft. Again following contemporary British practice, they were given a high bridge structure, in which an aircraft was accommodated, taking off from a light platform extending forward. Although this facility was soon removed in favour of a catapult, located abaft the funnels; the high bridge block remained.

The Tenryus were designed for 33 knots, the enlarged later groups for 36. Being fast and of a handy size, all were used extensively as fast transports. By 1944 American submarines infested every part of the western Pacific while carrier-based air strikes overwhelmed any ship encountered. Of the 13 units of the first three groups, just one survived the war. Of the other 11, all but two were destroyed in 1944–45.

ABOVE: **The six Nagaras were improved Kumas and designed primarily as leaders to destroyer and fleet submarine squadrons.** *Nagara* **is seen here after 1933, when her catapult and floatplane were moved aft. The curious funnel caps,**

fitted in the 1930s were probably to prevent flaming when supporting destroyers at night. LEFT: **Probably aboard the** *Kitakami*, **whose comprehensive torpedo armament was removed in 1943, and replaced by sided tracks for up to eight Kaiten I miniature submarines. These 8.5-tonne/8.4-ton craft, launched over the stern, had a single occupant and an explosive warhead.** BELOW: *Nagara* **during the 1920s. An original similarity with British light cruisers was the elevation of the bridge structure to provide housing for a scout plane, which lifted off from the short platform extending over the forward guns.**

ABOVE: **The** *Tenryu* **shows off her destroyer-like stern and starboard-side mine rails. No aircraft arrangements are visible, so this is probably a late 1930s picture. Few of these light cruisers survived the war, the** *Tenryu* **being sunk by submarine torpedo in December 1942.**

Tenryu, Kuma and Nagara classes

	Built	Commissioned
Tatsuta	Sasebo Navy Yard	March 31, 1919
Tenryu	Yokosuka Navy Yard	November 20, 1919
Kiso	Mitsubishi, Nagasaki	May 4, 1921
Kitakami	Sasebo Navy Yard	April 15, 1921
Kuma	Sasebo Navy Yard	August 31, 1920
Ooi	Kawasaki, Kobe	October 3, 1921
Tama	Mitsubishi, Nagasaki	January 29, 1921
Abukuma	Uraga Dock Company	May 26, 1925
Isuzu	Uraga Dock Company	August 15, 1923
Kinu	Kawasaki, Kobe	November 10, 1922
Nagara	Sasebo Navy Yard	April 21, 1922
Natori	Mitsubishi, Nagasaki	September 15, 1922
Yura	Sasebo Navy Yard	March 20, 1923

Nagara class (as designed)

Displacement: 5,781 tonnes/5,690 tons (standard); 7,315 tonnes/7,200 tons (full load)

Length: 152.3m/500ft (bp); 162.1m/532ft (oa)

Beam: 14.2m/46ft 6in

Draught: 4.9m/16ft (standard)

Armament: 7 x 140mm/5.5in (7x1) and 2 x 80mm/3.1in high-angle (HA) (2x1) guns; 8 x 610mm/24in torpedo tubes (4x2); 48 mines

Machinery: Geared steam turbines, 12 boilers, 4 shafts

Power: 67,113kW/90,000shp for 36 knots

Endurance: 1,300 tonnes/1,280 tons (oil) and 345 tonnes/340 tons (coal) for 11,112km/6,000nm at 14 knots

Protection: 63mm/2.48in (partial belt); 29mm/1.14in (partial armoured deck)

Complement: 450

ABOVE LEFT: *Sendai* shows her dated gun disposion with four singles forward (two flanking the bridge) and three aft. ABOVE: Another view of the nameship. The Sendais were influenced by the preceding British "D" class, not least in the heavy and lofty tripod foremast.

Sendai class

Of the final group of six planned Tenryu class derivatives only three were built, the 1922 Washington Treaty terms diverting interest to larger "treaty cruisers". Those actually constructed retained the dimensions and main characteristics of the preceding group. These included partial mixed-firing of boilers, unusual at this late date but probably indicative of the chronic Japanese oil shortage. A rearrangement of boiler spaces brought about an anachronistic reversion to four funnels of which the foremost was rather taller to reduce the smoke nuisance on the bridge. There were three boiler rooms with four units in each. Only the forward boiler room was fitted for mixed firing.

The Sendais were equipped from the outset with 610mm/24in torpedo tubes. Perhaps coincidentally, all were laid down in 1922, the same year as the British Nelson-class battleships, the only Royal Navy vessels ever to mount 610mm/24in torpedo tubes. The Japanese Type 8, 610mm/24in torpedo had been accepted into service in 1920 and should not be confused with the oxygen-fuelled Type 94 of World War II. Sixteen were carried, again permitting one reload per tube.

As with the Nagaras, the forward flying-off arrangement was considered unsatisfactory and probably never used. Following the visit of the Sempill mission in 1921, British influence on the embryonic Japanese naval air service was strong and the Mitsubishi 1MF (Type 10) fighter designated for use aboard the light cruisers was, in fact, designed by the Sopwith team.

All the light cruisers to date had been given a distinctive "boat bow", convexly curved, but *Jintsu* of the Sendai class adopted the double-curvature, "clipper" profile that would become closely associated with Japanese warship design.

All three of the class became war casualties, two of them in battle with American ships while leading their destroyers in the fierce nocturnal engagements that were a feature of the Solomons campaign.

Sendai class

	Built	Commissioned
Jintsu	Kawasaki, Kobe	July 31, 1925
Kamo		Cancelled
Kizu		Cancelled
Naka	Mitsubishi, Yokohama	November 30, 1925
Nayoro		Cancelled
Sendai	Mitsubishi, Nagasaki	April 29, 1924

Sendai class (as designed)

Displacement: 5,995 tonnes/5,900 tons (standard); 7,732 tonnes/7,610 tons (full load)
Length: 152.3m/500ft (bp); 162.1m/532ft (oa)
Beam: 14.2m/46ft 6in
Draught: 4.9m/16ft (standard)
Armament: 7 x 140mm/5.5in (7x1) and 2 x 80mm/3.1in HA (2x1) guns; 8 x 610mm/24in torpedo tubes (4x2); 48 mines
Machinery: Geared steam turbines, 12 boilers, 4 shafts
Power: 67,113kW/90,000shp for 35-plus knots
Endurance: 1,026 tonnes/1,010 tons (oil), and 579 tonnes/570 tons (coal) for 11,112km/6,000nm at 14 knots
Protection: 63mm/2.48in (partial belt); 29mm/1.14in (partial armoured deck)
Complement: 450

LEFT: **Another inherited feature of British wartime practice was the aircraft hangar in the bridge structure and flying-off platform.** *Naka*, **like her sisters, had them removed during the 1930s.**

Yubari

Although they carried seven guns, the later 5,588-tonne/5,500-ton light cruisers could use only six of them in broadside and three (theoretically) in chase. European trends were now favouring superimposed gun positions and it was posited that, if these were adopted, along with twin mountings, the same firepower could be developed by a smaller and less expensive vessel. If construction was kept light, a similar speed might also be possible. The result was the one-off experimental "light cruiser" Yubari, built at the same time as the Sendais.

Six 140mm/5.5in guns were arranged with singles in the "A" and "Y" positions, superfired by twins in the "B" and "X" positions. As all were located on the centreline, six were available on the broadside and three in chase, as before. The twins were enclosed in electrically

operated gunhouses, the singles only in shields, giving a superficial impression of a mixed armament.

A new Japanese "trademark" also made its appearance in the Yubari's exaggeratedly trunked funnel. All oil-fired, she had eight boilers distributed between three spaces, all being exhausted through a single large casing. This saved on the weight of separate funnels while keeping smoke well clear of the main director position, situated atop a tripod over the bridge.

By positioning two twin 610mm/24in torpedo tubes on the centreline, four were available on either broadside, similar to that of earlier ships with eight. This logical modification in armament layout permitted the hull to be shorter by some 21.9m/72ft.

Despite a shorter waterline length it was still hoped to make 35.5 knots on

TOP: **Due to her being considerably overweight, the Yubari's lower scuttles can be seen to be very close to the waterline.** ABOVE: **Yubari at Shanghai shows her very destroyer-like appearance. Note how her twin 140mm/5.5in gunhouses superfire single 140mm/5.5in guns in shields.**

a three-shaft machinery arrangement. Scantlings were very light (in fact, over-light) but the hull still emerged seriously overweight. Because of the resulting deeper immersion, she failed to make 35 knots. Her designed endurance was also reduced.

Yubari

Built: Sasebo Navy Yard
Commissioned: July 31, 1923
Displacement: 3,617 tonnes/3,560 tons (standard); 4,519 tonnes/4,448 tons (full load)
Length: 132.5m/435ft (bp); 139.4m/457ft 6in (oa)
Beam: 12m/39ft 6in
Draught: 3.9m/12ft 8in (standard)
Armament: 6 x 140mm/5.5in (2x2/2x1) and 1 x 80mm/3.1in HA guns; 4 x 610mm/24in torpedo tubes; 48 mines
Machinery: Geared steam turbines, 8 boilers, 3 shafts
Power: 43,176kW/57,900shp for 34.75 knots
Endurance: 931 tonnes/916 tons (oil) for 6,111km/3,300nm at 14 knots
Protection: 57mm/2.24in (belt over machinery spaces); 25–41mm/1–1.6in (partial armoured deck)
Complement: 330

ABOVE: **Another view of Yubari laying at Shanghai. Despite a further increase in topweight, the heavily trunked funnel needed to be raised by 2m/6ft 6in.**

LEFT: **For a year following World War II, *Kashima* was used for repatriation purposes, being conspicuously identified.** BELOW: **This view of *Kashima* shows her twin 140mm/5.5in gunhouse clearly. This pattern was shared with Yubari and Fubuki-class destroyers.**

Katori class

When, in December 1934, Japan abrogated the Washington Treaty and commenced rapid expansion of her fleet, she required modern vessels dedicated to the sea training of the growing number of midshipmen. The construction of four new 5,893-tonne/ 5,800-ton vessels was therefore authorized. Spread over the building programmes of 1937, 1939 and 1941, these ran foul of higher priority construction. The final hull consequently never reached launching stage before being dismantled.

Despite a record of duplicity in declaring the true size and function of its new vessels, those of the Katoris were exactly as stated by the IJN. Imposing for their size, they were usually referred to by the Allies as "cruisers", but were so only in the sense that they undertook training cruises. Never being intended

as combatants, they were built in a commercial yard and largely to mercantile standards.

For training purposes, armament, fire control, machinery, aircraft and catapults, boats, etc., all conformed to standard IJN practice, and it was the resulting external appearance that accounted for the Allies crediting them with cruiser-like qualities. The ships were, however, designed for a speed of only 18 knots, their lines being full and increasing internal space. Their high freeboard reflected accommodation spacious by contemporary IJN standards and intended to impress during foreign port visits.

Due to these unusually generous appointments, the wartime role of the Katoris was to act as flagships to second-line forces such as convoy escort and anti-submarine (ASW) groups.

From time to time, however, training of aspirant officers was still undertaken.

War saw their armament greatly supplemented by automatic weapons and by four high-angle (HA) 127mm/5in guns in twin mountings sided in the waist.

Only the *Kashima* survived hostilities. Fitted with extra topside accommodation, she was employed post-war in the repatriation of prisoners of war and garrisons of distant locations. This duty done, she was scrapped in 1947.

Katori class

	Built	Commissioned
Kashii	Mitsubishi, Yokohama	July 15, 1941
Kashima	Mitsubishi, Yokohama	July 31, 1940
Kashiwara		Cancelled
Katori	Mitsubishi, Yokohama	April 20, 1940

Katori class

Displacement: 5,985 tonnes/5,890 tons (standard); 6,858 tonnes/6,750 tons (full load)
Length: 123.5m/405ft 4in (bp); 133.5m/438ft 2in (oa)
Beam: 16.6m/54ft 6in (maximum)
Draught: 5.5m/18ft (standard)
Armament: 4 x 140mm/5.5in (2x2) and 6 x 127mm/5in (3x2) guns; 4 x 533mm/21in torpedo tubes (2x2)
Machinery: 2 sets geared steam turbines and 2 cruising diesels, 3 boilers, 2 shafts
Power: 5,965kW/8,000shp combined for 18 knots
Endurance: 611 tonnes/600 tons (oil) for 18,335km/9,900nm at 12 knots
Protection: None
Complement: 315 plus 275 trainees

ABOVE: **The training status of *Katori* is emphasized by the large freeboard hull resulting from extra accommodation. This feature defined her secondary role as station flagship.**

Oyodo and Agano class

By the 1930s the overweight 5,588-tonne/5,500-ton cruisers were proving deficient, their speed and endurance inferior to those of the new destroyers that they were expected to lead. Their broadside weight was also considered inadequate as was the reconnaissance potential of their single floatplane. As they could be replaced after 15 years of service by treaty definition, both "destroyer-and submarine-squadron flagships" were authorized during 1939.

The four destroyer leaders of the Agano class thus carried an increased main battery of six 150mm/5.9in guns in three twin turrets, two forward and one aft. Extensive trunking permitted a single, large funnel casing, with a prominent catapult abaft it. Two seaplanes (*Aichi* E13A1 "Jake") were accommodated, one on the catapult, the other on a platform over the eight torpedo tubes. Aft of the catapult, the mainmast provided a substantial post for a large aircraft handling crane.

The functions of the Japanese fleet submarine force emphasized reconnaissance as well as attack, necessitating a cruiser-flagship in addition to a depot ship, or tender. Two such flagships were authorized but only one, the *Oyodo*, was ever built.

To reconnoitre for her submarines, the *Oyodo* was designed to carry no less than six fast seaplanes of a new design. These demanded a large box hangar aft of amidships, and an after end devoted to a centreline catapult and aircraft handling facilities. The main battery was, therefore, concentrated forward in two triple 155mm/6.1in turrets. These were available following the up-rating of the Mogami-class cruisers. The aircraft never entered production and the ship was never employed as intended.

Of the Agano class and the *Oyodo*, only one ship (*Sakawa*) survived hostilities. Most capsized before sinking, possibly due to the centreline bulkheads that divided the machinery spaces.

Oyodo and Agano class

	Built	Commissioned
Agano	Sasebo Navy Yard	October 31, 1942
Noshiro	Yokosuka Navy Yard	June 30, 194
Sakawa	Sasebo Navy Yard	November 30, 1944
Yahagi	Sasebo Navy Yard	December 29, 1943
Oyodo	Kure Navy Yard	February 28, 1943
Niyodo		Cancelled

Agano class (as built)

Displacement: 8,027 tonnes/7,900 tons (standard); 8,667 tonnes/8,530 tons (full load)
Length: 162m/531ft 9in (bp); 174.5m/572ft 10in (oa)
Beam: 15.2m/49ft 11in
Draught: 5.7m/18ft 9in (standard)
Armament: 6 x 150mm/5.9in (3x2) and 4 x 80mm/3.1in HA (2x2) guns; 8 x 610mm/24in torpedo tubes (2x4)
Machinery: Geared steam turbines, 6 boilers, 4 shafts
Power: 74,570kW/100,000shp for 35 knots
Endurance: 1,443 tonnes/1,420 tons (oil) for 11,112km/6,000nm at 18 knots
Protection: 55–60mm/2.2–2.4in (partial side belt); 20mm/0.79in (partial armoured deck)
Complement: 800

ABOVE: **The *Oyodo* as originally completed as flagship for submarines. Her catapult is unusually long and the cranes that serve it are folded forward, against the after superstructure. Never employed as intended, the ship was later refitted with standard aircraft facilities.**

Furutaka and Aoba classes

These two very similar pairs were conceived as large scout cruisers, out-classing both the American Omaha and British Hawkins classes. Their design pre-dated the 1922 Washington Treaty, so that they were smaller and less heavily armed than so-called "treaty cruisers".

A notable new feature was the uniquely Japanese undulating sheerline. Variously interpreted as logical, a weight-saving measure or, simply, idiosyncratic, hull depth at key points was decided by adequate freeboard, either for seakeeping or for reserve stability, or for required strength. Different sections of the hull were thus governed by varying criteria, resulting in differing depths. The upper deck was connected then by a continuous sheerline that, from some angles, could appear distinctly odd. To save weight, armour was worked-in without backing plate. This design philosophy contrasts with that of the broadly contemporary British County class, who's great depth of hull conferred necessary stiffness, allowing scantlings to be significantly reduced.

As with American cruiser design, it was found that protection against 152mm/6in, rather than 203mm/8in gunfire, was only

ABOVE: *Kako* (here) and *Furutaka* were Japan's first pair of "treaty cruisers". Unusually, they displaced significantly less than the 10,160-tonne/10,000-ton limit while their 200mm/7.87in guns were of smaller calibre than the 203mm/8in limit. The single main-calibre turrets, shown here, were carried only until twins became available.

possible over a specific immunity band. This was compromised somewhat when, despite apparently careful control, the ships came out considerably overweight, submerging much of their belt protection. Machinery spaces were flanked by longitudinal bulkheads. The void spaces thus created, between bulkhead and shell plating were, together with a small integral bulge, intended to act as torpedo protection. In practice, it lacked sufficient depth to be effective. Again, machinery spaces were subdivided by a dubiously conceived centreline bulkhead.

The Furutakas' main battery comprised a newly developed 200mm/7.87in gun designed to out-perform the Hawkins' 191mm/7.5in guns. As completed, the ships accommodated six weapons in single centreline gunhouses, in two groups of

ABOVE:: Three twin 200mm/7.87in turrets later took the place of six singles. The *Furutaka* here shows the resulting gap left forward of the bridge structure. Note the "beaked" bow profile and the massive trunking to the forward funnel. RIGHT: Heavily retouched, this view of *Furutaka* appears to show a very obvious armoured belt, the side being slightly knuckled. Note the short funnels, later raised. The single 200mm/7.87in mountings were gunhouses rather than turrets.

three, one forward and one aft. The centre mounting superfired its neighbours. Although the arrangement must have influenced hull length, it was only temporary, pending the entry into service of a twin turret mounting. The Aoba pair was fitted with these from the outset, the Furutakas not being retro-fitted until their late 1930s modernization. Turrets gave a higher rate of fire per gun but imposed a further 102-tonne/100-ton or more load on the ship, whose structure needed strengthening.

Following the limitations imposed on capital ships by the Washington Treaty, the IJN increased emphasis on torpedo attack by cruisers, especially at night. All four ships were consequently fitted with twelve 610mm/24in torpedo tubes. These were fixed, firing in pairs on the beam from dedicated internal compartments, two of which were abaft the funnels and one forward of the bridge. Economizing on upper deck space, the arrangement also reduced the distance the torpedoes had to drop in firing. Rearrangement during the modernization nonetheless saw the arrangement superseded by two quadruple banks, sided on the upper deck. One reload was carried for each tube.

Fitted with prominent aircraft catapults in the late 1920s, the two pairs could be separately identified through their differing arrangements. In the Furutakas the catapult was located ahead of the mainmast, resulting in a large gap between mast and after funnel. The Aobas had their catapult sited immediately ahead of the after turret, resulting in the mainmast being located farther forward.

On completion, the Furutakas received four 80mm/3.1in high-angle (HA) guns, but these were later replaced by more effective 120mm/4.7in weapons to match those in the Aobas.

All four became war losses, all but the *Aoba* being destroyed during a three-month period of vicious nocturnal battles to decide sea superiority around the Solomon Islands, late in 1942. Following action damage to the *Aoba* in 1943, there were unfulfilled plans to convert her to carry six reconnaissance float planes, located aft.

ABOVE: *Aoba* (here) and *Kinugasa* were near repeats of the Furutakas, but carried twin turrets from the outset. They differed in appearance in carrying their catapult abaft the mainmast. Note the diminishing freeboard at the after end.
LEFT: A view of the nicely uncluttered foredeck of *Aoba*. The type was well designed, *Aoba* surviving hits by no less than twenty-four 152mm/6in and 203mm/8in projectiles at the nocturnal Battle of Cape Esperance in October 1942. She was torpedoed near Manila in 1944.
LEFT: Most surviving Japanese ships, crippled by lack of oil fuel, were sunk at their anchors by US naval aircraft during July 1945. *Aoba* settled in shallow water south of Kure. Her light automatic weapons have already been removed while foliage appears to have been used in a futile attempt at camouflage.

Furutaka and Aoba classes

	Built	Commissioned
Furutaka	Mitsubishi, Nagasaki	March 31, 1926
Kako	Kawasaki, Kobe	July 20, 1926
Aoba	Mitsubishi, Nagasaki	September 20, 1927
Kinugasa	Kawasaki, Kobe	September 30, 1927

ABOVE: **An early picture of *Kako* prior to her receiving twin turrets. All four of these early ships, led by the later *Chokai*, inflicted a sharp defeat on the Allies off Savo Island in August 1942. In the course of their withdrawal, *Kako* was torpedoed and sunk off Simbari.**

Furutaka (as built)

Displacement: 8,076 tonnes/7,950 tons (standard); 10,414 tonnes/10,250 tons (full load)
Length: 176.7m/580ft (bp); 185.1m/607ft 6in (oa)
Beam: 16.5m/54ft 2in
Draught: 5.6m/18ft 3in
Armament: 6 x 200mm/7.87in (6x1) and 4 x 80mm/3.1in HA (4x1) guns; 12 x 610mm/24in torpedo tubes (12x1)
Machinery: Geared steam turbines, 12 boilers, 4 shafts
Power: 76,061kW/102,000shp for 34 knots
Endurance: 1,118 tonnes/1,100 tons (oil) for 11,112km/6,000nm at 14 knots
Protection: 76mm/3in (belt); 35–48mm/1.38–1.89in (partial armoured deck); 19–25mm/0.75–1in (gunhouses)
Complement: 625

Myoko and Takao classes

Having gained considerable experience with the design of the radical *Yubari* and the 7,620-tonne/7,500-ton scout cruisers, the same constructor, Hiraga, was entrusted with the first four 10,160-tonne/10,000-ton "treaty cruisers", authorized in 1923, following the Washington Conference.

As intelligence indicated (incorrectly) that treaty-limited displacement would restrict foreign equivalents to eight guns, a prime Japanese requirement was to ensure superiority with ten. However, much the same thinking led the Americans to fit ten guns in the equivalent Pensacolas and, where they combined twins and triples in a four-turret main battery, the Japanese opted for five, centreline twins. This, together with the requirement for superior speed, resulted in longer and far finer-lined hulls.

The first Myoko group was strongly influenced by the preceding classes but overall gave a more massive impression. As before, three turrets were located forward, the centre mounting superfiring the others. To avoid the necessity for

three funnels the forward boiler space, sited directly below the bridge structure, exhausted via elaborate trunking through a heavily raked casing which, it shared with the central boilers.

Between the mainmast and after turrets was a considerable gap, directly above the machinery spaces. On the upper deck it was occupied by an off-centre rotating catapult, whose two associated aircraft were housed in a hangar immediately forward of it.

Beneath the catapult and above the machinery spaces were two under-deck compartments accommodating twelve 610mm/24in torpedo tubes. Grouped in threes, and fixed, all fired on the beam. Hiraga had opposed the arrangement on the grounds that an accidental warhead explosion could

LEFT: **Taken at the British Coronation Review in 1937, this picture shows a seaplane on either catapult. The standard outfit was three Mitsubishi F1M2 Type 0 reconnaissance floatplanes but, here, the *Ashigara* appears to be equipped with the earlier Nakajima E8N2 Type 95, known to the Allies as "Dave".** ABOVE: **The extraordinary mass and complexity of the *Chokai*'s bridge structure contrasts with the lightness of its masting. Trunking for the enormous forefunnel runs beneath the bridge structure. Note the distinctively shaped screens covering the torpedo tube mountings. Maintenance on ground tackle is being carried out forward.**

LEFT: **Continuing the British connection, *Ashigara* is here seen at Malta. The reverse sheer from her after turrets is marked, the line of lower scuttles descending to the horizontal boot topping. With so many Japanese cruisers being sunk by the Americans, it is interesting that both *Ashigara* and *Haguro* were destroyed by British forces.**

catastrophically damage the ship. During the 1934–35 modernization of the class, he successfully had them removed in favour of sided quadruple banks fitted on the upper deck.

A spardeck was also fitted at this time with a catapult sponsoned on both sides, and providing space for new 127mm/5in high-angle (HA) guns and directors.

Although relatively well protected, the Myokos' hull was lightly constructed, requiring later strengthening to correct weather-induced over-stressing.

Originally known as the "Improved Myoko class", the four Takaos followed on in response to numbers believed to have been authorized by the American and British navies. Virtually identical in size, they could be differentiated by much closer-spaced funnels and an even more monolithic bridge structure with a characteristically sloping forward side. Much of the internal volume of this structure was, in fact, consumed by the exhaust trunking from the forward boiler room.

From the outset, this group had two, sided catapults to serve three aircraft. Torpedo tubes were sited above the upper deck but enclosed by the spar deck above. Paired on rotating mounts, they fired through long, distinctively shaped but usually shuttered apertures in the side plating.

High power, a long hull and fine lines combined to give the classes a good turn of speed, although their designed endurance was only moderate. Protection comprised armour adequate to defeat 152mm/6in and some 203mm/8in gunfire, and longitudinal bulkheads inside a partially internal bulge ("blister") to minimize the effect of a torpedo hit.

Like the Americans, the Japanese were disappointed with their rate of fire, again governed by a fixed loading angle of 5 degrees. The main armament could be elevated to 70 degrees, but the rate of elevation or depression was only 12 degrees per second. It followed that the longer the range and the higher the elevation, the slower the rate of fire.

A further disappointment lay in the ships being overweight, their deeper-than-expected immersion detrimentally affecting both speed and endurance. As the problem of excess weight had been common to all the pre-treaty classes it suggests chronic under-estimation of weight and/or lack of building discipline rather than a deliberate flouting of agreed limits.

LEFT: **On November 5, 1944, *Nachi* was overwhelmed by US carrier aircraft in Manila Bay. Despite her rapid manoeuvring she finally sank after being struck by a claimed nine torpedoes and 20 bombs.**

Myoko and Takao classes

	Built	Commissioned
Ashigara	Kawasaki, Kobe	August 20, 1929
Haguro	Mitsubishi, Nagasaki	April 25, 1929
Myoko	Yokosuka Navy Yard	July 31, 1929
Nachi	Kure Navy Yard	April 30, 1929
Atago	Kure Navy Yard	March 30, 1932
Chokai	Mitsubishi, Nagasaki	June 30, 1932
Maya	Kawasaki, Kobe	June 30, 1932
Takao	Yokosuka Navy Yard	May 31, 1932

Myoko class (as built)

Displacement: 11,156 tonnes/10,980 tons (standard); 14,428 tonnes/14,200 tons (full load)
Length: 191.9m/630ft (bp); 203.7m/668ft 6in (oa)
Beam: 19m/62ft 4in
Draught: 5.9m/19ft 3in (standard)
Armament: 10 x 200mm/7.87in (5x2) and 6 x 120mm/4.7in HA (6x1) guns; 12 x 610mm/24in fixed torpedo tubes (4x3)
Machinery: Geared steam turbines, 12 boilers, 4 shafts
Power: 96,941kW/130,000shp for 33.5 knots
Endurance: 2,245 tonnes/2,210 tons (oil) for 13,890km/7,500nm at 14 knots
Protection: 102mm/4in (belt); 32–35mm/1.26–1.38in (armoured deck); 76mm/3in (turrets)
Complement: 765

Mogami class

The London Naval Treaty of 1930 took the heat out of the "treaty cruiser" race by capping the number of heavy cruisers (i.e. with guns of calibre exceeding 155mm/6.1in) that could be built by each signatory. Japan's allocation of 12 had already been committed but, as light cruisers could be built up to a global total of 102,062 tonnes/100,450 tons, four were ordered, two in 1931 and two in 1933. By the existing standards, they were large, their unofficial working figure of 8,636 tonnes/8,500 tons being nearer 9,652 tonnes/9,500 tons. The Naval General Staff required no less than five triple 155mm/6.1in turrets (which triggered an American response with the Brooklyns) and twelve 610mm/24in torpedo tubes. As an ambitious 37 knots was also stipulated, the resulting hull was as large as that of the preceding *Takao*. From the outset it was planned to exchange the gun mountings for twin 200mm/7.87in when required.

Hardly had the first pair launched in 1934 than a capsizing incident elsewhere brought about a general enquiry into the

ABOVE: **The four Mogamis could be recognized by their single funnel and forward turret layout. This picture shows the nameship, as built with five triple 155mm/ 6.1in guns, which were later changed for five twin 200mm/7.87in turrets.**

standards of stability acceptable to the IJN. Revised standards found the Mogamis deficient, causing them to be completed with a smaller bridge structure, no aircraft hangar and reduced deck heights. Welding, still developing as a technique, was used widely to save weight, but was responsible for many local structural failures at points of stress concentration.

The later pair, still building, had these modifications worked in, but at the expense of considerably increased displacement, due mainly to a further bulge being added outside the existing one, increasing the beam. While this measure satisfactorily raised the metacentre, it increased displacement to about 14,225 tonnes/14,000 tons. A new water-ballasting system was also added to preserve stability range in the "light" condition.

LEFT: **Still lacking some equipment, including directors and catapults, the *Mogami* is seen undergoing full-power contractor's sea trials in March 1935. Although she made a shade under 36 knots, her hull, which incorporated considerable welding, was distorted in places. Her displacement at the time was a treaty-breaking 13,170 tonnes/ 12,962 tons.**

ABOVE: **All four Mogamis were involved in the abortive attack on Midway in June 1942. Having collided with the *Mogami*, the damaged *Mikuma* (seen here) was attacked by aircraft from three US carriers. Wrecked by bombs, she was the first Japanese cruiser to be lost.** RIGHT: **More dramatic than accurate, this impression shows *Mikuma* under attack by SBD Dauntless aircraft, which also further injured the collision-damaged *Mogami*. The mainmast, seen toppling following an explosion of torpedo warheads, is noticeably absent in the photograph above.**

A single heavily trunked funnel casing served ten boilers located in four spaces in the first pair. The second pair had just eight boilers, each of higher capacity. Despite a designed output of 113,346kW/152,000shp, however, excess immersion and a fuller hull resulting from further bulging caused the operational speed and endurance to be reduced.

A light spar or shelter deck again provided space for the high-angle (HA) guns and aircraft arrangements. For the latter, two sponsoned catapults flanked an area laid out with rails for the movement of trolley-mounted seaplanes. Three aircraft were stored in the open, having lost their hangar in the quest to save topside weight. Their handling crane was stepped on a substantial tripod mainmast, located at the forward end of the handling area.

From the beginning of 1937 Japan considered herself to be no longer bound by treaties and, as part of a general fleet up-trading, the Mogamis exchanged their 155mm/6.1in triple turrets for 200mm/7.87in twins. The barrels of "B"-turret guns,

now being longer, would not tuck in behind "A" turret and needed to be elevated in order to be aligned fore-and-aft.

Badly damaged by bombing at Midway in June 1942, when her sister *Mikuma* was lost, the *Mogami* spent nearly 11 months under repair, in the course of which her after turrets were removed and a light aircraft deck added. Supported on stanchions this extended the existing deck almost to the stern. Rails and 11 seaplanes on trolleys were added, the purpose of which was to extend the reconnaissance horizon of the cruiser division.

Although the very maximum had been attempted on their displacement, the Mogamis could be counted as successful, giving very good service during the Pacific war. Other than the *Mogami*, all were lost in the Philippines following the Leyte Gulf landings of October 1944. All absorbed heavy damage before sinking; that to the *Suzuya* being caused by the progressive detonation of her own torpedo warheads, as feared by constructor Hiraga so long before.

ABOVE: **A further impression of the *Kumano* in her original, light cruiser configuration. An interesting point is that the later 200mm/7.87in guns were 50-calibre weapons, whose barrels were longer than those of the 155mm/6.1in guns that they replaced. The barrels of No.2 turret guns needed to be elevated to clear No.1 turret roof.**

Mogami class

	Built	Commissioned
Mikuma	Mitsubishi, Nagasaki	August 29, 1935
Mogami	Kure Navy Yard	July 28, 1935
Kumano	Kawasaki, Kobe	October 31, 1937
Suzuya	Yokosuka, Navy Yard	October 31, 1937

Mogami (as designed)

Displacement: 11,380 tonnes/11,200 tons (standard); 14,204 tonnes/13,980 tons (full load)
Length: 189m/620ft 5in (bp); 200.5m/658ft 6in (oa)
Beam: 20.6m/67ft 7in
Draught: 5.9m/19ft 4in (standard)
Armament: 15 x 155mm/6.1in (5x3) and 8 x 127mm/5in HA (4x2) guns; 12 x 610mm/24in torpedo tubes (4x3)
Machinery: Geared steam turbines, 10 boilers, 4 shafts
Power: 113,346kW/152,000shp for 36 knots
Endurance: 2,388 tonnes/2,350 tons (oil) for 14,168km/7,650nm at 14 knots
Protection: 25–140mm/1–5.5in (belt); 35–60mm/1.38–2.4in (armoured deck); 75–100mm/2.95–3.9in (barbettes)
Complement: 950

LEFT: **By July 1945, surviving Japanese heavy units were virtually tied to their bases, where they were systematically destroyed by rampant US carrier-based air power.** *Tone*'s **four twin 203mm/8in turrets, all forward, are clearly identifiable as she is bombed to oblivion in Kure.** ABOVE: **Struck by three heavy bombs and shocked by seven near misses,** *Tone* **began to settle. While still under attack, a tug valiantly pushed the cruiser into shallow water, where she was dismantled post-war. The mining effect of near-misses can be even more damaging than direct hits.**

Tone and Ibuki classes

As originally defined, the specification for the two Tone-class cruisers closely followed that of the Mogamis. They were laid down in 1934–35 but, before they reached launching stage, their role had been changed to that of "aircraft cruiser". Six, even eight, aircraft were to be accommodated to facilitate the ships acting as the reconnaissance element of a cruiser squadron. Their layout was changed drastically, the whole after end being devoted to the storage and operation of the aircraft. Four triple 155mm/6.1in turrets would, uniquely, be located forward, thus separating the ships' main functions.

These were major changes, and the ships were still unlaunched when, at the beginning of 1937, Japan renounced treaty obligations. This resulted in the exchange of the triple 155mm/6.1in guns for twin 203mm/8in weapons. Turret

weights were almost identical but the concentration of weight forward caused design problems with trim. The first, third and fourth turrets were located at the same level, only the second being superimposed.

Twelve 610mm/24in torpedo tubes were arranged in four triples. Located on the upper deck, they flanked the catapult pedestals.

The two Tones were completed in 1938–39, but a further pair was deferred in favour of more urgent construction. Eventually laid down in the spring of 1942, they were now intended to be repeat Suzuyas, with the mainmast relocated at the after end of the aircraft deck. This was the time of Midway, however, when the loss of three fleet carriers completely changed construction priorities. Although the first-of-class, *Ibuki*, was launched in May 1943, construction was halted, only

to be resumed in the December with the decision to convert the hull into that of a light carrier. This was still only 80 per cent complete when the war ended. The second hull never reached launching stage and both were scrapped.

Tone and Ibuki classes

	Built	Commisioned
Chikuma	Mitsubishi, Nagasaki	May 20, 1939
Tone	Mitsubishi, Nagasaki	November 20, 1938
Ibuki	Kure Navy Yard	
Kurama	Mitsubishi, Nagasaki	

Tone class (as built)

Displacement: 11,430 tonnes/11,250 tons (standard); 15,443 tonnes/15,200 tons (full load)
Length: 190.3m/624ft 8in (bp); 201.6m/661ft 9in (oa)
Beam: 19.4m/63ft 8in
Draught: 6.5m/21ft 6in (standard)
Armament: 8 x 203mm/8in (4x2) and 8 x 127mm/5in HA (4x2) guns; 12 x 610mm/24in torpedo tubes (4x3)
Machinery: Geared steam turbines, 8 boilers, 4 shafts
Power: 113,346kW/152,000shp for 35 knots
Endurance: 2,733 tonnes/2,690 tons (oil) for 14,816km/8,000nm at 18 knots
Protection: 55–145mm/2.17–5.71in (belt); 31–65mm/1.22–2.56in (protective deck); 70–145mm/2.76–5.71in (barbettes)
Complement: 875

LEFT: **Although unclear, this picture of** *Chikuma* **shows her four forward turrets while giving an idea of the spacious after deck, devoted to aircraft use. The centreline ramp access can be made out. She was sunk by a single air-dropped torpedo during the frantic battle off Samar in October 1944.**

ABOVE LEFT: **This picture of *San Giorgio* probably dates from World War I as she has been given a foremast and searchlight platforms. Her funnels have been shortened and a small navigating bridge added. Note the symmetry of the armament disposition, with four twin 190mm/7.5in turrets sided in the waist.** ABOVE: **From May 1940, the modernized *San Giorgio* acted as a floating defence for Tobruk. In January 1941, during the siege of the port by the British 8th Army, the vessel was destroyed by artillery fire.**

San Giorgio class

Of classic Italian design, the two San Giorgios were laid down in 1905–07. They were thus roughly contemporary with the last British armoured cruisers, the Minotaurs, but were sufficiently later to allow the second unit, *San Marco*, to be equipped with steam turbines.

The layout of the armament was typical of the time, with a main-calibre turret at either end and two secondary calibre turrets on either side in the waist. The long forecastle deck was narrow in order that the wing turrets could fire while in pursuit. Other than turrets, tophamper was minimal. The bridge structure was of insignificant size, the design depending upon two widely spaced pairs of lofty funnels for its "presence". The funnel spacing was a result of the boiler rooms being widely separated about the engine rooms. As built, there was only one mast, with a heavy boat derrick, stepped well aft of amidships but during their World War I service, a light foremast was added.

Both ships were dual-fired, mainly with coal, but with oil-spray for more rapid acceleration. By the early 1930s the pair was obsolescent. A new role was then found for the turbine-driven *San Marco* as a remotely-controlled target ship. During 1931–35 her original boilers were replaced by four oil-fired units developing 9,694kW/13,000shp for 18 knots. With all armament removed, her standard displacement was reduced to about 8,900 tonnes/8,750 tons.

In 1937–38 the *San Giorgio* was modernized for coastal defence. Reboilered with eight units, developing 13,422kW/18,000shp, she had an endurance of about 4,444km/2,400nm at 17 knots, sufficient for service in the Mediterranean and Red Sea. Now with just two funnels, she retained her heavy guns, these being supplemented by five twin 100mm/3.9in HA guns and six 37mm/1.46in cannon. She was sunk in the defence of Tobruk in January 1941, moored as a fixed AA and land bombardment platform.

San Giorgio class

	Built	Commissioned
San Giorgio	Cantiere di Castellammare di Stabia	July 1, 1910
San Marco	Cantiere di Castellammare di Stabia	February 7, 1911

San Giorgio class (as built)

Displacement: 10,160 tonnes/10,000 tons (standard); 11,278 tonnes/11,100 tons (full load)

Length: 131m/430ft (bp); 140.9m/462ft 6in (oa)

Beam: 21m/68ft 11in

Draught: 7.3m/24ft

Armament: 4 x 254mm/10in (2x2), 8 x 190mm/7.5in (4x2) and 18 x 76mm/3in (18x1) guns; 3 x 450mm/17.7in torpedo tubes

Machinery: *San Giorgio* – 2 sets triple-expansion engines, 14 boilers, 2 shafts; *San Marco* – Direct-drive steam turbines, 14 boilers, 2 shafts

Power: *San Giorgio* – 13,572kW/18,200shp for 23 knots; *San Marco* – 17,150kW/23,000shp for 23.5 knots

Endurance: 1,498 tonnes/1,475 tons (coal) 50 tonnes/49 tons (oil) for 5,741km/3,100nm at 12 knots

Protection: 200mm/7.87in (belt); 45mm/1.77in (protective deck); 180mm/7.1in (turrets)

Complement: 700

ABOVE: ***San Marco* is seen entering Brindisi in December 1916, passing close to the nearly submerged wreck of the battleship *Benedetto Brin*, which had blown up at her moorings in September 1915 and upon which salvage work is still being conducted.**

Bolzano and Trento class

First of the Italian "treaty cruisers", the *Trento* and *Trieste* are considered to be sisters, with the third unit, *Bolzano*, a sub-class. The importance of the new "heavy" cruiser to the Italian Navy was underlined by their being named after cities in territories ceded to Italy following World War I.

In treaty cruiser design, the American and Japanese emphasized firepower with a ten-gun main battery. The remaining Washington signatories opted for only eight guns but with improved protection and/or speed. Ever rivals of the neighbouring French, the Italians prioritized speed by which they could accept or decline action at will or, once engaged, dictate the range. With respect to the latter the Italians, talented gun designers, developed a 203mm/8in Ansaldo-Schneider weapon capable of ranging to 28km/17.5 miles at a maximum elevation of 48 degrees. This was improved to better than 31.5km/19.6 miles in the *Bolzano* and the *Zaras*. As with capital-ship armaments, these considerably out-ranged British equivalents during 1940–43, causing considerable tactical problems.

The Trentos' hulls were flush-decked, with no forecastle. The light armour belt extended from the forward to the after magazine, its scope evidenced in photographs by the lack of

ABOVE: The near-overhead light casts the *Trento*'s hull into sharp relief. The first Italian "treaty cruisers", the pair set the pattern for the remaining inter-war heavy cruisers, with symmetrical armament layout, a heavy tripod mainmast about the after funnel and foredeck aircraft catapult.

scuttles. A light protective deck extended over the same length, with local thickening in way of barbettes.

Machinery was arranged on the unit system, with boiler spaces preceding engine rooms. Considerably the larger, the forward funnel exhausted eight boilers against the after funnel's four. Although heavily trunked, both retained symmetry, lacking the exotic architecture of their Japanese counterparts.

The bridge structure was relatively low, but an impression of massiveness was given by a substantial, wide-legged pentapod foremast supporting main and secondary gunnery directors. Ahead of the after funnel was a powerful tripod bearing further secondary directors, a searchlight platform and a boat derrick.

During World War II three floatplanes, usually Ro.43 spotter/reconnaissance aircraft, were carried. Their catapult, unusually, stretched the length of the foredeck. Eight torpedo

LEFT: *Trento*, seen in Shanghai early in 1932. Before World War II it was customary for each nation with a trading concession to station a warship here to safeguard its interests. Her flush-decked hull has little sheer, the freeboard decreasing uniformly forward to aft with no discontinuity.

tubes were paired in two athwartships compartments at maindeck level. All were fixed, firing on the beam. To operate them, a "spoon" was extended outboard to support the tube until it was clear of the ship.

The pair's lack of protection attracted adverse criticism and they were followed by the slower, but more robust, Zara class. The *Bolzano* was built in parallel with these, a third but considerably modified *Trento.*

Laid down in 1930, the *Bolzano*'s sea-keeping was improved by the addition of a raised forecastle. The aircraft catapult was moved to a more conventional, less exposed location amidships, requiring the after funnel to be moved further aft. The bridge block was more monolithic and its designers, ever mindful of good aesthetics, blended it into the forward funnel. The same weight of armour was worked in but was rearranged for better effect in conjunction with more thorough subdivision. A handsome ship, she was the first of the big Italians to breach the Washington rules.

Torpedoed by the British submarine *Unbroken* in August 1942, the *Bolzano* was probably saved by her improved subdivision. Although put aground, her bridge and forward boiler space were gutted by fire. Salvaged, it was proposed that she be converted to a fast transport for the hazardous North Africa supply run. All main armament would be landed and magazine spaces and forward boiler room cleared for cargo. Except for sided funnels exhausting No. 2 boiler room, all the upper deck forward of the mainmast would be cleared for fighter aircraft, to be launched by a pair of catapults. The project progressed very slowly and, together with both Trentos, the *Bolzano* became a war loss.

ABOVE: Completed four years after the two Trentos, their quasi-sister *Bolzano* differed significantly in being given a forecastle deck and having a trainable catapult located amidships in place of the fixed forecastle track of the earlier ships. BELOW: Both of *Bolzano*'s funnels were capped from the outset, the forefunnel being incorporated into an enlarged bridge structure. The main director was supported by a short tetrapod. So modelled, the *Bolzano*'s profile could easily be confused with that of other Italian cruiser classes.

ABOVE: The *Bolzano* stemmed in drydock on an unknown occasion, but prior to 1942 as the ship is not camouflage painted. The platform was not part of the hull. Detail of the after hull is, unfortunately, in deep shadow but the double curvature of the extreme stern section is unusual.

ABOVE: A fine-looking cruiser, the *Bolzano*'s career was effectively ended when, in August 1942, she and the light cruiser *Attendolo* were torpedoed by the British submarine *Unbroken.* Gutted by fire, she was salvaged but was never again to see active service.

Bolzano and Trento class

	Built	Commissioned
Trento	Orlando, Livorno (Leghorn)	April 3, 1929
Trieste	Stab. Tecnico Triestino, Trieste	December 21, 1928
Bolzano	Ansaldo, Genoa	August 19, 1933

Trento (as built)

Displacement: 10,485 tonnes/10,320 tons (standard); 13,513 tonnes/13,300 tons (full load)
Length: 193.9m/636ft 6in (bp); 197m/646ft 6in (oa)
Beam: 20.6m/67ft 8in
Draught: 6.6m/21ft 8in (standard)
Armament: 8 x 203mm/8in (4x2) and 16 x 100mm/3.9in (8x2) guns; 8 x 533mm/21in torpedo tubes (4x2)
Machinery: Geared steam turbines, 12 boilers, 4 shafts
Power: 111,855kW/150,000shp for 35 knots
Endurance: 2,245 tonnes/2,210 tons (oil) for 7,685km/4,150nm at 16 knots
Protection: 70mm/2.76in (belt); 50mm/2in (protective deck); 100mm/3.9in (turrets)
Complement: 720

Zara class

Like the Trentos, the Zaras had a foredeck catapult but, having a greatly revised machinery layout, had a more compact appearance with closer-spaced funnels. Similar to the *Bolzano*, they had a forecastle deck.

Decisions regarding the over-light construction of the Trentos must have been taken without any experience with the class for the first of the Zaras, *Fiume*, was laid down less than four months after the completion of the *Trieste*. From the outset with the heavier new class, the Washington displacement of 10,160 tonnes/10,000 tons would be treated as a guide rather than a limit.

The same eight-gun battery was required, but on a hull with heavier scantlings and considerably more protection. To gain a proposed 200mm/7.87in belt, the Ministero della Marina was prepared to accept a sustained sea speed of 32 knots, slow by Italian standards.

British suspicions that the class did not conform to agreed limits was confirmed when, during the Spanish Civil War, the *Gorizia* suffered an incapacitating aviation fuel explosion and had to be towed to Gibraltar for emergency docking. Surreptitious but "careful" measurements of her underwater form indicated a normal displacement of "about 10 per cent"

greater than that declared. There was considerable variation between the four ships of the class but *Gorizia*, the heavier, was in fact some 17 per cent over limit.

Even with generous interpretation of limits, the desired 200mm/7.87in belt had proved impossible, the Zaras having 150mm/5.9in, tapering to 100mm/3.9in below the normal waterline. Extending from forward to after magazines, the belts were closed at either end by 120mm/4.7in transverse bulkheads. The same area was overlaid by a 70mm/2.76in maindeck and a 20mm/0.79in upper deck, thick enough to initiate the detonation of a bomb or projectile prior to deep penetration. Barbette protection, compared with that of the

ABOVE: The Italian Navy invested in battleships rather than aircraft carriers, a decision that proved severely limiting. Here, in March 1941, the *Pola* is wreathed in her own gun smoke as she tries, unsuccessfully, to avoid being torpedoed by British carrier aircraft.

ABOVE: Despite their size, the Zaras had an almost destroyer-like elegance, seen to good effect in this *contre-jour* study of the *Pola*. Last of the four, she differed from the rest in having the forefunnel casing merged, *Bolzano*-like, into the bridge structure.

ABOVE: **The Zaras operated as a coherent cruiser squadron and here the *Gorizia* lays in Taranto, with the *Fiume* in the foreground. Their funnels were trunked and carefully styled to enhance the ships' appearance. Note the unusual access arrangements to the bridge structure.**

ABOVE: **Seen in 1940, "Mediterranean-moored", stern-on to her berth, the *Gorizia* had two floatplanes on her forecastle catapult. Originally, these were Piaggio P.6 bis, changed for Ro.43 in 1938. The ship still retains a fourth twin 100mm/3.9in mounting, later removed, at the break of the forecastle.**

Trentos, was greatly increased. The Zaras were effectively proof against 152mm/6in and some 203mm/8in fire, and certainly do not deserve to be included in the general mythology that all Italian cruisers were "tinclads".

The major design concession was the reduction of installed power to 70,841kW/95,000shp and a waterline shorter than that of the Trentos by some 15m/49ft 3in. Careful hull design, including a bow bulb, nonetheless realized 32–33 knots, the *Fiume* and *Pola* being the slowest.

Their weakness lay in their unusual machinery layout. For the power, only two shafts were required. The eight boilers were arranged in an unorthodox fashion, with only three transverse pairs. The engine room for the longer starboard shaft lay to starboard with a seventh boiler on its port side. There was a reverse arrangement for the much-shorter port shaft. All the spaces were divided by a centreline bulkhead, a feature which, not for the first time, would prove disastrous.

On March 28, 1941, the *Pola* was hit by a single 457mm/18in torpedo from a British carrier aircraft. The starboard boiler space flooded and the starboard shaft that passed through them was damaged. The dangerous resulting list had to be corrected by counter-flooding the port spaces which, in turn, immobilized the port-side engines. All propulsive power was lost but, believing the pursuing British fleet to be at a safe distance, the Italian admiral ordered the *Fiume* and *Zara* to stand by her. With only a pair of destroyers in support the trio was surprised by the battleships of the British Mediterranean Fleet, being blasted at close range by 381mm/15in salvoes that no cruiser could withstand. In what became known as the night battle of Matapan, all the Italian vessels were lost, virtually without reply.

Zara class

	Built	Commissioned
Fiume	Stab. Tecnico Triestino, Trieste	November 23, 1931
Gorizia	Odero Terni Orlando, Livorno	December 23, 1931
Pola	Odero Terni Orlando, Livorno	December 21, 1932
Zara	Odero Terni Orlando, la Spezia	October 20, 1931

ABOVE: **Working up to maximum speed, the *Fiume* makes a fine sight. The picture shows clearly how the four legs of the tetrapod span the bridge structure proper, and support the platforms and main battery director above. Having considerable flare, the forecastle is sculpted to avoid excessive width at its after end.**

Zara (as completed)

Displacement: 11,847 tonnes/11,660 tons (standard); 14,498 tonnes/14,270 tons (full load)
Length: 180m/590ft 10in (bp); 182.8m/600ft (oa)
Beam: 20.6m/67ft 8in
Draught: 6.2m/20ft 3in (standard)
Armament: 8 x 203mm/8in (4x2) and 16 x 100mm/3.9in (8x2)
Machinery: Geared steam turbines, 8 boilers, 2 shafts
Power: 70,841kW/95,000shp for 33 knots
Endurance: 2,398 tonnes/2,360 tons (oil) for 9,908km/5,350nm at 16 knots
Protection: 150mm/5.9in (belt); 70+20mm/2.76+0.79in (protective decks); 150mm/5.9in (turrets)
Complement: 840

LEFT: **Although the light cruiser designers were not those of the heavy cruisers, there was much similarity in their approach, not least in the masting. The *Cadorna* was one of the second pair, which moved the mainmast ahead of the after funnel. This created a gap for angled aircraft catapults.**

da Barbiano and Cadorna classes

During the 1920s the French began constructing considerable numbers of what popularly became known as "super-destroyers". Mostly exceeding 2,743 tonnes/2,700 tons, several made 40 knots on trials and, carrying a respectable armament of five 138mm/5.43in guns and six torpedo tubes, constituted a threat not only to destroyers but, in an enclosed Mediterranean context, to trade. In response the Italian Navy laid down a quartet of small, but very fast, light cruisers in 1928. With their usual sense of history, the Italians named the ships after the Condottieri, the "soldiers of fortune". At about 5,283 tonnes/5,200 tons at what was "Washington standard displacement", they carried an adequate eight 152mm/6in guns and four torpedo tubes in paired mountings.

To match the speed of the French, about 44 per cent of waterline length was devoted to boilers and machinery (compared with about 39 per cent in the big 10,160-tonne/10,000-ton treaty cruisers (the "diecimille"). Run in the routinely ultra-light Italian trials condition, the lead ship notched up over 42 knots, but sustained sea speed was nearer 37.

Construction had to be very light, so light that even their crews referred to them as "*cartoni animate*". Too narrow for centreline bulkheads, machinery spaces were bounded by double light longitudinal bulkheads to limit flooding from light-calibre fire.

Two seaplanes, Cant 25s or, later, Ro.43s, were accommodated in the forward superstructure and transferred by rail to the foredeck catapult. On most, a mine cargo could be shipped.

The two Cadornas, effectively a sub-group, followed immediately. On the same dimensions, their slightly improved arrangements increased displacement and immersion, in turn reducing speed. Externally, they differed, mainly in having the catapult relocated aft, so that the tripod mainmast was moved ahead of the after funnel.

All except the *Cadorna* became war losses, three in surface action, and two to submarines.

ABOVE: **Like her 203mm/8in counterparts, *da Barbiano* had a catapult track laid into the foredeck. Just visible immediately abaft "B" turret is the door of one of two sided hangars for floatplanes. The pole mainmast, later considerably heightened, is abaft the after funnel.**

da Barbiano and Cadorna classes

	Built	Commissioned
Alberico da Barbiano	Ansaldo, Genoa	June 9, 1931
Alberto di Giussano	Ansaldo, Genoa	February 5, 1931
Bartolomeo Colleoni	Ansaldo, Genoa	February 10, 1932
Giovanni della Bande Nere	Cant. Castellammare di Stabia	April 17, 1931
Luigi Cadorna	CRDA, Trieste	August 11, 1933
Armando Diaz	Odeo Terni Orlando (OTO), la Spezia	April 29, 1933

da Barbiano (as built)

Displacement: 5,232 tonnes/5,150 tons (standard), 6,934 tonnes/6,825 tons (full load)
Length: 160m/525ft 2in (bp); 169.3m/555ft 9in (oa)
Beam: 15.5m/50ft 10in
Draught: 5.1m/16ft 9in (standard)
Armament: 8 x 152mm/6in (4x2) and 6 x 100mm/3.9in (3x2) guns; 4 x 533mm/21in torpedo tubes (2x2)
Machinery: Geared steam turbines, 6 boilers, 2 shafts
Power: 70,841kW/95,000shp for 37 knots
Endurance: 1,270 tonnes/1,250 tons (oil) for 7,037km/3,800nm at 18 knots
Protection: 18–25mm/0.71–1in (vertical); 20mm/0.79in (horizontal); up to 23mm/0.91in (turrets)
Complement: 505

FAR LEFT: **Like Italian architecture of the mid-1930s, Italian warships were stripped to pure functional style. The earlier tetrapod has become a cone, rising from the bridge to support the director of the *Attendolo*. The centreline amidships catapult is flanked by boat skids.** INSET ABOVE: **Some time in 1942, *Montecuccoli* was given this disruptive paint scheme. Note the paravane chains at the bows. Despite an active war she survived. Modernized, and with "B" turret removed, she served until the 1960s as the school ship for naval cadets.**

Montecuccoli and d'Aosta classes

The two Montecuccolis, laid down in 1931–33, comprised the "third group" of Condottieri. Their construction paralleled that of the French La Galissonniere class, to which their dimensions and displacement were very similar. Where the French opted for a greater beam and an extra gun, the Italians again chose speed, the lead ship making 38.7 knots on trials with machinery at about 19 per cent overload.

The third group were some 16m/52ft 6in longer than the second with only 1m/3ft 4in increase in beam. Armament remained the same and the extra displacement was due to improved protection. A 60mm/2.4in belt stretched from the forward to after magazines and was paralleled by an inboard longitudinal bulkhead of 25mm/1in. Over the length of the machinery spaces a third light bulkhead was interposed. A 20–30mm/0.79–1.18in protective deck overlaid the belted area. The ship's immunity zone

against 152mm/6in gunfire was calculated at 13,500–22,000m/14,764–24,059yds.

Great effort went into the ship's external appearance. The bridge block was reduced to a lower bridge surmounted by a two-decked conical structure which supported the main director. There was no foremast, a lofty tripod mainmast being tightly grouped with the after funnel. Secondary directors flanked either funnel, while aircraft and catapult were accommodated amidships. Up to 96 mines could be carried.

The two "fourth group" Condottieri, the d'Aostas, were, oddly enough, built at the same time as the Montecuccolis. Slightly beamier, slightly heavier and slightly better protected, they differed externally in having an upper bridge

below the level of the main director, and funnels of equal size. In the third-group ships the forward funnel exhausted four of the six boilers; in the fourth, each funnel exhausted three boilers.

Only the *Attendolo* became a war loss and this was to heavy bombers. Under peace treaty terms the *d'Aosta* was ceded to Soviet Russia and the *Savoia* to Greece.

Montecuccoli and d'Aosta classes

	Built	Commissioned
Muzio Attendolo	CRDA, Trieste	August 7, 1935
Raimondo Montecuccoli	Ansaldo, Genoa	June 30, 1935
Emanuele Filiberto Duca d'Aosta	OTO, Livorno	July 13, 1935
Eugenio di Savoia	Ansaldo, Genoa	January 16, 1936

Montecuccoli (as built)

Displacement: 7,508 tonnes/7,390 tons (standard); 8,977 tonnes/8.835 tons (full load)

Length: 166.7m/547ft 2in (bp); 182.2m/598ft 1in (oa)

Beam: 16.6m/54ft 6in

Draught: 5.6m/18ft 4in (standard)

Armament: 8 x 152mm/6in (4x2) and 6 x 100mm/3.9in (3x2) guns; 4 x 533mm/21in torpedo tubes

Machinery: Geared steam turbines, 6 boilers, 2 shafts

Power: 79,044kW/106,000shp for 37 knots.

Endurance: 1,676 tonnes/1,650 tons, (oil) for 7,222km/3,900nm at 14 knots

Protection: 70+35mm/2.76+1.38in (vertical); 30–35mm/1.18–1.38in (horizontal); 70–90mm/2.76–3.54in (turrets)

Complement: 578

ABOVE: **Visually, the pair of d'Aostas differed from the Montecuccolis in the upper bridge structure, now a stump conical section surmounted by a command bridge below the director. The clipper stem and clean lines gave an impression of grace and power. This picture shows *Eugenio di Savoia*.**

Abruzzi class

The final pair of Condottieri, the "fifth group", comprised the *Abruzzi* and *Garibaldi*. Of a size with the preceding d'Aostas, they were, nonetheless, far removed from the original concept governing the early groups.

Their authorization in 1933 coincided with the Italian Navy embarking on the extensive rebuilding of the Cavour-class battleships and the ordering of the two new Littorios, cornerstones to the Italian claim of "*Mare Nostrum*". Modern cruisers were required to complement the battle squadrons and robustness was more important than speed, for which the requirement was a sufficient margin over that of the capital ships.

Eight boilers, five large and three small, generated 74,600kW/100,000shp, a reduction on earlier cruisers. Although boiler spaces still alternated with engine rooms, extensive trunking enabled the two funnels to be closely spaced. Two catapults were fitted, flanking the after funnel and up to four aircraft could be accommodated.

Armour was arranged according to a new scheme with a 30mm/1.18in side belt backed by an arcing 100mm/3.95in bulkhead, which left a lenticular void space of a maximum 1m/3ft 4in depth. A further light longitudinal bulkhead ran inboard of this combination. The protective deck above was thickened to 40mm/1.57in.

TOP: **This pre-war picture of *Abruzzi* emphasizes the inherent simplicity of warships prior to the missile age. The heavy derrick, stepped on the mainmast, served both catapults and boats. The curved object on the ship's side, right aft, is a propeller guard, which was lowered when alongside.**

ABOVE: **The final pair of Condottieri reverted from the unit system of machinery layout employed earlier. By more closely grouping the boiler spaces, the funnels were closer together and flanked by the two catapults. "A" and "Y" turrets were triples, superfired by twins in "B" and "X" positions. *Giuseppe Garibaldi* is shown here.**

The Abruzzis were the only pair to mount ten 152mm/6in guns. These were distributed symmetrically forward and aft, with twin turrets superfiring triples. The guns themselves were of a new 55-calibre model, superseding the earlier ships' 53-calibre weapons. Improved muzzle velocity gave their 50kg/110lb projectiles a range of 24,900m/27,231yds, an increase of about 2,249m/2,460yds.

Longer than the Zara-class heavy cruisers, the Abruzzis' size was emphasized by their substantial forward freeboard, which was carried back to the forward funnel. Bridge structure was again kept low with, originally, no foremast other than a simple antenna pole. They were the only cruisers in the series to have a pole, rather than tripod, mainmast.

LEFT: **Scarcely recognizable following her rebuilding, the *Garibaldi* is seen here in the mid-1960s. Her after end is dominated by the search and guidance radar systems for a single Terrier SAM. Her funnels have been trunked into a single casing and, forward, she has two twin 135mm/5.3in mountings.**

LEFT: **Although the *Abruzzi* served in the post-war fleet until 1961, she was not converted to a missile cruiser. She was, however, thoroughly modernized, with considerably changed superstructure, masting and added electronics. She kept her original main-calibre armament.**

By early 1944 the Italian Navy was co-operating with those of the Allies and, with radars and improved communications being made available, the *Abruzzi* gained a light lattice foremast. Earlier dazzle painting gave way to a variation of Measure 12, a dark-grey hull with lighter grey upperworks, although the dark funnel caps were retained.

Both cruisers survived into Italy's full NATO membership, and electronics now proliferated. By the early 1950s the *Garibaldi* had joined a light foremast, crossed with a conventional yard, and a mainmast crowned with the outsized dish of an American SK series air search radar, an addition that did nothing for her appearance.

Although the nameship was scrapped in 1961, the *Garibaldi* underwent a near five-year rebuilding, emerging in 1962 as a guided-missile cruiser. Of the original ship, only the hull remained recognizable. A larger and more complex bridge structure was surmounted by one of two substantial lattice masts bearing a full range of American electronics. Aft were twin Terrier directors and launcher. Surprisingly, there were also four vertical-launch tubes for Polaris ICBMs.

(Dummy missiles were certainly fired but the policy on these remains unclear.)

A replacement set of boilers was trunked into a single, large, capped funnel and developed power for a reduced speed of 30 knots. All original guns were removed. The forward turrets were replaced by twin mountings for a new-pattern 135mm/5.3in dual-purpose (DP) gun, while eight single 76mm/3in weapons were distributed along either side of the waist.

This was a classic case of new wine in old bottles and, by the time that she went for disposal in 1978, the *Garibaldi* had seen 41 years of service. Her rebuilding had proved to be complex but had provided the necessary experience to progress to the next generation of purpose-built missile ships.

Abruzzi class

	Built	Commissioned
Luigi di Savoia duca degli Abruzzi	OTO, la Spezia	December 1, 1937
Giuseppe Garibaldi	CRDA, Trieste	December 20, 1937

ABOVE: **Very imposing in her original form, the *Garibaldi* lost much of her "presence" when she was extensively rebuilt in 1960–61. She is shown here laying to buoys.**

Abruzzi (as built)

Displacement: 9,581 tonnes/9,430 tons (standard); 11,725 tonnes/11,540 tons (full load)
Length: 171.8m/564ft (bp); 187m/613ft 10in (oa)
Beam: 18.9m/62ft
Draught: 6.1m/20ft (standard)
Armament: 10 x 152mm/6in (2x3/2x2) and 8 x 100mm/3.9in (4x2); 6x 533mm/21in torpedo tubes (2x3)
Machinery: Geared steam turbines, 8 boilers, 2 shafts
Power: 74,570kW/100,000shp for 33 knots
Endurance: 1,725 tonnes/1,695 tons (oil) for 7,408km/4,000nm at 13 knots
Protection: 100+30mm/3.94+1.18in (vertical); 40mm/1.57in (horizontal); up to 135mm/5.3in (turrets)
Complement: 640

Etna class

Together with destroyers, this pair of small cruisers was ordered to Siamese (Thai) account in 1938. With Italy's involvement in the war, work progressed slowly until, in December 1941 and shortly after Pearl Harbor, they were requisitioned.

As designed, they were diminutives of the later Condottieri, but with a single funnel and only one forward turret. However, just after being launched, they underwent considerable remodelling.

Responsibilities for the endless resupply of the Axis armies in North Africa were haemorrhaging the Italian merchant fleet. Fast warship/transports such as those used by the British to supply Tobruk and Malta were an attractive proposition, able either to make a high-speed solo overnight run, or to supplement and cover a convoy.

In place of the planned 152mm/6in battery, the pair was now fitted with

three twin 135mm/5.3in dual-purpose mountings, ten new-style 65mm/2.56in weapons in single mountings and six twin 20mm/0.79in guns.

Cargo spaces totalling about 525 cubic metres/687 cubic yards were arranged forward and aft, each served by a small crane. Short-term troop accommodation was also provided forward and in the after superstructure. Deck cargoes, typically cased petrol, could be stowed in the open space abaft the funnel, intended originally for aircraft and catapult.

Work progressed at a very leisurely pace for, although the ships had obvious utility, they overlapped with the programme for a dozen Capitani Romani which, capable of 40 knots and mounting a similar scale of armament on little over half the displacement, were considered more valuable. Both were competing for increasingly scarce resources as Italy's

ABOVE: **This picture is a digital rendition showing how the Etna class would have looked. As designed, the Etnas resembled reduced Montecuccolis, with one funnel and no superimposed forward turret. Note the torpedo tube aperture.** BELOW LEFT: **Conceived together, destroyed together. Neither ship survived to serve in either the Thai or Italian Navy.**

war effort stuttered to a halt. When Italy agreed an armistice in September 1943, the still-incomplete pair was taken by the Germans. Never progressed above the weather deck, both hulls were eventually found scuttled in shallow water off Trieste.

Etna class

	Built
Etna (ex-*Taksin*)	CRDA, Trieste
Vesuvio (ex-*Naresman*)	CRDA, Trieste

Etna class (as proposed for Italian AA cruisers)

Displacement: 5,985 tonnes/5,890 tons (standard); 6,512 tonnes/6,410 tons (full load)
Length: 141m/462ft 10in (bp); 153.8m/504ft 10in (oa)
Beam: 14.5m/47ft 8in
Draught: 5.9m/19ft 3in (projected)
Armament: 6 x 135mm/5.3in (3x2), 10 x 65mm/2.56in (10x1) and 12 x 20mm/0.79in (6x2) guns
Machinery: Geared steam turbines, 3 boilers, 2 shafts
Power: 29,828kW/40,000shp for 28 knots
Protection: 60+20mm/2.4+0.79in (vertical); 20–35mm/0.79–1.38in (horizontal); none (turrets)
Complement: 580 (projected)

ABOVE LEFT: **Although the *Attilio Regolo*, seen here, entered service as early as May 1942, only three of the 12 ships were ever completed. From forefunnel to the stern were tracks capable of stowing 70 mines. The eight torpedoes, in two banks, were decked over.** ABOVE: **The *Regolo* again, probably post-war. The 135mm/5.3in gun calibre was a new one for the Italians, and well-suited to the ship's limited size.**

Capitani Romani class

It will be recalled that French super-destroyers of the early 1920s begat the early Condottieri as an Italian response. Just five years later, however, the Condottieri had evolved into a quite different type of cruiser, but the French *contre torpilleur* had continued an uninterrupted line of development. Faced in 1938 with the new Mogadors (2,997 tonnes/2,950 tons, eight 138mm/5.43in guns, 40+ knots), the Italian Navy again sought a counter.

The Capitani Romani, with their resonant Roman names, were less than 6m/19ft 8in longer than the Mogadors but had machinery developing 20 per cent more power. Their main battery of eight 135mm/5.3in was similar and they were unprotected except for the use of toughened alloys in vital areas. An aircraft, without catapult, was planned but never adopted. Portable tracks along the side decks enabled up to 70 mines to be carried.

At only 3,805 tonnes/3,745 tons standard displacement they were classed officially as "*esploratori oceanici*" but were always known as light cruisers. Twelve were ordered during 1939, all

from commercial yards. These suffered badly from lack of resources, from bombing and from fluctuating priorities. As a result only three of the class were ever commissioned into the Italian Navy during the war. Several hulls remained incomplete due to sabotage or to bomb damage. Of those taken by the Germans at the armistice in September 1943 none was ever finished, with the near exceptions of *Caio Mario* and *Cornelio Silla*.

In 1948 the *Attilio Regolo* and *Scipione Africano* were ceded to France as war reparation, being renamed *Chateaurenault* and *Guichen* respectively. The *Pompeo Magno* and the salvaged *Giulio Germanico* went on to give the Italian Navy useful post-war service. Rearmed and re-equipped to NATO standards in the early 1950s, they served until 1975 as the *San Marco* and *San Giorgio* respectively.

LEFT: ***Attilio Regolo* and her sister *Scipione Africano* were ceded to France in 1948, being renamed *Chateaurenault* (here) and *Guichen* respectively. Rearmed with a mix of ex-German 10.5cm/4.1in and Bofors 57mm/2.24in guns, 12 AS torpedo tubes and new electronics, they served as Command Ships/Flotilla leaders until the 1960s.**

Capitani Romani class

	Built	Commissioned
Attilio Regolo	OTO, Livorno	May 14, 1942
Caio Mario	OTO, Livorno	
Claudio Druso	Cantieri del Tirreno, Riva Trigoso	
Claudio Tiberio	OTO, Livorno	
Cornelio Silla	Ansaldo, Genoa	
Giulio Germanico	Cant. di Castellammare di Stabia	January 19, 1956
Ottaviano Augusto	Cant. Navali Riuniti, Ancona	
Paolo Emilio	Ansaldo, Genoa	
Pompeo Magno	Cant. Navali Riuniti, Ancona	June 4, 1943
Scipione Africano	OTO, Livorno	April 23, 1943
Ulpio Traiano	Cant. Navali Riuniti, Palermo	
Vipsanio Agrippa	Cantieri del Tirreno, Riva Trigoso	

Capitani Romani class (as projected)

Displacement: 3,733 tonnes/3,675 tons (standard); 5,415 tonnes/5,330 tons (full load)
Length: 138.7m/455ft 3inn (bp); 142.9m/469ft 1in (oa)
Beam: 14.4m/47ft 3in
Draught: 4.1m/13ft 6in (standard)
Armament: 8 x 135mm/5.3in (4x2) and 8 x 37mm/1.46in (8x1) guns; 8 x 533mm/21in torpedo lubes (2x4)
Machinery: Geared steam turbines, 4 boilers, 2 shafts
Power: 82,027kW/110,000shp for 40+ knots
Endurance: 1,400 tonnes/1,375 tons (oil) for 7,871km/4,250nm at 18 knots
Protection: None
Complement: 420

Andrea Doria class

The conversions of the *Garibaldi* into an interim missile cruiser gave the Italian Navy operational experience in this new form of air defence while it was constructing purpose-designed ships. These, the Andrea Dorias, marked the transition from the traditional cruiser, essentially a surface-warfare ship with dual-purpose secondary artillery, to a multi-purpose task force component armed primarily for area air defence and the protection of a group against submarine attack. In that the Dorias were also a commitment to NATO multi-national forces they also marked the end of a long line of individual Italian cruisers, designed to work independently in purely national interests.

The Dorias, therefore, marked the transition from fast, protected, weight-critical warships to volume-critical vessels with considerable bulk but virtually no protection – the subtle objective being to avoid being hit rather than to trade direct blows with an opponent. However,

despite these differences in philosophy the ships retained their Italian individuality.

As built, each deployed a Terrier surface-to-air missile (SAM) system forward but, during the late 1970s these were modified for the standard SM-1 ER (extended range) weapon. This was supported by eight single 76mm/3in guns located along either side of the superstructure.

For the anti-submarine (AS) role the ships had hull-mounted sonar, supported by mobile sets deployed by any of three small helicopters accommodated in the after superstructure. These could also deliver AS torpedoes, in addition to those from the ships' six 324mm/12.75in tubes.

Because of the general stand-off nature of modern naval warfare, speed is no longer a major design priority. Two, well-separated, combined boiler and machinery spaces were installed that developed power sufficient for 30 knots.

The two ships were discarded in the early 1990s, *Caio Duilio* in 1990 and *Andrea Doria* in 1992.

Andrea Doria class

	Built	Commissioned
Andrea Doria (C553)	Cantieri del Tirreno, Riva Trigoso	February 23, 1964
Caio Duilio (C554)	Cant, della Navalmeccanica, Castellammare di Stabia	November 30, 1964

Andrea Doria class

Displacement: 6,620 tonnes/6,500 tons (standard); 7,430 tonnes/7,300 tons (full load)
Length: 144m/472ft 8in (bp); 149.3m/490ft (oa)
Beam: 17.3m/56ft 9in
Draught: 5m/16ft 4in (standard)
Armament: 1 x twin standard SM-1 ER launcher (40 missiles); 8 x 76mm/3in (8x1) guns; 6 x 324mm/12.75in AS torpedo tubes (2x3)
Machinery: Geared steam turbines, 4 boilers, 2 shafts
Power: 44,742kW/60,000shp for 30 knots
Endurance: 1,117 tonnes/1,100 tons (oil) for 11,112km/6,000nm at 15 knots
Protection: None
Complement: 485

Vittorio Veneto

Originally intended to have had a sister (reportedly to have been named *Italia*), the *Vittorio Veneto* remains a one-off larger version of the Andrea Dorias. Like them, she is termed a "cruiser" by virtue of size and capability.

Up to nine helicopters can be carried, hangared below the four-spot flight deck, forward of which are the interconnecting elevators. Because of the required hangar headroom, the after end has a greater freeboard than the forecastle deck, giving a hull form best described as a "raised quarterdecker".

As with the Dorias, the ship was designed around the Terrier surface-to-air missile (SAM) system. This was subsequently updated to the so-called Aster system, whose launcher can handle either standard SM-1 ER SAMs or ASROC anti-submarine (AS) missiles. For anti-submarine warfare (ASW) the ship has a triple-layered capability, consisting of helicopters, ASROC and ship-launched torpedoes. In anti-aircraft

warfare (AAW) the same applies, with SAMs, 76mm/3in and 40mm/1.57in guns, all with their own directors.

Where the smaller Dorias had little defence against surface ships, the *Veneto* has four canister-launched Otomat Mk2 "Teseo" Surface-to-surface missiles (SSMs), whose active homing head gives a theoretical capability out to 150km/93 miles. Her small AB-212 helicopters are also able to deploy air-to-surface missiles (ASM) such as the French AS-12.

To facilitate access to the two machinery spaces, to improve "sky arcs" and to minimize interaction between electronic systems, funnels and masts are combined in rather unlovely "macks".

Over the years, much of the ship's original American-sourced fire control radars have been replaced by indigenous equipment. With a 40x18.5m/131x61ft flight deck, the ship is far from the classic cruiser, whose handsome appearance has been lost in the high and spiky profile

inseparable from a multiplicity of modern systems. Long a favourite as a flagship by virtue of her size, she was decommissioned to the reserve in 2003.

RIGHT: **During 1981–83, the *Veneto* was extensively modernized, exchanging the Terrier system for Aster, capable of launching either Standard SM-1 ER or ASROC missiles. Four Otomat SSM launchers were sided in the waist and three, fully automatic, Dardo twin 40mm/1.57in mountings added.**

Vittorio Veneto (C550)	

Built: Cantieri Riuniti, Castellammare di Stabia
Commissioned: July 12, 1969
Displacement: 8,280 tonnes/8,150 tons (standard); 9,652 tonnes/9,500 tons (full load)
Length: 170.6m/560ft (bp); 179.6m/589ft 6in (oa)
Beam: 19.4m/63ft 8in
Draught: 5.5m/18ft (standard)
Armament: 1 x twin Aster launcher for standard SM-1 ER or ASROC missiles (60 missiles carried); 4 x Otomat Mk2 Teseo SSM; 8 x 76mm/3in (8x1) and 6 x 40mm/1.57in (3x2) guns; 6 x 324mm/12.75in AS torpedo tubes
Machinery: Geared steam turbines, 4 boilers, 2 shafts
Power: 54,436kW/73,000shp for 30.5 knots
Endurance: 1,219 tonnes/1,200 tons (oil) for 11,112km/6,000nm at 20 knots
Protection: None
Complement: 557

Duguay-Trouin class

Planned for 1914, the class design originally called for three-funnelled 4,572-tonne/4,500-ton vessels roughly equivalent to early British and German "Towns". Surprisingly, however, despite the French being allied to the Italians and opposed to the Austro-Hungarians during World War I, both with light cruisers, their yards were prevented by the war from building similar vessels.

It was not until 1922, and after the Washington Conference, that the French went ahead, not with German-style light cruisers (of which they had been ceded four in 1919) but with a larger type based broadly on the characteristics of the British E-class and the American Omahas, then building.

Armed with eight 155mm/6.1in guns and of a nominal 8,128 tonnes/8,000 tons displacement, the three Duguay-Trouins were, in no sense, "treaty cruisers", but shared their early failings of maximizing speed at the expense of protection.

More solid-looking than the Italian Condottieri, the trio was long and individually indistinguishable except for funnel markings. The hulls had a raised forecastle of adequate freeboard, with an aircraft catapult located on the quarter deck. The boat crane amidships had an extended jib to enable it to handle float planes. The two funnels were short and almost vertical, and the bridge was low and surmounted by a substantial tripod bearing the main fire control. In line with contemporary foreign practice there was a powerful torpedo armament of twelve 550mm/21.65in tubes.

Very lightly protected over only the turrets, conning tower and parts of the main deck, the ships were nonetheless considered reliable and good sea boats. Somewhat tender when "light", they were regarded as having inadequate endurance.

The nameship fought with the Allies and served until 1953. Her sisters, loyal to Vichy, were both destroyed by American attack, the *Lamotte-Picquet* at Saigon and the *Primauguet* at Casablanca.

ABOVE LEFT: **Contemporary French cruisers had generally similar characteristics in that they were all of raised forecastle form, with superimposed turrets forward and aft, two funnels, pole mainmast but a substantial tripod foremast. The three Duguay-Trouin light cruisers conformed, but were alone in having short, vertical funnels. This picture shows the nameship.** ABOVE: **An early picture of *Duguay-Trouin* on a port visit to Bordeaux. She still has a mainmast, apparently offset to starboard of centreline and a catapult track along the afterdeck. One aircraft was usually accommodated on the catapult, a second adjacent to the crane amidships.**

Duguay-Trouin class

	Built	Commissioned
Duguay-Trouin	Arsenal de Brest	November 2, 1926
Lamotte-Picquet	Arsenal de Lorient	March 5, 1927
Primauguet	Arsenal de Brest	April 1, 1927

Duguay-Trouin class

Displacement: 7,366 tonnes/7,250 tons (standard); 9,652 tonnes/9,500 tons (full load)
Length: 175.3m/575ft 5in (wl); 181m/594ft 2in (oa)
Beam: 17.2m/56 ft 6in
Draught: 5.9m/19ft 4in (standard)
Armament: 8 x 155mm/6.1in (4x2) and 4 x 75mm/3in HA (4x1) guns; 12 x 550mm/21.65in torpedo tubes (4x3)
Machinery: Geared steam turbines, 8 boilers, 4 shafts
Power: 76,061kW/102,000shp for 33 knots
Endurance: 1,219 tonnes/1,200 tons for 6,667km/3,600nm at 14 knots
Protection: 20mm/0.79in (vertical (bulkheads) in way of magazines); 20+10mm/0.79+0.39in (decks); up to 30mm/1.18in (turrets)
Complement: 580

ABOVE: **The very low profile, but generous freeboard, is apparent in this pre-war shot of *Lamotte-Picquet*. Serving in what was Indo-China as a unit of a squadron loyal to Vichy, she was effectively decommissioned for lack of spares by 1942. She was destroyed in 1945 when US carrier aircraft attacked Vichy and Japanese alike.**

Emile Bertin

Completed in 1926, the trio of Duguay-Trouins was a powerful incentive for the Italians to embark on their Condottieri. Considerably faster than the French ships, these also had their machinery arranged on the more survivable unit system which the French lacked.

In the 1930 Programme, the French therefore included a one-off which would combine the qualities of the recently completed cruiser-minelayer *Pluton* (later named *La Tour d'Avergne*) with the speed and firepower of a true fast cruiser. Six, more powerful, boilers in place of the earlier ships' eight reduced the length devoted to machinery so, despite their wider separation of the boiler spaces (evident externally in the widely spaced funnels) the ship, named *Emile Bertin*, was some 4.3m/14ft 1in shorter. This was facilitated also by the adoption of triple 152mm/6in turrets

of a new standard design, allowing an increased armament of nine guns to be accommodated in just three mountings.

Although a little shorter, the ship was proportionally less beamy, with the length/beam (L/B) ratio being increased from about 10.4 to 11.2, reflecting a finer hull. Thus, with the same installed power as the earlier trio, the *Bertin* managed nearly 40 knots on trials for a service speed of 34 knots. While similarly unprotected, she was the equal of contemporary Italian cruisers.

From the forefunnel aft, the ship was remarkably clear of tophamper, with necessary platforms grouped integrally with the after funnel. Lacking a mainmast, the layout gave exceptionally free arcs for the secondary and anti-aircraft armament.

The *Bertin*'s wartime career was typical of the dichotomy that affected

ABOVE: **Named after one of the greatest of French naval architects, the *Emile Bertin* carried three triple 152mm/6in turrets on a displacement of under 6,096 tonnes/6,000 tons, yet was capable of a sustained speed of better than 34 knots.**

French units. She fought alongside the British during the unsuccessful 1940 Norway campaign. With the French collapse she was demilitarized in the French Antilles until 1943 when she was refitted in the United States. With a Free French crew she then served with the Allied forces in the Mediterranean. She was discarded in the early 1950s.

Emile Bertin

Built: Penhoët, St. Nazaire
Commissioned: Late 1934
Displacement: 5,995 tonnes/5,900 tons (standard); 8,636 tonnes/8,500 tons (full load)
Length: 166.9m/548ft (bp); 177m/581ft (oa)
Beam: 15.8m/51ft 10in
Draught: 5.4m/17ft 9in (standard)
Armament: 9 x 152mm/6in (3x3) and 4 x 90mm/3.54in HA (2x2) guns; 200 mines; 6 x 550mm/21.65in torpedo tubes (2x3)
Machinery: Geared steam turbines, 6 boilers, 4 shafts
Power: 76,061kW/102,000 for 34 knots
Endurance: 1,828 tonnes/1,800 tons (oil) for 11,112km/6,000nm at 15 knots
Protection: 25–50mm/1–2in (protective deck)
Complement: 565

ABOVE: **Looking very similar to a French "super-destroyer", the *Bertin* is seen here at the end of the war, and in standard Allied two-tone colour scheme. Demilitarized until 1943, she was refitted in the United States, losing her aircraft facilities but gaining a new suite of electronics (note the foremast).**

La Galissonnière class

Judged to be very successful for their size, the six La Galissonnières were laid down between 1931 and 1933, exactly paralleling the six Italian Condottieri of the last three groups. These increased displacement successively from about 7,671–10,110 tonnes/7,550–9,950 tons but the French ships maintained 7,824 tonnes/7,700 tons and a standard design.

The *Emile Bertin* was also built over the same period, and there was a distinct commonality of design, but with the installed power reduced in order to release displacement for improved protection, notably a shallow side belt extending from forward to after magazines. The altered weight distribution necessitated a small increase in beam, with an overall speed penalty of about 3 knots maintained speed.

Contemporary Italian cruisers favoured two-shaft propulsion with each shaft delivering up to 41,000kW/55,000shp. Only with the La Galissonnières did the French adopt this lighter and less complex arrangement, albeit with lower loading per propeller.

The new and effective 152mm/6in main-calibre gun was retained in three triple turrets. As built, the after superstructure terminated in a bulky box hangar accommodating up to four small aircraft, although two large Loire 130 flying boats were more usual. A prominent pole mainmast supported two derrick-cranes, one each for boats and aircraft. The catapult was located atop the after turret, by which it could be trained. Mast and aircraft facilities were removed on the three of the class that served with Allied forces.

The other three, *La Galissonnière*, *Jean de Vienne* and the *Marseillaise*, were scuttled at Toulon in November 1942. The first two were salvaged by the Italians, who commenced their refurbishment. This was still incomplete when the Italians capitulated in September 1943, Taken by the Germans, the two, still unfit for sea, were destroyed by Allied bombing.

The three survivors continued in service until the 1950s.

ABOVE LEFT: **Although fighting under Free French colours alongside the Allies, the *Gloire* contrived for a period to sport what was probably the most extreme disruptive paint scheme of the war. This style of "dazzle painting" made a ship's heading difficult to estimate.** ABOVE: **Something of a puzzle. Along with her sisters, *Gloire* landed her mainmast to improve anti-aircraft (AA) defences. Here, however, equipped with radar and in post-war livery, she again caries her heavy mainmast with the distinctive crosstree, designed for spreading floatplane derricks.**

La Galissonnière class

	Built	Commissioned
Georges Leygues	Penhoèt, St. Nazaire	December 4, 1937
Gloire	Forges et Chantiers de la Girone	December 4, 1937
Jean de Vienne	Arsenal de Lorient	April 15, 1937
La Galissonnière	Arsenal de Brest	December 31, 1935
Marseillaise	Ateliers et Chantiers de la Loire	October 25, 1937
Montcalm	Forges et Chantiers de la Mediterranée	December 4, 1937

La Galissonnière class (as designed)

Displacement: 7,702 tonnes/7,580 tons (standard); 9,084 tonnes/8,940 tons (full load)
Length: 172m/564ft 7in (bp); 179.5m/589ft 2in (oa)
Beam: 17.5m/57ft 5in
Draught: 5m/16ft 5in (standard)
Armament: 9 x 152mm/6in (3x3) and 8 x 90mm/3.54in HA (4x2) guns; 4 x 550mm/21.65in torpedo tubes (2x2)
Machinery: Geared steam turbines, 4 boilers, 2 shafts
Power: 62,638kW/84,000shp for 31 knots
Endurance: 1,544 tonnes/1,520 tons (oil) for 10,186km/5,500nm at 15 knots
Protection: 75–120mm/3–4.7in (vertical); 38mm/1.5in (protective deck); 75–100mm/3–3.94in (turrets)
Complement: 540

LEFT: **Every inch a cruiser, *La Galissonnière* looks splendid as built and carrying neutrality colours painted-up on "B" turret. The Loire 130 flying boat is mounted on its catapult atop the after turret. A double hangar was housed in the after superstructure.**

Duquesne class

Lacking battlecruisers or fast battleships, the French Naval Staff required that the two Duquesnes, first of the French "treaty cruisers", act as scouts ahead of the battle fleet. To gain and maintain contact with the enemy would require speed, good seakeeping and endurance. A secondary requirement, that of preventing enemy ships interdicting essential lines of communication, required substantial armament. Probably the greatest influence on the design process, however, was the intelligence that the Italian Trentos would ship eight 203mm/8in guns and be capable of 34 knots. These were the lowest figures that the French could accept, but the weight required for armament and machinery left less than 5 per cent of the total displacement available for protection. The resulting hull, although very sea-kindly with its raised forecastle and generous freeboard, had thin protection only in way of magazines, turrets and conning tower. Subdivision, however, was thorough, and a stiffened longitudinal bulkhead paralleled the shell plating in way of the machinery spaces. The ships, nonetheless, were not proof against even destroyer gunfire.

Weight was saved by putting the design and supply of machinery out to commercial competition, but margins

RIGHT: **Between the wars, floatplanes were the obvious means of increasing the scouting radius of a cruiser. During World War II they were largely abandoned as a fire hazard and because a proliferation of aircraft carriers rendered them redundant. The torpedo-like object on the *Duquesne*'s bulkhead is a towed paravane.**

remained so tight that the specified 100mm/3.9in secondary weapons had to be downgraded to 75mm/3in guns.

An aircraft catapult was located between the after funnel and the pole mainmast. One aircraft was stowed on the catapult, a second sharing the boat deck between the funnels.

As with the Italians and the Americans, the French Navy had sufficient reservations about this, their first treaty cruiser, to authorize only two, with an eye to subsequent modification.

With war, the ships lay demilitarized and deteriorating at Alexandria until 1943. Reactivation for Free French service came too late for them to contribute significantly. Mainmast and aircraft arrangements were removed in 1945, but, by 1949, both ships had been reduced to static harbour training duties.

Duquesne class

	Built	Commissioned
Duquesne	Arsenal de Brest	January 25, 1929
Tourville	Arsenal de Lorient	March 12, 1929

Duquesne class (as built)

Displacement: 10,160 tonnes/10,000 tons (standard), 12,599 tonnes/12,400 tons (full load)
Length: 185m/607ft 3in (bp); 191m/627ft (oa)
Beam: 19.1m/62ft 8in
Draught: 5.9m/19ft 3in
Armament: 8 x 203mm/8in (4x2) and 8 x 75mm/3in HA (8x1) guns; 6 x 550mm/21.65in torpedo tubes (2x3)
Machinery: Geared steam turbines, 8 boilers, 4 shafts
Power: 89,484kW/120,000shp for 33 knots
Endurance: 1,869 tonnes/1,840 tons for 9,260km/5,000nm at 15 knots
Protection: 20–30mm/0.79–1.18in (in way of magazines); up to 30mm/1.18in (turrets)
Complement: 605

Suffren class and *Algérie*

The Duquesnes had the speed and seakeeping necessary to reconnoitre ahead of a slow battlefleet, but were vulnerable to the fire of even the large destroyers being built by Italy. With the rumoured speed of the planned new 152mm/6in Condottieri, the French Naval Staff looked for better protection, if not immunity, in the next group of French cruisers.

As the Duquesnes' new 203mm/8in twin turrets had proved to be effective, four were again specified, leaving a question of balance between protection and speed while remaining within the 10,160-tonne/10,000-ton limit.

Laid down in 1926–27 the first pair, *Suffren* and *Colbert*, while strongly resembling the Duquesnes, differed in having a much reduced power of 73,100kW/98,000shp, transmitted via three shafts. For a resulting penalty of about 1.5 knots it was possible to incorporate side belts of 50mm/2in and internal bulges.

Following on in 1928–29, the *Foch* and *Dupleix* were improved further with deep internal longitudinal bulkheads of 54mm/2.1in and 60mm/2.36in respectively, roofed by a protective deck of up to 20mm/0.79in and 30mm/1.18in respectively. Even this did not give the required 152mm/6in immunity zone and a major redesign was undertaken.

The resulting one-off, *Algérie*, saved weight at the expense of seakeeping through the elimination of the forecastle deck. Installed power was further reduced to 62,638kW/84,000shp. This was generated by six boilers of advanced design, but survivability was compromised somewhat by grouping them together in order that they could be exhausted through a weight-saving single funnel. This reduction in weight was slightly offset by a conservative reversion to four-shaft propulsion. Weight-saving permitted both 110mm/4.3in belts and a protective deck that was 80mm/3.1in thick over the axial half,

with 30mm/1.18in over the wing spaces. Longitudinal wing bulkheads were 20–40mm/0.79–1.57in thick. A full secondary armament of twelve 100mm/3.9in guns could also be included inside the mandated displacement limit.

Suffren class and *Algérie*

	Built	Commissioned
Colbert	Arsenal de Brest	1931
Dupleix	Arsenal de Brest	1932
Foch	Arsenal de Brest	1931
Suffren	Arsenal de Brest	1930
Algérie	Arsenal de Brest	October 19, 1934

Algérie (as built)

Displacement: 10,160 tonnes/10,000 tons (standard); 13,894 tonnes/13,675 tons (full load)
Length: 180m/590ft 10in (bp); 186.2m/611ft 3in (oa)
Beam: 20m/65ft 8in
Draught: 6.2m/20ft 4in (standard)
Armament: 8 x 203mm/8in (4x2) and 12 x 100mm/3.9in (6x2) guns; 6 x 550mm/21.7in torpedo tubes (2x3)
Machinery: Geared steam turbines, 6 boilers, 4 shafts
Power: 62,638kW/84,000shp for 31 knots
Endurance: 2,946 tonnes/2,900 tons (oil) for 14,816km/8,000nm at 15 knots
Protection: 110+20–40mm/4.3+0.79–1.57in (vertical); 30–80mm/1.18–3.1in (deck); 70–100mm/2.76–3.9in (turrets)
Complement: 620

LEFT: **Her hull already nearly 20 years old when commissioned, the *de Grasse* was completed as an AA/command cruiser. The lower mountings visible here are of 127mm/5in calibre, the higher mountings 57mm/2.24in. The single funnel is mounted farther forward than that of the *Colbert*.**

de Grasse and *Colbert*

Laid down at Lorient in November 1938 as a single-funnelled light cruiser, conforming to the new treaty limit of 8,128 tonnes/8,000 tons, the *de Grasse* was designed to carry three triple 152mm/6in turrets. Her construction was halted by war and she was finally launched in 1946. Towed to Brest, in 1951 the hull was taken in hand for completion as a large anti-aircraft cruiser, joined in 1953 by a near sister, *Colbert*.

Colbert's funnel was located further aft, and she lacked *de Grasse*'s forecastle deck. To reduce wetness, she had a knuckle, forward. By virtue of her transom stern, she was shorter, but she was also beamier. The *de Grasse* had more powerful machinery, developing 78,300kW/105,000shp for a maximum speed of 33.5 knots.

Both differed radically from earlier French cruisers in having a "pyramoidal" profile, rising from either end to a maximum amidships. Fitted out as a command cruiser and task force flagship, the *de Grasse* had a pole mainmast in contrast to the *Colbert*'s two lattice masts.

The ships' armament layout was identical and comparable only with that of the smaller American Atlantas in their original form. Sixteen 127mm/5in guns in twin mountings were arranged symmetrically, four forward, four aft, with two of each sided. Twenty Bofors-pattern, 57mm/2.24in guns, mainly sided, were also carried in twin mountings.

The prematurely aged *de Grasse* finished her career as a nuclear task force flagship in the Pacific but during 1970–72 the newer *Colbert* was thoroughly reconstructed as a missile cruiser. All 127mm/5in guns were landed in favour of just two new-style 100mm/3.9in mountings forward. Six twin 57mm/2.24in mountings were retained. Located aft was a French Masurca SAM system with a range of 48km/30 miles, while four canister-launched MM38 Exocet SSMs were sited to flank the forward bridge structure.

She served as Mediterranean flagship until finally discarded in 1997.

de Grasse and *Colbert*

	Built	Commissioned
de Grasse (C610)	Arsenaux de Brest et de Lorient	September 3, 1956
Colbert (C611)	Arsenal de Brest	May 5, 1959

ABOVE: **Although completed in much the same configuration as *de Grasse*, the post-war *Colbert* was heavily remodelled in 1970–72. She was given a French-built Masurca SAM system and helicopter pad aft and two single 100mm/3.9in guns forward. Six twin 57mm/2.24in mountings were grouped amidships.**

Colbert (as built)

Displacement: 8,636 tonnes/8,500 tons (standard); 11,176 tonnes/11,000 tons (full load)
Length: 174.9m/574ft 2in (bp); 181.9m/597ft 2in (oa)
Beam: 19.3m/63ft 6in
Draught: 5.7m/18ft 9in (standard)
Armament: 16 x 127mm/5in DP (8x2) and 20 x 57mm/2.24in HA (10x2) guns
Machinery: Geared steam turbines, 4 boilers, 2 shafts
Power: 64,130kW/86,000shp for 32 knots
Endurance: 7,408km/4,000nm at 25 knots
Protection: 50–80mm/2–3.1in (vertical); 50mm/2in (protective deck)
Complement: 975

LEFT: Designed as early as 1921, the *Emden* (III), Germany's first post-war cruiser, had features in common with both earlier and later ships. Her two forward turrets, closer-spaced funnels and high after superstructure differentiated her visually from the larger *Königsberg* that followed. ABOVE: *Emden* (III) as originally completed. The tall, slender foremast was later shortened to reduce vibration, and topped with a long-base rangefinder. Her funnels were also fully cased and brought to the same height. From the mid-1930s she carried a pole attached to the after funnel in lieu of the mainmast.

Emden (III)

Inheriting a famous name, the *Emden* (III) was the first major warship built for the renascent German Navy. This, still lacking its design facilities following World War I, used the hull form of the *Köln* (II) of 1918. Topside, the ship differed in adopting two more heavily trunked funnels in place of the earlier three. A new-style, heavy tubular "battlemast" was stepped through the bridge structure, topped-off with the main director, incorporating a long-base rangefinder. Prone to vibration, this had to be shortened as were, subsequently, the funnels for weight reduction.

As planned, the armament was to include eight 15cm/5.9in guns in new-pattern twin turrets, and eight torpedo tubes in paired mountings. The still-active Allied disarmament commission, however, objected to further gun design, the ship having to take eight single mountings, four of which had to be sided. Four torpedo tubes also had to be suppressed. Protection and subdivision were on a scale similar to the *Köln*, and much weight was saved through an early use of welding. Endurance was much improved, significant to her role as training cruiser for up to 160 officer cadets, who were accommodated in an enlarged after superstructure. As the command of the then-Captain Karl Dönitz, the *Emden* (III) made several world cruises.

During the 1930s the mainmast was suppressed in favour of a light pole, braced to the after funnel, in order to improve the firing arcs of the anti-aircraft (AA) armament. A plan to retro-fit the originally proposed armament of four twin 15cm/5.9in mountings and to improve the AA battery came to nothing with the onset of war in 1939.

As a one-off design, that of the *Emden* (III) was interesting in bridging those of the two world wars. Having spent the war in Baltic and Norwegian waters, she was scuttled near Kiel in May 1945.

LEFT: Seen leaving Kiel in the early 1930s, *Emden* (III) shows her handsome profile. Both the forward "battlemast" and mainmast have been shortened, and a foretopmast added. During 1934, her funnels were lowered by 2m/6ft 7in. Note the torpedo tubes, sided at the break of the forecastle.

Emden (III) (as built)

Built: Wilhelmshaven Naval Dockyard
Commissioned: October 15, 1925
Displacement: 5,388 tonnes/5,300 tons (standard); 7,102 tonnes/6,990 tons (full load)
Length: 150.5m/494ft (wl); 155.1m/509ft 1in (oa)
Beam: 14.2m/46ft 7in
Draught: 5.2m/16ft 10in (standard)
Armament: 8 x 15cm/5.9in (8x1) and 3 x 8.8cm/3.46in HA (3x1) guns; 4 x 50cm/19.7in torpedo tubes (2x2)
Machinery: Geared steam turbines, 10 boilers, 2 shafts
Power: 34,228kW/45,900shp for 29 knots
Endurance: 889 tonnes/875 tons (coal) and 1,219 tonnes/1,200 tons (oil) for 12,038km/6,500nm at 15 knots
Protection: 75–100mm/3–3.9in (belt); 20–40mm/0.79–1.57in (protective deck); 50mm/2in (gun mountings)
Complement: 475 plus 160 cadets

K-class, *Leipzig* and *Nürnberg*

Laid down in 1926, the three K-class were an extrapolation of the *Emden*. Some 18.5m/60ft 8in longer on the waterline, they carried nine 15cm/5.9in guns in three triple mountings, one forward, two aft. The two latter were staggered either side of the centreline to simplify ammunition handling.

The hull layout resembled that of the *Emden* (III) in that the short forecastle was continued well aft as a long centreline deckhouse. Four triple 53.3cm/21in torpedo tube banks were located on the side decks thus formed. A conspicuous crane served the floatplane catapult between the funnels. Three twin 8.8cm/3.46in HA mountings were grouped around the after superstructure.

Long endurance was important for trade warfare and the gearboxes driving the shafts could be powered by diesel engines as a more economical alternative to the steam turbines.

Although not particularly fast, the Ks were crank, despite efforts at weight-saving. The *Leipzig*, laid down two years later, therefore, had an extra 1m/3ft 4in on the beam for much the same length. Both boiler rooms exhausted through a single, heavily trunked funnel. All her main-calibre mountings were on the centreline. A further pair of 8.8cm/3.46in guns was added but 25mm/1in had to be shaved off the protection to the main gunhouses.

Five years later a fifth unit, the *Nürnberg*, was laid down. She was essentially a repeat, but some 4m/13ft 1in longer. Externally she differed in having a large bridge structure. Her catapult was abaft the funnel, the *Leipzig*'s before.

Both later cruisers had three shafts, with steam turbines on the outside and a cruising diesel in the centre.

All three of the K-class became war casualties, two by bombing, one by torpedo. The *Leipzig* was scuttled, laden with gas shells, by the British in 1946. The *Nürnberg* became the training cruiser *Admiral Makarov* in the Soviet fleet, more a trophy than a useful asset.

K-class, *Leipzig* and *Nürnberg*

	Built	Commissioned
Karlsruhe (III)	Deutsche Werke, Kiel	November 6, 1929
Köln (III)	Wilhelmshaven Naval Dockyard	January 15, 1930
Königsberg (III)	Wilhelmshaven Naval Dockyard	April 17, 1929
Leipzig (IV)	Wilhelmshaven Naval Dockyard	October 8, 1931
Nürnberg (III)	Deutsche Werke Kiel	November 2, 1935

K-class (as built)

Displacement: 6,096 tonnes/6,000 tons (standard); 7,823 tonnes/7,700 tons (full load)
Length: 169m/554ft 9in (wl); 174m/571ft 2in (oa)
Beam: 15.2m/49ft 11in
Draught: 5.6m/18ft 4in (standard)
Armament: 9 x 15cm/5.9in (3x3) and 6 x 8.8cm/3.46in HA (3x2) guns; 12 x 53.3cm/21in torpedo tubes (4x3)
Machinery: Geared steam turbines and cruising diesels, 6 boilers, 2 shafts
Power: 48,470kW/65,000shp (steam); 1,350kW/1,800bhp (diesel) for 32 knots maximum
Endurance: 1,372 tonnes/1,350 tons (oil) for 13,519km/7,300nm at 17 knots
Protection: 75–100mm/3–3.9in (belt); 75mm/3in (turrets)
Complement: 515

LEFT: An impression of *Nürnberg* at about 1936. She has a more built-up bridge structure than the earlier *Leipzig*, and no aircraft crane. Ceded to the Soviet Union post-war, she served the Russians as a training ship until the early 1960s.

LEFT: The *Hipper* was completed with a near-vertical stem that did nothing for her appearance. At her stem head she carries the crest of Admiral Franz Hipper, commander of the High Seas Fleet's battlecruiser squadron during World War I. Note the pronounced anti-torpedo bulge. ABOVE: In April 1940, the German Navy put troops ashore at six points in invading Norway. *Hipper* is seen here at Trondheim whence, together with four destroyers and four auxiliaries, she transported 700 military personnel with their equipment.

Blücher class

With no real design starting point, the designers of the Blüchers reportedly used the French *Algérie* as a yardstick although, in practice, there was little similarity. The Anglo-German Naval Agreement of June 1935 provided for the Germans to build up to 35 per cent of British tonnage in the major categories of surface ship. It was to be binding for six years, commencing January 1, 1937. Over this period the tabled German construction programme included no less than 18 cruisers, modern ships which would, qualitatively, pose real problems for the Royal Navy. British requests to slow the programme were ignored, with the first pair of heavy cruisers, *Blücher* and *Admiral Hipper*, being quickly laid down. The German action was completely legal in that the pair were permitted replacements for the (admittedly far smaller) *Berlin* and *Hamburg* of the rump fleet left to Germany by the Versailles Treaty. Before they were in the water, three further slightly enlarged units had been commenced.

Similarities with the *Algérie* included the flush-decked hull, of which the original bow design had quickly to be changed to one with increased sheer and freeboard, to reduce wetness and to improve overall seakeeping.

ABOVE: *Hipper* survived World War II only to come to this sorry end. Festooned with camouflage netting to safeguard against air attack, she was scuttled in a flooded dry dock in Kiel. Refloated, she was grounded nearby and scrapped.

In line with existing treaty requirements (to which Germany had not been a signatory), standard displacement was declared at 10,160 tonnes/10,000 tons, although the fact that this was exceeded (by over 40 per cent) was an open secret.

Earlier German armoured cruisers had employed an effective 21cm/8.2in gun, and the one concession made was to fit a new and untried 20.3cm/8in weapon to conform to Washington

LEFT: Following early forays into the Atlantic, *Hipper* spent most of her war in Norwegian waters. This view, from the signal bridge, looks over the lower rangefinder and forward turrets to the prominent air recognition insignia on the forecastle. The original design provided for triple 15cm/5.9in turrets. ABOVE: Too few to make any impact in ocean warfare, Germany's heavy warships were gradually confined to the Baltic and Norwegian waters, where *Hipper* is seen here, probably in company with the *Lützow* or *Scheer*. The threat posed by their presence prevented British units being sent to assist in the Pacific War.

standards. Like the Japanese, the Germans designed the ship to carry triple 15.5cm/6.1in guns but with the interchangeable option of twin 20.3cm/8in. The "light cruiser" version was never built.

Aesthetically, the ships were pleasing, business-like but graceful, their profile resembling that of the Bismarck-class battleship at a distance. The low navigating bridge was topped by a tower which replaced the earlier "battlemast". At its head was the main battery director, with back-up located lower down on both forward and after superstructures. Six twin 10.5cm/4.1in secondary mountings were carried, associated with four of the spherical-topped, stabilized "Wackeltopf" directors. Twelve torpedo tubes were fitted in four triple upper-deck mountings.

Although of a size that suggested commerce warfare, the Blüchers were not fitted with economical cruising diesels. Indeed, the advanced steam condition adopted for their machinery not only gave repeated problems but also resulted in a less than hoped for endurance.

A rotating catapult was located abaft the funnel. It was served by a pair of cranes, which handled both boats and the three hangared Arado 196 floatplanes.

Both *Admiral Hipper* and *Blücher* were completed in 1939. The former made a couple of raiding cruises but spent most of the war inactively in Norwegian waters. Barely six months after being commissioned, her sister was destroyed by Norwegian shore batteries while attempting to run German army units into Oslo during the invasion of April 1940.

The slightly enlarged *Prinz Eugen* was completed in July 1940 but, besides being involved in the high-profile episodes of the *Bismarck* pursuit (May 1941) and the up-channel dash of the *Scharnhorst* and *Gneisenau* (February 1942), she achieved little of note. As an American post-war prize, she was expended as a target ship in the course of the trials at Bikini Atoll.

ABOVE: **Following her cession to the United States in 1945, the *Prinz Eugen* was sailed there and much photographed. In contrast with the earlier *Hipper* (see opposite) she has the so-called "Atlantic" bow, with greater sheer and flare, and no external bulges. Note the complete radar outfit.**

Almost complete in 1942, the *Seydlitz* was dismantled for conversion to a light aircraft carrier, the project never being completed. Also never completed, the *Lützow* was transferred to the Soviet Navy in 1940 under the terms of the "non-aggression" pact.

ABOVE: **Following technical assessment and a publicity tour of American ports, the *Prinz Eugen* was expended by the US Navy in the 1946 Bikini A-bomb tests. Seen here on arrival, she is still complete with her Arado floatplane. Note the American ensign.**

Blücher class

	Built	Commissioned
Admiral Hipper	Blohm n. Voss, Hamburg	April 29, 1939
Blücher	Deutsche Werke, Kiel	September 20, 1939
Lützow	Deschimag, Bremen	
Prinz Eugen	Germania, Kiel	August 1, 1940
Seydlitz	Deschimag, Bremen	

Admiral Hipper

Displacement: 14,275 tonnes/14,050 tons (standard); 18,492 tonnes/18,200 tons (full load)
Length: 195.5m/641ft 9in (wl); 205m/672ft 10in (oa)
Beam: 21.3m/69ft 10in
Draught: 5.8m/19ft (standard)
Armament: 8 x 20.3cm/8in (4x2) and 12 x 10.5cm/4.1in (6x2) guns; 12 x 53.3cm/21in torpedo tubes (4x3)
Machinery: Geared steam turbines, 12 boilers, 3 shafts
Power: 98,432kW/132,000shp for 32 knots
Endurance: 3,688 tonnes/3,630 tons (oil) for 8,148km/4,400nm at 19 knots
Protection: 80mm/3.1in (vertical belt); 30–50mm/1.18–2in (protective decks); 70–105mm/2.76–4.1in (turrets)
Complement: 1,390

Kirov, Chapaev and Sverdlov classes

Following the 1917 revolution the Soviet Navy was neglected, its design and construction base eroded as the state wrestled with reorganizing its vast population, infrastructure and resources. Five-year plans were eventually instigated to modernize the fleet and, in the absence of indigenous expertise, design and construction supervision for a new class of cruiser, the *Kirov* was entrusted to the Italian firm of Ansaldo. The Soviet Union was not bound by the limitations of the Washington Treaty but the usually quoted figure of 8,941 tonnes/8,800 tons standard displacement was probably deliberately understated. The Kirov class was slightly longer, narrower and finer than the newly completed Italian Zara class. They were more lightly protected and carried three triple 180mm/7.1in guns, against the four twin 203mm/8in mountings of the Italians. The former were up to 19 percent heavier than officially stated and it is probable that the Kirov class were actually closer to 10,160 tonnes/10,000 tons.

ABOVE: **Ansaldo at Genoa are believed to be the source of the original design of the Kirov class. Dating from the late 1930s, it certainly echoes Italian style of the period, particularly in the heavy tetrapod structure above the bridge. This unit, unusually, has the tripod mainmast abaft the after funnel.**

Considerably disrupted by World War II, the programme saw only five (*Kalinin*, *Kirov*, *Maksim Gorki*, *Molotov* and *Voroshilov*) completed, with a further two (*Kaganovitch* and *Zhelezniakov*) destroyed before launch.

At the same time a class of 152mm/6in "light" cruisers, the Chapaev class was laid down. At 187m/613ft 6in by 17.5m/57ft 5in they were of a similar size with, but finer than, the Kirov class. In profile, they were very similar to the Italian Trento class but with four triple 152mm/6in turrets in place of the latter's four twin 203mm/8in. Powered for a respectable 34 knots, all could carry up to 120 mines on deck. All four of the class (*Chapaev*, *Chkalov*, *Kuibyshev* and *Zhelezniakov* [II]) were completed post-war, between 1948 and 1950.

LEFT: **Cleaning gun barrels aboard a Kirov. Unusually for so late a date, the guns can be seen to have been designed into a common sleeve and, therefore, not capable of being elevated or depressed independently.**
ABOVE: **An unidentified "Improved Kirov", which differs from the example above in having a prominent director tower located on the bridge structure ahead of a tripod foremast, and the mainmast moved ahead of the after funnel. Torpedo tubes have been landed in favour of large motor launches.**

At about 11,481 tonnes/11,300 tons, the Chapaev class offered a useful and balanced design that, suitably "stretched" by Soviet designers, begat the 13,716-tonne/13,500-ton Sverdlov class of the early 1950s. Handsome ships, these retained the old Italian features of a tower-type bridge structure and substantial tripod mainmast close ahead of the after funnel. The funnels themselves were more closely spaced, however, and the forecastle deck was extended well aft.

Larger even than the American Worcester class, the Sverdlov class was anachronistic, conventional, gun-armed cruisers born into the missile age. Of the 24 believed to have been planned, only 14 were actually completed. Their Cold War role was as commerce destroyers, a purpose for which they were endowed with considerable range.

From the outset, individual ships varied in details, particularly with respect to their electronic instrumentation. All appear to have had permanent mine rails let into the after deck.

As such large ships, they attracted some criticism for the choice of a 152mm/6in main battery. This was to overlook that Soviet ships were expected to operate in heavy northern and oceanic conditions. Size is of obvious benefit, contributing to dryness, steadiness and ability to maintain speed. The designers had been able to resist the common navy blandishments to arm the ship to the limit that it can accommodate, thus negating the size advantage.

During the early 1970s the *Admiral Senyavin* and *Zhdanov* were converted to command cruisers. Major topside modifications included the suppression of two and one after turret respectively to create helicopter facilities and accommodation for a short range SA-N-4 SAM system.

One unit (*Dzerzhinski*) was converted to deploy a medium-range SA-N-2 SAM system, the installation of which displaced the "X" turret. No others were similarly modified, the Russians repeating the American experience of finding that volume-critical systems do not fit satisfactorily into weight-critical hulls.

Totally obsolete by the 1980s, the Sverdlov class was, nonetheless, retired only slowly, being valuable as gun-armed fire-support ships and as impressive platforms for "showing the flag" in the Third World. They were among the last conventional cruisers in service.

ABOVE: In many respects, the Sverdlovs were enlarged Kirovs with a fourth triple turret. The last significant class of conventional cruisers, they were obsolete even when new. Note the size of the fully stabilized twin 100mm/3.94in mountings and German World War II pattern directors on the *Aleksandr Suvorov*.

Sverdlov class

	Built	Commissioned
Admiral Lazerev	Baltic Shipyard, Leningrad	November 1952
Admiral Nakhimov	Severodvinsk, Shipyard	1952
Admiral Senyavin	Severodvinsk Shipyard	July 1954
Admiral Ushakov	Baltic Shipyard, Leningrad	August 1953
Aleksandr Nevski	Marti Shipyard, Nikolaev	1952
Aleksandr Suvorov	Marti Shipyard, Nikolaev	1953
Dmitri Pozharski	Baltic Shipyard, Leningrad	1953
Dzerzhinski	Amur Shipyard, Komsomolsk	1954
Mikhail Kutuzov	Marti Shipyard, Nilolaev	1955
Molotovsk	Severodvinsk Shipyard	September 1954
Murmansk	Severodvinsk Shipyard	1955
Ordzhonikidze	Amur Shipyard, Komosomolsk	1952
Sverdlov	Baltic Shipyard, Leningrad	1951
Zhdanov	Baltic Shipyard, Leningrad	January 1952

ABOVE: This 1957 picture of *Sverdlov* clearly shows her Italian lineage. The class was built with an eye to commerce raiding but, as conventionally armed cruisers in a missile-controlled environment, they would have been vulnerable. Like their foreign peers, they were difficult to modernize.

Sverdlov class (as built)

Displacement: 13,716 tonnes/13,500 tons (standard); 18,594 tonnes/18,300 tons (full load)

Length: 200m/656ft 6in (bp); 210m/689ft 4in (oa)

Beam: 21.5m/70ft 7in

Draught: 7.2m/23ft 8in

Armament: 12 x 152mm/6in (4x3) and 12 x 100mm/3.9in (6x2) guns; 140 mines

Machinery: Geared steam turbines, 6 boilers, 2 shafts

Power: 82,027kW/110,000shp for 32 knots

Endurance: 3,860 tonnes/3,800 tons (oil) for 18,520km/10,000nm at 13 knots

Protection: 25–50mm/1–2in and 50–75mm/2–3in (protective decks); 75–100mm/3–3.9in (turrets)

Complement: About 1,000

FAR LEFT: **Old wine in new bottles.** *Mendez Nuñez* **was modernized and rearmed as an AA cruiser during 1944–47. Her 120mm/4.7in gun mountings were redesigned for higher elevation although there is little evidence that they were effectively radar-laid. Note two funnels and new bow form.**

ABOVE LEFT: **As built, the** *Mendez Nuñez* **shows her close relationship with British cruiser design of late World War I. The lack of forward sheer resulted in wet ships but, instead of a "trawler bow", the Spanish opted for the design at left.**

Mendez Nuñez class

Heavily influenced by the pre-World War I British Birmingham-class design, the one-off *Reina Victoria Eugenia* was completed by Ferrol Dockyard in 1922 as Spain's first "modern" cruiser. Her nine single 152mm/6in guns were necessarily disposed, however, so as to give only five in broadside. During the Spanish Civil War (1936–39), she was extensively rebuilt, her royal name being changed to *Republica*, and then again to *Navarra*. Funnels were reduced from three to two and an unlovely tower bridge structure added. By virtually eliminating masts, cutting down the after deck by one level and suppressing three mountings, it was possible to put six single guns on the centreline, permitting an improved six-gun broadside.

Building in parallel at Ferrol were the near-sisters *Don Blas Lezo* and *Mendez*

Nuñez, of the same length as the earlier ship but a full 1.2m/4ft less in the beam. This combined with an 80 per cent increase in shaft horsepower and a six-gun armament (supplemented by two twin torpedo tube mountings) permitted a 3.5-knot increase in speed. There was also a considerable decrease in the thickness of the belt armour. As completed, the pair was roughly equivalent to the British D-class of 1918. All three were seven to eight years under construction.

Following her sister's loss by stranding in 1932, the *Mendez Nuñez* was modernized during 1944–47. Rearmed as an anti-aircraft (AA) cruiser, she was given eight 120mm/4.7in guns on high-angle single mountings, unusually, three being superimposed at either end. The torpedo armament was increased to two triple tubes. The hull was reduced by one

level from the new blockhouse bridge, aft, while two capped and trunked funnels replaced the original three. A new, curved bow profile and increased forward sheer completed a distinctive and rakish new look. With the commissioning of new tonnage, the ship was stricken for disposal in the late 1950s.

Mendez Nuñez class

	Built	Commissioned
Don Blas Lezo	Ferrol Dockyard	November 4, 1924
Mendez Nuñez	Ferrol Dockyard	March 3, 1923

Mendez Nuñez (as rebuilt)

Displacement: 4,755 tonnes/4,680 tons (standard); 6,147 tonnes/6,050 tons (full load)
Length: 134m/440ft (bp); 140.7m/462ft (oa)
Beam: 14m/46ft
Draught: 4.4m/14ft 4in (standard)
Armament: 8 x 120mm/4.7in (8x1) guns; 6 x 533mm/21in torpedo tubes (2x3)
Machinery: Geared steam turbines, 12 boilers, 4 shafts
Power: 33,556kW/45,000shp for 29 knots
Endurance: 737 tonnes/725 tons (oil) and 812 tonnes/800 tons (coal) for 9,260km/5,000nm at 13 knots
Protection: 12–25mm/0.47–1in (belt); 25mm/1in (protective deck)
Complement: 370

ABOVE: **Never modernized, the** *Don Blas Lezo* **(or** *Blas de Lezo***) retained her original appearance until her disposal after 1945. Her World War I features included the prominent armoured conning tower before the bridge structure and the sided 15cm/5.9in guns flanking the forward funnel.**

Galicia class

Continuing the modernization of the Spanish fleet, the Ferrol Dockyard produced the three, more ambitious Galicia class in an overlapping programme with the Mendez Nuñez class, which were British-designed and effectively remodelled versions of the Royal Navy E-class. The nameship was built as the *Principe Alfonso*, becoming the *Libertad*, then *Galicia* during the Civil War. The *Cervantes*, last-built, had slight differences in armament.

As designed, the class had its eight 152mm/6in guns disposed messily, with twin mountings superfiring singles at either end and with a third twin mounting located amidships. Protection and propulsive power were on a similar scale to those of the E-class, although the machinery layout was more concentrated. For their day, the Galicia class was considered fast, being powered at 33 knots for the specific function of out-running enemy

commerce raiders. Only *Cervantes* took 12 torpedo tubes, the others six.

Original bridge structures were small, with fire control exercised from a short tripod foremast but, during the course of the 1940–46 reconstruction, this changed to a heavy, compact bridge with director tower and the light masting then typical of Spanish warships. The funnels gained prominent caps and the main battery was reorganized with four twin 152mm/6in mountings disposed in orthodox symmetry. This freed space in the after waist for an aircraft, and associated crane and catapult. By now somewhat anachronistic, these were only retained for any length of time by the *Cervantes*.

For secondary armament, *Galicia* and *Cervantes* had four twin 88mm/3.46in mountings, the *Cervera* two twin 105mm/4.1in guns. Both calibres suggest that the weapons may have been German sourced.

ABOVE: **The *Cervera*'s eight 152mm/6in guns were arranged unusually, with "A" and "Y" mountings (hidden by awnings) being singles, while "B", "Q" (amidships) and "X" were twins. This post-war picture shows her with her pendants painted up NATO-style and with new electronics.**

Although the *Cervantes* was heavily damaged by torpedo (from an Italian submarine) while serving as the Republican flagship during the Civil War, the class proved to be durable, giving good service until being stricken in 1966.

Galicia class

	Built	Commissioned
Almirante Cervera	Ferrol Dockyard	October 16, 1925
Galicia	Ferrol Dockyard	January 3, 1925
Miguel de Cervantes	Ferrol Dockyard	May 19, 1928

Galicia (as modernized)

Displacement: 8,382 tonnes/8,250 tons (standard); 10,059 tonnes/9,900 tons (full load)
Length: 175.2m/575ft (bp); 176.5m/579ft 6in (oa)
Beam: 16.5m/54ft
Draught: 5m/16ft 6in (standard)
Armament: 8 x 152mm/6in (4x2) and 8 x 88mm/3.46in (4x2) guns; 6 x 533mm/21in torpedo tubes (2x3)
Machinery: Geared steam turbines, 8 boilers, 4 shafts
Power: 59,656kW/80,000shp for 33 knots
Endurance: 1,727 tonnes/1,700 tons (oil) for 9,260km/5,000nm at 15 knots
Protection: 35–75mm/1.38–3in (belt); 25mm/1in (protective deck)
Complement: 565

ABOVE: **Built somewhat later, the *Cervantes* had her armament arranged conventionally, forward and aft. This allowed space abaft the funnels for a catapult and floatplane. The rather unusually configured handling crane jib was lowered to deck level when not in use.**

LEFT: The *Canarias* as rebuilt in the 1950s to the original two-funnelled design. She is probably laying in the eponymous islands, for the merchantman to the left is a Fred Olsen "tomato boat" that traded there regularly. ABOVE: The stump foremast, visible here, was an original fitting, but had been removed by the end of World War II. The original design trunked the funnels of a British County into two, but the Spanish took it a stage further with a single, arched casing that also incorporated searchlights.

Canarias class

The final British cruiser design acquired by the Spanish at this time was based on that of the County class. Two units were built, their construction taxing the nascent Spanish shipbuilding industry to the utmost. Laid down in 1928, they were not completed until 1936. The original British-built County class, with their gently raked funnels and masts had considerable dignity. The Spanish ships had near-identical hulls and main batteries, but were finished with bridge and funnel casing of extraordinary bulk and surpassing ugliness – "Odeon" architecture at its worst. Of proportions that would have graced an aircraft carrier, the funnel was heavily trunked to exhaust all boilers, while incorporating searchlight platforms. The huge block of bridgework appeared truncated in the absence of a foremast, all flag-signalling being conducted from a yard on the light mainmast.

Unlike the British, the Spanish were not tightly constrained by Washington Treaty limitations on displacement. They therefore added twelve fixed torpedo tubes, grouped in threes and firing on the beam from main deck level, to the secondary battery of eight 119mm/ 4.7in guns in open HA mountings. Considerably more protection was also worked in. However, although a catapult and aircraft facilities were originally specified, they appear to have never been fitted.

While still a comparatively new ship, the *Baleares* was torpedoed and sunk during March 1938 in the only event approaching a fleet encounter of the Civil War. She was serving as Nationalist flagship, while the Republicans were effectively under Soviet Russian command.

The lone *Canarias* underwent a major refit in the early 1950s, losing her torpedo tubes, and acquiring a light tripod foremast and the two vertical funnels with which she was first designed. Greatly improved in appearance, she served until 1975. Representing considerable investment, the pair were a disappointment in never being able to realize their potential.

Canarias class

	Built	Commissioned
Baleares	Soc. Español de Construccion Navale, Ferrol	1936
Canarias	Soc. Español de Construccion Navale, Ferrol	September 10, 1936

Canarias (as built)

Displacement: 10,841 tonnes/10,670 tons (standard); 12,446 tonnes/12,250 tons (full load)

Length: 181.6m/596ft (bp); 192,8m/636ft (oa)

Beam: 19.5m/64ft

Draught: 5.3m/17ft 4in (standard)

Armament: 8 x 203mm/8in (4x2) and 8 x 119mm/4.7in HA (8x1) guns; 12 x 533mm/21in torpedo tubes (4x3)

Machinery: Geared steam turbines, 8 boilers, 4 shafts

Power: 67,113kW/90,000shp for 33 knots

Endurance: 2,844 tonnes/2,800 tons (oil) for 14,816km/8,000nm at 15 knots

Protection: 36–50mm/1.4–2in (belt); 25mm/1in (turrets)

Complement: 765

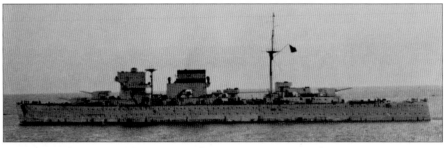

ABOVE: The ill-starred *Baleares*, torpedoed and sunk during the Civil War. For some reason, "Y" turret has been landed, although this may be because the twin 203mm/8in mounting, originally developed for the Counties, was known for its mechanical shortcomings.

Gotland

Traditionally neutral in modern times, Sweden has a long and relatively deserted coastline. Shallow and fringed with skerries, it is not easy to police by conventional naval craft, consequently aircraft are generally more effective.

Because the Swedish fleet is necessarily small, its ships need to fulfil more than a single function, and the *Gotland*, laid down in 1930, was configured as a small cruiser forward and aviation ship aft. Her concept pre-dated those of the Japanese Tone and Ise classes, and modern hybrids such as the Russian Moskva class, French *Jeanne d'Arc* and Italian *Vittorio Veneto*.

On an ice-strengthened, flush-decked hull, the *Gotland* had an unusual disposition for her six 152mm/6in guns. One twin turret fired forward, flanked by single weapons located in casemates, in the latter's last-recorded use. A second twin turret fired aft, across the flight deck.

The flight deck was a lightly constructed spar deck, which covered the after third of the ship's length. It was laid with three fore-and-aft tracks bearing eight self-propelled trolleys, each of which carried a Hawker Osprey floatplane with wings folded. Three more knocked-down aircraft could be stowed below. Forward of the tracks was a turntable-mounted, compressed air catapult which could be aligned with any of the tracks. Aircraft were recovered by a crane located right aft. The tracks had the alternative use, typical on Swedish ships, of accommodating up to 100 mines, which were laid over the stern.

Obsolete by 1943, the *Gotland* lost her aircraft-related equipment, which was replaced on the spar deck by modern anti-aircraft (AA) weapons. The ship served in the dual role of AA and training cruiser until 1955, when she was taken in hand for modernization. The two casemated 152mm/6in and all four

LEFT: **This late-1930s photograph shows the attractive lines of the *Gotland*'s ice-strengthened hull. The starboard 152mm/6in casemate and the strange "pillar-box" director tower are also evident. Soon afterward, the aviation fittings would be removed in favour of further AA guns.**

TOP: **Seen here in her original condition, the *Gotland* has one of her Osprey floatplanes right aft. Note how the bridge is flanked by single 152mm/6in guns in casemates. The after twin turret, not very evident, is flanked by triple torpedo tube mountings.**
ABOVE: **This outboard profile shows rather more clearly the arrangement of this hybrid cruiser/ aviation ship. The inherent weakness, of course, is that aviation ships are complex, fragile things that have no business pretending that they can absorb damage while acting as cruisers.**

75mm/2.95in guns were landed in favour of additional 40mm/1.57in weapons, together with modern fire-control equipment. The *Gotland* was sent for scrap in 1962.

Gotland (as built)

Built: AB Götaverken, Göteborg
Commissioned: December 16, 1934
Displacement: 4,826 tonnes/4,750 tons (standard); 5,639 tonnes/5,550 tons (full load)
Length: 130.2m/426ft 6in (wl); 133.4m/437ft 6in (oa)
Beam: 15.4m/50ft 7in
Draught: 5m/16ft 6in (standard)
Armament: 6 x 152mm/6in (2x2/2x1) and 4 x 75mm/2.95in (4x1) guns; 6 x 533mm/21in torpedo tubes (2x3)
Machinery: Geared steam turbines, 4 boilers, 2 shafts
Power: 24,600kW/33,000shp for 27.5 knots
Endurance: 853 tonnes/840 tons (oil) for 7,400km/4,000nm at 12 knots
Protection: 28–50mm/1.1–2in (protective deck); 28–50mm/1.1–2in (turrets)
Complement: 450

Tre Kronor class

Unique in appearance, the *Tre Kronor* (Three Crowns) and *Gota Lejon* (Gothic Lion) were laid down in 1943 to underline Sweden's intention to keep her water neutral. Neither, however, could be completed before 1947.

Due to their heavy, ice-class plating, the hulls looked beautifully faired, the belt being almost invisible. However, the two rows of scuttles that flanked the machinery spaces showed it to be quite shallow. The hull was of a long-forecastle type, with tripled torpedo tubes located at the break.

Unusually the main battery was of seven guns, disposed as a triple 152mm/6in turret forward and two superfiring twins located aft. All were of semi-automatic Bofors design and capable of a 70-degree elevation.

The ships were designed without masts, having only spreaders for W/T aerials. However, raked tripods were fitted prior to their entry into service. The funnels were also most distinctive. Being streamlined and with pronounced rake, they echoed mercantile conventions of the time, Sweden being a major shipbuilder.

As built, the bridge structure was also streamlined and with numerous platforms. Sweden's fear of a neighbouring nuclear exchange, however, resulted in the general enclosure and "cleaning-up" of a ship's structures. As a result, both ships acquired squared-off, blockhouse-style bridges in 1951–52. The secondary 40mm/1.57in armament was also considerably enhanced. Like most Swedish ships, they were equipped with permanent minelaying rails.

Tre Kronor had a comparatively short life, being paid off in 1964. Soon afterwards, Sweden adopted the policy that, as large fighting ships would not survive a nuclear exchange in the

ABOVE: **With their rather low profiles, the two Tre Kronors had an appearance of immense length, their 152mm/6in gun mountings seeming small in comparison. The picture was made after the mid-1950s, when the earlier, galleried bridge structure was rebuilt as a "block house".**

confined Baltic Sea, the future fleet would comprise only small combatants and submarines, housed in nuclear-bomb-proof shelters. All warships of destroyer size and above accordingly went for disposal. As part of this procedure, the *Gota Lejon* was purchased by Chile in 1971. As the *Latorre*, she served until the early 1980s.

Tre Kronor class

	Built	Commissioned
Gota Lejon	Erikoberg Mek. Verstad, Göteborg	December 15, 1947
Tre Kronor	Götaverken, Göteborg	October 18, 1947

Tre Kronor class (after 1951–52 refit)

Displacement: 8,128 tonnes/8,000 tons (standard); 10,160 tonnes/10,000 tons (full load)
Length: 180m/590ft 6in (wl); 181.9m/597ft (oa)
Beam: 16.5m/54ft 2in
Draught: 5.9m/19ft 6in (standard)
Armament: 7 x 152mm/6in (1x3/2x2) and 27 x 40mm/1.57in (1x4/10x2/3x1) guns; 6 x 813mm/32in torpedo tubes (2x3)
Machinery: Geared steam turbines, 4 boilers, 2 shafts
Power: 7,460kW/100,000shp for 33 knots
Protection: 75–125mm/2.95–4.92in (vertical belt)
Complement: 455

ABOVE: ***Tre Kronor*'s Bofors-designed 152mm/6in guns were credited with an exceptional 70-degree elevation, making them suitable for long-range AA barrage. On her mainmast is British-pattern air-search and height-finding radar of 1945 vintage. The surface search radar is Dutch-sourced.**

LEFT: **The complexity of large combatants taxed the resources of the small Dutch constructive design department to the limit and German influence is plain to see. Although much smaller and more lightly armed, the** *de Ruyter* **has more than a passing resemblance to the German "pocket battleships", then coming into service.** ABOVE: **Weight distribution was apparently a problem for the** *de Ruyter* **for, although she has two twin 15cm/5.9in aft, the forward twin is superfired by a single at O1 level. The unique funnel was designed to keep smoke clear of the bridge structure.**

Java class and *de Ruyter*

Neutral during World War I, the Netherlands nonetheless felt the need to update their naval presence in their extensive East Indies Empire. Two new ships, *Java* and *Sumatra*, were thus laid down in 1916. At 6,757 tonnes/6,650 tons and armed with ten 15cm/5.9in guns, they were rather larger and better armed, but slower, than contemporary British and German fleet cruisers.

Armament, machinery and considerable know-how stemmed from German sources and so it was not surprising that the delivery date of April 1918 was not achieved. By the time that the pair was completed in 1925–26,

cruiser design had moved on under the impetus of the 1921–22 Washington Treaty, and the ships were obsolescent. A third unit, the marginally larger *Celebes*, was approved in 1917 but, little advanced, was cancelled in 1919.

Alterations during the 1930s included the suppression of the tall signal masts in favour of a German-style "battlemast" forward and a stump mainmast. A gantry was added between the funnels to support lifting gear for two float planes.

During the early 1930s the Netherlands Navy again secured approval for a third cruiser. She, the *de Ruyter*, was criticized for being

under-armed but her fewer guns were much more efficiently arranged. In profile, she was strongly reminiscent of a German "pocket battleship", although with superimposed gun mountings. As built, her single vertical stack had a "parasol" cap, which was soon removed. The tower-like bridge structure was topped-off with a long-base optical rangefinder, and masting was confined to light poles and W/T spreaders. Finer-lined, the *de Ruyter* was 2 knots faster than the *Javas*.

Both *de Ruyter* and *Java* were lost in the Far East early in 1942 but the *Sumatra*, little used, was expended as part of the Gooseberry breakwater off Normandy in June 1944.

ABOVE: **A 1930s modernization saw the** *Java*'s **tall pole masts reduced, as shown here. The** *Java*'s **reduced armament reflects her training status.**

Java class and *de Ruyter*

	Built	Commissioned
Java	de Schelde, Vlissingen	May 1, 1925
Sumatra	Nederlandsche Sch. Maats, Amsterdam	May 26, 1926
de Ruyter	Wilton-Fijenoord, Rotterdam	September 16, 1936

de Ruyter

Displacement: 6,553 tonnes/6,450 tons (standard); 7,951 tonnes/7,825 tons (full load)
Length: 170.8m/560ft 8in (oa)
Beam: 15.7m/51ft 5in
Draught: 5m/16ft 4in (standard)
Armament: 7 x 15cm/5.9in (3x2/1x1) and 10 x 40mm/1.57in guns
Machinery: Geared steam turbines, 6 boilers, 2 shafts
Power: 49,216kW/66,000shp for 32 knots
Endurance: 1,320 tonnes/1,300 tons (oil) for 12,594km/6,800nm at 12 knots
Protection: 30–50mm/1.18–2in (belt); 30mm/1.18in (protective deck); 30mm/1.18in (gunhouses)
Complement: 437

Tromp class

Authorized in 1935, this interesting little pair equated roughly to the British D-class in terms of size and armament. Although more modern, they shared an auxiliary function as leaders of destroyer flotillas, also common to the Imperial Japanese Navy, which both were destined to meet. Their displacement was probably the smallest that could comfortably combine six 15cm/5.9in guns with a 32.5-knot speed

and light protection. Even so, their machinery was very concentrated and vulnerable to a single hit.

Fate decreed that the two, instead of being identical sisters, were completed very differently. The reason for this was that they were ordered from the same yard, which had only one suitable slipway. First-of-class *Tromp* was launched in May 1937. *Heemskerck* was commenced immediately but launched in mid-September 1939. With the German invasion of May 1940 (by which time the *Tromp* was already in the Far East), the incomplete *Heemskerck* was taken to Britain for completion. Portsmouth Dockyard armed her with five twin 102mm/4in high-angle (HA) guns, standard in the Royal Navy.

Significantly the Dutch contributed the advanced Hazemeyer stabilized fire-control system, later to be further developed by the British. The *Heemskerck* made an excellent anti-aircraft (AA) escort but, with the entry of Japan into the war in December 1941, she was sent east.

Both ships were fortunate. *Tromp*, the only one to carry the floatplane for which they were designed, was damaged in February 1942 and sent to Australia for

ABOVE LEFT: **The concept of an inexpensive light cruiser/destroyer leader was given a new interpretation in the two Tromps, probably the smallest ships that could carry three twin 15cm/5.9in mountings. Their destroyer-like appearance is belied by the long-base rangefinder atop the bridge structure.** ABOVE: **Late in her career,** *Tromp* **is seen at the 1953 British Coronation Review. She has been fitted with new, Bofors-pattern 15cm/5.9in mountings and a modern range of electronics. Aircraft fittings have long been removed but the modified funnel still appears to have an eddy problem.**

repairs. She thus missed the subsequent virtual annihilation of the ABDA (Australian, British, Dutch and American) forces. *Heemskerck* likewise missed this fate simply through arriving too late. Although prematurely aged by over-use both survived the war, served until the mid-1950s.

ABOVE: **Towed to Britain for completion in 1940,** *Heemskerck* **was given standard 102mm/4in twins and British electronics.**

Tromp

Displacement: 4,216 tonnes/4,150 tons (standard); 4,927 tonnes/4,850 tons (full load)
Length: 130m/425ft 6in (bp); 131.9m/433ft (oa)
Beam: 12.4m/40ft 9in
Draught: 4.6m/15ft (maximum)
Armament: 6 x 15cm/5.9in (3x2) and 4 x 40mm/1.57in (2x2) guns
Machinery: Geared steam turbines, 4 boilers, 2 shafts
Power: 41,759kW/56,000shp for 32.5 knots
Endurance: 874 tonnes/860 tons (oil) for 7,778km/4,200nm at 15 knots
Protection: 50–65mm/2–2.56in (belt); 36mm/1.42in (protective deck)
Complement: 380

Tromp class

	Built		Commissioned
Tromp	Nederlandsche Sch. Maats, Amsterdam	1939	
Jacob van Heemskerck	Nederlandsche Sch. Maats, Amsterdam	1941	

de Zeven Provinciën class

Intended as replacements for the Javas, this pair first resembled an extrapolation of the *de Ruyter* of 1936, but with ten 152mm/6in guns, disposed in two twin and two triple turrets. Barely commenced when the Netherlands were overrun in 1940, the two hulls were advanced slowly under German supervision. It was their influence that gave the *de Ruyter* the "Atlantic bow" which made her slightly longer than her sister.

By 1945, *de Zeven Provinciën* had been launched but the *Eendracht* (late *Kijkduin*) was still on the stocks. Long since ordered from Bofors, their gun mountings had been incorporated into the Swedish Tre Kronors.

It was decided to complete the two ships to a revised design that incorporated the advances made during the war. Again, an all Bofors outfit was specified – four twin 152mm/6in, four stabilized twin 57mm/2.24in and six twin 40mm/1.57in guns.

Machinery was rearranged on the unit system, requiring two funnels against the *de Ruyter*'s one. Soon after completion, the tripod mainmast was relocated from its position abaft the after funnel to a position immediately before it. The forward funnel was incorporated into the foremast.

Before completion, the *Eendracht* was renamed to commemorate the *de Ruyter*, lost in 1942. The ships also exchanged names.

During the early 1960s, both were slated for conversion to the American-sourced Terrier surface-to-air missile (SAM) system but cost considerations saw only the nameship so modified. In the process, she lost her after turrets and had the

after deck raised by one level, making the hull flush-decked.

In 1937 the unconverted *de Ruyter* was sold to Peru, being renamed *Almirante Grau*. Three years later she was joined by her sister, which, herself assumed the name *Grau*, the earlier ship being renamed *Aguirre*, Before transfer, *de Zeven Provinciën* was stripped of her Terrier system, her after end being modified for the accommodation and operation of helicopters.

de Zeven Provinciën class

	Built	Commissioned
de Ruyter	Wilton-Fijenoord, Rotterdam	November 18, 1953
de Zeven Provinciën	Rotterdam Drydock Company	December 17, 1953

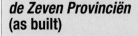

de Zeven Provinciën (as built)

Displacement: 9,906 tonnes/9,750 tons (standard); 12,116 tonnes/11,925 tons (full load)
Length: 180m/590ft 6in (bp); 185.5m/609ft (oa)
Beam: 17.3m/56ft 8in
Draught: 5.6m/18ft 6in (standard)
Armament: 8 x 152mm/6in (4x2), 8 x 57mm/2.24in and 8 x 40mm/1.57in guns
Machinery: Geared steam turbines, 4 boilers, 2 shafts
Power: 63,384kW/85,000shp for 32 knots
Endurance: 12,778km/6,900mm at 12 knots
Protection: 75–100mm/2.95–3.94in (belt); 25+25mm/1+1in (protective decks)
Complement: 965

LEFT: ***De Zeven Provinciën*** **in her original configuration. Following sale to Peru her after end, stripped of Terrier, was converted for flight pad and hangar space for three large helicopters. *De Ruyter* kept her full main battery but had two elevated platforms added amidships, supporting four Otomat SSM canister launchers on either side.**

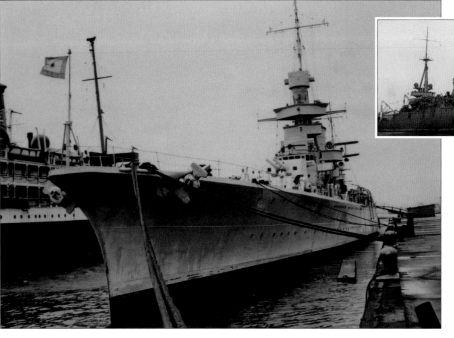

LEFT: **Built in Italy in the late 1920s, the two Browns bear comparison with contemporary Italian cruisers. The choice of 190mm/7.5in guns was unusual. A new calibre for the Argentinians, it had been a popular size in the British Royal Navy and was at that time fitted in the Improved Birminghams.** ABOVE: **The size of the *Veinticinco de Mayo*'s (*25 de Mayo*'s) guns is clearly visible. Although only three twin mountings were carried they, together with protection, made the pair considerably overweight and tender. As a weight-saving measure, the Italian-pattern director is supported on a tripod, rather than a more rigid tetrapod.**

Almirante Brown class

Included in the Argentine Navy's ten-year expansion and modernization programme of 1926 was a class of three heavy cruisers. This category of ship was much in vogue at the time because of the "cruiser race" developing between the signatories of the Washington Treaty. In the event, fiscal restraints reduced the class to only two ships.

At the same time Italy was constructing her first pair of "treaty cruisers", the Trento class. They were of strikingly attractive and modern design and the Argentine Navy, already operating ships of Italian origin, ordered what was effectively a pair of diminutives. The *Veinticinco de Mayo* (*25 de Mayo*) was laid down in the same yard as the *Trento*, just a month after the latter's launch in October 1927. She inherited a very similar arrangement of forward superstructure – funnel, heavy tripod foremast, bridge and superimposed turrets. In place of the

Trento's flush-decked hull, however, that of the Brown class was of the long forecastle deck type, with the break just forward of the after turret.

In British terms, the Brown class equated in size to the yet-to-be-built Leander class, to which there was also a passing resemblance, emphasized by the single, dominant funnel which, in both cases, exhausted adjacent boiler spaces. A major difference lay in the heavier 190mm/7.5in calibre of the Brown class main battery, an unusual size that may have had its origins in the Elswick-manufactured guns mounted uniquely in the earlier British Hawkins class. Because of their size and weight, only three twin turrets were mounted. A useful dual-purposes (DP) secondary battery of six twin 100mm/3.9in guns was also carried.

Other than the tripod for supporting the fire control arrangement, masting was very light. A catapult and floatplane (typically a Vought OZU Corsair) were located between funnel and mainmast.

Of well-balanced design, the Brown class served until 1961.

Almirante Brown class

	Built	Commissioned
Almirante Brown	Orlando, Sestri Ponente	September 16, 1931
Veinticinco de Mayo		
(*25 de Mayo*)	Orlando, Livorno	September 16, 1931

Almirante Brown class

Displacement: 6,909 tonnes/6,800 tons (standard); 8,941 tonnes/8,800 tons (full load)
Length: 163.1m/535ft 5in (bp); 166.2m/545ft 9in (oa)
Beam: 17.9m/58ft 7in
Draught: 5m/16ft 3in (standard)
Armament: 6 x 190mm/7.5in (3x2); 12 x 100mm/3.9in (6x2) guns; 6 x 533mm/21in torpedo tubes (2x3)
Machinery: Geared steam turbines, 6 boilers, 2 shafts
Power: 63,384kW/85,000shp for 32 knots
Endurance: 2,336 tonnes/2,300 tons (oil) for 14,816km/8,000nm at 14 knots
Protection: 36–70mm/1.18–2.76in (belt); 25mm/1in (protective deck); 50mm/2in (turrets)
Complement: 600

LEFT: **The *25 de Mayo* towards the end of her career in the 1950s. She has landed her catapult and pole masts, gaining an Italian-style tripod mainmast.**

LEFT: Built as a training cruiser by Vickers at Barrow, *La Argentina* (seen here) is little changed and quite clearly derived from the contemporary Arethusas, although with triple 152mm/6in turrets. The dark mass before the after funnel is the catapult-mounted aircraft with its wings in the folded position. ABOVE: The ship's Supermarine Walrus spotter-reconnaissance aircraft. Because of its length, the catapult is housed at an angle to the ship's centreline. The lowered handling crane is visible in front of it. Note the accommodation ladder in the stowed position, with its supporting davit lowered against the ship's side.

La Argentina

Following the worst of the 1930s recession, the Argentine Navy was able to order a third cruiser to complement the Brown class. Following considerable diplomatic pressure, British yards secured the order for not only the cruiser but also a flotilla of destroyers.

Bearing the proud name of *La Argentina*, the cruiser was laid down in January 1936. Although intended to be completed as part of a trio with the Brown class, the ship's design complicated logistics by introducing a new range of gun calibres.

Fitted as a training cruiser, the ship resembled the British Arethusa class, "stretched" by some 10m/32ft 10in. On a moderate 6,705 tonnes/6,600 tons displacement she carried three triple

152mm/6in mountings, (of the same pattern as those then being fitted to the British Southampton class) in place of the three twins of the 5,334-tonne/5,250-ton Arethusa class. Where the latter had a secondary armament of four twin 102mm/4in high-angle (HA) guns, *La Argentina* carried only singles. The British ships had a short forecastle deck but, in order to provide extra accommodation for her training role, the Argentinian had her forecastle extended to the after turret similar to the Brown class. This meant that the sided triple torpedo tubes, located amidships at upper deck level, had to be mounted behind screens.

A prominent feature was the enormous glazed wheelhouse area,

for the purpose of navigation instruction. Widely spaced boiler spaces and, hence, funnels, provided topside space for a catapult and two aircraft. As delivered, these were standard Walrus amphibians, but these were later replaced by Curtiss SOC-1 Seagulls, the last type of floatplane to be produced for the US Navy.

Following World War II (in which a neutral Argentina played no active part) the ship exchanged her 102mm/4in guns for 40mm/1.57in weapons, and acquired a mixture of radars. Her systems outdated, she was discarded in 1974.

ABOVE: Although replete with details from contemporary British cruisers, *La Argentina* is very different overall. The extended forecastle deck and two-level accommodation below the bridge structure betray her training status. The very large navigating bridge, for the purpose of instruction, is also evident.

La Argentina

Built: Vickers-Armstrong, Barrow
Commissioned: January 31, 1939
Displacement: 6,705 tonnes/6,600 tons (standard);
  7,747 tonnes/7,625 tons (full load)
Length: 155.4m/510ft (bp); 164.6m/540ft 2in (oa)
Beam: 17.2m/56ft 6in
Draught: 5m/16ft 3in
Armament: 9 x 152mm/6in (3x3); 4 x 102mm/4in
  (4x1) guns; 6 x 533mm/21in torpedo tubes (2x3)
Machinery: Geared steam turbines,
  4 boilers, 4 shafts
Power: 44,742kW/60,000shp for 31 knots
Endurance: 1,504 tonnes/1,480 tons (oil) for
  18,520km/10,000nm at 12 knots
Protection: 75mm/2.95in (belt); 50mm/2in (deck);
  50mm/2in (gunhouses)
Complement: 560 plus 60 cadets

Glossary

AS Anti-submarine.

Anglo-German Naval Agreement (1935)
Agreement for German fleet to be built up to fixed proportion of Royal Navy strength. This permitted 51,000 tons of heavy cruisers and 67,000 tons of light cruisers for Germany.

Armoured cruiser Generally, a cruiser fitted with belt (i.e. vertical) armour in addition to protective deck (horizontal).

bhp Brake Horse Power. The power developed at the engine, i.e. before deductions are made for mechanical losses.

BL Breech-loading (gun).

Ballast Permanent or temporary weight carried by a ship to improve stability or trim.

Barbette Vertical, armoured, tubular trunk upon which guns or their turrets revolve. It protects the ammunition supply path.

Barque (rigged) Vessel with three or more masts, all of which are square-rigged except the aftermost (mizen), which is fore-and-aft rigged.

Barquentine (rigged) Uusally a three-masted vessel, square-rigged on only the foremast, fore-and-aft rigged on mainmast and mizen

Beam The maximum width/breadth of a ship at the waterline.

Belt Vertical side armour, usually about the waterline.

Belted cruiser Early style with thick side armour, of limited area, but little other protection.

Blister (or Bulge) Outer layer of hull compartmentation, added usually to improve a ship's resistance to torpedo damage.

Boiler, cylindrical Similar to locomotive boiler, in which water surrounds hot flue with steam drawn from the top. Heavy, due to weight of water.

California (CGN.36)

Boiler, water tube Water passes through lengths of large/small bore tube supported within combustion chamber. Lighter; less water in boiler.

Bowsprit Spar which extends forward from the bows. Its length is extended by the associated jib boom.

Brig Two-masted vessel, square-rigged on both masts.

Brigantine (rigged) Usually, a two-masted rig, with square sails on the foremast and fore-and-aft on the mainmast.

Bulwark Solid planking or plating along the deck edge to afford protection.

Bunkers Embarked fuel. A bunker is a fuel storage compartment or tank.

C-in-C Commander-in-Chief.

CIWS Close-in Weapon System.

Calibre Bore or diameter of a gun barrel, e.g. 5in. The length of the barrel is expressed in "calibres", e.g. a 54-calibre barrel is 270in in length.

Cantilever To support a structure or member at one end only.

Casemate Gun position, usually armoured, built into the hull or superstructure of a warship. The gun may often be run in and its aperture closed-off by shutters.

Casing, funnel The casing forms the outer funnel, enclosing the hot smoke pipe(s). Some cruisers, especially German, had half-cased funnels to save topweight.

Catapult Aboard a cruiser, the means to directly launch an aircraft. Usually powered by cordite charge or compressed air.

Cellular (layer) Level immediately above a protective deck, closely subdivided to limit flooding in the event of damage.

Compound armour Composite plate of tough iron substrate with welded-on hard steel facing.

Compound engine Double-expansion engines. Having expanded partially in the high-pressure cylinder, steam is transferred to expand further in a larger-

diameter, low-pressure cylinder before being exhausted to a condenser.

Coppered Having underwater hull surfaces covered in thin copper plates in order to reduce fouling and to maintain speed.

Corvette Three-masted, ship-rigged, flush-decked warship, with a single gundeck and no forecastle or poop. Classified as a Sixth Rate.

Counter stern Style of stern where the above-water hull, supported on cant frames, projects well abaft the rudder.

Cruiser stern Style of stern where the hull abaft the rudder is fully plated, increasing waterplane area and buoyancy.

Derrick Spar, pivoted at lower end and rigged for lifting and transferring cargo or boats.

Displacement, full load or "deep" Weight of ship (expressed in tons of 2,240lb) when fully equipped, stored and fuelled.

Displacement, standard Weight of ship less fuel and other deductions allowed by treaty.

Draught (or Draft) Mean depth of water in which a ship may float freely.

Fighting top Platform, usually circular, located on lower mast for the mounting of light, anti-personnel weapons.

Flare Curved overhang of hull at bows and stern, designed to throw water clear and to dampen pitch amplitude.

Floatplane (or Seaplane) Aircraft with external floats intended, usually, to be launched by catapult and to be recovered from the water.

Fore-and-aft Parallel to the major axis of the ship.

Freeboard Usually, the vertical distance from waterline to weather deck. Effectively, it is the vertical height between the waterline and the lowest aperture through which the ship can flood.

Gunhouse Revolving, covered gun mounting not based on a barbette.

Marsala

Belfast

Medea

Gloire

Grand Fleet Usually, the wartime title of the British battle fleet.

Gross registered tons (grt) Measure of volumetric capacity of a merchant ship. One gross ton equals 100 cubic feet (2.83cu m) of reckonable space.

Guerre de Course Sustained campaign against commercial shipping.

Gunport Aperture, usually square, cut in side of ship to permit broadside fire. Closed by portlid when not in use.

Harvey Nickel steel armour plate introduced in early 1890s. Homogenous composition but with hardened face and tough annealed back.

High Sea(s) Fleet The primary German battle fleet of World War I.

Horsepower Unit of power equal to 746 Watts.

ihp Indicated horsepower. Specifically, the power delivered by the pistons of a reciprocating steam engine.

Kite balloon Aerostat deployed by ships for observation purposes.

Knuckle Line of discontinuity in curvature of side plating, usually to avoid excessive flare at weather deck level.

Krupp An improvement on Harvey armour, introduced about 1896. A nickel-chromium-manganese steel was used, selectively heated and water-chilled.

Length (bp) Length, between perpendiculars. Usually the distance between the forward extremity of the waterline at standard displacement and the forward edge of the rudder post. For American warships, lengths on "designed waterline" and "between perpendiculars" are synonymous.

Length (oa) Length, overall.

Length (wl) Length, waterline. Measured at standard displacement.

London Treaty First of 1929–30, Second of 1935–36. Treaties reaffirming and modifying the Washington Treaty of 1921–22.

MLR Muzzle-loading Rifle.

Main deck In British practice, the level below the upper deck.

Metacentric height Relationship between a ship's centres of gravity (fixed) and buoyancy (variable). Essential component of stability.

NATO North Atlantic Treaty Organization.

nm Nautical mile. One nautical mile per hour equals one knot.

Naval Defence Act Usually, that of 1889, which provided for the Royal Navy to be built up to the "Two Power Standard", maintaining it at the strength of the next two largest navies combined.

Plan "Orange" American war plan, periodically updated, for use against Japan.

Protected cruiser One whose protection comprises an armoured deck, usually vaulted, overlaid with a "cellular" layer, closely subdivided.

Quick-firing (QF) Guns, up to 152mm/6in calibre, which accepted "fixed" ammunition, i.e., charge and projectile combined. In American parlance, Rapid Fire.

RFA Royal Fleet Auxiliary.

Running rigging That part of a ship's rigging used for setting and trimming the sails.

shp Shaft horsepower. Power is transmitted by a shaft at a point ahead of the stern gland. It does not, therefore, include mechanical losses in stern gland and A-bracket, if fitted.

Seaplane *See* **Floatplane**.

Schooner (rigged) Vessel with two or more masts, fore-and-aft rigged on both, or all.

Scuttle Correct term for what is popularly termed a "porthole".

Sheer Curvature of deckline in fore-and-aft direction, usually upward toward either end.

Sheathed Simply "coppered" or, less frequently, a metal hull, timbered below water, then coppered.

Sheer strake Run, or strake, of plating along ship's side adjacent to the upper deck and following sheer line. May be highly stressed, so fashioned from heavier plate.

Shell plating General term for all plating that forms the outer skin of a vessel.

Ship (rigged) A three-masted vessel, square-rigged on all three masts.

Emperador Carlos V

Sided Situated toward the side(s), as opposed to the centreline, of a ship.

Sloop In context of this book, a small unrated warship with two or three masts, square-rigged throughout. These were termed Brig Sloops and Ship Sloops respectively.

Spar deck A deck of light construction, one level above the uppermost strength deck.

Splinter deck A thin armoured deck, situated beneath a thicker one and designed to stop any fragments being projected downward.

Stability range Total angle through which, from a position of equilibrium, a ship is statically stable.

Sponson In warships, platforms projecting beyond the line of the hull, usually supporting guns which can thus be trained closer to the ship's main axis.

Standing Rigging That part of a ship's rigging supporting masts and spars.

Triple-expansion Three or four-cylinder engine in which the steam expands progressively through high, intermediate and low pressure stages.

Tumblehome Much the reverse of Flare. Higher decks are made progressively narrower to reduce topweight and to facilitate sponsoning of guns.

Turbine, steam Multi-stage, bladed rotor which revolves under the action of steam passing through the blades. Virtually vibration-free.

Two Power Standard *See* **Naval Defence Act**.

Upper deck The uppermost continuous deck of a ship.

Uptake Conduit conducting products of combustion to the funnel.

W/T Wireless Transmission, i.e. radio.

Waist That part of the upper deck between forecastle and quarterdeck.

Warsaw Pact Eastern military bloc. Essentially a counter to NATO.

Washington Treaty Arms limitation agreement of 1921–22 that had a profound effect on the development of the cruiser.

Index

California (CA.6)

Nürnberg

Acknowledgements

Research for the images used to illustrate this book was carried out by Ted Nevill of Cody Images, who supplied the majority of the images.

The publisher and Ted Nevill would like to thank all those who contributed to this research and to the supply of additional pictures:

Anova Images; ArtTech; Richard Cox; Jim Culbertson; Photographic Section, Naval Historical Center, Washington, DC, USA; Still Pictures, National Archives and Records Administration, College Park, Maryland, USA; US Merchant Marine Academy, Kings Point, NY, USA; US Navy.

Chester

Key to flags

The nationality of each ship or ship class is identified in the relevant specification box by the national flag that was in use at the time of the vessels' commissioning and service.

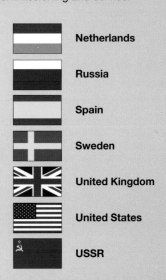

Argentina

Austria-Hungary

France

Germany: World War I

Germany: World War II

Italy

Japan

Netherlands

Russia

Spain

Sweden

United Kingdom

United States

USSR